Imperial Endgame

BRITAIN AND THE WORLD
Edited by The British Scholar Society

Editors
James Onley, University of Exeter, UK
A. G. Hopkins, University of Texas at Austin
Gregory Barton, The Australian National University
Bryan Glass, University of Texas at Austin

Imperial Endgame: Britain's Dirty Wars and the End of Empire is the first book in the *Britain and the World* series, edited by The British Scholar Society and published by Palgrave Macmillan. From the sixteenth century onward, Britain's influence on the world became progressively profound and far-reaching, in time touching every continent and subject, from Africa to South America and archaeology to zoology. Although the histories of Britain and the world became increasingly intertwined, mainstream British history still neglects the world's influence upon domestic developments and British overseas history remains largely confined to the study of the British Empire. This series takes a broader approach to British history, seeking to investigate the full extent of the world's influence on Britain and Britain's influence on the world.

Benjamin Grob-Fitzgibbon's book is a work of considerable insight, breadth, and originality. It controversially argues that British decolonisation policy throughout the empire in the 1940s and '50s was carefully and intentionally orchestrated to ensure that independence happened on British terms. The British government did this by waging coordinated counterinsurgency campaigns to isolate insurgents from the general population, by transferring power to those wishing to maintain links with Britain and supporting them after independence, and by persuading many former colonies to remain within a British and American sphere of influence during the Cold War. This is not a story you have been told before. We hope you will enjoy reading it as much as we did.

Forthcoming titles in the *Britain and the World* series include:

SCIENCE AND EMPIRE: KNOWLEDGE AND NETWORKS OF SCIENCE IN THE BRITISH EMPIRE, 1850–1970
Brett Bennett and Joseph M. Hodge (eds)

MUSE OF EMPIRE: THE CLASSICS, BRITISH IMPERIALISM AND THE INDIAN EMPIRE, 1784–1914
Christopher Hagerman

THE PAPER WAR: ANGLO-AMERICAN DEBATES ABOUT THE AMERICAN REPUBLIC, 1800–1830
Joe Eaton

BRITISH IMAGES OF GERMANY: ADMIRATION, ANTAGONISM AND AMBIVALENCE, 1860–1914
Richard Scully

Britain and the World
Series Standing Order ISBN 978–0–230–24650–8 hardcover
Series Standing Order ISBN 978–0–230–24651–5s paperback
(*outside North America only*)

You can receive future titles in this series as they are published by placing a standing order. Please contact your bookseller or, in case of difficulty, write to us at the address below with your name and address, the title of the series and one of the ISBNs quoted above.

Customer Services Department, Macmillan Distribution Ltd, Houndmills, Basingstoke, Hampshire RG21 6XS, England

---

Imperial Endgame

Britain's Dirty Wars and the End of Empire

Benjamin Grob-Fitzgibbon
Assistant Professor of History, University of Arkansas, USA

First published 2011 by
PALGRAVE MACMILLAN

Palgrave Macmillan in the UK is an imprint of Macmillan Publishers Limited, registered in England, company number 785998, of Houndmills, Basingstoke, Hampshire RG21 6XS.

Palgrave Macmillan in the US is a division of St Martin's Press LLC, 175 Fifth Avenue, New York, NY 10010.

Palgrave Macmillan is the global academic imprint of the above companies and has companies and representatives throughout the world.

Palgrave® and Macmillan® are registered trademarks in the United States, the United Kingdom, Europe and other countries

ISBN 978–0–230–24873–1   paperback

This book is printed on paper suitable for recycling and made from fully managed and sustained forest sources. Logging, pulping and manufacturing processes are expected to conform to the environmental regulations of the country of origin.

A catalogue record for this book is available from the British Library.

A catalog record for this book is available from the Library of Congress.

10   9   8   7   6   5   4   3   2   1
20   19   18   17   16   15   14   13   12   11

Printed and bound in Great Britain by
CPI Antony Rowe, Chippenham and Eastbourne

For my wife, Amanda,
and my children,
Sophia, Isabel, and Kieran

The central purpose of British Colonial Policy is simple. It is to guide the Colonial Territories to responsible self-government within the Commonwealth in conditions that ensure to the people concerned both a fair standard of living and freedom from oppression from any quarter.

Arthur Creech Jones, Secretary of State for the Colonies, 1948

There is nothing in the colonial record of Great Britain for which we have cause to hang our heads. I claim that The Queen's peace, the advance of enlightenment and knowledge, the increased prosperity, the rising standard of life, freedom from fear, which we have brought with us, are achievements with which we can face the verdict either of history, or of a still higher judgement, with pride and confidence.

Oliver Lyttelton, Secretary of State for the Colonies, 1953

As I see it the great issue in this second half of the twentieth century is whether the uncommitted peoples of Asia and Africa will swing to the East or to the West. Will they be drawn into the Communist camp? Or will the great experiments in self-government that are now being made in Asia and Africa, especially within the Commonwealth, prove so successful, and by their example so compelling, that the balance will come down in favour of freedom and order and justice? The struggle is joined, and it is a struggle for the minds of men. What is now on trial is much more than our military strength or our diplomatic and administrative skill. It is our way of life.

Harold Macmillan, Prime Minister, 1960

Contents

List of Plates		ix
Acknowledgments		xi
Maps		xiv
Prologue		1
1	The Attlee Years, July 27, 1945, to October 26, 1951	5
I.	A promised land, but to whom?	5
II.	The American intervention	23
III.	The terror begins again	31
IV.	The end of compromise	48
V.	Into the abyss	58
VI.	The Endgame in Palestine	80
VII.	Trouble comes to Malaya	100
VIII.	The appointment of Sir Harold Briggs	127
IX.	The Special Air Service, the Briggs Plan, and progress in Malaya	140
X.	The end of the Attlee years	166
2	The Churchill Years, October 26, 1951, to April 7, 1955	173
I.	A new government, a new approach	173
II.	The carrot and the stick	189
III.	The challenge of Mau Mau	208
IV.	The General's stamp in Malaya	226
V.	"The Horned Shadow of the Devil Himself"	233
VI.	Dirty wars, dirty deeds	251
VII.	A fresh start in Kenya?	264
VIII.	The end of the Churchill years	275

Contents

3   The Eden Years, April 7, 1955, to January 10, 1957   297
        I.   Problems in paradise   297
       II.   Templer's return   310
      III.   The Dirty wars become even dirtier   324
       IV.   Suez   338
        V.   The endgame for Anthony Eden   349

Epilogue: The Imperial Endgame after Eden   351

Notes   378

Bibliography   446

Index   458

List of Plates

Plate 1   The explosion of a second bomb at the King David Hotel in Jerusalem, Palestine, 22 July 1946. © Imperial War Museum.

Plate 2   Damage done by terrorist bombs to a police station in Jaffa, Palestine, 1946. © Imperial War Museum.

Plate 3   A derailed mail train in Johore, Malaya, c. 1950. © Imperial War Museum.

Plate 4   A New Village in Malaya, c. 1952. © Imperial War Museum.

Plate 5   Members of the Malayan Home Guard receiving hand grenade training, c. 1950. © Imperial War Museum.

Plate 6   A Dyak tracker being instructed in Malaya, c. 1949. © Imperial War Museum.

Plate 7   A suspected Mau Mau insurgent being taken for interrogation, 1955. © Imperial War Museum.

Plate 8   Sir Evelyn Baring inspecting the King's African Rifles in Kenya, 1957. © Imperial War Museum.

Plate 9   A British Army lorry burnt out by EOKA in Cyprus, 1955. © Imperial War Museum.

Plate 10   The British Army on patrol in the Western Aden Protectorate, July 1955. © Imperial War Museum.

Plate section appears between pages 172 and 173.

Acknowledgments

This is my third book. It has been by far the most satisfying and the most challenging. For that reason, I have accumulated a debt of gratitude to many. At the University of Arkansas, I have received generous financial and moral support. I am particularly grateful to the Dean of the Fulbright College of Arts and Sciences, Bill Schwab, and to my department chair, Lynda Coon, both of whom have stood behind me throughout this enterprise. Fulbright College has provided me with much financial assistance, as has the Cleveland C. Burton professorship (of which I am the inaugural holder), the Nolan endowment, the Robert C. and Sandra Connor endowment, and the E. Mitchell and Barbara Singleton endowment. In the department of history, I am grateful for the support of my colleagues, particularly Randall Woods, Elliot West, Dan Sutherland, Patrick Williams, Joel Gordon, Tom Kennedy, and especially Calvin White, Jr.—I have come to value their friendship and good judgment on a daily basis. Thanks also to Beth Juhl and the other staff at Mullins Library and Dean Bob McMath of the Honors College.

Outside the University of Arkansas, I must acknowledge the history department at Duke University. Although not contributing directly to this project, the faculty there made me the historian I am. In particular, I must recognize the late John W. "Jack" Cell, who taught me how to be an imperial historian; and Alex Roland, John Herd Thompson, and Martin Miller, who stepped into the breach without hesitation upon Jack's untimely death. I would also like to thank R. J. Q Adams at Texas A&M University and Sir David Cannadine, now at Princeton, for the encouragement and inspiration they have offered me at this early stage of my career.

Beyond academia, I have benefited from generous hospitality at the homes of Paul and Alicia Fraser and Norman and Robyn

Edwards in Kew, from the master and staff at Churchill College, Cambridge, and from Donna McDaniel and Kate Simcoe at the C. S. Lewis Foundation Study Center at the Kilns, Oxford. Finally and perhaps most importantly, at archival institutions I owe thanks to the helpful staff at the Bodleian Library, Oxford; the British Library, London; the Churchill Archives Centre, Churchill College, Cambridge; the Imperial War Museum, London; the Liddell Hart Centre for Military Archives, King's College, London; the National Archives, Kew; the Rhodes House Library, Oxford; the Special Collections Department at the University of Birmingham; and the Templer Study Centre at the National Army Museum, London.

This book is published in Palgrave Macmillan's "Britain and the World" Series, in association with the British Scholar Society. I am greatly appreciative of the enterprising Bryan Glass, founder and president of the society, for all he has done for British history in recent years. I am also grateful to Wm. Roger Louis, Gregory Barton, and James Onley, all of whom have supported this project unceasingly. In preparing this book for publication I am indebted to the staff at Palgrave Macmillan, particularly my editor Michael Strang and assistant editor Ruth Ireland. I also owe thanks to Haunani D. Verzon of Verzon Mapping & Graphics, LLC, who drew up the maps.

The images on the cover and within this book are used with the kind permission of the Imperial War Museum, which holds the copyright. I must also offer thanks for permissions and copyright for written materials to Helen Langley (Curator, Modern Political Papers collection, Bodleian Library, Oxford); Anne, Lady Attlee; Simon, Lord Boyd; Jan William of Taylor Wessing; the Trustees of the Late Harold Macmillan's Papers; the British Library; the National Army Museum; the Trustees of the Liddell Hart Centre for Military Archives at King's College, London; Lucy McCann (Archivist, Bodleian Library of Commonwealth & African Studies at Rhodes Houses); Clarissa Eden, Lady Avon; W. H. Thompson; Jane Jefford; Susan Towers-Clark; John Green; Norman Martin; Peter Head; Roy Hammerton;

Sue Scott-Cole; Brigid Dolby; R.H. Clark; Ian Gibb; A.M. Hodges; and the copyright holder for the papers of Brigadier D. F. A. Baines. Every effort has been made to trace copyright holders for those papers held at the Imperial War Museum, most of whom are listed above, but the museum would be grateful for any information which might help to trace those whose identities and addresses are not currently known.

Portions of this work draw on content previously published as "Securing the Colonies for the Commonwealth: Counterinsurgency, Decolonization, and the Development of British Imperial Strategy in the Postwar Empire," *British Scholar*, Volume 2, Issue 1 (September 2009), pp. 12–39. Used with permission by *British Scholar*; and "Counterinsurgency, the Interagency Process, and Malaya: The British Experience," in Kendall D. Gott and Michael G. Brooks, eds, *The US Army and the Interagency Process: Historical Perspectives* (Fort Leavenworth, KS: Combat Studies Institute Press, 2008), pp. 93–104. Used with permission by the Combat Studies Institute Press; and "Intelligence and Counter-Insurgency: Case-Studies from Ireland, Malaya and the Empire," *RUSI Journal*, Volume 156, Number 1 (February/March 2011). Used with permission by the *RUSI Journal*.

Finally and above all else I must thank my family, to whom this book is dedicated. My wife, Amanda, has continually supported my frequent trips to England's green and pleasant land, my daughters Sophia and Isabel provide me with authentic enjoyment, and my newborn son, Kieran, gives me hope for the future—children, mum says you must not read this book for at least another sixteen years due to its disturbing content. I promise someday I will write a book with less chilling subject matter. Until then, you must know this is all for you.

The British Empire, c. 1945*

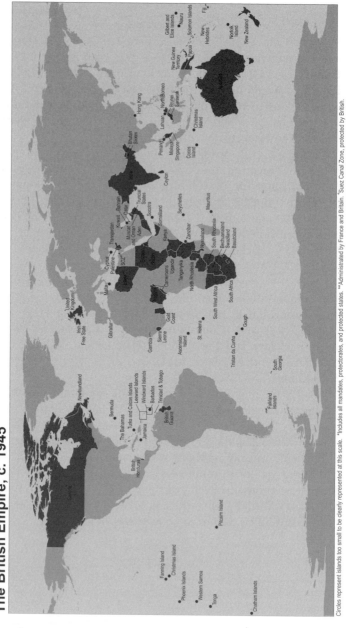

Circles represent islands too small to be clearly represented at this scale. *Includes all mandates, protectorates, and protected states. **Administrated by France and Britain. °Suez Canal Zone, protected by British.

The Commonwealth of Nations, c. 2010

Circles represent islands too small to be clearly represented at this scale.

Prologue

The story of the British Empire in the twentieth century is one of decline, disarray, and despondency. Or so we have been told. Historians have generally viewed Britain's postwar imperial journey through the lens of reactive defeat. Ronald Hyam best captures this consensus in his work *Declining Empire: The Road to Decolonization, 1918–1968* when he uses a cricketing analogy to describe the four main interpretations of Britain's end of empire: "Either the British were bowled out (by nationalists and freedom-fighters), or they were run out (by imperial overstretch and economic constraints), or they retired hurt (because of a collapse of morale and 'failure of will'), or they were booed off the field (by international criticism and especially United Nations clamor)."[1] The key point here is that in each of these cases, Britain lost the match. Hyam adds his own voice to this cacophony of defeat: "'[S]uccess' is not a theme or prediction that history can endorse for the twentieth-century British empire."[2]

This viewpoint is prominently held in the literature on decolonization, where it is implied that prior to Prime Minister Harold Macmillan's famous "wind of change" speech in 1960, decolonization—like the birth of empire—occurred in a fit of absence of mind.[3] Historians have overwhelmingly held that Britain's end of empire was a mismanaged disaster. Those who administered it were paralyzed by uncertainty, inaction, and a general lack of direction, and those in charge received contradictory and conflicting advice that crippled proper governance. At first blush, it is not hard to see the source of this stance. For the fifteen years following the Second World War, the British

1

Empire was ablaze with insurgencies: in Palestine, insurrectionary bombings and an underground terrorist organization; in Malaya, a powerful communist revolt; in Kenya, the Mau Mau uprising; in Cyprus, a terror campaign waged by EOKA (*Ethniki Organosis Kyprion Agoniston*—the National Organization of Cypriot Fighters); and in Aden, Oman, and Dhofar, tribal rebellions. Throughout it all, British politicians, colonial administrators, and the security forces struggled to put out the flames to prevent empire's end.

Yet British counterinsurgency policy in the postwar empire was not merely a matter of military strategy, nor did the British government view each campaign in isolation. In this book, I reveal that the policy developed by the government was in fact one carefully calculated to allow decolonization to occur on British terms rather than those of the indigenous people. With remarkable consistency, and in response to the insurgencies in Palestine, Malaya, Kenya, Cyprus, and the Middle East, the British government crafted an imperial strategy that was designed to guide much of the formal empire into the British Commonwealth and, as such, into the British and American sphere of influence during the Cold War. When necessary, the government employed counterinsurgency techniques to achieve this end, isolating potential troublemakers—whether nationalists, communists, or tribal rebels—from the general populace while winning the hearts and minds of the majority of colonial subjects. The government's hope was that these territories might remain within the British world rather than leave it when finally granted independence.

This is not the story we have been told. It has become conventional wisdom to argue that Britain's postwar counterinsurgency campaigns were an ad hoc and uncoordinated reaction to immediate events on the ground. As such, they have not held a prominent place in our accounts of imperial decline. For example, John Darwin's otherwise comprehensive *Britain and Decolonization: The Retreat from Empire in the Post-War World* devotes just three pages to events in Cyprus, despite a five-year conflict there, and only four pages to the twelve-year Malayan emergency. Darwin makes little attempt to connect the campaigns one to the other and offers no suggestion that those in Kenya or Aden were even mildly aware of what was occurring in Malaya or Cyprus.[4] Studies that have been dedicated to the insurgencies and counterinsurgencies of the 1940s, 1950s, and 1960s—such as Charles Townshend's *Britain's Civil Wars: Counterinsurgency in the Twentieth Century*, Thomas Mockaitis' *British Counterinsurgency, 1919–1960*, and John Newsinger's *British Counter-Insurgency: From Palestine to Northern Ireland*— have failed to place such events in the larger context of British decolonization, instead compartmentalizing each conflict and exploring them in the context of violence and state control using the tools of the military historian.[5]

The few works that have addressed colonial insurgencies in the framework of decolonization have done so only as national case studies, such as Caroline Elkins' *Imperial Reckoning: The Untold Story of Britain's Gulag in Kenya*, David Anderson's *Histories of the Hanged: The Dirty War in Kenya and the End of Empire*, Daniel Branch's *Defeating Mau Mau, Creating Kenya: Counterinsurgency, Civil War, and Decolonization*, and R. F. Holland's *Britain and the Revolt in Cyprus*.[6] In each of these works, the fact that the colonial office was simultaneously struggling with insurgencies in numerous territories, and that administrators, soldiers, and policemen alike were being constantly transferred from one colony to the other does not merit mention. Yet British decolonization policy, and the counterinsurgency campaigns that supported it, did not pigeon-hole each territory into separate sections, with one viewed in isolation from the others by different government departments. Rather, the British government developed a concerted imperial strategy designed to secure the colonies for the Commonwealth in an orderly transfer of power while maintaining British influence in the region and strengthening overall Western dominance in the Cold War world. This book argues that in this endeavor the government met with considerable success.

That is not to say, of course, that these counterinsurgency campaigns were clean, for they were not. These were Britain's dirty wars of empire, wars that defied any attempt to place them into the neat categories of black and white and were instead fought in the gray shadows of empire and morality. The British government's decolonization strategy was predicated on notions of liberal imperialism, on Rudyard Kipling's "white man's burden." British prime ministers, colonial secretaries, and foreign secretaries in both the Labour and Conservative parties drafted policy with the belief firmly in mind that the values and society Britain had achieved over the previous 700 years—based on democracy, good governance, the sanctity of property, and respect for the rule of law—were universal in nature, and that it was the British government's unique responsibility to present these gifts to the world.

As it became clear that twentieth-century populations rejected the authoritarian methods that Britain had used to inculcate these ideas into the minds of colonial subjects in the Victorian age, the government changed tack to instead steer with the winds of self-governance and national independence. For those within colonial societies who were willing to follow Britain's timetable toward sovereignty and to do so within the confines of the Commonwealth, the government promised education, social welfare, training in the arts of administration and security, and eventual power. For the minority who rejected Britain's way, however, there could only be the hard hand of the military. For as has always been the case with liberal imperialism, illiberal measures are required to protect it. These dirty wars of empire were Britain's imperial endgame. This is their story.

1

The Attlee Years

July 27, 1945, to October 26, 1951

I.   A promised land, but to whom?

George Henry Hall had been His Majesty's colonial secretary
for less than three months when, together with the foreign secretary Ernest Bevin, he met with Chaim Weizmann, president
of the World Zionist Organization, and Moshe Shertok, head
of Palestine's Jewish Agency. It was early on the morning of
November 2, 1945, and despite the elegance of the foreign office
building in which they sat, their conversation was as grim as the
November day outside.[1] Dispensing with all normal diplomatic
pleasantries, Bevin at once accused the Jewish Agency of collaboration in the shocking events of the day before, when terrorists in Palestine had sunk three police naval vessels, severed
the railway in 242 places, bombed the stationmaster's office in
Jerusalem, and badly damaged seven locomotives. Bevin asked
whether the British government was now to assume that the
Jews wished to settle the Palestine question by force, warning
that if so, the British would respond in kind.

Weizmann and Shertok insisted that they deplored the violent
acts, and Weizmann quoted a resolution passed by the agency to
make his point: "The Agency repudiates recourse to violence, but
finds its capacity to impose restraint severely tried by the maintenance of a policy which Jews regard as fatal to their future."
Bevin immediately dismissed the resolution as a half-hearted
statement, pointing out that the latter part of the sentence even

seemed to condone violence. The meeting ended on a sour note, with disagreement between Bevin and Weizmann over the level of access the British government had given to the Jewish Agency and with Weizmann reluctantly agreeing to issue a second categorical denunciation of all violence in Palestine. The four men had spoken for less than an hour. The colonial secretary, although technically responsible for the Palestine Mandate, had been a mere observer, overshadowed by the more charismatic Bevin.[2]

This was not how Hall had imagined his first three months as colonial secretary would end. He had come to the office with a great sense of optimism, one shared by most members of his party. The general election had taken place on July 5, 1945, although it was not until July 26 that the electoral commission declared the results and only on July 27 that King George VI officially asked Clement Attlee to form the new government.[3] And what an election it had been. Parliament had sat uninterrupted for the previous ten years, all elections suspended during time of war, and although Winston Churchill had formed a national coalition government upon entering Downing Street in May 1940, the cabinet had still been dominated by members of the Conservative Party. Indeed, a Labour prime minister had not held the reins of power since Ramsay MacDonald submitted his letter of resignation amid the great economic crisis of 1931.[4] In late May 1945, however, with the Nazis beaten on the continent and the defeat of Japan seemingly imminent, the Labour Party withdrew from the national coalition, forcing the king to dissolve Parliament and call the first general election in a decade.[5] Despite Churchill's wartime success, the Labour Party inflicted a shock defeat on the Conservatives, picking up 239 new seats and a majority of 145 over all other parties.[6] It was just the sort of mandate Clement Attlee needed in order to achieve his ambitious program of socialist reform. It was a good time to be a member of the Labour Party.[7]

Even so, it had taken the new prime minister a nail-biting week to finalize his cabinet, and Attlee had only called upon Hall to take charge of the colonial office on Friday, August 3.

Hall had expected a ministerial role in the government, having served the Labour Party faithfully since 1922 and acted successively throughout the war as parliamentary undersecretary of state for the colonies, financial secretary to the admiralty, and parliamentary undersecretary of state for foreign affairs, but being named colonial secretary exceeded all his hopes and dreams.[8] There was real power in the colonial office, and the territories over which he now presided spread from Canada in the west, across much of Africa, the Middle East, and South Asia, to Australia and New Zealand in the east. It was truly an empire upon which the sun never set, and in 1945 it was at its greatest geographic expanse.[9]

The three months that followed his appointment, however, quelled all of Hall's initial enthusiasm, and although November 2 was the first time he had actually met with Weizmann and Shertok, it was not his first encounter with the Jewish Agency or the Palestine question. Quite the opposite, it had been the most dominant issue encountered since he had become colonial secretary. British forces had seized Palestine from the Ottoman Empire during the First World War to prevent it from falling into German hands. On November 2, 1917, A. J. Balfour, the British foreign secretary, issued the Balfour Declaration, which read in part: "His Majesty's Government view with favour the establishment in Palestine of a national home for the Jewish people, and will use their best endeavours to facilitate the achievement of this object."[10] The problem was that in 1915, Sir Henry McMahon, the British high commissioner in Egypt, had already promised Palestine to Husain ibn Ali, the Grand Sharif of Mecca, in return for Husain raising Arab armies against the Ottomans in the initial British conquest; and in 1916, the British and French governments had secretly agreed that Palestine would go neither to the Jews nor to the Arabs but would instead, together with the rest of the Middle East, be partitioned into British and French colonies.[11] Ultimately, none of these three promises were fulfilled. In 1922, the newly formed League of Nations delegated to the British the Palestinian territory as a mandate, under which the British government would administer Palestine but the Palestinian people would remain sovereign rather than British subjects.[12] To all intents and purposes, Palestine was a British colony but, on paper at least, there was the possibility for both Jewish and Arab independence from British rule.

The Jewish Agency formed shortly thereafter, in 1923, and was established according to the twenty-seven articles laid down by the League of Nations at the creation of the Palestine Mandate. Taking their lead from the Balfour Declaration, these articles committed the British government to nurturing Palestine towards the establishment of an eventual "Jewish National Home" by creating the economic, political, and administrative conditions under which Jewish independence from the British Empire could be achieved.[13] An Arab Agency, designed to protect Arab interests in light of this generally pro-Jewish charter, was rejected by Arab leaders, thus creating an imbalance in the mandate that would continue for the subsequent two and a half decades.[14] For the five years after the beginning of the mandate, from 1923 to 1928, the Arab population struggled to form a response to the declared British policy of a Jewish national home, all the while contending with increased Jewish immigration into Palestine. While the Jewish Agency strengthened its hold on Jewish-Palestinian society, liaising with the British government to ensure that those newly arrived Jews received proper housing, jobs, and other necessities of life, there was a distinct lack of leadership in the Arab community.[15]

All this changed in September 1928. On the twenty-fourth of that month, on *Yom Kippur* (the Jewish day of atonement), Jewish leaders placed a screen on Jerusalem's Western (Wailing) Wall to separate Jewish men from women. This wall, however, was regarded by Palestine's Muslim population as sacred, being the spot where Prophet Muhammad had tethered his horse after his journey from Mecca to Jerusalem. The precedent laid down by the Ottoman rulers was that no foreign objects could be attached to places perceived as holy by either religion, a policy known as the principle of *status quo*. Under mandate rule, the

British continued this practice. Edward Keith-Roach, the British deputy district commissioner in Jerusalem, therefore ordered the police to remove the screen, which they duly did. The Arab leadership in Palestine pointed to the *Yom Kippur* incident as evidence of Jewish foul play and began a propaganda campaign aimed at enhancing Muslim claims on Palestinian land. This campaign was accompanied by Arab building work directly next to and above the Western Wall, from which bricks would occasionally be dropped onto Jewish persons praying below.

Tensions between the two communities rose throughout the spring and summer of 1929 and climaxed on August 16, when the Arab community held a demonstration after Friday morning prayers at the Muslim *Haram ash-Sharif* (the Temple Mount) by the Western Wall, during which thousands of Muslims raised banners, listened to sermons, and burned Jewish prayer books. For the next week, there was a strained stand-off between Jerusalem's Jewish and Muslim populations until on August 23 a number of bloody riots erupted, beginning in Jerusalem but spreading throughout Palestine. In all 133 Jews and 116 Arabs were killed, and a further 339 Jews and 232 Arabs wounded. Following these riots of 1929, the situation in Palestine worsened considerably.[16] In response, in October 1930, the British government published a White Paper that sought to reduce Jewish immigration into Palestine and limit the purchase of land by Jews from Arabs. Following opposition from the Conservative and Liberal parties, however, the Labour prime minister withdrew the White Paper's policy recommendations in February 1931 and immigration continued unabated.[17] Between November 1931 and December 1946, 350,800 Jews immigrated to Palestine, with a further natural increase (births minus deaths) of 116,900, compared to Muslim immigration of just 100,000 and a natural increase of 271,000. Consequently, while in 1931 the Jewish population constituted 20 percent of the total population of Palestine (174,600 Jews; 693,000 Muslims; with a negligible number of Christians), by 1946, it had risen to 37 percent (625,000 Jews; 1,044,000 Muslims).[18]

For the four years following the 1929 riots, there was an uneasy quiet in Palestine, but in October 1933, rioting again broke out, with fifteen people killed in Jaffa on the twenty-seventh of that month. Clashes continued throughout the final days of October, and by the end of the month 27 people had been killed and 243 wounded, 46 of whom were in serious condition.[19] This time, in contrast to the aftermath of the 1929 riots, the British government made no policy changes and the anger in the Palestine Arab community continued to grow. It was only a matter of time before the tensions underlying this anger bubbled to the surface. In 1936, riots escalated to an Arab general strike followed by an all-out Arab revolt for independence, lasting till 1939.[20]

The outbreak of the Second World War brought great change to Palestine. In May 1939, just four months before Adolf Hitler's Panzer troops invaded Poland, the British government published a new White Paper in response to the Arab revolt. It declared that the government would move towards an independent Palestine within ten years and placed restrictions on Jewish immigration and land purchases over a five-year period, the former capped at 75,000 for that half decade. Immigration subsequent to this five-year period would be dependent on Arab consent.[21] The Muslim population in Palestine had rebelled against British policy and, as a consequence, had been granted their demands. This lesson was not lost on Palestine's Jewish population. If force could work for the Arabs, so too could it work for the Jews. A war on the European continent, where the British government was distracted by and ultimately engaged in a struggle for survival with Nazi Germany, provided the perfect backdrop against which to launch a campaign of violence.[22]

Nevertheless the majority of Zionists in Palestine decided to suspend agitation against the British government until after Nazi Germany was defeated; a violent minority was not so accommodating. The *Lohamel Herut Israel* (LEHI—Fighters for the Freedom of Israel) formed in 1939 as a breakaway group from the *Irgun Zvai Leumi* (the IZL—National Military Organization), the militant wing of Zionism, which had largely allied itself with the British on the outbreak of war.[23] LEHI's founder, Avraham Stern, was heavily read in the literature of Europe's revolutionary past; he formulated LEHI as a seditious organization that would employ terror against the British Empire, in his view the chief enemy of Zionism. Once the British were defeated and expelled from Palestine, he believed the Zionists would be free to set up the state of Israel, a true national home for the Jews.[24]

The leadership of the IZL initially condemned Stern's campaign of violence, seeking to instead work with the Jewish Agency towards a peaceful resolution of the Palestine question. The situation changed dramatically in the autumn of 1943, however, when one of the Irgun's inner leadership circle, Arieh Ben-Eliezer, returned to Palestine from the United States with confirmation that the rumors of a Jewish Holocaust on the European continent were true. This infused a new sense of urgency into the IZL and convinced it that an independent Jewish homeland was needed sooner rather than later. Despite growing revelations of this Holocaust, the British government refused to amend in any way the restrictions placed on Jewish immigration by the 1939 White Paper. This policy decision seemed murderous to many Jews. Consequently, together with Yaacov Meridor, the head of the IZL, Ben-Eliezer approached a recent Polish immigrant named Menachem Begin. They informed him that the Irgun had lost its way and that its leadership—including Meridor—had become old and devoid of ideas. A fresh commander was needed. They asked Begin if he would be that man. With a heavy heart, and fully knowing the consequences of the decision for his life, Begin accepted.[25]

Menachem Begin was an unlikely guerilla warrior. A bespectacled man with a short stature, he was born on August 16, 1913, in Brest-Litovsk, at that time a Russian territory. His early years were spent as a war refugee moving from village to village in the face of the German advance and Russian counter-advance. In 1923, at ten years old, he joined *Hashomer Hatzair*, a Zionist-scouting organization of sorts, and five years later progressed to *Betar*, a radical Zionist fascist party not unlike Germany's Nazi Party in ideology.[26] Here he came under the leadership of Vladimir Ze'ev Jabotinsky, the founder of the Zionist-Revisionist movement, which was dedicated to the immediate establishment of a Jewish state. Following a time at Warsaw University where he studied law, Begin became a political organizer for *Betar*, rising to become head of its Propaganda Department in September 1935 and *Betar* commissioner in Poland in April 1939. With the outbreak of the Second World War and the partition of Poland, Begin found himself a political prisoner in the Soviet Union's Lukishki prison and Pechora labor camp throughout 1940 and 1941. He was released only in early 1942 under the condition that he would fight the common German enemy as part of the Polish Free Army. In May of that year, he first set foot in Palestine, brought there by the army he had been forced to join as it made its way through Iran and Iraq.[27]

As an intellectual supporter of Zionism, a party organizer, and a soldier with the rank of private, Begin had never held a leadership position in a militant organization, nor did he have any experience of directing organized violence. His selection as IZL commander in late 1943 was, therefore, surprising. Nevertheless, the 30-year-old Begin approached his new position with vigor. He immediately settled on a strategy of targeted terrorist attacks against institutions of British authority. To carry out this strategy, he reorganized the IZL along the lines of an underground guerilla army, dividing Palestine into military districts and placing each under a senior officer with assault teams, propaganda units, and recruitment officers. Each member of the IZL was given a military rank, and Begin established an intelligence department to carry out reconnaissance on potential British targets. Finally, on February 1, 1944—just three months after taking command—Begin published a declaration of revolt against the British, proclaiming that the armistice between the IZL and British forces was over. On February 12, less than two weeks after this declaration, the IZL began its campaign of terror, simultaneously bombing immigration offices in Jerusalem,

Tel Aviv, and Haifa.[28] The Palestine problem, simmering since the establishment of the mandate in 1922, had finally come to a boil in open insurgency.

In February 1944, however, the British government had greater concerns before it. Beginning on February 12 and continuing until May 17, British soldiers were bogged down in the three battles of Cassino in Italy, where their repeated assaults on German positions at the monastery of Monte Cassino were viciously repelled. Further to the east, on March 12, the Japanese army launched its offensive towards Imphal and Kohima, where British and Indian troops courageously held ground, but only at great cost in lives and material. In the world's oceans, allied losses at sea continued, with the Germans sinking seventy-one merchant ships between January and March 1944. Finally, the preparations for Operation Overlord, the invasion of Normandy, had been set into place in late 1943 and by February 1944 the planning was well underway.[29]

Nevertheless, the British cabinet kept a close eye on developments in Palestine. To assist it in this task, Palestinian police secured the services of an informer within the IZL, Jankelis Chilevicius. Based on the information he provided, in late March 1944, the police arrested fifty individuals for "recent terrorist outrages," including Ben-Eliezer. In return for this information, the police promised Chilevicius passage to the United States. However, American immigration authorities insisted that the normal visa procedures be followed, with a delay of up to six months. Concerned for his safety, the British authorities in Palestine moved Chilevicius to Egypt. Unfortunately, the police in Cairo received information from informers that the IZL knew where he was located. On April 15, 1944, therefore, Sir Harold MacMichael, the British high commissioner in Palestine, sent a telegram to the colonial secretary, Oliver Stanley, requesting that Chilevicius be moved to South Africa.[30] Stanley, rightly realizing that the sanctity of the British intelligence system rested upon its ability to protect informers, immediately contacted William Ormsby-Gore, 4th Baron Harlech, the British high commissioner in South Africa. Harlech, however, told MacMichael that there was a "large Zionist population in South Africa" and that if Chilevicius were to come there, "it seems certain that they would learn of it and it is not impossible, though perhaps improbable, that he would be in danger here." He suggested that it would be better to hold Chilevicius in "some other British territory where there [were] no local Jewish militant factions."[31] MacMichael reluctantly agreed.[32]

Consequently, Chilevicius was given secret passage to Casablanca on an American military aircraft. However, British authorities in Morocco were not informed of his impending arrival. It was with some confusion, then, that the British consul in Casablanca wrote to the colonial secretary to inform him that a Palestinian had arrived at his office on May 15, 1944, refusing to give his name as anything other than "John," claiming that he was on an "official mission," and requesting that the British government help him obtain a French exit visa for the United States. Stanley forwarded the consul's telegram to MacMichael, who informed him that "John" was Chilevicius. Stanley gave the matter serious consideration and on June 2 ordered the consul in Casablanca to assist Chilevicius in obtaining his visa for the United States. By mid-summer 1944, Chilevicius had settled in New York.[33] In the first intelligence operation in its campaign against the IZL, the British government had successfully infiltrated the organization, gained information leading to the arrest of fifty suspects, and protected its informant with safe passage to the United States. It was an achievement to be proud of.

Nevertheless, the situation in Palestine continued to worsen. Following the attacks of February 12, the IZL exploded bombs on February 27 at income tax offices in Jerusalem, Tel Aviv, and Haifa. It then turned to target the Palestine police, bombing the Criminal Investigation Department (CID) stations at Haifa, Jerusalem, and Jaffa on March 23. At Haifa, these bombs killed three police constables and wounded a fourth; at Jaffa, the CID station was destroyed but without loss of life; and at Jerusalem, the Irgun shot dead a police assistant superintendant who disturbed the bombers. That same day, LEHI—in recent weeks overshadowed by the IZL—renewed its terror campaign, assassinating the British chief clerk at the Tel Aviv district police headquarters and shooting two police constables in Jerusalem, one of whom died. In all, on March 23, Zionist terrorists murdered four police constables, one police superintendent, and one chief clerk; seriously wounded two other police constables; and destroyed three CID stations.[34] It was a deadly day for the British in Palestine.

Moshe Shertok of the Jewish Agency was aghast at the Irgun's campaign. The agency believed that it, rather than the IZL or LEHI, held the true leadership of the Jewish community in Palestine. As such, it felt that it had a responsibility to broach a cease-fire. Between February 18 and March 3, 1944, representatives of the Jewish Agency met with members of the Revisionist Party—long associated with the IZL—five times, but to no avail. On April 2, therefore, the agency articulated an official policy of opposition to the terror campaign, a policy which contained three parts: "(1) efforts to stop extortion and terror, (2) increased propaganda, [and] (3) isolation of the separatists."[35] Despite this opposition, the terror campaign continued unabated. On July 14, the IZL attacked the Land Registry Office in Jerusalem, with the resulting deaths of two police constables; on July 15, it assassinated a British constable and hijacked a British truck carrying explosives; and on August 9, it riddled High Commissioner MacMichael's car with bullets, although he escaped unharmed.[36]

In the face of such continued violence, the British government placed more pressure on the Jewish Agency to control the Jewish population, accusing it of guilt by association and inaction. On October 10, 1944, the government officially requested "active collaboration with the forces of law and order" from the Jewish Agency.[37] This the agency agreed to, but from the British perspective it did so only half-heartedly. On December 22, Sir John Shaw, the British chief secretary in Palestine, wrote to Sir Arthur

Dawe, deputy undersecretary at the colonial office, detailing the collaboration offered by the agency. He revealed that between September and December 1944, the agency had provided information to the CID on 561 persons alleged to be involved with terrorism. Of these, 284 had been traced and arrested, 219 of whom had been detained under emergency regulations, 28 of whom had been released under police supervision, and 37 of whom had been released with no restrictions. Despite this impressive haul, Shaw noted that the lists provided by the Jewish Agency "did not include particulars of any *leading* terrorists; rather, the names seem to have been taken from old records and relate to unimportant members of illegal organizations." Furthermore, the value of the information given had been "poor" and the Jewish Agency seemed to be using collaboration with the British authorities more for the "working off of political scores" than for truly eliminating terrorism. Finally, the agency had been encouraging the larger Jewish population to come to it with information about terror suspects rather than to the police so that any information could be filtered before being offered up to British authorities. Shaw concluded that "there has been carefully rationed and regulated 'collaboration' which has been of some value to us. But it is not 100% sincere: it is controlled by a careful policy of Ca'canny and it is political in motive."[38]

Little changed in the new year, and on March 1, 1945, the British administration in Palestine sent a telegram to Stanley at the colonial office stating that although Jewish Agency collaboration had "in some respects improved in quality," including the receipt of information that led to the capture of Meridor, the agency's list of alleged terrorists continued to include "many persons unconnected with terrorism but politically objectionable to the Agency." Not only did this waste police time, who had difficulty "separating sheep from goats," but also marginalized an important segment of the Jewish community and potentially drove them further into the arms of the Irgun. Yet this was not the agency's only sin. It had also developed the habit of kidnapping suspects before the Palestine police could arrest them, claiming that the agency's methods of interrogation were "superior" to those used by the police. Kidnapped persons were eventually released but were "more or less the worse for wear."[39] The agency, it seemed, did not trust the British government; it could not in turn be trusted. Since October 1944, the government had attempted to delegate its responsibility for keeping Palestine safe to the Jewish Agency. By March 1945 it was clear that any information provided by the agency would be of limited value at best. It was now time to turn to other methods and other agencies.

Of the various options available to the British government, MI5 (the Security Service) seemed the most suitable. Since its founding in 1909, MI5 had been tasked with intelligence gathering and counter-subversion in the empire as well as the United Kingdom and thus had developed an empire-wide network of contacts and informants. Furthermore, while the government had been busily putting all its eggs into the basket of the Jewish Agency, MI5 did not sit idle. In September 1944—on the eve of the British decision to turn to the Jewish Agency—MI5 commissioned Richard Catling, deputy head of Palestine's Special Branch, to travel to the United States to assess Zionist influence in that country. Catling had first joined the Palestine police in 1935, traveling from his home in rural Suffolk to take employment in a part of the world he had never visited before. On the outbreak of the 1936 Arab revolt, he transferred to the CID in Jerusalem and was promoted sergeant shortly thereafter. In 1938, he moved from Jerusalem CID to the Special Branch in Jaffa, before being promoted assistant superintendent in charge of the Haifa coastal watch unit on the outbreak of the Second World War. He returned to Jerusalem's Special Branch in 1940 and became deputy head of that unit with the rank of full superintendent in early 1944.[40] It was in this role that MI5 first approached him.

Upon returning from his trip to the United States on October 10, 1944, Catling submitted a lengthy report to MI5. He had arrived in America on September 29 and spent his first full day

(September 30) fulfilling official engagements. On October 1, however, he turned to the real reason for his visit, travelling to New York to meet with an MI5 informant whom he identified only as Y 32 but who was in fact Jankelis Chilevicius. Since arriving in New York, Chilevicius had liaised with Hillel Kook, the nephew of the Palestinian Rabbi Kook, who was using the assumed name Peter Bergson and who had established a Zionist terror organization in the United States known colloquially as the Bergson Group. Chilevicius infiltrated this group, claiming to be a member of the IZL who had escaped the police roundup in March (the same roundup that was brought about by his information). Upon joining, Chilevicius quickly realized that the Bergson Group was supplying the Irgun with considerable sums of money raised in the United States and was directing some of its operations. Unfortunately, he was compromised after only two months when Eric Jabotinsky in Palestine sent a cable to Bergson revealing the extent of Chilevicius' cooperation with the Palestine police. Chilevicius was undeterred, however, and continued to probe the activities of the Bergson Group. In September, he travelled to Washington, DC, and provided his information to American Army Intelligence (G2 Branch), who in turn contacted MI5. MI5 then asked Catling, who had previously worked with Chilevicius, to travel to the United States on its behalf to verify the information.

Catling met with Chilevicius over a period of five days, from October 1 to 5. The information he secured was of an alarming nature. The Bergson Group, led by eighteen prominent Zionists (nine of whom were exiled Palestinians known to Jerusalem CID as IZL members), planned to lead a "full-scale Jewish uprising in Palestine," scheduled to begin two or three months after the Allies defeated Germany. The Bergson Group had dispatched Ben-Eliezer from New York to Palestine in the autumn of 1943 to reorganize the IZL, and it was at Bergson's prompting that Meridor had resigned as Irgun leader, allowing Begin to take the helm. The anticipated Jewish rising had a similar plan to the infamous 1916 Easter Rising in Ireland, with members of the IZL and LEHI tasked to seize the Jerusalem General Post Office, the Ramallah broadcasting station, the British Secretariat, Government House (the residence of the British high commissioner), and the district offices in Jerusalem, Haifa, Jaffa, and Tel Aviv. The Bergson Group gambled that they would be able to hold these positions against the police, and once the government called in British soldiers "the propaganda value of a wail that British soldiers were killing Jews in their own homeland would turn world opinion" in favor of the Irgun. Once the uprising began and once international opinion favored the guerilla campaign, the Bergson Group believed that Jews from the world over would flock to Palestine to fight, and thus the British forces would be easily defeated. In October 1944, Chilevicius could provide no further details. He hoped, however, that more information would soon be forthcoming, as he was on "intimate terms" with Ruth Kaplan, Samuel Merlin's mistress and second in command of the Bergson Group.[41]

While in New York meeting with Chilevicius, Catling also contacted representatives of the Federal Bureau of Investigation (FBI), who supported the information provided by Chilevicius with hard evidence. E. W. Bavin of British Security Coordination and Ian McEwen, the New York British passport control officer, were likewise able to substantiate Chilevicius' claims. On October 5, Catling returned to Washington, DC, where he met with Isaiah Berlin at the British Embassy, who gave further credence to the existence of the Bergson Group and its direction of certain aspects of IZL strategy. On October 7, Catling met with special agents Burton and Roach of the Washington office of the FBI, who confirmed that Bergson was a "racketeer." Finally, Catling met with Evan Wilson, head of the Palestine desk in the American state department, two other members of the state department, three members of G2, and one employee of the justice department, each of whom were aware of the existence of the Bergson Group. In his final report to MI5, Catling concluded: "We know that what Y 32 [Chilevicius] told us regarding the Irgun in March this year was correct and I believe that what he communicated to me in New York has basis in fact, although the information is sketchy. It is sufficient to indicate, in my opinion, that the Bergson Group is connected with the Irgun in Palestine and seemingly supplying funds for the terrorist activity."[42]

Catling's report sent shockwaves through the British intelligence establishment. On December 13, 1944, Guy Liddell, director of MI5's B Division (counter-espionage), contacted the FBI foreign attaché in London, requesting that the FBI in New York keep a close eye on Chilevicius and give MI5 "their estimate of his reliability." The FBI agreed to do so, but before carrying out any investigation first consulted with the colonial office on the legality of the operation. On December 19, Christopher Eastwood, formerly private secretary to the British high commissioner in Palestine and now in the colonial office, wrote to Liddell explaining the difficulties of liaison with the FBI (the latter famously territorial). He requested that the bureau be fully briefed on the position of Chilevicius before further cooperation was sought. Liddell complied with this request but at great cost to his mission. The FBI was furious, complaining to Liddell on January 26, 1945, that Catling had "at no time revealed the real purpose of his visit to the country or the fact that he had interviewed or intended to interview a British informant residing in the U.S.A." The FBI now demanded to know why neither MI5 nor Catling had informed them that British intelligence was running an informant in the United States. Liddell's colleague in MI5, A. J. Kellar, explained to Eastwood that this questioning by the FBI was an "unfortunate and unexpected development since, knowing how sensitive the F.B.I. are in such matters, we had warned Catling that it would be wiser to take the Bureau fully into his confidence and enlist their cooperation." Catling, when questioned, explained that he had not fully informed the FBI of Chilevicius because "they were evidently not au fait with the details of the Bergson Group" and thus did not need to know. MI5 accepted his excuse and pursued the matter no further.[43]

In March 1945, however, with relations between the British government and the Jewish Agency collapsing, the colonial office again approached MI5 to ask that they repair their relationship with the FBI and take the lead role in intelligence gathering in Palestine.[44] Within a month, MI5 had gathered more information on the IZL than the Jewish Agency had provided in six months. In particular, Liddell wrote to Eastwood on April 19, 1945, explaining that MI5 had received an "urgent signal" from Security Intelligence Middle East (SIME) revealing that "V-Day in Europe may be regarded as D-Day by the Irgun Zwi [sic] Leumi and Stern Group [LEHI], the two terrorist organizations in Palestine." The information was credible, having come directly from Meridor, the former leader and present second in command of the IZL. Meridor was at that time under interrogation in Cairo but he had been cultivating a friendship with a British warden, who he hoped would assist him in his eventual escape. Meridor, believing that he had won the warden's confidence, revealed the plan to him. Although MI5 could not verify with absolute certainty the truth behind this revelation, Liddell informed Eastwood that the warden had "shown himself in the past to be a truthful reporter" and was an "unimaginative man" with "no motive for exaggeration" who was "unaware of the importance of his statement." Meridor, in contrast, was "by nature a boastful man. There is therefore nothing inherently improbable in his making such an important disclosure to an outsider." SIME believed that this information "should be given its full value" and asked MI5 that they be informed 48 hours prior to expected victory in Europe so that they might better prepare for the anticipated revolt. Liddell contacted the war cabinet, which assured him that he would be informed of such impending victory, although it was unlikely that he could be given the full 48 hours advance notice. He was authorized to share what notice he was given with Brigadier Douglas Roberts, head of SIME.[45]

On April 24, just five days after Liddell wrote to Eastwood, John Rymer Jones, the inspector general of the Palestine police, gave further credence to MI5's information, writing in a report to the chief secretary that although it would be "difficult, possibly unwise, to attempt to forecast the future development of Jewish terrorism," there was nevertheless a "distinct feeling in many quarters that the Irgun is about to renew activity." His report was forwarded to the colonial office.[46] In the days that followed Jones' report, events on the European continent proceeded quickly towards the anticipated allied victory over Germany. On April 23, Soviet forces entered Berlin; the city fell on May 2. By that point, Adolf Hitler had committed suicide (he did so on April 30). On May 4, German forces in Holland, Denmark, and northwest Germany surrendered to the allies, followed on May 7 by a complete and unconditional surrender by the entire German army. This surrender was accepted by the allies on May 8. Victory-in-Europe Day had finally arrived, and with it, the expected D-Day of the Jewish insurgent campaign in Palestine.[47]

The information provided by Chilevicius, as well as the intelligence gained by MI5, SIME, and the Palestine police, seemed to have been erroneous, however. On May 12, the police did discover a collection of mortars buried throughout the mandate, and on May 14 the IZL destroyed 400 telegraph poles in an act of communications sabotage, but this was more of the same rather than a heightened level of violence. The anticipated widespread revolt did not materialize.[48] Indeed, in the weeks following VE-Day, the Jewish Agency found a new assertiveness and the Irgun announced a temporary cease-fire to assess British intentions now that the war in Europe was over. On May 22, two weeks after the German surrender, the agency sent a list of demands to the British government: first, it had to declare immediately its desire to establish a Jewish state; secondly, it had to grant the Jewish Agency the power to welcome an unlimited number of Jews; thirdly, it had to secure an international loan to assist in the transportation of one million Jewish immigrants; fourthly, it had to obtain reparations from Germany on behalf of the Jewish people for the suffering inflicted during the Holocaust; and finally, it had to cooperate internationally to ensure the smooth operation of Jewish immigration into Palestine.[49] If any one of these demands were not met, the

Jewish Agency warned that it would find it very difficult to condemn any further actions by the Irgun.

Churchill's national coalition government did not respond immediately to these demands. Following the Labour Party's withdrawal from the government, however, Labour leader Clement Attlee immediately issued a statement of pro-Zionist intentions and pledged his support to an eventual Jewish state, a platform his party held to throughout the general election campaign. With the Labour Party victory on July 26, the Jewish Agency was buoyed at the prospects of the soon-to-be Jewish national home, and the IZL kept in place its cease-fire. The only question now remaining was how long it would take for the Labour government to fulfill its campaign promises and finally create an independent Jewish state in Palestine.[50]

Despite these political changes in London, the realities of imperial administration on the ground remained very much the same. On July 29, just two days after Attlee formed his government, Christopher Eastwood wrote to Sir Miles Lampson, 1st Baron Killearn, the newly appointed undersecretary of state for foreign affairs. He gave him a brief summary of recent intelligence activities in Palestine and then informed him that a suspected terrorist had been arrested for the 1944 murder by LEHI of Lord Moyne (Walter Edward Guinness, 1st Baron Moyne), the former colonial secretary. The suspect, a man named Joseph Sytner, was in the process of being extradited to Egypt for trial.[51] In Westminster, the government may have changed but in Palestine the counterinsurgency campaign continued as before, regardless of any purported cease-fire on the part of the Irgun. As far as the British security forces and colonial administration were concerned, Palestine still had to be watched, and watched carefully.

II.   The American intervention

When George Henry Hall became colonial secretary on August 3, 1945—five days after Eastwood wrote to Killearn—he too was briefed by the colonial office civil servant; was given detailed information on the interactions between MI5, SIME, and the FBI; and was provided with an account of all that had transpired with Chilevicius. The colonial office gave the same briefings to the foreign secretary Ernest Bevin, the war secretary Jack Lawson, the first lord of the admiralty Albert Victor Alexander, the air secretary Lord Stansgate (William Wedgwood Benn, 1st Viscount Stansgate), the chancellor of the exchequer Hugh Dalton, and the prime minister Clement Attlee. The colonial office and security forces made the new cabinet well aware of the problems that had dogged Palestine throughout the war, as well as the terror campaign waged by the IZL and LEHI.

This new information challenged the cabinet members, particularly those with instinctive Zionist sympathies, and made it considerably more difficult for them to honor their election pledges to bring about the immediate implementation of a Jewish state. They also had to consider the question of the Palestinian Arabs, who had been given frequent guarantees for their future in that land by British statesmen and soldiers since 1915. In his memoirs, Attlee succinctly articulated the difficulty his government confronted in Palestine upon taking power in July 1945:

> We were faced with a legacy of the past in the incompatible assurances that had been given to Arabs and Jews. The sufferings of the Jews under the Nazi regime, the romantic adventure of the Palestine experiment, and the wealth of sentiment for the Jewish national home enlisted great support for the Jews ... On the other hand, the Arabs, as the inhabitants of Palestine for centuries, had a case which was sometimes ignored. They commanded support throughout the Moslem world, and there are many Moslems in the British Commonwealth and Empire.[52]

This problem was further conflated by the fact that with all the challenges the government faced that summer, Palestine was simply not a priority. In the first days of August, Japan was as yet undefeated, and even after the dropping of the atomic bombs on Hiroshima and Nagasaki on August 6 and 9 and the Japanese surrender on August 15, the question of what to do with Japan plagued the cabinet.[53] Germany too remained an occupied power and needed to be dealt with, a problem enhanced by its partition between east and west.[54] The advent of the nuclear age increased tensions with the Soviet Union, tensions that had already seemed close to boiling point at the Potsdam Conference of July 16 to August 2. Even before the allies dropped the atomic bombs, the post-hostilities planning staff presented to the war cabinet a report titled "The Security of the British Empire." It noted that "the U.S.S.R. has proved herself to possess the war potential to constitute a serious threat to the British Empire" and listed as the number one imperial defense commitment, "The safeguarding of British territories and of Imperial communications against Soviet aggression."[55] These beginnings of the Cold War forced the British government into a "new terrifying era" in which the troubles in Palestine seemed quite small.[56]

The international situation was undeniably grave. Yet even with all of these issues at hand, imperial and foreign policy was not the Labour government's primary consideration upon taking power. Indeed, the party's 1945 electoral manifesto had contained just one sentence on the empire, referring vaguely to "the planned progress of our Colonial Dependencies."[57] More important to the government was rebuilding at home, in particular the nationalization of British industry and the establishment of a robust welfare state. Attlee wrote that the "ultimate objective" of his party upon taking power was "the creation of a society based on social justice ... in our view, this could be attained only by bringing under public ownership and control the main factors in the economic system."[58] Attlee was quick to act on this belief and between 1945 and 1949 various elements of the British economy were nationalized: "The Bank of England, civil aviation, cable and wireless, and coal in 1946; railways, long-distance road transport, and electricity in 1947;

gas in 1948; [and] iron and steel in 1949."[59] The government supported this program of nationalization with the implementation of the welfare state, the centerpiece of which was a national health service, complemented by a national insurance scheme, a government housing program, the creation of a comprehensive secondary school system, and government-backed free education through the undergraduate level.[60] With such an ambitious domestic program to execute, the government had little time to devote to the empire. Consequently, colonial affairs took a back seat in cabinet discussions.

Nevertheless, under the Labour Party the colonial office remained one of the six largest ministries in Whitehall, having doubled in size between 1939 and 1945.[61] Furthermore, of all the issues the colonial secretary had before him in 1945, none was more pressing than Palestine and it was to Palestine that George Hall devoted most of his time.[62] This was particularly accentuated by the pressure placed on Britain's government by the American administration of President Harry S. Truman. On July 24, just three days before Attlee came to power, Truman wrote to Winston Churchill, the sitting prime minister, informing him of the "passionate protest from Americans" that continued to greet the 1939 White Paper restrictions placed on Jewish immigration and imploring him to lift "the restrictions which deny to Jews, who have been so cruelly uprooted by ruthless Nazi persecutions, entrance into the land which represents for so many of them their only hope of survival."[63] By the time the letter reached Downing Street, Churchill's government had been replaced by the Labour government and it was therefore Attlee's responsibility to send the response. This he did on July 31, curtly replying: "I cannot give you any statement of policy until we have had time to consider the matter."[64]

Truman did not let the issue rest, however. On August 16, he informed the press corps that he had "asked Churchill and Attlee to allow as many Jews as possible into Palestine."[65] Two weeks later, he wrote again to Attlee, stating that "no other single matter is so important for those who have known the horrors of concentration camps for over a decade as is the future of the immigration possibilities into Palestine," and telling him that "the American people, as a whole, firmly believe that immigration into Palestine should not be closed, and that a reasonable number of Europe's persecuted Jews should, in accordance with their wishes, be permitted to resettle there."[66] Truman included with his letter a report by Earl G. Harrison, dean of the University of Pennsylvania Law School and a U.S. congressman who served on the House of Representatives' intergovernmental committee on refugees. Harrison's report suggested that an additional 100,000 Jews ought to be allowed into Palestine. Truman assured Attlee that he was in full agreement with the report's findings.[67]

Attlee immediately dismissed Truman's suggestion, informing him that British immigration authorities had "very grave difficulties" and that the British government as a whole had "endeavoured to avoid treating people on a racial basis." Attlee then reminded Truman that "we have the Arabs to consider as well," particularly as there were in British India alone "ninety million Moslems, who are easily inflamed." For that reason, he rejected Harrison's recommendations, believing that they would have "very far-reaching implications."[68] Committing to an eventual Jewish home in the Palestine mandate was one thing, but immediately altering the demographics in favor of the Jewish population at the expense of Arab public opinion empire-wide was quite another. It simply could not be done. Attlee confirmed this judgment on October 25, 1945, telling Truman that the cabinet "had the problems of Palestine and of helping the Jews urgently before it," but stressing that these two problems "were not necessarily the same."[69]

The British government stood behind Attlee on this issue. From September 5 to 17, the foreign secretary chaired a conference of British representatives in the Middle East that explored future British policy in the region, attended by the British ambassadors to Baghdad, Cairo, and Teheran, the British ministers at Beirut and Jeddah, the British high commissioner for Palestine and Transjordan, representatives from the British

Middle East Office in the foreign office, and the director-general of the Middle East Supply Centre. Bevin made it clear that the conference was not to consider the "Jewish-Arab problem in Palestine," which was only a small part of the larger picture. He also stressed that the Middle East was to "remain largely a British sphere of influence." As such, Bevin publicly announced that the British government would "not make any concession that would assist American commercial penetration into a region which for generations has been an established British market."[70] The Palestine committee of the cabinet likewise insisted that the "attitude of the Arabs" was of the "first importance" since the Middle East was a region of "vital consequence" for the empire and the Middle East was, of course, largely populated by Arabs.[71]

The British government could not entirely ignore the wishes of the American administration, however, and Attlee could not continue to defy Truman without risking a rift in the Anglo-American relationship that was so important to postwar rebuilding in Britain. This was especially true as the United States seemed to be taking a leading role in world political and economic affairs. Only weeks before Bevin's conference on Middle East policy, the British ambassador to the United States, Lord Halifax (E. F. L. Wood, the 1st Earl of Halifax), sent a dispatch to Bevin, warning him that in the United States "the concept has steadily gained ground ... that Great Britain has come to occupy a position on the world stage which in terms of power and influence is inferior to that of the United States." This was heightened by a fear among the American public that following the election of the Labour government, Britain was "about to embark on a Socialist experiment." The American administration was "apprehensive lest Britain, for all her temperamental caution, will now commit herself to a thoroughgoing system of State trading with its attendant features of subsidies, bulk purchases and quotas which might effectively defeat any sound working of the reciprocal trade programme." For this reason, Halifax cautioned, "Our official pronouncements will be eagerly awaited: the development of our economic and foreign policies will be scrutinised with the utmost care."[72] The US government was certainly open to British proposals regarding foreign affairs, but it would not hesitate to act unilaterally if these were not forthcoming. The United States no longer felt compelled to seek British cooperation and advice.

With Halifax's warning on his mind, Bevin proposed to the cabinet that a joint Anglo-American committee of inquiry be formed to address the question of European Jewish refugees. His hope was that a solution could be found that was acceptable to American public opinion but would not tie the British government's hand in formulating a policy for Palestine that pleased the empire's Arab populations.[73] The colonial office initially balked at the proposal, declaring that American participation in the committee would ultimately prejudice its results due to their strongly held and publicly stated sympathy for Jewish immigration into Palestine. The result of such shared policymaking, it claimed, would be "a complete loss of face [for the British] in the Middle East."[74] Less than a week later, however, at a meeting of the Palestine committee Bevin persuaded the colonial secretary that the implications for future Anglo-American relations made the Palestine question more of a foreign affairs issue than a colonial issue and thus the colonial office should defer to the judgment of the foreign office. As he would do throughout his time in the cabinet, Hall gave way to Bevin, agreeing against his civil servants' wishes to the formation of an Anglo-American committee on the Jewish refugee problem in Europe.[75]

On October 11, the cabinet approved the terms of reference for the new committee, and on October 18, Bevin granted Halifax permission to present the proposal to the American government. The draft submitted to the American secretary of state, James F. Byrnes, listed the purposes of the committee in the following way:

(1) To examine the position of the Jews in Europe,
(2) To make an estimate of the number that could not be settled in their own countries of origin,

(3) To examine the possibility of relieving the position in Europe by immigration into other countries outside Europe, including the United States,

(4) To consider other available means of meeting the needs of the immediate solution.[76]

Significantly, Bevin's proposal made no mention of Palestine.

Byrnes carefully considered the proposal and he and Halifax met twice, on October 19 and 22, before Byrnes handed an amended and generally unrecognizable draft of the committee's terms of reference to Halifax. The draft began by boldly requiring the committee to "examine the political, economic and social conditions in Palestine as they bear upon the problem of Jewish immigration and settlement therein, and the well-being of the peoples now living therein." The second term of reference pledged the committee to "examine the position of the Jews in those countries in Europe where they have been the victims of Nazi and Fascist persecutions, and the practical measures taken or contemplated to be taken in those countries to enable them to live free from discrimination and oppression, and to make estimates of those who wish, or will be impelled by their conditions, to migrate to Palestine or other countries outside Europe." The third and final term of reference declared that the committee would "hear the views of competent witnesses including representatives of Arabs and Jews on the problem of Palestine ... and [would] make recommendations to the governments of the United States and Great Britain for the ad interim handling of these problems as well as for their permanent solution."[77] In a single bureaucratic brushstroke, Bevin's committee of European Jewish refugees without reference to Palestine had become a committee on the Palestine problem.

There followed a diplomatic wrangling between Bevin and Byrnes, with Halifax caught in the middle. Bevin refused, Byrnes pushed, Bevin retreated, Byrnes conciliated, and ultimately an agreement was reached on November 7, 1945, which declared that the committee's primary responsibility was to explore

"Palestine's potential to solve the refugee problem," although with the caveat that "other countries outside Europe" would also be considered for the eventual resettlement of Jewish refugees.[78] Bevin's original plan—to placate the Americans without prejudicing British action in Palestine—had failed miserably. An Anglo-American committee had indeed been set up, but an investigation into Jewish settlement in Palestine was at its heart. The British government had, in effect, abdicated its sole responsibility for the future of the Palestine mandate, introducing an American element into decision making and requiring future consultation with the government of the United States. All British action in Palestine would henceforth be scrutinized across the Atlantic.

Yet Bevin had larger concerns to worry about, for just six days before this agreement was reached, the IZL renewed its campaign of terror and he and George Hall made it clear to the leadership of the Jewish Agency that violence on the part of the Jewish population in Palestine was unacceptable. There could be no backing down from that stance. Regardless of American pressure, the British counterinsurgency campaign was about to escalate dramatically.

III. The terror begins again

While Attlee was wrestling with Truman, Bevin with Byrnes, and the Jewish militants with each other, British intelligence continued to closely monitor the situation in Palestine. On August 22, 1945, Sir David Petrie, director-general of MI5, wrote to A. F. Giles, head of police CID in Palestine, to discuss the future of Agent Y 32, Jankelis Chilevicius. He regretfully informed Giles that from June 9, 1945, the FBI had refused to run Chilevicius on behalf of British intelligence. MI5 had no official mandate to operate in the United States and MI6 (the Secret Intelligence Service) could not approach Chilevicius for fear of offending American intelligence. Agent Y 32 had ceased to exist as a British asset, therefore. Nevertheless, MI5 was through undisclosed methods continuing to watch the main Jewish-Palestinian suspects in the United States. As a sign of the continuing good faith between MI5 and the Palestine police, Petrie sent with his letter intelligence reports on two of MI5's most watched men, Abraham Abrahams and Jeremiah Helpern, the latter of whom Chilevicius had singled out as the expected leader of the Jewish revolt.[79]

Two days after Petrie wrote to Giles, MI5's A. J. Kellar sent a telegram to Christopher Eastwood at the colonial office, informing him that an agent of the Defence Security Office (DSO), the local MI5 station in Cairo, had been murdered on August 20. The agent, Joseph Davidesca, was the man primarily responsible for the capture of Joseph Sytner in Egypt (Lord Moyne's murderer). Kellar had received intelligence to suggest that LEHI was responsible, despite its purported cease-fire. Furthermore, on August 16, the Palestine police had captured three persons with two Thompson submachine guns, two rifles, fourteen pistols, four grenades, and a quantity of explosives. These men also carried with them several IZL pamphlets. The police believed that they were on an Irgun training mission. The murder of Davidesca, together with these arrests, seemed to confirm that any cessation of terrorist violence in Palestine was fleeting.[80]

It was not only MI5 and the Palestine police who were concerned about a resumption of hostilities. The Royal Air Force (RAF), likewise, was preparing for a fight with the IZL. Liaising with the army, the RAF determined that it would need a minimum of two fighter squadrons and one tactical reconnaissance squadron to support the expected three army divisions that would be deployed to Palestine on the outbreak of a new terrorist campaign. The reason for this was that "Army operations when they commence must almost inevitably lead to large scale unrest with a corresponding scale of air operations."[81] On August 31, 1945, Group Captain E. R. E. Black wrote to Air Commodore H. D. McGregor, the commanding officer of RAF Levant, recommending that "Although it is not visualized that there will be any great need for bombing and the chances of it are unlikely, it is essential that some stocks should be held so that if the need should arise it can be met."[82] By September 12, McGregor and Black had developed an "Administrative Plan for Internal Security Operations in Palestine," which stipulated that tactical stations operating internal security squadrons in the Middle East would be given "first priority in supply and maintenance." It then laid down eight expected missions that the RAF would be involved with in Palestine: "(a) Demonstration flights; (b) Tactical Reconnaissance; (c) Area Reconnaissance; (d) Protection of trains and convoys; (e) Supply and leaflet dropping; (f) Laying of smoke screens; (g) Maintenance of Internal and External Communications [and] (h) Evacuation of casualties."[83] While the channels of American and British diplomacy remained choked with debate over what level of Jewish immigration could be sustained in Palestine, RAF leaders were planning for war.

When this war finally arrived on November 1, 1945, it did so with the bombing of police naval vessels and the Palestinian railway system, including the railway lines, the stationmasters' offices, and the trains themselves. Following these attacks Hall and Bevin hastily met with Weizmann and Shertok on November 2 at the foreign office. The colonial office immediately sent reports of this meeting to the high commissioner of Palestine, as did the foreign office to the British ambassador in Washington, DC, and the dominions office to the prime ministers of Canada, Australia, New Zealand, and South Africa.[84] Hall and Bevin, acting on behalf of the British government, had put the Jewish Agency on notice and they wanted the world to see this. Tellingly, Bevin instructed Lord Halifax, the British ambassador to the United States, to "inform Mr. Byrnes [the American Secretary of State] of [the] substance of this interview."[85] The British government had warned the Jewish leaders that if violence continued in Palestine, the security forces would increase the intensity of their counterinsurgency campaign. From November 6, the American government was well aware of this stance.

With the United States informed of British intentions, the cabinet felt that the way was clear for more aggressive action. There were sufficient troops in place to conduct such an operation. When the Irgun renewed its terror campaign on November 1, the British Army in Palestine consisted of one infantry division, one airborne division, and one independent infantry brigade. Together, these units provided twenty-nine infantry battalions (including airborne battalions), four armored regiments, and eight artillery regiments, numbering about 25,000 men in all. These field formations were supported by a further 75,000 troops in noncombat roles. The mandate was then divided for the purposes of administration and command into three military sectors. The army within each of these sectors was commanded by the General Officer Commanding (GOC) British troops in Palestine and Transjordan, at that time Lieutenant General J. C. D'Arcy. The GOC also had control over the Palestine police, providing absolute coordination in security matters, although on a day-to-day basis the police were commanded by their inspector general, in 1945, Captain J. M. Rymer Jones. The police force numbered about 20,000 men and was divided into six police districts. Various intelligence agencies then supported the police and the army, with MI5 playing the lead role. Each of these elements of the security forces answered to the civilian authority of the British high commissioner in Palestine and Transjordan, Field Marshal Viscount Gort (John Standish Vereker, 6th Viscount Gort).[86]

On November 6, the day Bevin ordered Halifax to brief American Secretary of State Byrnes, General D'Arcy ordered additional airborne troops into Haifa in a show of force.[87] Just days earlier, on November 1, he had imposed a road curfew and established roadblocks to ensure that it would be enforced.[88] Further operations were delayed by a change in the civilian leadership, however. On November 2, Viscount Gort was diagnosed with cancer and tendered his resignation.[89] His replacement, Lieutenant General Sir Alan Cunningham, arrived in Palestine six days later, on November 8. Cunningham was well known in military circles. Commissioned in 1906, he had served on the western front during the First World War, where he was awarded both a Military Cross and the Distinguished Service Order. Following the war, he rose through the officer ranks to become commander of the 5th Anti-Aircraft Division by the Second World War. In 1940, Sir Arthur Wavell chose him to act as GOC East Africa in the campaign to retake Abyssinia. By April 1941 his men had "covered 1,700 miles, liberated nearly 400,000 square miles of country, and taken 50,000 prisoners, all at the cost of 500 casualties." In June, Sir Claude Auchinleck appointed him commander of the British Eighth Army. In this position he performed less well, however, and Auchinleck relieved him before the end of 1941, at which time he returned home to England to serve as commandant of the Staff College. It was while in this post that he was called upon by the war secretary to take up the civilian position of British high commissioner in Palestine.[90]

While Cunningham settled in, the rhetoric in London heated up. On November 5, Attlee told the House of Commons that there was "no excuse for violence," echoing the words spoken three days earlier by the colonial secretary, George Hall, who expressed "feelings of abhorrence at this dastardly series of outrages" and pledged that "Unless [the wanton resort to force] is stopped and suppressed [by the Jewish community], then progress in relation to Palestine will be impossible."[91] The House of Commons staged its first full debate on the issue on November 13, when the foreign secretary briefed those gathered on the agreement he had just reached to establish the Anglo-American committee of inquiry. He began by reminding his fellow parliamentarians of the difficulties the British government faced in Palestine, explaining that "since the introduction of the Mandate it has been impossible to find common ground between the Arabs and the Jews." He then gave his rationale behind establishing an Anglo-American committee, before revealing its terms of reference. Taking a sudden twist, however, he informed the House that ultimately the British government would not be tied to the recommendations of the committee: "So far as Palestine is concerned, it will be clear that His Majesty's Government cannot divest themselves of their duties and responsibilities under the Mandate while the Mandate continues." He pledged, therefore, to "consult with the Arabs" at every step of the way and declared that the government reserved the right of "devising other temporary arrangements for dealing with the Palestine problem" if the committee's findings were unacceptable either to the British government or to the Arab population.[92]

To the outside world, it appeared that Bevin was backtracking on the Labour government's manifesto promise to create a Jewish home in Palestine, as well as implying that the Anglo-American committee of inquiry was a mere ruse for keeping in check an unhappy American populace. Bevin confirmed this impression when a journalist asked him to explain further at a press conference in Parliament following his speech. He bluntly stated that "Britain had never undertaken to establish a Jewish state but rather a Jewish home."[93] Among the Zionist population in Palestine, the anger was immediate and deadly. When news of Bevin's statement reached the mandate, day-long rioting in Jerusalem and Tel Aviv killed three people and injured a further thirty-three civilians and thirty-seven soldiers.[94]

Sir Alan Cunningham, the new British high commissioner in Palestine, could wait no longer to order action. He immediately contacted the GOC, General D'Arcy, who implemented Operation Bellicose, an action orientated toward the heart of the trouble in Tel Aviv. At just before seven o'clock in the evening on November 14, 1945, C Company of the eighth battalion, the Parachute Regiment (8 PARA), advanced into the city with their bayonets fixed, the horns of their vehicles blaring, and carrying signs that read in English, Arabic, and Hebrew, "Disperse or We Fire." When the crowd responded with stone throwing, the company commander co-opted the services of a local magistrate to reiterate the army's demands. When he too failed to move the crowd, the commanding officer ordered select marksmen to fire carefully placed warning shots in the direction of those protesting. This was done without any injury to the Jewish protesters, and the crowd, for the most part, simply relocated to another area of town and continued to riot. The remaining companies of 8 PARA arrived shortly thereafter and by ten o'clock they had quieted the city.

Following the evening's violence, the British administration in Palestine instituted a curfew in Tel Aviv, which the city's population broke as soon as the sun rose on November 15. Consequently, General D'Arcy approved the deployment of two more battalions of the Parachute Regiment into the city by nightfall and brought in a further infantry battalion and two armored-car regiments on November 16. On November 17, these soldiers distributed a proclamation issued by Cunningham that "directed all citizens to behave in an orderly manner and warned that the government would take all measures necessary to maintain order."[95] Cunningham's words seemed to strike the right cord and rioting in the city ceased. On November 20, the high commissioner lifted the curfew and the army battalions returned to their camps. Operation Bellicose was over.

To the extent that such serious rioting would never occur again in the subsequent three years of British rule, Bellicose was a success. However, Palestine as a whole was anything but quiet. On November 23, just three days after Cunningham lifted the curfew in Tel Aviv, Jewish militants stole two truckloads of explosives from an RAF base. Two days later, the Haganah, which as the military arm of the Jewish Agency had been formed to protect Jewish settlements during the communal riots of the 1920s and 1930s, attacked a police station at Givat Olga wounding four policemen. That night, the Haganah also ambushed a coastal patrol station at Sidna-Ali, wounding a further ten policemen. In response, the following day the British Sixth Airborne division, together with the Palestine police, mounted a 10,000-man search operation on the Plain of Sharon and in Samaria, where Sydna-Ali was located. The objective of this operation was to find the stolen armaments and capture those who had launched the Haganah attacks. The soldiers, however, met with universal resistance from the Jews whose homes they wished to search. Rioting soon broke out and by the end of the day the soldiers had shot dead eight Jews and wounded seventy-five; sixty-five British soldiers and sixteen policemen were also wounded in the operation. The security forces did arrest 337 people, although they found very few arms and 140 of those detained were subsequently released due to mistaken identity and overenthusiasm on the part of the soldiers in their initial roundup. On December 11, 120 more were released, leaving just 77 of the original 337 in state custody.[96] The number of Jews living in Samaria and on the Plain of Sharon who had been isolated by these actions and were thus more prone to give sympathy to the IZL, LEHI, and Haganah was incalculable. While some Jews who were insurgents had indeed been captured, many more who were innocent had suffered along with the guilty.

Not only was this search operation a public relations disaster for the British, but it also failed to quell the violence. On December 27, the IZL, working in coordination with LEHI, pulled off its most ambitious attack to date, targeting the Jerusalem CID headquarters, the CID station in Jaffa, and the workshop of the British army's Royal Electrical and Mechanical Engineers (REME) regiment at the Tel Aviv exhibition grounds. No soldiers were killed at the REME workshop, but in Jerusalem the explosive devices used to enter the police station killed one constable and four Basuto guards who were on imperial service in Palestine, as well as wounding another five constables. In Jaffa, a police superintendent and five constables were sprayed with machine gun fire by the IZL, which killed one and wounded the other four. During the Irgun's withdrawal, the gunmen shot dead three more constables who were attempting to cut off their escape. In all, on that cold December evening, ten members of the British security forces lost their lives and a further twelve were wounded—the greatest number killed in a single night since the beginning of the Irgun's revolt in 1944.[97]

Immediately following the attacks, the high commissioner summoned Moshe Shertok, who was back from his trip to London, and David Ben Gurion, the coleader of the Jewish Agency, to Government House. He demanded to know, first, "to what extent is the Jewish Agency associated with or dissociated from these incidents," and second, "to what extent [is] the Jewish Agency prepared to co-operate with the Government in tracking down those responsible?" Ben Gurion, taking the lead in the conversation, told Cunningham that the Jewish Agency "entirely dissociated itself" from the terrorist attacks but confessed that the agency "could neither co-operate in bringing law breakers to the book, nor call on the Jewish community to keep the law," because the law itself had lost all respect and validity for the Jewish population. Cunningham asked Ben Gurion if this was his way of admitting that the Jewish Agency had "lost control over the people," to which both Ben Gurion and Shertok nodded their concurrence.[98]

The following day, December 29, Cunningham wrote to Hall, providing the colonial secretary with a report on the situation in Palestine as it stood at the end of the year. He began by explaining that the Jewish Agency had now lost all control and credibility within Palestine, a fact admitted by its leaders. He then turned to the security situation. Thus far, British policy had been to limit operations to "establishment searches" in the "vicinity of incidents." D'Arcy, the GOC, had suggested that the conditions in Palestine might now "call for widespread seizure of persons, and searches for arms." For the time being, Cunningham had decided against this recommendation, his reason being that it would provoke an outcry that could derail the investigations of the Anglo-American committee, thus delaying indefinitely the settlement of the Palestine question. Cunningham was quick to point out, however, that "government troops and police have shown [the] greatest tolerance in the face of [the] most severe provocation." If the situation continued to worsen, he would have no qualms about "instituting full scale operations against Jewish illegal military organisations in this country." He further encouraged Hall to make frequent public announcements stating that the government and security forces were willing to take the "strongest measures" if necessary, so that "the patience, constantly manifested by His Majesty's Government in the face of these continuous outrages, should not be misconstrued as weakness."[99]

Upon receiving Cunningham's report, Hall summoned the undersecretary of state for colonial affairs, Arthur Creech Jones, and asked him to prepare a detailed report on Palestine in advance of the cabinet meeting scheduled for January 1, 1946. In this report, Creech Jones summarized the meeting that Cunningham had held with Ben Gurion and Shertok, as well as Cunningham's report to Hall, before providing a more comprehensive account of the Jewish Agency. He noted that on December 30, just two days after its meeting with Cunningham, the agency issued an "unequivocal assertion that His Majesty's Government are no longer entitled to rule the country," a defiant attitude that Cunningham now believed could not be ignored. Creech Jones cautioned, however, that if the government decided to act, it could do so in only one of two ways. First, it could shut down the Jewish Agency, arrest its leaders, and deport them from Palestine; or second, it could ostracize the agency within Palestine, refuse any further meetings between it and the government, and instruct the police to trail its leaders. Whichever of these two paths the government followed, the inevitable consequence would be a weakening of the political moderates in the agency and strengthening of the extremists, boycotting by the Jewish community of the Anglo-American committee, and "virtual certainty of serious civil war or at any rate of widespread disorders." Against Cunningham's wishes Creech Jones therefore suggested that the government ignore the defiance of the agency and continue as before.[100]

Hall travelled to Downing Street on the morning of January 1, 1946, to meet with the prime minister and cabinet. He brought along Creech Jones, for whom he had obtained special permission to attend. The colonial secretary circulated Creech Jones' report and then, after allowing him to present a summary, assured all those who had gathered that he stood behind the recommendations of his undersecretary. Sir Alan Brooke, the chief of the imperial general staff, immediately took issue with Creech Jones' predictions of civil war, stating that if the cabinet decided to take a more aggressive stance against the Jewish community, "adequate military forces would be available to deal with the situation." The meeting then turned to Jewish immigration into Palestine. Hall once again stepped aside to allow his undersecretary to present the colonial office viewpoint. Creech Jones indicated that the 1939 White Paper's ceiling of 75,000 immigrants had almost been reached, yet no agreement had been arranged with the Palestinian Arabs or the surrounding Arab states for continued immigration beyond that limit. A cabinet member whose identity was not disclosed in the minutes noted that High Commissioner Cunningham believed that most of those who were illegally immigrating were simply trying to reunite with family members already in Palestine. He suggested that this reality "might afford an opportunity to make a humanitarian gesture." Other ministers agreed that this approach might "be sympathetically received by the Arabs," and the cabinet as a whole decided that once the 75,000 limit had been reached, immigration would not be cut off absolutely: "While it was right to consult the Arab States and to endeavour to obtain their concurrence in continued immigration, His Majesty's Government would in the last resort have to take their own decision in the matter."[101]

As the New Year progressed, rumors of a possible war with Russia in Eastern Europe began to overshadow colonial affairs. Foreign Secretary Ernest Bevin worked especially hard, therefore, to convince the cabinet defense committee that the Middle East, as the bridge between the Mediterranean Sea and the Indian Ocean, was as important to Britain's security as the threat from the Soviet Union. On March 13, 1946, Bevin sent to the committee a memorandum in which he outlined "the whole problem of defence in the Mediterranean, Middle East and the

Indian Ocean." At the heart of the matter, he argued, was the fact that the Mediterranean was the area "through which we bring influence to bear on Southern Europe, the soft underbelly of France, Italy, Yugoslavia, Greece, and Turkey." Put simply, if the British government were to "move out of the Mediterranean, Russia will move in, and the Mediterranean countries, from the point of view of commerce and trade, economy and democracy, will be finished." Beyond that was the question of Egypt, a country which as host to the Suez Canal was vital to British trade and defense interests. Finally, Bevin asserted that Britain represented the "last bastion of social democracy," a unique and moderate way of life placed between "the red tooth and claw of American capitalism and the Communist dictatorship of Soviet Russia." Any weakening of the British position in the Mediterranean would ultimately lead to a loss of social democracy in that region and the adoption of either full-fledged capitalism or autocratic communism. Stability in Palestine, as the bridge territory between the Mediterranean and Middle Eastern worlds, was essential for the maintenance of the British presence in the region. And that presence was an important aspect of overall British Cold War strategy.[102]

Bevin's message was apparently shared by the chiefs of staff, who wrote to the cabinet defense committee on April 2, just three weeks after Bevin. Concluding that a "conflict with Russia is the only situation in which it at present seems that the British Commonwealth might again become involved in a major war," they insisted that the Middle East would form an important battlefield in that possible war. It thus had to be held at all costs. This was because the Middle East held a fivefold strategic importance to Britain: first, it formed the land-bridge between Europe, Asia, Africa, and the Mediterranean world, and provided the easiest route to the Indian Ocean and hence the immense resources of the Indian subcontinent; second, if the Soviets were to gain control of Palestine and Egypt they would have a base area from which to directly attack Western interests in Africa, particularly in the north, east, and south of the continent; third, continued British control of the Middle East would provide a buffer zone between potential enemy forces in Eastern Europe and critical resources in India and Africa; fourth, in a British offensive operation, the Middle East offered the best launching point for an invasion of the Russian industrial and oil-producing regions of the Caucasus, as well as the best air bases from which to deter Russian aggression; and finally, the immense oil supplies of the Middle East were a crucial factor of both British national security and British economic security. Due to this strategic importance, if the British government were to withdraw from the Middle East "[t]he security of the United Kingdom would be directly threatened."[103] By May 1946, Bevin and the chiefs of staff had convinced the cabinet defense committee and, in turn, the cabinet as a whole that the Middle East was an essential region in the emerging Cold War with the Soviet Union. Colonial affairs were thus inextricably linked with the larger national security of Britain.

Of the many issues confronting the postwar colonial office, Palestine remained the most pressing, where the violence continued unabated. On January 12, 1946, seventy members of the Jewish insurgency activated an explosives charge on the railway line near Benyamina, destroying the engine of and derailing the first train to hit it. A raiding party then descended on the hapless locomotive, stealing £35,000 worth of payroll and injuring three police constables who attempted to protect the money. A week later, on January 17, the Irgun attempted to blow up the Palestine Broadcasting Service, followed within days by attacks on the coast guard station at Givat Olga and the RAF radar station on Mount Carmel. On January 29, eighteen members of the IZL dressed in RAF uniforms brazenly drove through the gates of the RAF base at Aqir, near Gaza, bound and gagged the four genuine RAF men at the arms hut, and escaped with twenty Bren-guns and hundreds of Sten-guns. The RAF raised the alarm immediately and within hours the British security forces recovered most of the arms, but the damage to British prestige had been done. The government attempted to make amends and within two days the British administration in Palestine fired all Jewish lorry drivers who were servicing RAF bases. This was a nonsensical and counterproductive decision, however, given that the Irgun had been disguised as RAF servicemen rather than civilian Jewish drivers, and the measure served only to create unemployed men who could be preyed upon to join the insurgency. In any case, the security attempt failed, as on February 3, eight members of the IZL, again dressed in RAF uniforms but driving a taxi rather than a lorry, successfully stole four Sten-guns, eleven rifles, and three pistols from an RAF medical unit in Tel Aviv.[104]

Such actions continued throughout the spring of 1946, provoking the British to respond more aggressively. Curfews, searches, and seizures became the norm, and by the end of June the security forces had conducted more than fifty-five major search operations. In addition to these planned searches, the army and police also manned road blocks, undertook constant patrols, and launched raids on specific targets based on active intelligence.[105] Most vigorous of the security forces were the Parachute Regiment battalions of the Sixth Airborne division who, according to one soldier serving in a neighboring unit at the time, were "being vilified by much of the Jewish Press with accusations that they were acting like the Gestapo." Much of this behavior was excused by their compatriots, who recognized that they had been "highly trained for the aggressive action required at that time [the Second World War], and were now having to be retrained in the far more sensitive techniques required for a totally different type of campaign."[106] The British in Palestine reasoned that under the circumstances, violent excesses were to be expected and could be forgiven. Such behavior, of course, did nothing to help win over the Jewish moderates to the side of the British.

Despite the aggression, throughout the first six months of 1946 the security forces were, to a certain extent, restrained by government policy. General Sir Bernard Paget, commander in chief Middle East Land Forces (MELF), complained bitterly that, "the Army has not yet initiated any offensive action: any fighting that has been done has been carried out in support of police operations."[107] This was particularly galling when placed against the increasing level of insurgent violence in Palestine. At no time was this shown more clearly than on April 25 when LEHI mounted an operation in the car park of the Sixth Airborne division, directly opposite the Apak police station in Tel Aviv. As machine gun fire rained down on the unsuspecting soldiers, six were killed immediately and a British constable fell wounded. When soldiers scattered to escape the fire, they encountered mines that had been previously laid by LEHI. A hapless paratrooper was killed instantly as he stepped on one, and three others around him were injured by the resulting blast, bringing the death toll up to seven with four wounded. LEHI retreated without casualties and no men were later found or arrested.[108] Despite these losses, the British government continued to counsel restraint.

This policy changed abruptly, however, when the British security forces launched Operation Agatha on June 29, 1946. This about-face was prompted in the short term by a series of attacks that included the destruction of eleven road and railway bridges by LEHI bombings on the night of June 16/17, an IZL kidnapping of six British army officers on June 18, and the theft of £40,000 worth of diamonds from a polishing plant on June 26.[109] In the long term, it was provoked by the sustained level of violence in Palestine, which by the army's count had included forty-seven major incidents of terrorism between November 1, 1945, and June 1, 1946, resulting in the deaths of eighteen British army personnel and nine Palestine police officers, the wounding of 101 soldiers and sixty-three police officers, and damage to property valued at a little over four million pounds sterling. For political reasons, in particular American scrutiny, it had "not previously been possible to take drastic action against those persons considered responsible," but in June the British cabinet decided that "the situation could no longer be tolerated." It authorized Cunningham, the high commissioner, to "take such steps as he considered necessary." He in turn transferred responsibility to the army commander, Lieutenant General Sir Evelyn Hugh Barker, who had replaced General D'Arcy as GOC on March 10.[110]

The purpose of Operation Agatha was fourfold: first, to occupy the buildings of the Jewish Agency in Jerusalem to search them for "incriminating documents"; second, to arrest prominent Jewish political figures who were either implicated in terrorist attacks or were deemed guilty of "inciting the people to violence"; third, to occupy and search buildings in Tel Aviv that were considered likely headquarters of terrorist organizations; and finally, to arrest as many members as possible of the militant Jewish groups. Because of the difficulty of separating the insurgents from the general civilian population, and because the Jewish groups were known to have an efficient intelligence organization, the British maintained certain operational precautions in the lead-up to Agatha. Until the final day, all but the most senior commanders were kept in the dark about the timing and scope of the operation; all meetings were held away from army headquarters, with officers attending these meetings in disguise so as not to alert the insurgents that anything unusual was afoot; those in mid-level command positions received sealed orders that they were only to open an hour before the operation; the troops taking part were informed of their role only following their confinement in camp; detention camps were erected under the excuse that they were required for illegal immigrants; no army leave was canceled until the day of the operation; and the night before the operation, most Jewish and Arab civilian employers working within military camps were detained to prevent them from spreading the word that a buildup was underway.[111] British military planners believed Operation Agatha was their best chance to break the back of the insurgency, and it was absolutely crucial that nobody tipped off the targeted Jewish organizations.

The launch date for Operation Agatha was Saturday, June 29, with the chosen hour at 4:15 in the morning, a day and time when army planners believed most people would be at home in bed. Just ten minutes before this, at 4:05 a.m., soldiers from the Royal Signals seized all telephone exchanges in Palestine and cut off all telephone communication for the next three hours. At the same time, parties of military police imposed road curfews in four districts by erecting roadblocks and checkpoints, and complete curfews were emplaced in all the main cities. Then, at 4:15 a.m., 10,000 British army soldiers and 7000 Palestine policemen descended on the three cities of Jerusalem, Tel Aviv, and Haifa, together with 30 other rural settlements.[112] At the top of the target list was the Jewish Agency headquarters, and the army immediately established an inner and outer cordon surrounding it. Following confirmation that it was secure, police and army personnel entered the building at exactly 4:30 a.m. and arrested the three caretakers found within. These men offered no resistance and, by providing the keys to the offices and safes, allowed the police to remove all documents with minimal damage to the building.[113]

Similar search operations commenced at other important buildings and settlements throughout Palestine, and on average the army and police cordons remained in place for seven hours, allowing the buildings to be thoroughly searched and the occupants carefully screened.[114] Those who raised suspicion or resisted were arrested. By July 1, 2718 such persons had been taken into British custody, although 2000 of them were subsequently released after only a short period of detention. Among the 700 kept for longer interrogations and internment were four members of the Jewish Agency executive committee and seven Haganah commanders. The searches also uncovered thirty-three weapons caches, from which over 500 arms were seized. The documents taken at the Jewish Agency headquarters provided compelling evidence that the agency had been actively supporting Jewish resistance to British rule and had developed a fairly intricate espionage system to spy on the British civic and military establishment.[115]

In a statement issued to Parliament in early July, the colonial secretary laid out the conclusions the government had reached from Operation Agatha. These were threefold: first, the Haganah, "working under the political control of prominent members of the Jewish Agency," had engaged in "carefully planned movements of sabotage and violence"; second, the IZL and LEHI had worked "in co-operation with the Haganah High Command" on some of these operations; and finally, the broadcasting station *Kol Israel*, which worked under the direction of the Jewish Agency and was dubbed "the voice of the Resistance Movement," had actively supported each of these organizations. Hall noted that insurgent operations throughout the spring had been "widespread in character and caused very extensive damage." When followed by the kidnapping of six British officers, it was "no longer possible for His Majesty's Government to adopt a passive attitude." It was for these reasons that the government carried out Operation Agatha, which it believed was justified.[116] Following Agatha and with the information that it had revealed, the British government felt it could no longer cooperate with the Jewish Agency; it now regarded the agency with as much suspicion as the IZL, Haganah, and LEHI.

By almost all measures, Operation Agatha was a success for the British. The government had confirmed suspicion of the Jewish Agency's guilt; leading figures in both the Jewish Agency and the Haganah were arrested; the arms haul was such that the Haganah would never again be able to operate against the British to any significant degree; and the six British hostages taken earlier that month were released. However, the operation had failed in one crucial regard. The Irgun Zvai Leumi was left untouched.

IV. The end of compromise

At 12:15 p.m. on July 22, 1946—just three weeks after the close of Operation Agatha—a police constable walking his beat in Jerusalem informed Inspector J. C. Taylor at the Palestine police control center of an upheaval occurring outside the King David Hotel. The hotel served a dual role in Palestine, housing the working offices of British chief secretary Sir John Shaw and high commissioner General Sir Alan Cunningham, as well as functioning as an upscale hotel for foreign dignitaries and the well-to-do of the British establishment. Buildings across from the hotel housed the headquarters of the British military police and its Special Investigations Branch (the military CID). The entire area was consequently surrounded by a barbed wire cordon. Despite this security, those Britons resident in Palestine regarded the hotel as the heart of the mandate's social scene, and within its walls British officials drifted between business and pleasure with very little transition, physical or mental.

The police constable informed Inspector Taylor that two explosions had occurred beside the hotel, one at the south end about fifty yards from its grounds, the other at the north end in a lane leading to the French consulate. In all the commotion, a lorry had driven past security barriers and parked beside the hotel kitchen, where its occupants unloaded seven large milk churns. On closer inspection, the police constable found each to be marked "Mines—Do Not Touch." An ostensible hotel waiter turned a machine gun on a second constable who stopped to inquire about the lorry. When this second constable struggled to grab the weapon, a passenger of the lorry shot him dead. Receiving this information, Taylor dispatched a patrol car to investigate. By the time it arrived, the lorry and its occupants had disappeared and the milk churns had been moved from the kitchen to the central pillars at the southwest of the hotel, the section that housed the British administration's offices. As it was now clear that a terrorist attack was imminent, Taylor issued an immediate alert and the terrorist warning siren began to sound from the hotel. Inside, a telephone operator informed her assistant manager that an anonymous message had been left directing staff to evacuate the hotel as a bomb would explode in thirty minutes. Taylor received a similar message from the *Palestine Post*, and a telephone call from the French consulate indicated that the diplomats within had been told to open their windows to avoid damage by bomb blast.

At 12:31 p.m., Superintendent K. P. Hadingham of the Palestine police arrived at the hotel and ordered the siren turned off. He walked inside, found the hotel manager, and was escorted upstairs to the hotel offices. With the exception of the terrorist warning siren, which was now silent, no communication had been given to employees or guests about the impending attack, and no evacuation was ordered. Most inside presumed that the siren was in response to the earlier explosions of twelve noon. The chief secretary continued to work in his office, guests mingled in the lobby, and socialites enjoyed their lunches in the hotel's restaurants. In the Palestine mandate of July 1946, the sound of explosives and terrorist warning sirens was not out of the ordinary, and life continued as it had on every other day. But then, at exactly 12:37 p.m.—thirty minutes after the lorry had delivered its deadly cargo—the milk churns exploded, stopping all electric clocks in the building and sending a mushroom cloud of brown smoke hundreds of feet into the air. The southwest wing of the building crumbled, floor hitting floor, until it resembled nothing more than a pile of rubble. The debris from the explosion damaged nearby buildings and coated the passengers of a No.4 bus that had just pulled up outside the hotel. There was a moment of silence, and then the screaming began.[117] Captain Ridley Hugh Clark, commanding an army duty company that day, was immediately ordered to set up a cordon around the bomb site. He later recalled that "watching the rescue teams digging out the dead bodies was a horrible sight." So horrible, indeed, that Clark had to carefully watch his own men for fear of reprisal: "The first night on curfew, the Company Sergeant Major was so mad and worked up by the killing of innocent civilians, that I took charge of his pistol for the night as I was sure that he was going to shoot someone."[118] In all, the attack killed ninety-two people and injured sixty-nine, most of whom were civilian employees of the mandate secretariat. It was by far the worst atrocity the IZL perpetrated in Palestine.[119]

The prime minister did not make an immediate statement. With the parliamentary debate over recommitting his National Health Service bill scheduled to begin that day at 3:40 p.m., it was little wonder that Attlee did not find time to address Palestine.[120] After all, pushing through a plan for a comprehensive national health service under the controversial circumstances of opposition from the British Medical Association was a far higher priority for Attlee's Labour government than the security of a far-flung colonial mandate.[121] The following day, however, Anthony Eden, deputy leader of the Conservative Party, asked the prime minister if he would like to make a statement. Having previously warned Attlee that his request was imminent, the prime minister had a statement prepared. He proclaimed that this "insane act of terrorism" was by far "the worst" that had been committed in Palestine to date. He assured the House that "[e]very effort is being made to identify and arrest the perpetrators of this outrage," and noted that the "work of rescue in the debris ... still continues." Calling the attack a "dastardly outrage," he reminded the House that "His Majesty's Government are at this moment in consultation with the Government of the United States with a view to arriving at proposals for a just settlement," and asserted that they would "not be diverted by acts of violence."[122]

Perhaps surprisingly, as the dust settled from the King David Hotel bombing, the summer in Palestine passed into autumn in a quieter manner. Searches, curfews, and arrests continued, but the Irgun seemed content with the splash it had made on July 22. Furthermore, on August 23, the Jewish Agency finally dissolved its partnership with the IZL and LEHI, withdrawing the support of its 45,000 members and ordering the Haganah to play no further role in the campaign against the British.[123] For those in colonial service in Jerusalem, the remaining weeks of the summer were a time for rest and recuperation. Not so for those in London. On April 30, 1946, the Anglo-American Committee of Inquiry had published its findings. Of its ten recommendations, seven were widely agreed upon but three proved controversial: first, the British government was to admit 100,000 Jews into Palestine immediately; second, the Jewish Agency was to be brought back into the fold to cooperate in the suppression of illegal organizations; and finally, Palestine was to become neither a Jewish nor an Arab state.[124] Immediately, American President Truman endorsed the findings, noting that the figure of 100,000 was the same as he had proposed in 1945. This public comment sent Foreign Secretary Bevin into a "black rage" and he immediately reacted by informing the American secretary of state James Byrnes that Jews in Palestine were "murdering British soldiers," and that until all Jewish illegal armies and formations were disbanded, no more Jews would be allowed into the territory.[125]

Once tempers had cooled, however, Bevin recognized that his position was untenable. Although Attlee had issued a statement in the House of Commons that stressed "the practical difficulties of absorbing a large number of Jewish immigrants into Palestine in a short time," Bevin agreed to enter talks with an American cabinet committee composed of representatives from the state department, the war department, and the treasury.[126] Chaired by Ambassador Henry F. Grady, the former assistant secretary of state, the American delegation restated its support for each of the ten proposals and assured its British counterparts that it had President Truman's full backing on the matter. The British at first appeared conciliatory, noting the American position and asking only that American troops be deployed to Palestine to assist in the inevitable fallout that would occur upon the implementation of the committee recommendations. However, the kidnapping on June 18 of the six British army officers in Jerusalem, followed by the American chiefs of staff's refusal on June 21 to entertain the notion of American troops in Palestine, caused the British position to harden. They reasserted Bevin's original stance that further immigration could only continue once Jewish militant organizations were disbanded. When the British launched Operation Agatha on June 29, it was in part to ensure that this was carried out. Attlee informed Truman of British intentions vis-à-vis Agatha only hours before the first soldiers hit the ground. Those involved in the Anglo-American talks were not consulted at all.[127]

Following Agatha, the British government quickly soured on the idea of cooperating with the Americans to find a solution to the Palestine problem. On July 11, Hall presented to the cabinet a paper that argued that the Anglo-American committee recommendations were "unworkable." His conclusion was backed by the chiefs of staff, who informed the cabinet that if the recommendations were implemented, an additional two infantry divisions with three extra battalions attached and one armored brigade would need to be dispatched immediately to the Middle East, together with reinforcements from the navy and Royal Air Force. These forces, they warned, could not be produced "save at the expense of withdrawing from other commitments from which, in fact, withdrawal is not possible."[128] Taking such dire predictions into account, Hall presented a new proposal: Palestine should be partitioned into two provinces, one Jewish and one Arab, each with semiautonomous governance under the direction of a central trustee government run by the British. This would be a temporary arrangement to remain in place only until tensions calmed, at which time the British could arrange talks between the Jews and Arabs to decide upon either eventual partnership within a single federal state or final partition into two independent states.

Bevin immediately opposed Hall's plan. He questioned whether it would provide a long-term solution and worried that it would unnecessarily isolate the Americans by rejecting all aspects of the Anglo-American committee recommendations. He instead suggested that the majority of Arab territory in Palestine be incorporated into Transjordan and Lebanon, with a single Jewish state created that would be large enough to accept the 100,000 immigrants proposed by Truman. He acknowledged that Hall's plan might need to be implemented in the short term, but argued against either a federal state or a two-state partitioned Palestine. The cabinet seemed to agree that the Anglo-American committee recommendations ought to be rejected as a whole. Some members argued strongly in favor of Bevin's plan. They believed that if partition were to be the eventual outcome, better to implement it immediately than wait. The new Jewish state could then determine its own immigration quotas and, more importantly, be left with the financial burden of managing such. Lord Tedder, the chief of the air staff, rejected this view, noting the strategic importance of the Middle East to the United Kingdom and reminding the cabinet that Britain's position there depended on the goodwill of the Arabs. After much discussion, the cabinet agreed to put forward Hall's plan as a short-term solution, while keeping an open mind on Bevin's plan for the long term.[129]

The following day—July 12—an American delegation led by Ambassador Grady arrived in London, and on July 13, Sir Norman Brook—secretary to the cabinet and the civil servant authorized by the secretaries to negotiate with Grady—presented the new proposal. Grady was immediately impressed, later noting, "We went to London with a plan for a bi-national government under the Trusteeship of the United Nations. ... Much to our surprise, on our arrival in London, the British presented us with a proposal for a federal government in which there would be semi-autonomous Jewish and Arab provinces."[130] He asked for a copy of the plan in writing, which Brook gave him on July 15, and on July 19 he recommended it to the American secretary of state.[131] Byrnes was not as enthusiastic as his ambassador. He preferred the original committee recommendations, wedded in particular to the immediate immigration of 100,000 Jews.[132] It was at this point in the negotiations that on July 22 the Irgun bombed the King David Hotel. This terrorist atrocity at the heart of the British administration in Palestine changed everything. Grady testily informed Byrnes that the new plan was the best the Americans could hope for under the circumstances and warned that the American government better accept it before the British moved toward a harder line. He then took it upon himself to inform the British cabinet that the plan had been accepted. Clement Attlee was ecstatic, wanting nothing more than to solve the Palestine problem so he could renew his focus on domestic affairs. He immediately proposed to Truman that they make simultaneous announcements in the House of Commons and at the White House on July 31, after which the British and American governments could work in concert to get world opinion behind their scheme.[133]

The problem was that Attlee's letter was the first from which Truman had heard of the new plan. He dispatched Byrnes to meet with Attlee and Bevin in Paris on July 28 to get a full account of the proposed agreement. Although Byrnes was angry with Grady for his rogue diplomatic behavior, after his face-to-face consultations with the prime minister and foreign secretary he recognized that Grady was right. The British were in no mood to compromise. He therefore recommended to Truman that the British plan be accepted.[134] Unfortunately, while in Paris, Byrnes let slip at a press conference that the American government was shelving its proposal for 100,000 immigrants. Jewish Agency representatives in Paris immediately contacted their offices in Washington, DC. Within hours, the machinery of the American Jewish lobby was put into motion. By the morning of July 30, Leo Kohn, the Jewish Agency representative in DC, had copied the Paris telegram to Rabbi Abba Hillel Silver (a leader of the American Zionist movement) and David Niles (one of only two of President Roosevelt's political advisors to be retained by Truman); Niles conveyed Jewish opposition directly to Truman; Robert Nathan (economist and member of the War Refugee Board) spoke with Sam Rosenman (White House Counsel) and Secretary of War Robert Patterson; Leo Kohn spoke by telephone with Supreme Court Justice Felix Frankfurter, who contacted Dean Acheson (undersecretary at the State Department), War Secretary Patterson, and Treasury Secretary John W. Snyder; and New York Senators James Mead and Robert Wagner, together with James G. MacDonald (later appointed the first US ambassador to Israel in 1948), met personally with Truman.[135]

In an American cabinet meeting on July 30, after two days of constant lobbying by the Jewish community, Truman lost his temper when he was informed by Secretary of Commerce Henry Wallace that the British proposal was "loaded with political dynamite." "Jesus Christ couldn't please them when he was here on earth," the president snapped, "so how could anyone expect that I would have any luck?"[136] Nevertheless, the following day Truman agreed to meet with a delegation of New York congressmen, all of whom were opposed to the British proposal, and later that day—as British Member of Parliament Herbert Morrison (standing in for Bevin) presented the plan to the House of Commons—Truman announced that the American government was delaying its decision on the new proposals. On August 1, Rabbi Silver declared publicly a victory for Zionism, stating: "Zionist pressure ha[s] narrowly averted political disaster by bringing influential opinion to bear on the President."[137] Truman was outraged and Silver never again set foot in the White House. Nevertheless, the damage had been done. The British government waited for a response from Truman for another week, and then on August 7 informed him that they were moving ahead unilaterally with a conference in London that would attempt to bring the Jews and Arabs together in an acceptable compromise. Truman gave no immediate reply, but on August 12 telegrammed Attlee that he was formally rejecting the British proposal, explaining that "the opposition in this country to the plan has become so intense that it is now clear it would be impossible to rally in favor of it sufficient public opinion to enable this Government to give it effective support."[138] The Anglo-American negotiations, opened in October of the previous year, had finally broken down, and the British were left once again to their own devices to solve the Palestine problem.[139]

Even without American support, the British government hoped it would be able to implement Hall's plan. It was mistaken. Following the breakdown of talks with the United States, the British government immediately sent invitations to the Arab states for delegates to attend the conference in London. It sent similar invitations to the Arab High Executive and, in an extension of the olive branch, to the Jewish Agency. There followed four weeks of flurried diplomacy, as British officials sought to arrange the conference and find common ground between the Jewish and Arab delegations before either arrived in London. It was not to be. Each would settle for nothing less than their own sovereign state, with each laying claim to the holy sites, including Jerusalem. When the conference finally convened on September 10, only the representatives of seven Arab states together with the secretary-general of the Arab League attended; there was no Jewish representation whatsoever. The Arab delegates immediately criticized the British plan not only for its concept of eventual partition, but also for creating a "Jewish state [which] will be a grave menace to the neighboring Arab countries, and will be a jumping off stone that may enable the Jews to overrun the whole Arab World in the East."[140] They instead proposed an independent, unitary, democratic state in which the Jews would be formally recognized as a protected "religious community" but would have to exercise any political clout within the traditional structures of a first-past-the-post democratic system. Within that state, there could be no additional Jewish immigration.[141]

After three weeks of tense negotiations, during which the Arab delegates refused to compromise on any of their demands, the conference met for the final time on October 2. Bevin gave a brief statement to close its proceedings. He confirmed that he understood the Arab position but explained that he must now hear the Jewish case. He then suspended any further sessions, pledging that the conference would not reconvene again until December 16 at the earliest. It had all been, in the words of one scholar, "an unmitigated waste of time."[142] Two days later, on October 4 (the Jewish *Yom Kippur*), President Truman publicly chastised the British government for its approach to Palestine, issuing a statement that summarized the recommendations of the Anglo-American committee, reaffirmed the US commitment to the immediate immigration of 100,000 Jews into Palestine, and closed with the words: "it is my belief that a solution along these lines would command the support of public opinion in the United States. I cannot believe that the gap between the proposals which have been put forward is too great to be bridged by men of reason and goodwill. To such a solution our Government could give its support."[143]

His words were a damning verdict on the previous three months of British diplomacy and negotiation. They also ensured that the British government would keep its distance from the US government in the immediate future, as the trust between the two shattered over the Palestine question. In a handwritten letter to Truman that "radiate[d] white-hot anger," Attlee vented furiously, accusing the president of "refusing even a few hours' grace to the Prime Minister of the country which has the actual responsibility for the government of Palestine in order that he might acquaint you with the actual situation and the probable results of your action."[144] From that moment forth, the British government was unwilling to share any information or proposals with the Americans. Coming just two days after the collapse of the talks in London, Truman's statement spelled the end of compromise in Palestine.

V. Into the abyss

Henry Gurney arrived in Palestine on October 1, 1946, just as the talks in London were collapsing. He had come to replace Sir John Shaw as chief secretary and, like his predecessor, had vast experience in colonial administration. After service during the First World War and a spell at University College, Oxford, Gurney joined the colonial service in 1921 with an appointment as assistant district commissioner in Kenya. After fourteen years there, he was promoted to assistant colonial secretary of Jamaica before being transferred for a short stint at the colonial office in London. In 1938, he became secretary to the East African Governors' Conference, a post he remained in until 1944 when he was appointed colonial secretary of the Gold Coast. He was in this position when George Hall approached him in the autumn of 1946 to request that he go to Palestine.[145] Gurney found his first week in the Middle East to be "[t]horoughly bewildering, but intensely interesting and pleasantly difficult." He wrote to his friend John Martin, assistant undersecretary at the colonial office, stating that his new post was "a fairly catholic sort of life that includes philosophical politenesses with Patriarchs, personal understanding with the Army, the whole range of administration and a persistent environment of security and barbed wire."[146]

That environment of security and barbed wire increased soon after Gurney took up his position. Captain Ridley Hugh Clark, the army officer who had set up the cordon following the King David Hotel bombing, noted that in the second week of October, "the troubles started up once again." This, of course, corresponded with the collapse of talks in London. For Clark and his soldiers, this meant an increase in residential searches for weapons dumps, which was a "rotten job ... search[ing] right through someone's home looking in cupboards and sometimes having to lift the floorboards."[147] Gurney found the sudden swell in violence and its reasons mystifying. He admitted to Martin that "it is sometimes difficult to discover which particular century some people are living in."[148] Nevertheless, he still had to contend with the violence, particularly as British soldiers were bearing the brunt of its bloodshed. Gurney concluded that the best way to do this was not through increased army offensives, but rather with a determined policy of restraint by the security forces and renewed engagement between the British government and the Jewish Agency. In this new policy, he had the support of the colonial office in London, which was undergoing its own change of leadership. On October 4, 1946—the day Truman issued his blistering remarks—George Hall resigned from the House of Commons to join the House of Lords as Viscount Hall. He also resigned as colonial secretary. In his place, the prime minister promoted Hall's deputy, Arthur Creech Jones.

Creech Jones was more than ready to tackle the Palestine question. He had, after all, played a major role in formulating Hall's plan for the territory and he made the achievement of a peaceful settlement without resort to violence his primary aim in holding office. Since his earliest years of adulthood, Creech Jones had resisted force, even suffering three years of imprisonment from September 1916 to April 1919 for his stance of conscientious objection during the First World War. Barred from returning to the civil service because of his detention, Creech Jones worked on the issue of prisons for the Labour Party's research department, and became heavily involved in the trade union movement. Throughout the late 1920s and early 1930s, he became an active member of the New Fabian Research Bureau, a hothouse of radical and socialist ideas, and in 1935 won election to the House of Commons as Labour Member for Shipley. He immediately became involved in colonial affairs, visiting Palestine during the Arab revolt of 1936–1939 and cofounding the Fabian Colonial Bureau in 1940. In 1943, Creech Jones became chairman of the parliamentary advisory committee on imperial questions; also that year he was appointed to the colonial office advisory committee on education in the colonies. In August 1945, he moved permanently to the colonial office, becoming undersecretary of state for colonial affairs in October of that year. Now, exactly one year later, he won promotion to full colonial secretary, a position for which all his previous experience had prepared him well.[149]

As a socialist, peace advocate, and frequent visitor to Palestine, Creech Jones was convinced that force alone could not bring peace to the territory and thus he fully supported Gurney's notion of reengagement with the Jewish Agency. In early November, therefore, he gave Gurney permission to suspend all army residential searches and on November 5 he instructed High Commissioner Cunningham to order the release of three members of the Jewish Agency's executive committee who had been held in internment without trial since Operation Agatha, four months and seventeen days earlier.[150]

Despite this change in policy at the governmental level, the IZL's terror campaign continued. The new chief of the imperial general staff, Viscount Montgomery (Bernard Law Montgomery, 1st Viscount Montgomery of Alamein), warned the prime minister on November 19 that he was becoming increasingly "disturbed about the situation in Palestine."[151] The following day, Montgomery again raised the issue at a meeting of the cabinet defense committee, attended by the prime minister, the colonial secretary, the first lord of admiralty, and the various defense chiefs. He began by stating that the violence in Palestine over the past six weeks had "seriously perturbed him," where since October 1 (the day Gurney arrived as chief secretary) Jewish militants had killed seventy-six army servicemen and thirty-three police officers. Incidents of sabotage had also increased and rail communication was now at a "standstill." The police force was 50 percent below strength, and needed an additional 3000 recruits to reach full strength. The strain of being short-handed was beginning to show. On November 17, a police lorry had hit a mine in Tel Aviv, killing three British police constables and one RAF sergeant and injuring four others. That evening, in an act of retaliation, a gang of young British constables went on a rampage through several cafes on Tel Aviv's Hayarkon Street, injuring twenty-nine Jews. Montgomery worried that "outbreaks of this kind ... might spread to the army." He lamented that the government had forced the army in recent weeks to "adopt a defensive role" and argued that with the situation "rapidly deteriorating," the "only means of stamping out this type of warfare was to allow the Army to take the offensive against it."

Creech Jones agreed with Montgomery's appraisal of the worsening situation, but challenged his notion that an increase in military force was necessary. He believed that there were "signs that there was a rally of moderate opinion behind the Jewish Agency, and a real desire to stamp out terrorism." He pleaded with the cabinet defence committee to allow the new policy of negotiation and a soft hand to run its course. The prime minister was sympathetic to Creech Jones' position. He reminded the committee that when in June the cabinet had given the security forces authority to "break up the illegal organisations in Palestine" with Operation Agatha, it had been "assured that the power of these illegal organisations would be seriously crippled." This, however, had clearly not happened, as "terrorist activity was, in fact, increasing." That tempted Attlee to support the new approach taken by Creech Jones and Gurney, particularly as he was "not certain what was required by a request to allow the Army to take the offensive against terrorism."

Montgomery, clearly exasperated, insisted that when in June the army had been given such responsibility, it had in fact "destroyed the organisation of the Hagana and Irgun." It was only since the October restrictions had been placed on the army that the Jewish militants had "been allowed two months in which to reorganise, and consequently, terrorist activity was increasing." More aggressive military action had worked, he assured the committee. The change of policy introduced by Gurney and Creech Jones was now undermining the successful results of previous army operations. Taking his lead from Montgomery, George Hall, now first lord of the admiralty, suggested that the time had come for British security forces to attempt a general disarming of the entire Palestinian population, Jewish and Arab. Attlee agreed that such action might be necessary but demanded a detailed report on the situation in Palestine before a general disarming could be authorized. The prime minister having had the final word, the meeting then closed. Neither Montgomery nor Creech Jones left the meeting happy with the outcome.[152]

While the cabinet defense committee debated which levels of government force were most conducive to quelling the insurgency, the Jewish guerillas continued to attack. On November 20, 1946, Gurney was writing another letter to Martin when he was interrupted by "a large detonation" that had "blown up what I am told is the Income Tax Office." This did not deter him from the direction he was steering policy as he believed there were "signs of returning common sense on the part of the [Jewish] Agency leaders here." Still, there would be consequences to his approach, as he explained to Martin: "Our whole short-term policy as I see it is to drive the terrorist groups into a corner. This process, combined with their nature, will make them more desperate as the net closes, and we are therefore facing the unpleasant prospect of continued terrorism for some time." Although he believed fervently that his policy would eventually lead to peace, the violence would get worse before it got better, and Gurney found the "immediate local outlook in the terrorist field ... discouraging." Nevertheless, he felt it was absolutely essential that Creech Jones' arguments triumph over those of Montgomery. Further troop action would only exacerbate the situation.[153]

Gurney was supported in this position not only by Creech Jones but also by General Sir Alan Cunningham, the high commissioner in Palestine. On November 23, Cunningham forwarded to Creech Jones an exchange he had conducted with General Sir Miles Dempsey, Paget's successor as commander in chief MELF. Dempsey, perhaps encouraged by Montgomery, informed Cunningham that in his view, "the time has come when we must take action. Directly an outrage occurs, we should thoroughly search the area for arms and explosives and impose a fine on the locality. We know that terrorism is tacitly accepted by all and sundry. Were this not so, these murderers would soon be apprehended. The people, therefore, must take the consequences." That Dempsey should have held this view is not surprising. Having been commissioned an army officer in 1915, he served first on the western front where he was awarded the Military Cross for bravery, before moving to Iraq in 1919, taking part in counterinsurgency operations there during which large-scale civilian reprisals were an important part of British military strategy.[154] Cunningham disagreed with Dempsey, and Creech Jones distributed his reply to twenty-two others in the government, including the private secretary to the prime minister, Hall at the admiralty, the private secretary to the foreign secretary, the private secretary to the war secretary, Christopher Eastwood (now at the cabinet office), A. J. Kellar at MI5, and, in what was surely a blatant act of defiance, to Montgomery himself.

Cunningham began by assuring Dempsey that he was "as concerned as you are regarding the incidence of casualties to my police and the Army, and in the constant ways and means of dealing with terrorism." However, he disagreed with Dempsey's characterization of the Jewish population as tacitly accepting of terrorism, pointing out that "All Jewish institutions, all Jewish press and illicit Hagana wireless have made statements of varying intensity against terrorism." Furthermore, on November 22, Cunningham had visited the head of the Jewish Agency and although he could not reveal to Dempsey what was said (he had promised a seal of secrecy on the conversation), he was "satisfied that they [the Jewish Agency] had, in fact, a plan and were fully conscious of the need from their point of view of doing all they could to eradicate the evil." He next turned to Dempsey's recommendation to "institute searches for arms in, and to impose fines on, areas in the vicinity of incidents even though there is no indication that the perpetrators either came from or retreated to that area; what, in fact, amount to reprisals." This, he believed, was folly; the "results of such action would only serve to alienate if not to send over to terrorists those elements of the population who are now showing signs, if not of co-operation, then of taking action themselves with a view to the same end as ourselves." Reprisals would not have the "slightest effect in reducing terrorism and might well increase it." With the examples of Ireland and the Arab rebellion before him, he was "dead against reprisals as such."[155] He promised Dempsey that the morale of troops was "constantly in [his] mind" but also noted that "it would not be right to take action which would imperil [an] imminent political solution to this thorny problem." Finally, he assured Dempsey that he had not ruled out searches when actual intelligence was available and, perhaps in an attempt to reemphasize his commitment to the campaign, added: "I have always been clear that the best method of dealing with terrorists is to kill them."[156]

Less than a week after Creech Jones forwarded Cunningham's recommendations to the cabinet, Montgomery travelled to Palestine to see for himself the situation and to meet directly with Gurney. While it is not clear what exactly transpired between the two, Montgomery evidently was still not on board with Creech Jones' policy. Following the meeting, Gurney wrote to Martin: "I have had Monty in for nearly an hour this morning. ... It is becoming increasingly difficult to go on carrying out a lack of policy with which nobody agrees!"[157] Montgomery continued to keep abreast of developments in Palestine, travelling again on December 15 to obtain a briefing from Colonel C. R. W. Norman, the chief of military intelligence in Palestine.[158] Montgomery and Creech Jones continued to be at odds in cabinet meetings. Indeed, so conflicted was government policy that on December 17 at a MELF commander in chief's briefing, General Sir Harold Pyman, the chief of staff for MELF, noted that there was "unlikely to be an early settlement to this problem."[159]

It became clear on December 19 how very divided the cabinet was when the cabinet defense committee received a memorandum prepared jointly by the war office and the colonial office on the use of armed forces in Palestine, in accordance with the prime minister's November 20 request for such a report. Part I of the memorandum laid out the views of the war office. Part II laid out the views of the colonial office. The two were completely opposed to each other. The civil servants who prepared the memorandum (L. C. Hollis and M. S. Murrie) "invited" the committee to "decide between the two possible courses of action."[160]

The war office held that the role of the army in Palestine was to "assist the police to maintain law and order and to protect life and property," which it would do by: "(a) apprehending those who commit murder and sabotage; (b) removing arms and explosives from those who use them to commit murder and sabotage and from any other as may be ordered; [and] (c) protection against sabotage." In order to achieve these objectives, "the minimum numbers should be employed on purely defensive tasks, leaving the maximum numbers free to act offensively against disturbers of the peace. Only thus can the initiative be seized and held, and peace maintained." The memorandum explicitly criticized the high commissioner, claiming that his recent decisions had "put a restrictive interpretation on the general principle of the employment of troops." These restrictions included the following:

(a) Although possession of arms is illegal and punishable by death, action is limited to searching for known Irgun Zvai Leumi dumps. Searches for arms throughout the whole Jewish community are not permitted.
(b) In pursuance of the policy of establishing better relations between the Palestine administration and the Jewish community the high commissioner decided that
    (i) No offensive action was to be taken against illegal armed organizations except as a direct result of intelligence information.
    (ii) No offensive action was to be taken after an outrage unless it is considered that there is a definite connection between the perpetrators and the locality concerned.
    (iii) No major offensive operation is to be undertaken without the permission of the high commissioner.
(c) A further defensive commitment to the extent of twelve battalions has been laid upon the army by the necessity of protecting the railways.

The memorandum charged that "[t]he effect of these restrictions is so great that the object as a whole cannot be achieved. ... Viewed from the military standpoint appeasement has failed." The memorandum concluded: "In the view of the War Office, the measures being taken to maintain law and order in Palestine are totally inadequate; the country is in the grip of lawlessness; the Police Force is unable to deal with the problem; a large Army is in the country but it is not being used properly with the result that lawlessness and terror are on the increase."

The colonial office view was quite different. Bypassing the question of armed force altogether, the colonial office memorandum stated:

The object of His Majesty's Government is to reach a political decision in Palestine. ... An important factor affecting the attainment of this object is the existence in Palestine of a large and highly organised Jewish community, with whose acknowledged leaders His Majesty's Government are bound to negotiate. The immediate political object is to create conditions in which such negotiations ... will have some prospect of success.

The colonial office had commissioned Sir Charles Wickham, formerly the inspector general of the Royal Ulster Constabulary in Northern Ireland, to carry out an "examination of police methods and organisation." Wickham agreed with Cunningham that "reprisals or punishments inflicted on the general public, unless direct connection between a section of the community and specific terrorist acts can be demonstrated, will not defeat terrorism but merely further alienate the populace on whose nascent co-operation present hopes of eliminating the scourge of violence are based." The memorandum acknowledged that "[g]eneral searches, curfews and collective fines might contribute towards the morale of the troops," but argued that such would be interpreted by the Jewish population as an attempt to "terrorize the Jewish community" and would destroy the influence of the moderate Jewish leaders.[161]

In sum, the war office held that the Jewish population in Palestine should be punished as a whole for every terrorist action carried out by the Jewish insurgents, forcing them through fear of reprisal to provide any information they might have on those committing the violence. The colonial office argued that an end to terrorism was reliant upon the goodwill of the larger Jewish population, most of whom opposed terrorism. Only through political negotiation could a long-term solution be reached; reprisals and state violence would only embitter the population, make them less likely to take the British government at its word, and more likely to turn to the insurgents for protection from the state. It was up to the cabinet defense committee, including both Creech Jones and Montgomery, to determine an acceptable policy based on these contrasting and contradictory viewpoints.

Such agreement would not come before Christmas, or even New Year's Eve, but on January 1, 1947, the members of the cabinet defense committee gathered once again at No. 10 Downing Street to discuss the problem of Palestine. Creech Jones opened the meeting by reinforcing the colonial office view, telling his colleagues that "in existing circumstances political considerations should weigh heavily in deciding the role that should be adopted by the Armed Forces." He warned that the "adoption of more aggressive tactics" would "upset the political balance and make the task of achieving a settlement in Palestine more difficult." He also assured the committee that the high commissioner in Palestine supported his rather than the war office's view, and added that there was "the fullest cooperation and harmony between the civil and military authorities in Palestine."

Ernest Bevin spoke next. He agreed with Creech Jones that the political process had to be paramount in the committee's considerations, but questioned what exactly the political process was, arguing that any decisions taken by the cabinet were inevitably "bound up" with "our ultimate intentions" in Palestine, which at that moment were not at all clear. He argued that during the past month, "our whole position in the Middle East [has] weakened," and noted that "the impression seemed to be growing that we [have] lost the ability and, indeed, the will to live up to our responsibilities." Bevin reminded the cabinet of the importance of the Middle East to British strategic interests, and warned that without "its oil and other potential resources" there was "no hope of our being able to achieve the standard of life at which we [are] aiming in Great Britain." The success of Attlee's welfare state, his nationalization of industry, and the socialist rebirth of Britain were all dependent on the economic resources of the Middle East. For that reason, Bevin suggested the government "make up our minds on what solution we [are] going to impose and recognise that any solution which we might think it right to impose [will] be met with opposition from both Jews and Arabs."[162]

A. V. Alexander, the minister of defense, asserted that in the long term, "the retention of our position in Palestine [is] a strategic necessity." Consequently, he believed Britain's ultimate policy ought to be to maintain British influence rather than devolve sovereignty either to the Jews or to the Arabs. In the short term, "all necessary discretion should be given to the Army to prevent and punish terrorism," particularly because of "the cruelty and indignities to which members of the Armed Forces were being subjected." As things stood, British inaction was "having a most serious effect on our prestige in the Middle East." Lord Pakenham, the undersecretary of state for war, agreed that the army was "being placed in an impossible and unfair position" and requested that they "be authorised to take stronger military action on the lines proposed in the War Office paper."

It was then Montgomery's turn to speak. He disputed the colonial office claim that "the Jewish Agency had the extremists under control" and offered as evidence the fact that "the terrorists operated exactly when they liked and were not subject to any control." He argued that the army was more than capable of solving the problem, but that they needed a "clear-cut objective." He therefore suggested that "the country be flooded with mobile columns of troops who would move about from place to place under close wireless control. On receipt of information of an outrage, columns in the neighbourhood would converge on the spot, surround it, and comb it thoroughly." If this occurred, he argued, "the confidence which [is] now lacking would be restored, and things would be made more and more difficult for the terrorists."

With the colonial and war office views explained, other ministers chimed in and a broad consensus (excluding Creech Jones and to a certain extent Bevin) emerged that the restoration of law and order ought to be the first priority, and the army in Palestine ought to be used along the lines suggested by Montgomery. Attlee, summing up the meeting, stated that there was "every indication that further outbreaks of terrorism would take place and no reliance [can] be placed on co-operation from the moderate elements, who were intimidated by the terrorists." He therefore ordered Creech Jones, "in consultation with the War Office," to draw up a directive to the high commissioner in Palestine outlining the new policy.[163] Ironically, the cabinet had agreed to employ a strategy which the colonial secretary, the high commissioner, and the chief secretary were opposed to and the foreign secretary had grave reservations about. It was a policy based on army operations rather than political engagement, one in which the primary emphasis was on the insurgent rather than the civilian. It was a defining moment in the history of the British mandate in Palestine.

Montgomery was ecstatic and on January 2 sent a cipher to General Pyman, the chief of staff MELF, informing him that the cabinet defense committee had ruled that the high commissioner must "use the Military and Police forces at his disposal to maintain proper order in Palestine with no nonsense about it." Montgomery also ordered Pyman to inform General Barker, the GOC in Palestine, that this new strategy, which was a "change over from the policy of appeasement," should be "carried through firmly and relentlessly and despite world opinion or Jewish reaction in America."[164]

Montgomery was not content merely to inform Pyman of the impending directive. Well aware that it was the colonial office that would draft the directive, and having discovered that High Commissioner Cunningham was flying from Palestine to London to meet with Creech Jones directly, Montgomery suggested that he be present at the conference between the two men.[165] This Creech Jones assented to and at the meeting that took place on the evening of Friday, January 3 (just hours before Montgomery was to fly to Moscow), Cunningham and the chief of the imperial general staff clashed terribly, the former holding the same objections to the new policy as Creech Jones. So inflamed was Montgomery by what he considered a lack of deference by Cunningham that he immediately drafted a letter to the colonial secretary and sent it the following morning. He thanked Creech Jones for his hospitality at the meeting but declared that as "professional head of the British Army," he considered it his duty to say "certain things very clearly." If for "political reasons" Creech Jones chose to "disregard [his] military advice," any responsibility for the repercussions that might follow would be his alone. He then laid out his viewpoint:

(a) It is my considered and definite opinion that the army is not being properly used in Palestine.

(b) The country is in the grip of terrorism and disorder: to deal with this menace we have a police force *and* an army; the army totals about 100,000 men and is a very powerful weapon.

(c) I consider that if the police force and the army are used properly, the present state of disorder in Palestine could be held in check and eventually brought under control.

(d) To carry out (c), more effective and robust methods must be employed than is the case at present. The present methods are neither effective nor robust.

(e) It is quite useless to imagine that we can counter terrorism without annoying and upsetting Jewish areas that are seemingly quite friendly; such a restriction would merely cramp the initiative of the armed forces and help the terrorists. If for political reasons such a restriction is necessary, then we will have no success in our efforts to control terrorism and we must face this fact.

He acknowledged that his opinions differed from Cunningham's, but claimed that the high commissioner's efforts to maintain order in Palestine "are futile, are quite ineffective, have definitely failed, and will continue to fail." Finally, he reminded Creech Jones that the ministers in the cabinet had spoken on the matter and that "the first responsibility of Government is to maintain law and order; that is not being done."[166]

Left with little choice, Creech Jones wrote the directive for Cunningham, laying out a policy with which he disagreed completely and which he believed would have terrible consequences for the political process in Palestine. He completed it and sent it to Cunningham and Gurney on January 15, 1947. The responsibility for implementing this policy was now left to these two men, each of whom was equally as opposed to it as the man who drafted it.[167] Meanwhile, those in the military chain of command were enthusiastic about the new flexibility they had been granted. On January 3, Pyman wrote to General Dempsey, commander in chief MELF, informing him that while Cunningham was in London, General Barker (the GOC Palestine) had taken temporary control of the territory. Upon reviewing the situation, Barker hoped to carry out "a whole series of town searches" and place "curfews and restrictions on civilian movement and trade." Barker had drawn up a plan to "isolate the Tel Aviv area from the rest of Palestine" and to "convene summary military courts."[168] When Pyman learned from Montgomery that he had succeeded in his political battle with Creech Jones, he noted with pleasure in his diary that Barker was now free to "crack about" with his soldiers and "be aggressive in Palestine until the end of March."[169]

Gurney was well aware of the military's viewpoint and on January 16 informed Martin that General Barker was "quite content with the present decision to continue searching and searching wherever terrorists are likely to be found." The chief secretary, however, remained unconvinced that more searches would change the dynamics on the ground, as the Jewish Agency leaders were now "thoroughly frightened of the monster they have helped to rear." In his opinion, continued engagement with the Jewish moderates, who now saw the dangers of terrorism, would yield better results than aggressive military patrolling. But it was out of his hands. The cabinet had spoken.[170]

The impact of this new policy was felt immediately, although not in the manner Montgomery had hoped. Rather than stamping out insurgent violence, the increasingly hard-line taken by the army only seemed to incite it. Furthermore, in addition to the terrorist threats to their lives, the army now faced new hardships. Beginning on January 15, and coinciding with Creech Jones' directive, Cunningham introduced a set of restrictions on the movements of the armed forces intended to lessen their vulnerability. With immediate effect, Cunningham prohibited all British soldiers from visiting cafés, cinemas, and other public areas, and mandated that they move on or off duty in groups no smaller than four. He also ordered that physical security in Palestine be increased, which necessitated the building of more barricades and check points, the laying of more barbed wire and sandbags, and the employment of more guards.[171] Dempsey went a step further, informing his commanders on January 21 that "any soldiers kidnapped in Palestine should be regarded as losses and that their recovery should not form an excuse for any alteration of the present policy of breaking the power of the extremists."[172] When these steps failed to quell the Irgun attacks, Cunningham instituted Operation Polly. Beginning on February 2, all nonessential personnel and families were evacuated from Palestine. For those essential personnel who remained, the army created security zones in Haifa and Jerusalem, beyond the wire of which they could not venture. As one historian has written, "The British in the name of security had transformed the Mandate into a prison, and locked themselves in as well."[173]

Such restrictions were clearly felt by those serving in Palestine. Colonel Norman, the chief of military intelligence, informed his mother on February 2 that life had become "rather grim and dismal," although admitted that "it's no use trying to govern this country saddled with a lot of people whom you can't protect."[174] Following a week's worth of restrictions, his mood darkened further. He wrote: "[T]he situation is very tense indeed and it looks as if almost anything might happen. This week seems to have been endless. There's been an enormous amount of work to do and so far as I can see, next week will be just as bad."[175] Gurney, too, sensed a tangible change in the atmosphere, writing to Martin that "the strain here has been pretty heavy and now that the remaining British are all behind wire we are beginning to wonder how long it will be possible to carry on civil administration at all."[176] Even Montgomery was "absolutely horrified at what is happening in Palestine." In contrast to Norman and Gurney, however, he believed that the security forces were still not doing enough, telling Creech Jones on January 28 that "we have been led into this unpleasant situation by weak and spineless handling of the problem. ... [W]e have only ourselves to blame for what is going on. ... It is vital to maintain order in Palestine. This we are not doing. Until we show that we mean to do it, we will get nowhere."[177]

Meanwhile, in London, the second peace conference began on January 26, although again without any Jewish representation. Bevin once more tried to encourage the Arab representatives to seek compromise and accommodation with the Jews, but following an outright rejection of any solution involving partition or the creation of a Jewish state, Bevin called off talks on February 4.[178] It was the last time the British government attempted to broker a deal between the Jews and Arabs. Its commitment to Palestine had been tried one too many times.

Besides, by February 1947, the cabinet was wrestling with another colonial problem. The Second World War had produced dramatic change in India, Britain's most important holding. Beginning in 1942, the Indian National Congress launched the

"Quit India" Movement, which, because of the preemptive arrest of its leaders, resembled most closely a peasant revolt, an unco-ordinated and spontaneous outbreak of violence against British rule on a level unseen since the 1857 Indian Mutiny. Those who rebelled attacked government property, destroyed railway stations, pulled up railway tracks, and pulled down telegraph lines. In the Indian province of Bihar alone, "170 police stations, post offices, and other government buildings were destroyed."[179] The rebellion was easily crushed by fifty battalions of British troops, and the British Indian administration kept the congress leaders imprisoned for the remaining three years of the war, but the Quit India Movement was a sign of things to come.[180]

Because of the loss of Hindu support in India owing to the suppression of the movement, the British government turned to India's Muslim population, represented most prominently by the Muslim League. Consequently, army recruitment efforts in India shifted from the traditional Hindu "warrior" castes to an all-inclusive approach. The result was that by the end of the war, India "possessed an army, 'national' in all except its topmost ranks, prepared to lead the country into independence."[181] Furthermore, the famed Indian Civil Service, which admitted its first Indian employee in 1864 and had only twenty-eight Indians in its ranks by 1900, was by 1945 more than half Indian.[182] This meant that as the war came to a close, within India the British government not only contended with a discontented population of 400 million people and a Hindu leadership cadre that had only just been released from three years' imprisonment, but also had to manage a professional army and civil service made up primarily of Indian rather than British employees who believed they could settle their own affairs without outside guidance. When the government staged elections in India in the winter of 1945–1946, the picture became clear. All minor parties were swept from the stage and the Indian National Congress and Muslim League dominated, with the Congress winning 90 percent of the open (non-Muslim constituencies). The Muslim League took all 30 reserved Muslim seats in the central legislature and 442 of the 500 Muslim seats in the provincial assemblies.[183]

With the Indian population so sharply divided between Hindu and Muslim constituencies, the leader of the Muslim League, Muhammad Ali Jinnah, began to claim that Muslims in India could never reach parity with Hindus and thus should be granted their own state, which he termed "Pakistan." Almost immediately, Pakistan took on a meaning of its own among the Muslim population of India: "It was, as a modern nation-state for India's Muslim peoples, the logical culmination of the long process of colonial Muslim politics. At the same time, however, as a symbol of Muslim identity, Pakistan transcended the ordinary structures of the state. As such it evoked an ideal Islamic political order, in which the realization of an Islamic life would be fused with the state's ritual authority."[184] In March 1946, the British cabinet sent a delegation to India, the purpose of which was to reach a solution. After speaking with Muslim and Hindu representatives, it devised a plan whereby the British government would give India its independence, but India would be divided into a three-tiered federation with Muslim and Hindu provinces. This plan faced opposition from both the Indian National Congress and the Muslim League and the talks collapsed in July 1946. The following month, India descended into an anarchy of communal violence between Hindus and Muslims. In the so-called Great Calcutta Killing of August 16–20, 4000 people were murdered in neighborhood purges, with the deaths of 7000 Muslims in Bihar quickly followed by several thousand Hindus in Bengal.[185] The Indian subcontinent, part of the British Empire in one form or another since the early 1600s and the most important and seemingly stable crown colony since 1858, was quickly coming unstuck. With the rapid surge of both Hindu and Muslim nationalism, there seemed little the British government could do.

On December 20, 1946, the cabinet's India and Burma committee finally succumbed to the pressure of communal violence on the subcontinent, drafting a statement declaring that Britain would withdraw from India by March 31, 1948, at the latest. Attlee, however, persuaded the committee to postpone making such an abrupt announcement. Many in the cabinet feared that the loss of India "might be regarded as the beginning of the liquidation of the British Empire" and argued that it would be better to manage a "voluntary transfer of power to a democratic government." This could only be done if the British government first nurtured and maintained a viable government in India, which would take time. A sudden declaration, they claimed, would lead to chaos rather than ordered democracy.[186]

By February 1947, the political situation in India had worsened so dramatically that ministers realized that the one luxury they most certainly did not have was time. On February 18, 1947, therefore, the cabinet authorized the secretary of state for India, Lord Pethick-Lawrence (Frederick William Pethick-Lawrence, 1st Baron Pethick-Lawrence), to issue a statement pledging an end to British rule in India by June 1948.[187] Two days later, on February 20, Attlee publicly proclaimed that "on behalf of the people of this country [the British government express] their goodwill and good wishes towards the people of India as they go forward to this final stage in their achievement of self-government."[188] The jewel in the crown of empire had lost its sheen and the government pledged to dislodge it within sixteen months. As it turned out, the end would come much sooner than that.

It was not only in the empire that the British government faced trouble. At home, too, the situation was worsening. In early January 1947, the road haulage workers launched a strike in response to wage freezes imposed by the government.[189] By January 8, the lorry drivers were striking nationally and food supplies into London were being held up.[190] Such a cut in supply could not have come at a worse time. Throughout 1946, Hugh Dalton, the chancellor of the exchequer, had followed a policy of cheap money, cutting general interest rates to 2.5% and replacing local loans with irredeemable treasury bonds in October 1946, which also bore interest of only 2.5%.

Such bonds became known colloquially as "Daltons" and were a colossal failure, most being sold off in January 1947 after only three months. This caused a collapse in the gilt-edge market for the first time in British history.[191] This problem was conflated by an American loan the British government had negotiated in December 1945, the money becoming available in July 1946. Beginning in January 1947, however, there was a worldwide drain on the dollar, caused by a food and raw materials shortage that left the United States as one of the world's sole suppliers. This caused US prices to rise sharply that, according to Dalton, knocked $1 billion off the value of the original loan, although the loan of course had to be repaid in full. Consequently, the British economy faced a trade imbalance with the United States, with the balance of payments turning sharply against Britain in the first quarter of 1947.[192]

Even the climate seemed to be conspiring against the British people in early 1947, with the *Annual Register* recording "the most severe [winter] since 1880–1." On January 27, heavy snow fell across the land, which caused electricity cuts in many locales.[193] As the weather continued to worsen, the sea in Folkstone harbor froze, preventing the landing of any supplies; coal ships were stranded in the River Tyne due to stormy weather; and the continuing presence of snow prevented coal shipments by road or rail. By February, the government coal stocks had fallen short, and on February 7, Emanuel Shinwell, the minister of fuel and power, announced in the House of Commons that "fuel for industry in the South-East, the Midlands and the North-West of England could not be supplied for the time being; and that the use of domestic electricity was also to be banned in the same areas between 9 [a.m.] and 12 a.m. [*sic*; p.m.] and 2 and 4 p.m."[194] Writing in his diary three days later, Sir Cuthbert Headlam, the Conservative Member of Parliament for Newcastle North, noted, "If this weather continues the situation may really become disastrous—coal cannot be moved and the railway lines are congested—sea transport largely suspended."[195] His mood grew worse as the weeks progressed and on March 2 he wrote: "The mess and confusion everywhere—at home and abroad—continue and things seem to be getting worse not better. The Government clearly cannot cope with the situation and we appear to be heading for economic disaster."[196] In this assessment, Headlam seemed to be correct. On February 11, the government announced that the publication of all weekly periodicals would be stopped for two weeks to save fuel; and on February 15, the government reported that owing to the closure of factories due to the fuel shortage, unemployment had hit 2,319,400.[197]

It was with these events as backdrop that the government decided to let Palestine go. On February 14, the cabinet officially abandoned its quest for a political solution. In the short term, it would simply seek to reduce the level of violence through force of arms. Then, in September 1947, it planned to refer the Palestine problem to the General Assembly of the newly created United Nations. For the eight months from February to September, the British government would engage itself in an operation of damage control, but would do no more.[198] The IZL immediately tested Britain's new apathy to see if it extended to the security forces. On March 1, it launched eighteen major operations, including bomb attacks on the British officers' club at Goldschmidt House, within the security wire. This bomb alone killed twenty and wounded thirty. The next morning, the *Sunday Express* ran a headline calling on the government to "Govern or Get Out."[199] Colonel Norman saw the attacks and decided to put pen to paper in a letter to his mother: "I saw the Goldschmidt Club go up. It's only about 300 yards away. I was in my room and when I heard rifle shots I went to the roof and I was just in time to see the explosion. One of my own officers, Michael Gibbs, lived there and had a very lucky escape. Now of course we are going to impose martial law in certain parts of the country and will be further from a peaceful settlement than ever."[200] Norman's words were prescient. At eight o'clock on the morning of March 2, 1947, Cunningham proclaimed statuary martial law with a full curfew in effect throughout most Jewish areas.[201] The British government, having lost the will for a political solution, had placed Palestine fully into the hands of the military.

VI. The Endgame in Palestine

A new military strategy demanded a new military commander and for that role Montgomery hand-selected Major General Sir Gordon MacMillan, formerly director of weapons and development at the war office, to replace General Barker as GOC, Palestine. MacMillan implemented martial law with an aggressive edge previously lacking in army operations. The movement of all trains, buses, and taxis was prohibited; the army distributed all food; postal services were suspended; civil courts were abandoned in place of military tribunals; and all soldiers were given police authority, with permission to shoot any Palestinian who was purportedly disobeying their orders. In Tel Aviv, the army launched a 10,000-man search operation code named Operation Elephant. A similar offensive, Operation Hippo, commenced in Jerusalem. All Jews were rounded up and screened by police CID for their possible involvement in insurgent activities. Within a day of Cunningham's declaration of martial law, the security forces had shot dead two Jews, one of whom was a four-year-old girl—the military hierarchy failed to ascertain what order she had disobeyed, and the military police launched no investigation to judge the actions of her shooter.[202]

This turn of events greatly dismayed Henry Gurney, who wrote to Martin on March 5, saying, "This is a most tricky child that we have been handed to look after … [A]ll warnings have been apparently ignored by those responsible for decisions in London … I hope it is clear that we are very near war with the Jews."[203] By all accounts, it would seem that Gurney had misspoken: the British security forces *were* at war with the Jews, or, at least, with those Jews involved in the insurgency. On March 3,

1947, the day after Cunningham declared martial law, the IZL injured five soldiers and four civilians in three attacks; on March 5, the Irgun launched further attacks in Haifa and Jerusalem, including the complete destruction of the Haifa Municipal Assessments Office; three days later, on March 8, three attacks were launched within the Tel Aviv security zone and the staff car of Brigadier Robert G. C. Poole, commanding officer of the third infantry brigade, was blown up with him in it—he only narrowly escaped death. And it was not only the IZL that was engaged in this insurgent campaign. On March 12, LEHI contributed to the chaos, attacking the Middle East headquarters of the Royal Army Pay Corps, also within the security zone. Six other attacks, some Irgun and others LEHI, were launched that day.[204]

Gurney was not the only official second-guessing the introduction of martial law. Montgomery, previously so keen on enhanced military action, also began to have doubts. On March 4, he sent a top-secret cipher to Dempsey asking his opinion of the military situation in Palestine.[205] Dempsey replied immediately, downplaying the level of violence and suggesting that there were as many murders in England as in Palestine. The difference, he claimed, was that in England the "murderer is caught because the people of the country are on the side of law and order and assist the police. In Palestine the people do not assist the police and the murderers are not caught." Demspey concluded that regardless of British policy, "Outrages will continue. We will go on picking up a few terrorists and I hope lessen their activities. But so long as there are fanatical murderers at large in the country and so long as the people are not on the side of law and order we will not stamp out the menace."[206] Dempsey's report was not optimistic, but one that was borne out by the evidence on the ground. The fact was that Operations Elephant and Hippo were producing few results. In their first five days, despite thousands of screenings, the British security forces arrested only twenty-five insurgents. Even after bringing in the Jewish mayors of Tel Aviv and Petva Tikva, warning them of unspecified consequences if more intelligence was not forth-coming, the number of arrests continued as a trickle rather than a gush.[207] So long as martial law remained in place, the British would have no hope of bringing Jewish people over to the "side of law and order."

Consequently, those within the cabinet began to question the wisdom of martial law. Montgomery, despite his doubts, became its sole supporter. On March 12, he wrote again to Dempsey, explaining, "I have said [to the cabinet that] its value lies in the power it gives to the Army to take action in a number of matters without always having to get prior permission from the Govt. It gives the power to arrest on suspicion. It enables the Army to do its stuff properly. Far from being remitted soon it should be extended. It is in fact bearing good fruit."[208] His efforts were in vain. On March 17—after seventy-eight arrests—Cunningham, in consultation with Gurney, decided he could no longer imple-ment a failed policy. Martial law had lost the support of all but Montgomery, and day by day it was isolating more and more of the Jewish community. Cunningham therefore lifted the restrictions, suspended Elephant and Hippo, and restored public services.[209] Montgomery was outraged and wrote to Dempsey asking for a restoration of martial law. On March 20, however, Dempsey replied to Montgomery that he did not recommend martial law at the present time. Furthermore, he downplayed his previous concerns, claiming that "The Army today is not hampered by the civil government in any way in striving to attain its object. True the G.O.C. has to consult and obtain permission from the High Commissioner before carrying out a large operation such as the recent cordoning off of Tel Aviv. But he is free to carry out his continuous searches where and when he will."[210] Cunningham, now supported by the cabinet, had clearly reasserted his authority upon the military hierarchy. Montgomery, in contrast, had been hung out to dry.

With martial law a clear failure, the question for the British government was what to do next in Palestine. Even those ele-ments of the Jewish community that had been sympathetic to

British governance were now marginalized. Moderate opinion, in the past held by the silent majority of Jewish Palestinians, had been exorcized by the guns and dogs of martial law and the Irgun reaped the benefits. This was a lesson not lost on General MacMillan. On March 23, less than a week after Cunningham lifted martial law, he sent a memorandum to Montgomery titled "Appreciation in Note Form of the Measures Necessary to Maintain Law and Order in Palestine." Describing the consequences of martial law, he wrote: "Jews received severe shock; considerable financial loss running into millions; unemployment; organized labour realized need for stopping outrages; ... Possibility of re-imposition much feared by the Jews; this threat is powerful deterrent and incentive to assist security forces." He warned, however, that this "powerful weapon" should in future be "imposed with discretion," acknowledging that "if kept on too long will turn the whole YISHUV [Jewish community] against us and considerably aggravate internal security situation." He suggested that the reimposition of martial law over the whole country was "most undesirable" and instead recommended that "Civil Government should continue" with increased security in selected areas where and when necessary.[211] In the larger debate over the applicable use of armed force in Palestine, Creech Jones rather than Montgomery had been correct. The problem was the government had given up its quest for a political solution. Now that Montgomery's approach had also failed, the government had nothing left on the table.

By late spring 1947, the pressure of applying a policy that was unworkable had become numbing to those in Palestine. Gurney commented to Martin on May 22 that there was "a danger here of our most extraordinary conditions of life and government being regarded as normal, so accustomed are we all becoming to the day to day adjustments and problems arising in the task of trying to make something work that was never meant to work at all."[212] Colonel Norman, likewise, had become so habituated to the constant violence that on May 25 he chastised his worrying mother for paying "too much attention to the BBC and the papers," reassuring her that "they're quite wrong."[213] In reality, the situation in Palestine between the ending of martial law on March 17 and the last days of May had been quite grave. On March 31, LEHI bombed the Haifa oil refinery, causing a blaze to light up the night sky for the subsequent three weeks, only being completely extinguished on April 18.[214] In response to this attack, the high commissioner introduced the death penalty as punishment for terrorist actions. The British hanged their first four members of the IZL at 4:00 a.m. on April 17. Four days later, two prisoners—one IZL and one LEHI—held onto each other in their cell and detonated a smuggled grenade, preferring to die on their own terms than be hanged by the British at dawn.[215]

Meanwhile, the Jewish insurgent attacks continued, capital punishment failing to provide the deterrent Cunningham had hoped. On April 21, the Irgun attacked three separate military convoys; on April 23, insurgents ambushed a train, killing eight people; on April 24, an army lorry hit a mine, injuring four soldiers; on April 25, a bomb attack on a police billet killed four and wounded six; and on April 26, the CID chief in Haifa and three constables in Tel Aviv were assassinated.[216] The insurgents' most spectacular event occurred in May, however, at 4:22 a.m. on the morning of Sunday, May 4, when IZL and LEHI volunteers detonated an explosion on the outside wall of the Acre prison. Inside, thirty-four LEHI and IZL prisoners were waiting, ready to pour out of the hole and into four lorries idling outside. In the confusion of the blast, the prison descended into anarchy. Not only did the thirty-four planned escapees pass through the hole; eighty-six other Jews and 131 Arabs also left the prison, bringing the total number of escapees up to 251. The Jews were easily rounded up, standing out in the all-Arab old city. By the evening of May 5, just twenty-one of the Jewish escapees remained at large. The Arabs blended into their surroundings and thus were harder to track down, but within a week most had been recaptured.[217] Although ultimately a failure for the Jewish insurgents, the week-long saga epitomized the

British experience in Palestine during the spring of 1947. They were reacting to rather than preventing violence.

The government in London recognized its position was untenable and decided to bring forward its appeal to the United Nations. On April 2, Sir Alexander Cadogan, the British representative at the United Nations, requested a special session of the General Assembly to discuss the Palestine problem. This he was granted, and on April 28, 1947, talks opened at Lake Success, New York.[218] The Zionist representatives, led by Rabbi Hillel Silver, realized they would get a better hearing from the United Nations than the British and thus made the most of the convention. They argued that as the surviving remnants of an ancient people whose numbers had been greatly reduced by the Holocaust and who were now living as unwanted refugees on a hostile European continent, the Jewish people deserved a country of their own in their historic homeland of Palestine. The Arabs, however, also recognized that the United Nations was a more impartial body than the British government and thus might be more ready to sympathize with the Zionists. They therefore argued that the Palestine problem was one to be solved by the British and Arab states working in coordination, with no interference from the United Nations. They held that Palestine had never been and never should be partitioned and that as tragic as the Holocaust was, it was "irrelevant to the basic, obvious fact: Palestine had been [an] Arab [territory] for many centuries."[219] The UN delegates, with British agreement, decided that a neutral investigating committee should be formed, and on May 15, they appointed the United Nations Special Committee on Palestine (UNSCOP), composed of representatives from the eleven nations of Australia, Canada, Czechoslovakia, Guatemala, India, Iran, the Netherlands, Peru, Sweden, Uruguay, and Yugoslavia. The committee planned to travel to Palestine to carry out its investigations in mid-June.[220]

Meanwhile, the killing continued. On June 9, the IZL kidnapped an off duty police sergeant and constable bathing at a public swimming pool at Galei Gil. They were taken to a safe house in Herzlia, where they were bound, gagged, and threatened with execution if five Irgun members on trial for the Acre prison escape were executed. After nineteen hours, the Irgun guards stepped outside and the police officers were able to free themselves and escape to the street, still wearing their swimming trunks, directly into the arms of a passing army patrol.[221] Just seven days later, on the day UNSCOP arrived in Palestine, a British tribunal passed sentence on the five members of the IZL; three were awarded the death penalty, the remaining two got fifteen years' imprisonment each.[222]

With UNSCOP actively meeting with Palestinian Jews and the Arabs refusing to cooperate because they did not recognize the authority of the United Nations to intervene, Colonel Norman composed a review of the situation in Palestine. He declared that "[a]t the present time it is the Jews who are causing most of the trouble" but, taking note of the Arab boycott of UNSCOP, warned, "this position may easily be reversed in September if and when a decision on the Palestine problem is made by the Assembly of the United Nations." With the arrival of UNSCOP and the eyes of the world now upon Palestine, Norman predicted that the violence would lessen and that both the Jews and the Arabs would most likely "hold their hand until September." However, once UNSCOP's report was published, and "in the very likely event of the UN recommendations being contrary to their [both Jews and Arabs] aims," he suspected the violence would flare up again, perhaps to an even greater extent than before.[223]

Norman did not have to wait until September for the flare up of violence; it arrived within a week of his writing. On June 30, LEHI fired on a party of British soldiers in Tel Aviv, instantly killing one, fatally wounding another, and leaving two more with injuries. That evening, a LEHI team in Haifa opened fire into a restaurant frequented by British citizens, wounding three off duty officers and the barman. In response, the British government rejected UNSCOP's request that the death sentences of those convicted on June 16 be commuted, reconfirming them on July 8. The IZL promised that if the three were executed, members of the British security forces would be hung in turn. On July 12, in order to make good on its promise, the Irgun kidnapped two off duty Palestine police sergeants in Natanya, together with a civilian war department clerk with whom they were walking. The clerk was released within hours, but the two police sergeants were taken to an underground bunker.[224] The strain of the situation showed on Norman, who confessed to his mother on July 13 that he was "beginning to feel I'd like another holiday. The kidnapping of two sergeants yesterday was about the last straw."[225] In response to the kidnappings, Cunningham launched Operation Tiger, a 5000-man search operation in Natanya, which required the implementation of a complete curfew for forty-eight hours. British soldiers took town residents from their homes in groups of thirty to forty until all 1427 had been interrogated, but they were unable to turn up any intelligence and only seventeen of those questioned were detained as possible Irgun suspects. The sergeants were not found.[226]

On July 18, only days after Cunningham lifted the curfew in Natanya, the British received a further setback. The refugee ship *Exodus*, one of the last refugee blockade runners to remain in service, arrived close to Palestinian territorial waters, carrying on board 4554 Jewish refugees. Two British destroyers were sent to prevent its landing and closed in on either side, ramming the vessel and subsequently boarding it using tear gas and firecrackers. In the process, a sixteen-year-old refugee and an American volunteer crew member were killed by British sailors. The *Exodus* was forced into the harbor at Haifa, where the refugees were transferred by gangplank to three prison ships, never setting foot on Palestinian soil beyond the harbor piers. From there they sailed through the Mediterranean to Sète in France. Upon docking on July 29, the Jewish refugees refused to leave. There followed a four-week standoff lasting until August 22, during which time the Jews were kept on deck in cages, burning under the sun of a French heat wave. Five infants were born, the heat wave turned to rain, and the Jews, without shelter, launched a hunger strike. Still the British insisted that they disembark, making no secret of the fact that they had allowed the conditions on board to deteriorate so that the Jews would be forced to leave. On August 22, the ship sailed from France to Hamburg, where on September 9 the refugees were greeted by 3000 British soldiers and 1500 German policemen. There the police and soldiers forced them off with high-pressure hoses, truncheons, and riot shields. Their final destination was two camps at Poppendorg and Amstau, where they were kept in barracks overlooked by watchtowers and British soldiers. The whole six-week saga inflicted irreparable damage on British prestige, with the images of herded Jews on the newsreels seeming so similar to those recently seen of the Holocaust. Coming just weeks before the UN General Assembly session in September, it ensured that the British delegation would be met with skepticism and distrust.[227]

While the *Exodus* languished in France and Germany, on the Palestine mainland, the violence continued. In Tel Aviv, Colonel K. G. F. Chavasse, commanding officer of the second battalion, Royal Irish Fusiliers, received a telephone call in the officers' mess informing him that the building would be blown up in fifteen minutes. Chavasse was unimpressed by the warning: "My reaction was that I was damned if I was going to turn the battalion out in the streets, possibly for nothing, and be laughed at by the Jews! So I took a quick glass of sherry and rang the Brigadier at [Brigade] headquarters and told him that if he heard a large bang or saw a cloud of dust going into the air it would be us being blown up by the 'thugs.'"[228] Thankfully for Chavasse and his men, the phone call was a bluff. Yet other incidents were more serious. On July 18, the IZL killed a British soldier in Jerusalem and wounded another seven, prompting Norman to describe the week as "truly atrocious."[229] The following day, the IZL launched six attacks, one of which killed a police constable. Finally, on July 29, the British authorities led their three convicted Irgun prisoners to the gallows.[230]

The IZL response was swift and deadly. Less than an hour after the hangings, the Irgun dragged the two captured British police sergeants from their underground bunker. They too were hung, as promised. The British administration, security forces, and public were outraged and expressed their anger. In the United Kingdom, crowds held anti-Semitic demonstrations in London, Manchester, and Glasgow, where Jewish shop windows were broken; in Liverpool, mobs looted Jewish stores; and throughout the country, individuals desecrated Jewish graves and offensive graffiti appeared on synagogues. In Palestine, the British security forces went on a rampage. Most seriously, in Tel Aviv, British soldiers and armored cars fired into Jewish buses and cars, killing five people and seriously injuring fifteen more. At the funeral of three of those killed, an RAF armored car opened fire on the procession, although it failed to leave any dead.[231] It was, to use Colonel Norman's words, "a pretty grim week."[232]

Following the deaths of the two police sergeants and the subsequent British reprisals, it was clear to the British government that a continued presence in Palestine was no longer viable. On August 3, General Sir John T. Crocker, who had replaced Dempsey as commander in chief MELF in July, sent a telegram to Emmanuel Shinwell, recently promoted war secretary, to inform him that the situation in Palestine was "at [a] critical stage." He continued: "So to speak the battle is on. Terrorists unlikely to call off present intensive effort unless further convinced of futility."[233] The following day, the vice-chief of the imperial general staff tersely informed Shinwell, "I doubt whether there are any further steps that Generals Crocker and MacMillan can take in order to ensure that the Terrorists do not 'pick up' any further British soldiers."[234] The starkest counsel of all, however, came from Hugh Dalton, the chancellor of the exchequer, in a letter written to the prime minister. Putting pen to paper on August 11, Dalton laid out his case in plain terms. His correspondence deserves to be quoted at length:

> I am quite sure that the time has almost come when we must bring our troops out of Palestine altogether. The present state of affairs is not only costly to us in man-power and money, but is, as you and I agree, of no real value from the strategic point of view—you cannot in any case have a secure base on top of a wasps' nest—and it is exposing our young men, for no good purpose, to most abominable experiences, and is breeding anti-Semites at a most shocking speed. I appreciate that we cannot take decisive action until we have the U.N. Report, but I shall press once more, as soon as this last stage in the long drawn out affair is reached, for a decision in the sense indicated above. It is high time that either we left the Arabs and the Jews to have it out in Palestine, or that some other Power or Powers took over the responsibility and the cost.[235]

Attlee agreed with Dalton and ordered the security forces to take a lower profile in Palestine until after the UN meeting. Those on the ground accepted this stance, as Gurney confessed to his friend Martin: "Lying low and saying nothing is not an attitude that commends itself to me at any time, but it is clear that we here shall have to be very careful to do so for the next couple of months."[236] The situation had now been taken from the hands of the military and placed into the care of the United Nations.

Yet it was not only in Palestine that the British were taking leave of their colonial responsibilities. On August 15, 1947, just four days after Dalton suggested to Attlee that British forces leave Palestine, the government awarded India its independence. Ever since the British had agreed on February 18, 1947, to leave India by June 1948, events in the colony had moved forward at a rapid pace. Rioting erupted in Punjab in early March, and on the fifth of that month the House of Commons held a debate over Attlee's policy. By a vote of 337 to 118, the members supported the decision to withdraw from the subcontinent. In India itself, the violence intensified, with more than 1000 people killed, more than 1000 people seriously wounded, and more than 60,000 refugees created in the first two weeks of March alone. Into this atmosphere a new viceroy, Lord Louis Mountbatten, arrived, being officially sworn in on March 24, 1947. After meetings with Gandhi, Jinnah, and Nehru, Mountbatten concluded in mid-April that Jinnah's notion of partition and of a Muslim Pakistan was right. It was, he believed, the only way to quell the communal violence. Once Mountbatten had made his decision, there was little point in the British remaining in India. By June 3, Mountbatten had developed a plan for a peaceful transfer of power. Over the subsequent ten weeks, the lines of partition between India and the new state of Pakistan were hammered out. Finally, on August 14, Mountbatten handed over power to the new dominion of Pakistan and on August 15 transferred power to the dominion of India. On that day, Britain's Indian empire had ceased to exist.[237]

Elsewhere in the empire, UNSCOP remained in Palestine until early August and thus witnessed the IZL and LEHI bombings, the kidnapping of the police sergeants, the British executions, the Irgun reprisals, the British reaction to them, and the whole debacle with the *Exodus*. After a short stay in Beirut to meet with representatives from the Arab states, the committee proceeded to Geneva, Switzerland, where between August 6 and August 15 it held ten lengthy meetings to hammer out a solution to the Palestine problem. By the close of these meetings, all present agreed that the British mandate must come to an end. The only question was what to do with Palestine once the British government left. Ultimately, no agreement could be reached; and on August 31, UNSCOP published both a majority report (supported by Canada, Peru, Czechoslovakia, Guatemala, the Netherlands, Uruguay, and Sweden) and a minority report (supported by India, Yugoslavia, and Iran), with Australia refusing to give its assent to either solution. The minority report was the closest to the original British plan of the previous year, proposing a three-year transitional period under the auspices of the United Nations after which a federal Palestinian state with both Arab and Jewish provinces would be born. But it was not the minority report that mattered. The majority report recommended a two-year transitional period under both British and UN auspices, during which time 150,000 additional Jewish immigrants would be admitted into the territory. Following this two-year period, the United Nations would partition Palestine three ways into a Jewish state, an Arab state, and an international district in Jerusalem that would remain under UN administration.[238]

UNSCOP circulated its reports to the British cabinet, which met to discuss them on September 20, 1947. Encouraged by Bevin, the cabinet rejected UNSCOP's recommendations outright. Although partition now seemed an inevitability, the cabinet found the proposed borders to be "manifestly unfair to the Arabs" and held that the two-year transitional period where British forces were expected to remain in Palestine was unacceptable. The cabinet decided instead that it would issue a declaration stating that it intended to evacuate at the earliest possible date. If the United Nations could not come up with more equitable lines of partition before then, the Jews and Arabs would have to sort out their problems on their own. This Creech Jones announced at the UN General Assembly on September 26, succinctly stating: "In order that there may be no misunderstanding of the attitude and policy of Britain I have been instructed by His Majesty's Government to announce, with all solemnity, that they have decided that in the absence of a settlement they must plan for an early withdrawal of British forces and of the British Administration from Palestine."[239] Despite the terseness of his words, those in the UN General Assembly continued to act as if they had not been spoken, each issuing statements relating to UNSCOP's reports. Creech Jones therefore repeated his declaration on October 16, stating, "My government desire that it should be clear beyond all doubt and ambiguity that not only is it our decision to wind up the mandate but that within a limited period we shall withdraw."[240]

This time, Creech Jones' message registered. The UN ad hoc committee on Palestine set up two subcommittees on October 22 to study in detail the majority and minority reports. By November 10, they had reached a compromise. Palestine would be partitioned into a Jewish state and an Arab state, with the lines of partition drawn more closely in line with the present demographics, although allowing for some continued immigration of Jewish refugees. The British mandate would come to an end on May 1, 1948. The two-year transition period would be cut to two months, and by July 1, 1948, all British forces would be withdrawn. The cabinet considered the new proposal and, after consulting with the chiefs of staff, informed the UN subcommittees that the earliest a military withdrawal could be completed would be August 1, 1948, although the continued presence of British troops did not necessarily mean that British administrative control of the mandate need continue for that long. This the ad hoc committee agreed to and on November 29, the proposals came up for a full vote of the UN General Assembly. That afternoon, at the UN site in Flushing Meadows, New York, the delegates voted in favor of partition by thirty-three votes to thirteen, with ten abstentions. Thirty years after the Balfour Declaration and almost four years from the original IZL declaration of revolt, the United Nations had given the Jews their state.[241]

However, the vote did little to quell the violence in Palestine. On the contrary, in many ways it exacerbated it, introducing a further complicating factor. For while the Jewish population was overjoyed at the United Nations' decision, the Palestinian Arabs were outraged and immediately rejected the resolution. As Colonel Norman wrote on November 30, "The Jews have got their State to-day [sic] and are very pleased with themselves. The Arabs are furious and have already started trouble shooting up a bus and killing 3 Jews. What a country!"[242] The British, having nullified the grievances of the Jewish insurgency, were now facing a low-level civil war between the Arabs and Jews. By the morning of December 10, less than two weeks after the partition vote, ninety-three Arabs, eighty-four Jews, and seven members of the British security forces had lost their lives. Later that day, Arab militants killed another ten Jews and wounded four when they ambushed their vehicles on the Jerusalem-Hebron road. The Haganah retaliated in Haifa, killing six Arabs and wounding 32 more with gunfire. By December 12, a further 32 Arabs and 11 Jews had been killed, together with two more British soldiers.[243]

Norman believed it was "the Jews' fault to begin with really, by rejoicing so ostentatiously and arrogantly when Partition was announced," although he declared both Jews and Arabs to be "fools."[244] In a report written for army commanders on December 11, he painted a gloomy picture of Palestine. He suggested that once the British mandate ended on May 1, 1948, there would be "military intervention" by surrounding Arab states determined to prevent partition. Alongside this intervention, there would be "guerilla activity." Before then, "the disorders of the past week may continue and extend in scale until they amount to a general rebellion." It was "inevitable that the [British] security forces will become involved in hostilities, possibly on a large scale with the Arabs, with serious harm to general Anglo-Arab relations." The start of this process was "already in evidence." As for the Jewish population, Norman argued that although the "aim of the Jewish leaders is to secure the establishment of a Jewish state without conflict with the Arabs," the Arab attacks already occurring showed that "Jewish restraint quickly wears thin." The consequence would be "a continuous cycle of reprisal and counter-reprisal. ... Attempts by Government to curb this tendency will be represented as sabotage of Jewish self-defence and the security forces may themselves become the target of Jewish attack." He concluded: "It may well be that, even before the Mandate is laid down, large parts of Palestine, Jew and Arab, may have passed out of the effective control of the Government; and that Palestine's economy may be virtually paralysed by cessation of labour by intimidation, fear or interruption of communication."[245] A directive issued by General Headquarters MELF two weeks later was no more optimistic. Seeing that the end of the Palestine mandate was near, it suggested that the British security forces should not unnecessarily endanger their lives in pursuit of an aim (peace in the Middle East) that might never come. It therefore limited the role of the army to being an "Aid to the Civil Power, [but only in areas] where the maintenance of Law and Order is a BRITISH Responsibility."[246]

The situation was no calmer in the New Year, and on January 7, 1948, the Irgun detonated a van-bomb at a bus stop in Jerusalem, killing seventeen Arabs and wounding over fifty.[247] The mood of this winter was well captured in Colonel Norman's increasingly pessimistic letters to his mother. On February 22, he noted, "I had to stop [writing this letter] for half an hour. Jewish terrorists have just murdered an army chaplain and a soldier in the street ... What it is to live in a country almost entirely populated by madmen!"[248] A week later, he wrote: "I've just heard that a train has been blown up on the coast and it looks like there'll be a lot of casualties. But [I] simply can't cope with maniacs. I've spent hours in the last few weeks in complicated negotiations with all sorts of people trying to keep things peaceful, and I might just as well have not wasted my time."[249] In March, the situation went from bad to worse. On the fourteenth of that month, Norman told his mother, "I've had a very trying week indeed and am thankful to-day is Sunday"; on March 20 he wrote, "The whole country's in a dither again"; and on March 27 he noted, "I've had an abso-lutely maddening week and am absolutely exhausted and thoroughly stale."[250] Norman's pessimism was matched by the soldiers serving alongside him. Second Lieutenant R. Hodges, a young man on national service, penned a letter on March 24 explaining to his friend in the United Kingdom that things had become "pretty critical ... pretty b——- grim. Battles are going on all round, shots pinging over the camp, snipers sniping and gunners gunning, it's all quite crazy. ... I dread to think what will happen when we clear out and the Jews and Arabs really set to."[251]

It was not long before the British administration and troops did indeed "clear out." At the beginning of April, the United Nations pushed the date for the end of the mandate back from May 1 to May 15/16. Yet even this date was uncertain. Cunningham wrote to Creech Jones on March 31 stating that he had engaged in a conversation with the army general officer commanding in Palestine, who had stated categorically that "unless the trends of the security situation change, every day longer we remain in Jerusalem makes its evacuation without loss of life more difficult." Cunningham continued: "He [the GOC] states that he is certain, without a change in present tendencies, that to remain in Jerusalem as late as May 15th will entail loss of life during extrication. The reason for this is that both Arabs and Jews are clearly at present proposing to undertake all out hostilities on the day the Mandate has been stated to end which will hamper seriously the physical withdrawal of the troops from their difficult situation in Jerusalem. In this situation even 10 days may make all the difference."[252]

Two days later, on April 2, General Crocker, the commander in chief MELF, wrote to Montgomery claiming that the situation in Palestine was "deteriorating," that "civil authority is really no longer exercising effective mandatory control in Palestine," and that "there is no hope of any other competent authority taking over from us in Jerusalem on 15 May." He acknowledged that "[m]ilitarily we cannot leave Jerusalem tidily under after 20 Apr[il]," but suggested the "sooner we do it after that date the more orderly I believe our departure will be. ... I fully appreciate that there may be serious political objections to any date earlier than 15 May but militarily I must recommend you strongly to support advancement."[253] Cunningham sent a second plea to Creech Jones ten days later, informing him that "the advice given to the Cabinet by the Chiefs of Staff [for a May 15 withdrawal date] did not agree either with the opinion of the

G.O.C. here or that given by the C-in-C. MELF." Like Crocker, Cunningham suggested that the date be brought forward:

Since the trends following on the [UN General] Assembly recommendations of November 29 became apparent and the decision to leave Palestine was irrevocable, my view on the date for the termination of the Mandate has always been the same. Looked at purely from the point of view of the Civil Government the longer we stayed here the more would our authority weaken, and, therefore again purely from our point of view, the sooner we went the better. ... In the event our authority has progressively weakened to a greater extent than what even I had foreseen. ... If we are required to remain here for political reasons we will do our best to do so, though I would suggest that if it becomes apparent that [the] U.N. can do nothing by May 15 the matter might be reconsidered. After April 20 there would not appear to be military reasons for staying.[254]

On April 13, Sir Hugh Dow (whom the government had designated to act as its consul general in Jerusalem once the mandate ended) and Cyril Marriott (designated consul general in Haifa) arrived for a visit with Cunningham. Major P. F. Towers-Clark, Cunningham's military assistant, was taken aback that neither man had "any practical experience of Palestine," which he believed would make their job "very difficult." He was also surprised that "neither of them seemed to have been briefed at all for the job," a fact clearly highlighted when "Sir Hugh compared stopping the fighting here with the quelling of a riot in India which he had accomplished with two companies of troops; he did not seem to appreciate the difference!"[255]

It was not only Dow and Marriot who seemed ignorant of events on the ground. On April 16, the UN General Assembly met again to see if it could produce a better solution to the Palestine problem than had been realized with the vote the previous November. Towers-Clark, writing in his diary, did not hold much hope for success: "There are but 29 days left before we go and out here we have given up any real expectation of getting a successor authority to take over from us on May 15th. Presumably the [United Nations] session will take at least a fortnight, which leaves only two weeks to get the new plan working." He was particularly discouraged that those in Palestine had not been consulted, lamenting in his diary that "we do not use any liaison officers to keep our delegation in touch with up-to-date developments in Palestine, relying entirely on telegrams. ... It is astonishing to me that the Secretary of State [for colonial affairs] can go to America especially for the General Assembly meeting and that nobody should go from Palestine to brief him on the background."[256]

This problem of communication dogged the talks in New York, with the Security Council continuing "to delude themselves that we are going to stay on here after the Mandate expires. ... Even if we did wish suddenly to alter our minds, it would not be possible to do so now, quite apart from any political considerations, for our military withdrawal has already gone too far."[257] As the UN negotiations dragged into a fourth day, the talk in Westminster and Whitehall turned toward the possibility of bringing forward the end of the mandate from May 15 to May 5. To Towers-Clark, the answer was an obvious one: "The military situation continues to deteriorate and there is no practical advantage whatever in staying for the last ten days."[258] When those involved in the negotiations failed to reach a resolution, Towers-Clark became exasperated, writing angrily, "By now any governmental control is largely theoretical ... and the military position is extremely precarious ... A full-scale civil war is inevitable and we are not going to make any difference to the eventual result by staying ten days longer. ... Two more Englishmen killed today and three yesterday. And they are surprised that we are fed up with Palestine!"[259]

By April 26, the British situation was becoming unsustainable and still no decision had been made in the cabinet about the end date. Most of army headquarters had been withdrawn and the number of government officers, including Towers-Clark, had been reduced to thirty-seven. On that date, he wrote in his diary:

> Sir Alan [Cunningham, the high commissioner] is now in a very difficult position. He cannot but accept the opinion of his two military commanders that it is necessary, from the military angle, to evacuate Jerusalem not later than May 5th. In fact he is entirely in agreement with them and has been pressing the point for a long time. He cannot, however, at this moment get the Government to agree to give up the Mandate on that date.[260]

Ultimately, Cunningham failed in his endeavors. On April 27, Montgomery wrote to Crocker that the cabinet would not grant the Palestine administration's requests for a May 5 withdrawal.[261] The following day, the cabinet officially notified Cunningham of its decision. Those Britons who remained in Palestine, now reduced to just twenty-two officials, would "have to stay to the bitter end." Ironically, to ensure their survival in those final two weeks, the war secretary had to move an additional army battalion and two Royal Marine commandos (each equivalent in size to an army battalion) into Palestine to provide extra security.[262]

Alongside Towers-Clark and Cunningham, both Gurney and Norman stayed until May 15. Gurney sent his final letter to John Martin at the colonial office on April 27, saying, "The situation is deteriorating very rapidly now. We get no sleep, as the nights are like a continuous air-raid. ... [Our] impotence is of course having disastrous effects and is itself the cause of progressive decline in security and everything else. There is no more we can do here now except send telegrams and even this may not be possible in a week or two."[263] Norman, sending his last letter home on May 2, told his mother:

> It has been an absolutely grueling week and we've been working all hours of the day and night in continuous and

rather futile efforts to restore peace in the country. The whole situation is now absolutely chaotic and Palestine is rapidly disintegrating—Arab refugees flocking out of their towns in thousands, prices rising, profiteering, black marketing and all the horrors of economic disruption. As usual, it is the innocent and harmless people who are suffering. The general [Cunningham] is absolutely worn out and if he doesn't have a rest soon will become a nervous wreck.[264]

On May 15, less than two weeks after Norman penned these words, the British administration officially withdrew from Palestine. The day before, the Jewish Agency declared independence and officially proclaimed the state of Israel, encompassing all Palestinian territory without partition. Even as the British forces pulled back, troops from Egypt, Syria, Jordan, Lebanon, and Iraq arrived to violently confront the new Jewish state in the first Arab-Israeli War. Second Lieutenant Michael Jefferson of the Royal Leicestershire Regiment noted that the withdrawal "was a text book action. For our part it was orderly, well organised and we exchanged, and took, no fire from either Arab or Jew. We passed many units of the Egyptian army on their way up to engage in actions against the Jewish settlements that were determinedly defended."[265] In all, the government in Palestine suffered the loss of 338 British citizens.[266] Its counterinsurgency efforts had failed spectacularly and on May 15, 1948, the imperial endgame in Palestine arrived.

VII. Trouble comes to Malaya

Sir Henry Gurney had been back in the United Kingdom for less than two months when Arthur Creech Jones, the colonial secretary, called upon him to take up a new role. The British high commissioner in Malaya, Sir Edward Gent, had been killed in a plane crash on July 4, 1948, and since that time the colony had been without executive leadership. On June 17, less than three weeks before his death, Gent had declared a state of emergency in Malaya, citing evidence from the Malayan Security Service of an "organised campaign of murder by Communist organisation(s)." The emergency regulations included "liability to death penalty for unlawful possession of arms, power of detention of any persons, search of persons and premises without warrant, and power to occupy premises."[267]

British businessmen had immediately questioned his declaration. They were heavily invested in the Malayan rubber plantations and tin mines and were concerned that a declared emergency might affect their bottom lines. Between June 22 and 25, Creech Jones and Malcolm MacDonald, the commissioner-general for British territories in Southeast Asia, exchanged several telegrams discussing the matter, culminating in MacDonald's request that Creech Jones recall Gent. Through no fault of his own, Gent had lost the confidence of the British business community, and as Malaya was first and foremost an economic resource for the government, it was vital that this confidence be restored. On June 26, therefore, Creech Jones sent Gent a telegram requesting that he return to England at the "earliest opportunity," with the understanding that he would resign as soon as his plane touched the ground. Gent agreed to return, although he made it clear that when he did so he would make his case to remain as high commissioner. He left Singapore on June 28 and, following a short stopover in Sri Lanka, boarded a York freighter on the morning of July 4. As this plane approached Northolt airport in West London later that day, it collided with another, instantly killing Gent.[268]

Even before the high commissioner's untimely death, MacDonald had suggested to Creech Jones that the colonial office appoint "a successor who has the qualities required not only for dealing with the immediate emergency, which (barring accidents or a serious deterioration) should not last more than 6 months, but also for leading the Federation through the next 5 years." He suggested that his top choices were Lord Milverton

(Sir Arthur Richards), General Sir Archibald Nye, and Sir Alexander Grantham. MacDonald suspected Creech Jones might already have Gurney in mind due to his experience in Palestine, but feared that "[not] enough prestige attaches to his name to make it one which would quickly restore confidence in administration in Kuala Lumpur."[269] Creech Jones immediately replied to MacDonald that Gurney was indeed at the top of his list, stating, "I doubt whether we are likely to improve on his clear mind and calm temperament, his administrative qualities and his capacity to delegate and to gain the confidence and respect both of his staff and of unofficials."[270] Furthermore, Gurney had written to Creech Jones on June 18 revealing that he would be "grateful" to be considered for "any governorship."[271] Gurney was therefore likely to accept the position if offered, and time was of the essence.

MacDonald, however, continued to press for Milverton. His hopes were dashed on July 7, though, due to concerns over Milverton's health.[272] Creech Jones immediately instructed Cunningham to contact Gurney and see if he was interested in going to Malaya. Cunningham did so and on July 14 informed Creech Jones that Gurney had replied "in rather non committal form" that "other people are probably better suited than he." Nevertheless, Cunningham believed that if pushed "he would take on the job, as indeed he should, gladly."[273] Creech Jones next dispatched Sir Thomas Lloyd, permanent undersecretary of state at the colonial office, to assess Gurney's likelihood of accepting the position. Like Cunningham, Lloyd reported on July 22 that Gurney was "not at all keen on going to Malaya," but would take the position "if pressed to do so as a matter of duty." Gurney did, however, insist that he could not leave the United Kingdom until September due to family concerns at home that needed to be resolved.[274] Undeterred, Creech Jones continued to push for Gurney's appointment throughout the summer. At the end of August, MacDonald finally relented and Gurney agreed to take up the post. His appointment was made public on September 2, and Gurney arrived in Kuala Lumpur as the new British high commissioner for Malaya on October 6, 1948—less than five months after leaving Palestine.[275]

The British government had been interested in Malaya since the earliest days of its empire, when in the first years of the seventeenth century the newly formed English East India Company opened a trading post at the mouth of the Kedah River. Trade was expanded greatly a century later, and between 1765 and 1800 the British government signed a number of treaties with the sultan of Kedah that granted the British Penang Island and a strip of land opposite in exchange for an annual income payable to the sultan. An invasion from Siam in 1821 temporarily expelled the British from the island, but in 1894 a British consul returned with the permission of the Siamese government, and in 1909 the British once again brought Kedah under their direct control with the signing of the Anglo-Kedah Treaty. Meanwhile, the British captured Malacca on Malaya's western coast from the Dutch in 1795. Expansion on the peninsula continued until in 1819 the government signed a treaty with the ruler of Johore that gave the British the right to settle on Singapore Island. In 1867, the government united Singapore with the west coast of Malaya (including Malacca) to form the Crown Colony of the Straits Settlement.[276]

From the Straits Settlement colony, the British government exercised considerable informal control over the ostensibly independent Malay States, signing treaties with Perak, Selangor, and Sungei Ujong in 1874 and Pahang in 1888, under which a British resident was appointed to the court whose mission was to replace the traditional feudal structure of Malay society with Western law and market-based economics. In 1896, these four states merged to form the first Federation of Malaya (also known as the Federated Malay States), with a central government in Kuala Lumpur. The British government signed further treaties with Malay rulers establishing British residents in Kedah, Kelantan, Trengganu, and Perlis in 1910, followed by Johore in 1914. In each of these states, the British government posted British engineers, doctors, and civil servants alongside the

British residents, each responsible to the British high commissioner for Malaya, who at that time was resident in Singapore.[277] Although the Malay States were not officially British colonial possessions, they were nevertheless an integral part of the British Empire. British residents opened a Malayan railway system in 1884, cleared the swamps to prevent the spread of malaria in the late nineteenth century, and introduced domestic and international flights with Empire Airways in the early twentieth century. Most importantly, the residents engineered the replacement of coffee with rubber as the staple crop of the Malay economy. By the eve of the Second World War, Malaya (encompassing both the Straits Settlement and the Malay States) exported a quarter of a million tons of rubber, two-and-a-half million gallons of latex, and eighty thousand tons of tin and tin ore each year.[278]

However, the British and Malays were not the only peoples to inhabit the peninsula. To find workers for the rubber plantations and tin mines, the British government embarked upon a large-scale immigration scheme from China and India, the result being that by 1945 Malaya's population of 5.3 million people included 49% Malays, 38% Chinese, and 11% Indians, together with 12,000 Europeans, most of whom were British. While the Chinese were willing to work for the British estate managers, they were indignant about being employed by Malays, whom they believed to be their inferiors. Ethnic quarrel thus became an ingrained aspect of Malayan society in the twentieth century.[279] This Chinese separation from Malay culture and economics was further increased by the formation of the Malayan Communist Party (MCP) in 1930, which had evolved from the earlier South Seas branch of the China Communist Party (established in Singapore in 1925). Led from 1939 by Lai Tek, the MCP played a decisive role against the Japanese army following the latter's invasion and occupation of Malaya in December 1941. Within ten days of the invasion, Lai Tek offered communist assistance to the British administration and the MCP began to send ethnically Chinese Malays for training to Lieutenant

Colonel Freddie Spencer-Chapman's 101 Special Training School.[280] Their efforts were in vain, however. By January 11, 1942, Kuala Lumpur had fallen to the Japanese army and on January 31 the remaining Britons resident in Malaya fled across the Johore Bahru causeway to Singapore. There they held out for less than three weeks; General Arthur Percival surrendered all British forces to General Tomoyuki Yamashita on February 15, 1942.[281]

Facing the Japanese occupiers alone, the MCP formed the Malayan People's Anti-Japanese Army (MPAJA) in September 1942, a communist guerilla force established along the lines taught by Spencer-Chapman and committed to overthrowing the Japanese occupiers. By 1945, this army had grown to 7000 men. For the first two years of its campaign, the British government remained uninvolved, all resources focused instead on Montgomery's campaign against the Germans and Italians in North Africa. Following the appointment of Lord Louis Mountbatten as supreme allied commander Southeast Asia in August 1943, however, British policy in the region was transformed. Beginning in December 1943, the British government directly supplied arms, ammunition, and medical supplies to the MPAJA, and Force 136 (the Far East division of Britain's Special Operations Executive) established substantial links with Lai Tek, providing training to members of the MPAJA and a sum of £3000 a month to aid their anti-Japanese insurgency. By August 1945, there were eighty-eight British officers resident in Malaya working with the MPAJA.[282]

While the MPAJA and Force 136 waged their guerilla war on the peninsula, in Whitehall government officials and civil servants developed plans for Malaya once the Japanese army was defeated. In the spring of 1944, the colonial office announced a radical department from previous British policy in the region, seeking both an "unprecedented direct rule in the short term" and a British commitment to "Malayan self-determination in the long term." For the first time in British rule on the peninsula, the government articulated as its primary goal the grant of self-governance to the indigenous people. The colonial office sought to achieve this through a Malayan Union, a peninsula-wide amalgamation of the Malay States and the Straits Settlement whereby the British government would strip from the provincial rulers all authority and sovereignty and would instead create a single, Malayan citizenry with a central administration run by the British. Once the Malayan Union was functioning in an efficient and unified manner, the government would gradually devolve power until Malaya became an independent state within the British Commonwealth.[283] The MPAJA's victory over the Japanese army on September 28, 1945, made this vision a reality, and on October 10, the British Parliament announced the establishment of the Malayan Union. Consequently, the government cut off all funding for the MPAJA, staged an official disbandment ceremony in December 1945, and in March 1946 appointed Sir Edward Gent as the new union's first governor.[284]

Initially, the MCP sought to cooperate with the British government, operating as a legitimate constitutional party within the union in what amounted to an explicit recognition of Britain's colonial authority. That it should have done so is not terribly surprising. The party had, after all, received much funding and support from the British government throughout the Japanese occupation, and its army—the MPAJA—had been trained by British soldiers and agents. The party also had great support from the Malay people—including those of non-Chinese ethnic groups—due to the substantial role it played in defeating the Japanese. The union seemed the perfect vehicle with which to assert Chinese supremacy on the peninsula and spread the doctrines and practices of communism. Almost immediately, however, dissention formed within the ranks of the party. In particular, suspicion of the leadership of Lai Tek became pronounced. Rumors circulated that he had betrayed the party to the Japanese during the occupation, and in the summer of 1946 the central standing committee of the MCP banned Lai Tek from the organization committee, instead relegating him to the political bureau. He remained secretary-general of the party, but in February 1947 criticism against him climaxed. On the twenty-eighth of that month the central standing committee issued a summons for him to attend their next meeting. When the appointed time arrived on March 6, Lai Tek failed to show. It later transpired that he had escaped to Singapore, from whence he went to Hong Kong, remaining in hiding until a Chinese "killer squad" tracked his movements and assassinated him sometime in late 1948.[285] With Lai Tek dead, the communist leadership felt less inclined to work with the British, instead hoping to take the country for itself.

It was not only the MCP that expressed dissent from the union. The rulers of the Malay States also boycotted the April 1, 1946, installation of Gent as governor, forming a parallel administration called the Pan Malayan Malay Congress, which was renamed as the United Malays National Organization (UMNO) in May 1946. UMNO was committed to the defeat of the union, and its leaders called for an immediate return to independent, self-governing Malay states. Facing such opposition, Gent began to question the feasibility of the union as a permanent political fixture, and by the end of 1946, the British government decided to abandon the Malayan Union altogether. It instead created the Malayan Federation, which gave limited autonomy to the Malay States within the framework of a British-ruled federation.[286] Throughout 1947, the colonial office drew up proposals for a new Malayan constitution. The cabinet approved these proposals in early July 1947 and Parliament gave its assent. later that month. After further negotiation and refinement, on January 21, 1948, the rulers of the Malay States agreed to the creation of the federation. Eleven days later, on February 1, the government appointed Gent high commissioner to the new federation of Malaya. UMNO had been appeased, but the MCP remained unyielding.[287]

Following Lai Tek's defection in February 1947, the central standing committee reorganized itself, drawing closer both to the Chinese and to the Soviet communist organizations and distancing itself from constitutional government within the union. Following the federation's birth in February 1948, the MCP withdrew its cooperation from the British government completely. At the fifth plenary session of the central standing committee on May 10, 1948, the MCP called for a general strike in Malaya, describing the "increased exploitation and oppression and even the use of violent attacks of the British Imperialists." The party also declared that "without resolute action, concerted struggle and the use of violence when necessary it will not be able to repel the enemy and achieve victory."[288] On May 5—just five days before this declaration—the MPAJA reconstituted itself the Malayan People's Anti-British Army (MPABA) in preparation for the armed struggle announced at the MCP's fifth plenary session.[289] Finally, on June 15, the MCP, with the MPABA acting as its armed wing, issued a call to arms:

> Imperialism orders its running dogs and their followers to oppress us: then we will use the same method against them. All in all, for the sake of our lives, we cannot procrastinate any more nor can we give in any further but to fight our way out through struggle. Today the British Imperialists' cruel fascist countenance has been completely exposed. Imperialism is fascism and their violence and outrages are the same as those of [the] Japanese. The people of Malaya can never forget the bloody role of the Japanese fascists. At the same time they will remember the methods used against the fascists.[290]

The next day, June 16, the MPABA murdered three British rubber planters and their Chinese assistants. It was following this action that on June 17 Gent declared a state of emergency in Malaya.[291]

Coming only a month after the British government had extricated itself from Palestine, the cabinet was naturally troubled about this latest emergency, a concern most explicitly manifested in Gent's recall. To assuage their fears, on July 1, Creech

Jones composed a memorandum making clear precisely why the declaration of emergency was necessary. He explained that it was in the British interest to have "encouraged and supplied with arms" the "subversive movements against the Japanese occupation" during the war. However, once the war was over and the Japanese threat had been removed it was "no wonder that some of the resistance groups which sprang up at that time should—as happened also in Europe—prove after liberation an embarrassment to their Governments." This was particularly the case with Chinese communist guerillas, who at the time of the Japanese surrender controlled large parts of Malaya. Creech Jones explained that in the three years from 1945 to 1948, these Chinese communists had attempted to form trade unions that would disrupt labor practices in the union and later federation. In the spring of 1948, they became more militant, and in April began to seize British estates. On June 1, seven Chinese laborers were killed when 200 Malay policemen retook control of an estate the communists had seized in Johore. In response, by June 12 communist laborers had murdered five Malays and attempted the murders of two more. On June 16, they killed their first European planters.

Following Gent's declaration of emergency on June 17, the situation worsened further. Between June 18 and June 29, there were fifteen murders and fifteen attempted murders. The purpose of these murders, Creech Jones explained, was to "produce the maximum industrial unrest and disruption of economic life of the country, with a view amongst other things to destroying the Government's authority." Evidence gathered by the Malay police force suggested that these campaigns had evolved "from fomenting labour disputes to a policy of picking off the managerial staff of installations and mines." Furthermore, the British government in Malaya had received information that the "mobilisation and training of guerillas in jungle hide-outs is now coming into force." These guerillas were "well organised and armed and their activities [would] include attacks on villages and small towns to commit murders and robberies and to dislocate transport systems with the ultimate objective of controlling certain areas." Creech Jones did not need to remind the cabinet that these were the same guerillas that had effectively defeated the Japanese army during the Second World War.

Having outlined the problem, the colonial secretary next summarized the steps that had been taken to defeat the communist guerillas. To execute the emergency regulations, the police force had been strengthened throughout Malaya. In particular, Creech Jones had sent to the colony W. N. Gray, formerly inspector general of the Palestine police, who had "special experience in combating terrorism." Gray's mission was to "discuss all measures likely to increase the efficiency of existing police action against terrorism." He had already made several recommendations to Creech Jones, including strengthening the Malayan police force with recruits from the recently disbanded Palestine police and recruiting an additional sixty experienced police officers to act as assistant superintendents, many of whom would be brought from Palestine where they had experience in counterinsurgency techniques.

In addition to strengthening the police force, the army and Royal Air Force had begun planning for operations, and civil and military authorities were cooperating in the newly established defence coordination committee, Far East. This committee had outlined a two-phase operational strategy to defeat the insurgency. Phase 1 aimed to "restore law and order in settled areas of the territory and ... maintain the economic life of the country and restore morale." It would achieve this through "offensive operations to round up the gangsters," establishment of roadblocks and checkpoints, sweeps in the area of murders, and increasing protective security on institutions such as power stations, prisons, factories, docks, and the like. Once law and order was restored, phase 2 could begin, which would "comprise the operations necessary to liquidate the guerilla bands whose headquarters are in the jungle," including the "destruction of their camps, cutting off of food supplies, and uncovering dumps of arms and equipment." While phase 1 would primarily be a police operation, phase 2 would be carried out by the army and air force.[292]

Such a plan would take time, of course, and while it was being implemented, the violence in Malaya escalated. By July 19, the guerillas had murdered another twenty-six people, one of whom was a British plantation owner, bringing the total to more than fifty.[293] These guerillas were organized into mobile units of the *Lau Tong Tui*, the Special Service Corps of the MPABA. The purpose of these mobile units, each of which was made up of four or five insurgents, was to kill those deemed complicit in British rule, including economic aspects of that rule. The units operated from camps in the jungle and their attacks were characterized by surprise and overwhelming force. Two such attacks carried out in the week ending July 15 were representative of their actions. The first occurred in Johore, where a unit of four armed guerillas killed a vegetable gardener for refusing to supply the insurgency with food; the second, also in Johore, was the shooting of a Chinese schoolmaster who was allegedly cooperating with British rule by educating young Chinese Malays using British standards and conventions.[294]

Yet the operation of these small mobile units was not the MPABA's only tactic. It also employed larger-scale and more brazen attacks, such as the one on July 13 when five separate units of guerillas descended on the coal-mining village of Batu Arang in Selangor at seven o'clock in the morning. While one party went into town to silence the population, a second stormed the local police station, and a third entered the coal mine, killing a mining superintendent, three miners, and a lorry driver, and destroying excavator equipment and generators. Simultaneously, a group of up to forty guerillas entered the railway station, imprisoning the station staff, seizing the recently arrived train from Kuala Lumpur, and robbing the passengers of their valuables. A separate gang then halted a bus arriving from Kuala Selangor, likewise depriving its occupants of their belongings. In all, more than eighty guerillas were evolved in this coordinated

111

attack.[295] In the face of such intensifying violence and having received "conclusive evidence that the Malayan Communist Party was actively responsible for planning and directing this campaign of violence and terrorism," on July 19 the cabinet proscribed the MCP, declaring all those who were members of or associated with the party liable to immediate arrest.[296] This proscription did very little to quell the violence, however, and when Gurney arrived in Malaya on October 6, 1948, the murder of plantation owners and workers continued unabated.

Part of the problem was the lack of a British security force presence in the federation. When the emergency erupted in June 1948, there were just twelve army battalions spread across three districts, supported by one RAF squadron of Spitfires, one squadron of Sunderland flying boats, one photographic reconnaissance squadron of Austers, and one Dakota transport squadron. These soldiers and airmen were spread thinly on the ground. In Johore, for example, with an area of 7300 square miles and a population of 730,000 people, there was just one squadron from the RAF Regiment and three companies of Seaforth Highlanders.[297] These army and air force units—numbering less than 8000 men for the whole of Malaya—were supported by a police force of just 9000, many of whom had only recently been brought into the force and consequently lacked both training and experience.[298] Furthermore, although Creech Jones had appointed Gray as commissioner of police in August with the charge to lead emergency operations, the army general officer commanding (GOC) Malaya, Major General Sir Charles Boucher, was convinced that the emergency could only be solved by military means and thus tended to ostracize Gray.[299] In addition to the police, army, and air force, 200 Dyaks were also brought to Malaya from Sarawak as jungle trackers, but their use was limited by agreement to just three months. Following protests against their employment from around the colonial world, ninety-six were returned to Sarawak in November, with the remaining trackers leaving the peninsula in December 1948.[300]

With such limited numbers, army and police operations were necessarily reactive. When insurgents carried out an attack, the army made "sweeps" through the jungle in the locality of the incident. The idea of such sweeps was to "locate and trap" the guerrillas, at which point they could be destroyed. The soldiers carrying out these sweeps, however, had largely been trained "on the wide-open flats of England's Salisbury Plain" and had little experience in jungle warfare. Consequently, the "major effect of these mass movements of troops was to telegraph their advance so that the guerillas were alerted well before the troops arrived."[301] The army in fact killed few guerillas in such sweeps, and as the police were kept in an ancillary role, no arrests were made. This problem was accentuated by General Boucher, who was convinced that the guerillas would soon receive reinforcements from communist countries outside Malaya. He therefore planned for a large-scale war, keeping troops in reserve and preparing for a decisive battle rather than small-scale but continuous counterinsurgency operations.[302] With the success rate so low on those operations that did occur, the morale of both soldiers and officers began to fall.

One such officer was Lieutenant I. S. Gibb, a Seaforth Highlanders' platoon commander who was stationed in Malaya when the emergency erupted. Describing these early operations, he wrote: "Initially we had to react to the enemy moves. ... Get away [for the guerillas] was no problem. Simply disperse in small groups in the opposite direction from advancing or attacking troops and regroup a mile or two away in a preselected new camp site." This constant game of cat-and-mouse bred frustration, as is evidenced in Gibb's writing: "It always seemed to me from an early time that at my level we should go onto the offensive all the time or as often as possible. Not only would we gain the moral superiority but we would cause disruption. ... Force them into smaller groups, force them into deeper jungle." But that was not Boucher's plan: "Initially we were on the defensive in a strategic sense, probably most of the time I was there [from 1948 to 1950]." These defensive sweep operations were "a platoon commander's war. It was very basic. ... Later there was to be much more control. Much more organization, more troops with helicopters and other sophisticated instruments of warfare. At the beginning there was little." Such lack of organization and resources placed considerable stress on young platoon commanders, both physically and mentally: "This Emergency meant we lived in semi-civilized conditions. Perhaps in sheds, tents or an old planters bungalow on the edge of the jungle. ... Psychologically it was difficult sometimes. ... This was it, day after day, week after week, month after month with a small team of soldiers in search of an elusive enemy."[303] It was no way to wage a counterinsurgency campaign, a fact that the security forces themselves realized by the autumn of 1948. When Gurney arrived in Malaya in October, an army operational analysis concluded that "the value of large and elaborate sweeps is doubtful."[304] The strategy of fighting an insurgency with the same tactics that conventional enemies had been fought with during the Second World War had failed. This was a lesson Gurney had already learned in Palestine, and he could not have agreed more with the army's conclusion.

Writing to Sir Thomas Lloyd, permanent undersecretary of state at the colonial office, two days after his arrival, Gurney suggested that the first task of the British administration in Malaya was to "create confidence in [the] Government's ability to exterminate the bandits." Once such confidence was restored, Gurney believed the British administration and security forces would be able to secure "more active co-operation from the Chinese," which, in turn, would "cut the popular support out from under the insurgency."[305] He argued that this could best be accomplished by removing the Chinese squatters who had illegally settled on plantation lands during the Japanese occupation, most of whom were susceptible to communist ideology and who as a community "constituted a state without a state."[306] On October 25, Gurney provided a fuller account of his thoughts in a telegram to Creech Jones. He explained that British efforts so far had "to some extent restored confidence, increased the flow of information, and killed or captured a number of bandits." The security forces now protected most rubber estates and tin mines, and the vast majority of European residents lived in secure communities. However, "whole fields of operation lie wide open to the bandits," including roads, railways, power lines, and water pipelines. In the week prior to his writing, there had been seventy-three attacks on such targets, thirty more than the previous week, and Gurney feared that "our troubles from terrorism have scarcely begun." Consequently, he argued that the administration must make "an immediate and serious attempt to deal with alien Chinese squatters who are providing bases from which bandits operate and are helping them, in some cases under duress and in many others willingly with food, arms, money, and other means of resistance to our Forces." Gurney's suggestion was to round up the squatters and repatriate them to China. This, he argued, could not be regarded as banishment, as it would "merely involve sending back to their own country alien elements who have illegally entered the Federation and who are illegally occupying land there." He requested Creech Jones' permission to issue an emergency regulation that would immediately repatriate the 3800 Chinese aliens currently held in one-year detention under emergency powers, as well as any others who might be captured subsequently.[307]

After deep consideration and with a great deal of reluctance, the colonial secretary granted Gurney's request. Coming from anyone else, he might have denied it, but after their experiences together grappling with the Palestine problem, Creech Jones trusted the high commissioner's instincts. Repatriation was not as clinical as the term suggested, however, which was what concerned Creech Jones. As Hugh Humphrey, a member of the Malayan Civil Service at the time and later secretary for defence and internal security in Malaya, remembered:

[W]e immediately set up a series of shipping movements to move Chinese detainees in thousands. ... There were distressing things to have to do because when you picked up a detained man, for example, you didn't necessarily get his wife and his children. Now, a deportation order made against the man automatically applied to his dependents, which were all defined of course in the regulations, but it wasn't always that easy to find them and nor in some cases did they want to be found. So I am afraid it is the case that the speed at which the deportation of Chinese took place, and the circumstances, led to a great deal of distress. ... It was ruthless and quite often when these people were being put as deck passengers on these ships, there were some quite distressing scenes—you know, women breaking down and children screaming and all this sort of thing.[308]

Humphrey never doubted the soundness of the plan and believed that repatriation was a "necessary measure in the interests of restoring law and order in Malaya, but to deny that it was ruthless could not be a fair comment."[309] By August 1949, the government had rounded up 15,000 illegal Chinese squatters, 10,000 of whom had been deported back to China.[310]

Yet the problems in Malaya went far beyond illegal Chinese aliens. While most of the insurgents were indeed ethnically Chinese, the vast majority had been born in Malaya and thus could not be repatriated. The return of Chinese squatters to China, although potentially disruptive of the supply lines of the insurgency, had very little effect on the guerillas themselves. This situation was complicated further by the British government's refusal to acknowledge an actual insurgency, or even to concede that those engaged in the killings were politically motivated. As J. D. Higham, head of the colonial office's Eastern Department, noted in a letter in November 1948, "It has been decided that the criminal elements engaged in acts of violence in Malaya should be referred to as 'bandits.' On no account should the term 'insurgent,' which might suggest a genuine popular uprising, be used."[311] Although this was in large part an ideological stance rather than an actual failure to understand the situation on the ground, it nevertheless limited the approach the security forces could take with the insurgency. Such limitations were not in and of themselves a hindrance. Contrary to General Boucher's view, Gurney, Creech Jones, and the colonial office as a whole were convinced that the emergency in Malaya required a civil rather than a military solution, a lesson the failed counterinsurgency campaign in Palestine had imprinted on their minds.

Gurney and Creech Jones were not the only officials to have reached this conclusion by the end of 1948. General Hugh Stockwell, commander of the Sixth Airborne division in Palestine from 1947 until the withdrawal in May 1948, had accepted an appointment as commandant of the Royal Military Academy, Sandhurst, following his departure from Palestine. Based on his experiences there, Stockwell had become convinced that "in peace time the major operational task of the British Army will be one of Imperial Policing carried out in much the same conditions as prevailed in Palestine." This was a facet of soldiering that had not yet been incorporated into officer education at Sandhurst, however.[312] Consequently, in the early autumn months of 1948, Stockwell contacted many of the officers who had served under him in Palestine, asking for their impressions of the counterinsurgency campaign and for their insights into what lessons had been learned.

Lieutenant Colonel John Hackett, commander of the 8th Parachute battalion from 1946 to 1948, was the first to reply. In a lengthy essay, he argued in favor of reprisals and curfews. Contrary to "what the politicians say," he claimed that every soldier on the ground knows "by bitter experience" that "when the security forces have to deal with a thoroughly non-cooperative, unscrupulous, dishonest and utterly immoral civil population such as the Jewish Community in Palestine, who systematically and continually hide and refuse to give up to justice the perpetrators of murderous outrages, reprisals are the only effective weapons to employ, saving time, money and unnecessary bloodshed." He believed that the confiscation and

117

destruction of property was the "most effective" way to do this and listed two examples to support his claim: first, when shots were fired from a house in Palestine at British soldiers, that house was destroyed by three Sappers of the Royal Engineers in a matter of twenty minutes, providing a deterrent to its neighbors at very little cost to the army; second, when a vehicle was mined in the vicinity of an orange grove, that grove was destroyed by a single tank in twenty minutes. Closely tied to reprisals were curfews. These had to be "strictly enforced" or would lose all value. Finally, he warned against confining troops to barracks following a "terrorist outrage," which was the standard approach in Palestine: "This played into the hands of the Jewish propagandists. Every terrorist outrage which takes place should be suffered by the civil population. They it is who should suffer the curfew and NOT the troops."[313] That the examples of reprisals Hackett gave had been expressly forbidden by Cunningham and Gurney could not have gone unnoticed by Stockwell, but the general chose to ignore them. After all, Hackett was not the only officer in a dirty war to contravene standing orders, nor would he be the last.

By the end of November, Stockwell had heard from five other high-ranking officers. He compiled their essays into a single report and distributed it both to his cadets at Sandhurst and to the wider military community. Taking a less aggressive tone than Hackett, Major Taylor argued that "orthodox military methods will never succeed against underground fighters," and recommended that the war office establish a "branch of the Army trained in the appropriate methods of counter-action." Lieutenant Colonel Nelson claimed that "It is low level intelligence gleaned by IOs [Intelligence Officers] on unit level which counts as much as, if not more than, the high level stuff in Formation Intelligence Summaries. Time is well spent in getting to know more and more of the local inhabitants, their history and intrigues." Lieutenant Colonel Birkbeck agreed, writing: "Good Intelligence: This factor was probably the most important of all relating to success of IS [Internal Security] ops. All ranks should become intelligence-minded and the collection and collation of it at unit tac[tical] HQs must be highly organised. The best type of intelligence has an immediate bearing on the current local situation." Finally, Brigadier Colqhoun suggested that the army was not "'politically and police' trained to carry out their difficult jobs without making certain mistakes which annoyed the civil and police authorities." For a counterinsurgency campaign to succeed, he argued, both sides—military and police—had to "[understand] the job of the other better."[314]

The conclusions laid out in Stockwell's report were threefold: first, conventional military units were not best suited to carry out counterinsurgency operations; second, the army had to give greater respect to policing and civil authority; and lastly, efforts had to be made to separate the civilian population from the insurgents, whether through the use of reprisals, curfews, or some other method. On each of these points, Gurney was in complete agreement. Boucher, however, had not yet reached the same conclusions, and in the winter of 1948 in Malaya it was the general's opinion that mattered.

No incident better illustrates the difficulties of using military troops trained in conventional warfare to wage a counterinsurgency campaign than the events of December 12, 1948, at the village of Batang Kali in Selangor province. On that day, soldiers of the 2nd Battalion, Scots Guards, engaged in an operation at a rubber plantation that was believed to be infiltrated by communist insurgents. Unable to differentiate between those who were hostile and those who were not, the Scots Guards herded all residents into a central area of the village before separating the men from the women and children. The women and children were placed on lorries while the men were divided into groups of four to six, each guarded by a few soldiers. What occurred next is unclear to this day. As the women and children were driven away they heard the sound of machine gun fire. The soldiers deposited the women and children in the nearest town before returning to Batang Kali. After a week or so, the women were permitted to return to their village, where they found their huts burned to the ground and the bodies of twenty-four people rotting and bloated. One of the women describes what happened next: "[We] had to use some kind of chemicals with wads of cotton wool to cover [our] mouths and to carry with [us] much bundles of incense to kill the smell in order for [us] to go and identify the bodies. And identification was only by the clothing, not by the faces, because they had already rotted." One of the few men to survive did so only because he fainted when the men were being divided into groups. Upon awaking, he found the other male villagers dead and the soldiers forced him to carry their ammunition. The army then sent him to Kuala Lumpur, where he was interrogated for a week before being released without charge.[315]

There is no evidence to suggest Gurney had any knowledge of the events of December 12. He was, however, well aware of the problems of using the army as the lead security agency. On January 8, 1949, he sent a dispatch to Creech Jones, insisting that "The day is past in which a clear dividing line [can] be drawn between the responsibilities of the police for maintaining law and order and the role of the military forces in defence against external attack." Gurney described the Malayan police as the "only Force which has the information and intelligence necessary for the conduct of an underground war," and suggested that the force could only be effective if it was "built up well in advance with long and thorough training." In January 1949, the police had been increased from its June 1948 composition of 9000 all-ranks to 245 officers (chief inspector and above), 237 inspectors, 500 British sergeants (no Malays were authorized to hold this rank), and 14,291 constables. In general, the police now had sufficient numbers to tackle the insurgency. Nevertheless, Gurney insisted that reorganization was vital. In particular, it was "urgently necessary" to improve the work of the Special Branch of the CID. Gurney argued that the special branch should be increased by at least 200 officers, most of whom should be ethnically Chinese and familiar with the Chinese communities in Malaya. To achieve this goal, the high commissioner requested additional funding from the British government to the sum of £7½ million in 1949 and £2½ million in both 1950 and 1951, bringing total expenditure on internal security in Malaya to £13½ million in 1949 and £8½ million in 1950 and 1951.[316] This was a significant cost. Under the Colonial Development and Welfare Act of 1948, the entire Far East region—including Hong Kong, Borneo and Sarawak, and Malaya—had just £7.5 million allocated for colonial development.[317]

By the end of February 1949, Gurney's stress on bolstered police action and an emphasis on the special branch were paying off. He informed Creech Jones on the twenty-eighth of that month that the police had been following a plan of action established by Gray, whose remit since being appointed police commissioner in 1948 had expanded gradually to place him "in charge of operational planning" for the emergency. Gray's plan hinged upon "mopping up the [communist] killer squads and the gradual turning over of 'clear' areas to normal but intensified police work." This would be done by "increased probing of the jungle areas, on a basis of complete and centralised knowledge of all jungle tracks, with a view to surprise air strikes on enemy concentrations and ambushing of their communications." Gray's hope was that little by little, Malaya could be returned to a sense of normalcy, with those areas in which fighting was taking place becoming fewer and fewer. By February 1949, Gurney reported, the British security forces were "killing bandits at the rate of 3 or 4 a day, and arresting about 50 a day," with a corresponding "steady flow" of surrendered arms.[318] The colonial office likewise reported that by February 1, 1949, 468 communist insurgents—457 of whom were ethnically Chinese—had been killed in operations, at the cost of 371 civilian casualties, 258 of whom were Chinese.[319] The situation was slowly beginning to turn around.

Nevertheless, in the short term, such a strategy unavoidably placed a larger operational impetus on the army and air force than the police, with the latter serving as an auxiliary force despite its lead role on paper. Gurney recognized as much when he proposed to Creech Jones on April 11 that "military forces should maintain a continuous and heavy pressure on the main bandit bodies in the remoter jungle areas to which they have retired or are retiring."[320] General Boucher and his military subordinates were well aware of their essential role and took advantage of their position to carry out aggressive patrolling in Malaya. When told of Gurney's preference for police action, Boucher dismissively told a friend that it was unthinkable that "a bunch of coppers should start telling the generals what to do."[321] By the end of 1950, Boucher had convinced the war office to dramatically increase the size of the army force in Malaya from twelve infantry battalions to twenty, with a corresponding jump in supporting units.[322]

This extensive military buildup concerned Gurney, and in mid-April he told Creech Jones that "the lesson has not apparently yet been generally learnt that the answer to Communist terrorism equipped with modern arms is not the soldier but the policeman. ... It is of immense political advantage in restoring confidence if the inhabitants of this country can be organised and led to put their own security house in order, rather than have the impression that it is being done for them by troops on whose inevitable departure there will be no guarantee of peace."[323] The army might be necessary in the short term, but it was a necessary evil rather than good. The police, Gurney insisted, must hold overall command and must be allowed to play an increasingly prominent role in operations.

Gurney expanded these thoughts in a dispatch to Creech Jones on May 30. "Terrorism equipped with modern automatic weapons and political aspirations is a new development in the British Commonwealth," he declared. "It is a method of warfare to which the training and traditions of our police and military forces have not yet been adapted." He noted that terrorism was impossible to defeat completely, for "the terrorist tends always to have the initiative. It is impracticable to defend against assassination all the individuals who may be attacked, or to defend against sabotage all the railway tracks, telephone and electric power lines, factories, Government offices and other installations that are vulnerable." Communist terrorists were "completely ruthless" and employed the "technique of sheer intimidation," something even the Irgun in Palestine had shied away from. The difficulties the British faced were amplified because there was "an obvious reluctance on the part of any civil authority, particularly one nurtured in the British tradition, to administer drastic remedies." Gurney pointed out that it had "been the practice in the past to hand to the military authorities the unpleasant job of restoring law and order," the result often being martial law. Keeping in mind his experiences in Palestine, Gurney argued against this practice, stating that "the withdrawal of the civil power and the substitution of military control represent the first victory for the terrorists," as the civil administration would necessarily appear "too weak to carry on" and thus lose all credibility in the eyes of the indigenous people. It was essential that power remained in the hands of the civil authority.

To achieve this, Gurney suggested that all military forces in any counterinsurgency campaign be "at the disposal of the Commissioner of Police and operate under his general direction." This was as necessary in Malaya as in any other disturbed colony. Military commanders would, of course, determine tactical issues, but there could be no debate that ultimately the police commissioner was responsible for overall security operations. To facilitate the smooth operation of such civilian control, in the spring of 1949, Gurney had instituted a weekly conference attended by the army's GOC, the air officer commanding (AOC), the chief secretary, the commissioner of police, the federation's secretary of defense, and the naval liaison officer. The Malayan secretary of defense had also established an internal security committee whose membership included representatives from the police force, the military services, and various civilian departments. Finally, the police commissioner had arranged weekly meetings with the heads of the various civilian departments. Gurney hoped that coordinated command would allow for successful, police-led operations, which in turn would convince the Malayan people—both ethnic Malays and ethnic Chinese—that the government was working for them and with them to defeat a criminal menace. It was most certainly not an occupying power no better than the Japanese.[324]

Despite Gurney's convictions, throughout 1949 and into 1950, the army continued to take an aggressive approach in defeating the MPABA, which from February 1949 was renamed the Malayan Races Liberation Army (MRLA). On June 13, the army issued a revised version of its manual "Imperial Policing and Duties in Aid of the Civil Power." This document clearly stated that "Once a request has been made for military assistance of any kind, the military commander, irrespective of his rank, is entirely responsible for the form which the action shall take and the amount of force used."[325] In direct contradiction to Gurney's wishes, the army reasserted that when called up, it would be army commanders rather than the police or civil authorities who would make the important decisions. Operating under this guidance, Boucher continued to treat the Malayan campaign as he would any other, sending battalions into the jungle to hunt and kill the communist insurgents. The consequence was that each operation "took the better part of a day, with more than a thousand soldiers, to get an effective cordon even a half-mile square around a jungle camp." By the time this cordon was established, the guerillas, "hearing the soldiers crashing through the jungle into position," were long gone, and "all the soldiers ever found was an empty camp."[326]

The experience of a single regiment suffices to illustrate this point. The war office dispatched the Green Howards to Malaya in September 1949. By the end of that year, the regiment had encountered the MRLA just five times, had killed just one guerilla, and had suffered only one casualty itself, despite insurgent attacks on civilian and police targets of some fifteen to twenty a day, and insurgent murders of more than 200 policemen and civilians each month in September, October, November, and December.[327] The MRLA was active and expanding, but the army could not find it. On those few occasions when the two did clash, the encounters could be deadly. Norman Martin, a young soldier on national service, witnessed the ambush of one of his unit's trucks, which resulted in ten deaths and twelve injuries. He described the incident as follows:

There were the dead laying in all sorts of twisted positions. There were pieces of hair and skin and bone stuck to the side of the truck, the truck itself was like a sieve. It was shot to pieces, there was not a square foot of it without a bullet hole in it. ... There was so much blood, it was everywhere. ... The hardest job of all was to get the dead from out of the back of the truck, we gently lifted their bodies out and laid them on the estate road until we could put them in another truck.[328]

For many of the soldiers serving in Malaya, it was becoming increasingly difficult to see any good coming from their operations. The civilian leadership in Kuala Lumpur felt the same way.

By the end of 1949, Gurney had become convinced that the defense planners were approaching the problem from completely the wrong direction, attacking symptoms rather than seeking to cure the underlying disease. On January 12, 1950, he wrote to Creech Jones, asserting that "The enemy in Malaya is Communism, with all its implications, and is not merely some 3,000 bandits." Militarily, the security forces had achieved as much as they could. Between July 1, 1948, and November 30, 1949, they had killed 942 insurgents, wounded 303, captured 569, and accepted the surrender of 241. Of those captured, the government had tried and hung seventy-seven. The security forces had also seized 3600 rifles, 45 machine guns, 1488 hand grenades, and 565,000 rounds of ammunition. These efforts were supported by the repatriation of 10,000 aliens back to China and the detention of 5000 individuals for supporting the insurgency. Nevertheless, "[a]lthough a large number of bandits have been disposed of and larger numbers of sympathisers detained or deported, the political brains behind the Communist effort remain for practical purposes untouched and unlocated."[329] In operational terms, the military campaign was succeeding but the insurgency was by no means defeated. The emergency in Malaya needed a political solution, and until the civil authorities took firm control of all planning, with the police as their lead agency, such a solution would be impossible.

Gurney thought long and hard about this problem and then, on February 23, put pen to paper in a telegram to Creech Jones. In this wire—perhaps the most important of his career—he suggested a radical department in British counterinsurgency strategy in Malaya. He noted that he had "for some time" considered appointing a single civilian officer to "plan, co-ordinate and generally direct the anti-bandit operations of the police and fighting services." Over the previous fourteen months, he had become convinced that the army was the wrong agency to lead the campaign and preferred police leadership. Now that the conflict had reached the stage of "protracted guerilla warfare," however, he believed that even the police commissioner was incapable of directing operations. Gurney thus found himself in a complicated position: for political reasons, he could not allow the army to direct the campaign, but for practical reasons, the police had become unsuitable. Civilian control of the security forces was essential, yet there was no civilian official other than himself who had the authority to give directions to both the army's general officer commanding and the police commissioner. Gurney needed a civilian with insider military knowledge whom the chain of command would respect. He therefore recommended that the government send to Malaya a high-ranking military officer, preferably retired, who would be appointed in a civil post with the following duties:

> He would be responsible for the preparation of [a] general plan for offensive action and the allocation of tasks to the various components of the security forces. In consultation with

heads of the police and fighting services he would decide priorities between these tasks and general timing and sequence of their execution. He would exercise control through heads of police and fighting services and aim at achieving co-ordination and decentralisation by this means. ... He would work directly under myself [the British High Commissioner] and within the framework of the policy laid down by this Government. He would be in close touch with civil authorities responsible for essential features of the campaign, such as settlement and control of squatters, propaganda, immigration control and settlement of labour disputes, and would have [the] right to make representation to me in such matters affecting the conduct of [the] anti-communists campaign as a whole.[330]

Gurney was proposing a position without precedent in British imperial experience. Alas, he sent his telegram at a highly inopportune time. For in the United Kingdom, Clement Attlee's Labour government found itself in deep trouble and the emergency in Malaya was suddenly less important than the emergency spreading through Labour's parliamentary constituencies. On February 23, 1950—the day Gurney sent his missive—the Conservatives forced the government to hold a general election. In the rout that followed, Creech Jones—colonial secretary since 1946 and member of Parliament since 1935—lost his seat. With the checking of an electoral ballot box, the support from the colonial office that Gurney had come to rely upon was cast into doubt.

VIII. The appointment of Sir Harold Briggs

The Labour Party's troubles began soon after its election in July 1945. The British press immediately typecast the party's leader Clement Attlee as a political lightweight, with some scoffing that when he replaced Churchill at the Potsdam conference "the Big Three became the Big Two-and-a-Half."[331] Others wondered if Attlee was capable of steering Britain through the infested waters of the immediate postwar period. After all, the problems facing the government were enormous. The Germans had destroyed half a million homes during the war and these had yet to be rebuilt. Countless millions more had been damaged but not destroyed and were in desperate need of repair. Factories, shops, and warehouses fared no better, and one third of Britain's prewar shipping tonnage had still not recovered from wartime losses. In addition to physical destruction, the government was forced to sell off £1000 million worth of foreign investment and ended the war with £3500 million of debt. In the words of John Maynard Keynes, in the war's aftermath Britain faced a "financial Dunkirk."[332] This economic catastrophe reached its climax in February 1947 when industrial production fell by 50% and unemployment rose to 2.5 million.[333] The British economy continued to struggle throughout 1948 and into 1949, and on September 18 of that year Stafford Cripps, the chancellor of the exchequer, devalued the pound sterling by 30%, from $4.03 to $2.80.[334]

It was in the midst of this continuing economic crisis that the government withdrew from India, waged and lost its counterinsurgency campaign in Palestine, and declared an emergency in Malaya. Such actions provoked concern among the parliamentary opposition. On June 4, 1948—less than three weeks after the British withdrawal from Palestine—Winston Churchill, still leader of the Conservative Party, wrote to Montgomery expressing his "anxiety" about "the world situation and about the state of the British Services." In particular, Churchill was concerned that "should trouble come" the armed forces would be "even less well-prepared than we were at the beginning of the late war."[335] Montgomery shared this apprehension, writing on the seventh of that month, "You could not be more anxious about the general situation than I am, and in particular about the measures being taken to deal with it. ... Unless a firm grip is taken from the top, we shall drift to disaster." He offered to "come and tell you about it, and give you the whole story; I consider it *very necessary* I should do so."[336] That a sitting chief of the imperial general staff, present at many cabinet meetings and privy to confidential governmental memoranda and discussion, should have made such an offer to the leader of the opposition is extraordinary. That Churchill should have accepted is equally noteworthy. On Sunday, June 13, the two men met alone for a long lunch at Chartwell, the Churchill family home in Kent. It is not known what was said between them but three days prior to their meeting Montgomery promised to "tell you [Churchill] all you want to know."[337] Judging by the tone of Montgomery's letters, it is highly likely that confidential cabinet information was disclosed.

It was not only Montgomery and Churchill who were concerned about the Labour government. On January 14, 1949, Harold Macmillan—a Conservative MP since 1924, who had served briefly as Churchill's secretary of state for air in the two months prior to the 1945 electoral defeat—told a crowd in his Bromley constituency that "the Middle East muddle is really intolerable." He continued:

> We find ourselves, after thirty years of generous effort on their behalf, bitterly hated by the Jews. We are suspected by the Arabs. We have failed to win the sympathy or the co-operation of the Americans. We are being out-maneuvered by the Russians. Yet the Middle East is vital to our security, strategically and economically. We have almost thrown away, in a few months, the fruits of years of peaceful labour and of two bloody wars.[338]

Macmillan was joined in this criticism by Oliver Lyttelton, another rising star in the party, who wrote to Churchill on March 4, 1949, that while "nothing could be more unfair, or for that matter shortsighted, than to pretend that the present Socialist Government is other than a bitter enemy of Communism," socialism was nevertheless "the weakest bulwark against Communism on the Continent, and in fact often prepares the ground for Communism by weakening the respect for tradition and the individual." Furthermore, while "people like Attlee, Morrison, Bevin, and for that matter Dalton, are bitter enemies of Communism, I should doubt if that was either true of Shinwell or Strachey, and even if it were there are Warbeys and Tiffanys and fellow travellers who are still under the pink umbrella."[339] This was particularly worrying to Lyttelton. After all, the government was engaged in a war against communist insurgents and ideology in Malaya, a point he had taken pains to make "on the Front Bench [of Parliament] last night."[340]

It was not only Conservative opposition to government policy and the economic crisis that confronted the Labour Party. There was also a general sense of the passing of an era, well articulated in the diaries of Sir Cuthbert Headlam, member of Parliament for Newcastle North, who wrote on December 31, 1949, "it is very painful ... to have lived to see the end of an epoch when England meant so much to the rest of the world and when one had such pride in being an Englishman."[341] Sensing that the mood of the country was turning against his party, on January 5, 1950, Attlee wrote to King George VI asking for a dissolution of Parliament. This he was granted, and in the early morning hours of January 11 Attlee announced that the election would be held on February 23, with the last day of the current parliament being Friday, February 3.[342]

When polling day arrived, the Labour Party witnessed a swing from it to the Conservatives of 3.3 percent. Although not enough to secure victory for Winston Churchill's party, the number of Labour seats was cut from 393 to 315, leaving a slim majority of just nine seats over all other parties. Hugh Dalton, formerly chancellor of the exchequer and in 1950 chancellor of the Duchy of Lancaster, remarked that it was "the worst possible result ... We have office without authority or power, and it is difficult to see how we can improve the position."[343] Cuthbert Headlam agreed, writing in his diary that the result was "a strange and unsatisfactory state of things," which would entail "before long" another general election to give one party or the other a more decisive majority.[344]

Headlam, at least, kept his seat in Parliament. Not so for Arthur Creech Jones, who lost by just eighty-one votes. His constituents clearly felt the same as his good friend Harold Locker, professor at the London School of Economics, who wrote to him on January 30 explaining his decision not to campaign for Creech Jones in the imminent election:

> You are the one man who might, in my view, have prevented from the period of your appointment as Colonial Secretary, the terrible tragedy of Bevin's policy in Palestine. By choosing to accept it, and indeed to be responsible for some of its terrible consequences, was to me as big a disappointment as I can remember in many a day, and therefore, much as I should have wished to speak for Arthur Creech-Jones, for whom I have real affection and a long-standing friendship, I could not speak for the Secretary of State for the Colonies, who was the main co-operator of the Foreign Secretary in imposing a policy that was both a denial of specific pledges given by the Party and an outrage upon our good name as a country all over the world.[345]

On that frosty Thursday in February, Creech Jones perhaps lost more than his constituency seat.

With Creech Jones gone, Attlee had to fill his position at the colonial office. Creech Jones' parliamentary undersecretary, David Rees-Williams, had also lost his parliamentary seat, so the prime minister offered the job to Hugh Dalton. Despite being a distinct promotion from the largely ceremonial role of chancellor of the Duchy of Lancaster, Dalton refused, telling Attlee, "This is not my Kingdom," and declaring that he had no desire to visit "pullulating, poverty-stricken nigger communities, for whom we can do nothing in the short run, and who the more one tries to help them, are querulous and ungrateful."[346] Dalton instead accepted the position of minister of town and country planning. Attlee therefore turned to James Griffiths, his minister of national insurance, a man whom Oliver Lyttelton believed to be "absolutely hopeless ... swayed entirely by sentiment" and whose cabinet colleagues soon nicknamed the "minister of tears."[347] Griffiths accepted the position and committed himself to furthering Creech Jones' agenda in the empire.[348] This made him particularly well suited for cooperating with Sir Henry Gurney, who wasted no time in apprising the new colonial secretary of his plans for a change of strategy in Malaya.

Gurney briefed both Griffiths and Emmanuel Shinwell, the new minister of defense, on his intention to appoint a single civil official to oversee all emergency efforts. Shinwell met with the chiefs of staff to ascertain if they had any objections, and finding none, he informed the prime minister that he was "satisfied" that "the proposed appointment is a step in the right direction and is one which will materially improve the combined operations of the Police and Military which under the existing arrangements have need for greater co-ordination."[349] On March 9, two days after Shinwell wrote to the prime minister, Gurney sent a telegram to Griffiths providing more information on his plan. He suggested that a lieutenant general (serving or retired) be appointed for a minimum of one year, and recommended that this position be titled the Director of Operations with the same civilian rank as the chief secretary. Gurney then provided Griffiths with the wordings of a press release the government could issue to announce the post, specifically proposing that the release make clear, "His primary function will be to secure full and effective co-ordination."[350]

Field Marshal Sir William Slim, who succeeded Montgomery as chief of the imperial general staff in January 1949, suggested to the cabinet that they approach his good friend Lieutenant General Sir Harold Briggs for the position, who had been in retirement in Cyprus since 1948. Only fifty-five years of age, Briggs had spent much of the Second World War in the jungles of Burma and was thus well suited for the position.[351] After initial hesitation, Slim persuaded Briggs to take up the post, and on March 21, the government announced that the first director of operations for Malaya had been selected. Following a whirlwind series of meetings in London to explain and discuss the position, Briggs arrived in Kuala Lumpur on April 3, 1950.[352]

The appointment of Briggs as director of operations was not the only innovation to emerge following the February general election. The government also created a Malaya committee within the cabinet, the likes of which had been absent for the previous twenty months of the emergency. Its formation was prompted by Shinwell's belief that "the campaign is [not] being taken sufficiently seriously here in Whitehall."[353] Chaired by Shinwell, the committee held its first meeting on April 5—two days after Briggs landed in Malaya—and was tasked by the cabinet to "keep the situation in Malaya under review" and to "authorise such measures they may think necessary to preserve law and order in the Colony."[354] The committee hoped that emergency measures in Malaya would begin to more accurately reflect the guidance offered by a recent memorandum from the colonial office. This memorandum reminded all ministers that the colonies were "held and administered on the principle of trusteeship, which means, briefly, that, mainly through education in its widest sense, Colonial people are helped along the road of social and economic development with the ultimate object of attaining the highest possible standard of living for the people at large and the greatest possible measure of self-government for the communities to which they belong."[355] It was the government's belief that all peoples of the world could obtain a quality of life similar to that of postwar Britain. The role of the colonial office was to ensure that Britain's overseas territories were afforded an equal opportunity to achieve this objective.

This was a vision that had been lacking in Palestine but was at the heart of Gurney's mission in Malaya. Even before Briggs' appointment, Gurney had declared that March 1950 would be "anti-bandit" month, where the British administration would encourage the Malayan population to volunteer for emergency service and become part of the solution to the problems ailing the colony. In all, half a million Malays volunteered, each of whom was placed into auxiliary police units to safeguard villages, resettlement teams to assist the relocation of squatters, or propaganda units to combat the MCP's dogma. Such was the success of anti-bandit month that after consultations with the newly arrived director of operations, Gurney made public a plan to implement many of its features on a permanent basis. On April 5, he issued an official statement laying out the government's proposals:

(a) In the main towns of the Federation a uniformed Auxiliary Police Force [will be] formed. This will have its own volunteer officers and S.P.O.'s [Special Police Officers].
(b) In rural areas the present system of Kampong guards and coast watchers will be extended and placed on a more permanent basis in order to safeguard villages from attacks and to close the coasts to illegal immigration.
(c) Resettlement teams which have functioned successfully in many areas during the month will be increased in number so that the vitally important task of bringing all squatters into touch with the local administration may be pressed forward with all possible speed.
(d) Propaganda work will be developed with the aid of volunteer workers so that the evils of communism may be brought home to those who are exposed to pressure and propaganda from the bandits and who normally have little access to information from Government sources.[356]

When Briggs arrived in Kuala Lumpur, just days after anti-bandit month came to a close, he was met at the airport by Sir Robert Thompson. Thompson was the Surrey-born son of an English clergyman who had joined the Malayan Civil Service in 1938 and was the Chinese Affairs Officer when the emergency erupted. Having served with the Royal Air Force as a Chindit in Burma during the Second World War, Thompson left the

Chinese Affairs office to serve as a member of the short-lived special operations Ferret Force during the first months of the emergency.[357] Upon Gurney's arrival, he was immediately transferred to the Government Secretariat in Kuala Lumpur, where he was tasked, among other things, with handling and coordinating all intelligence reports.[358] Holding unparalleled knowledge of the counterinsurgency campaign in Malaya thus far, and with a shared war history from Burma, Gurney felt Thompson would be the ideal man to make Briggs' introduction to the colony and its people. It was for this reason that he instructed Thompson to meet Briggs at the airport. In this as in so much else, Gurney's judgment proved correct. Briggs immediately asked Thompson to his house for dinner, during which Briggs told Thompson that "the whole key to the war lies in getting control of the squatter areas," a strategy that was contingent on providing adequate security for the resettled squatters. As Briggs put it, "The people matter—they are vital—but you can't expect any support from people you can't protect."[359] Thompson agreed entirely, and by the end of the evening Briggs had asked him to move from the secretariat to be his civil staff officer, a transfer Gurney approved.[360]

Following several more dinners with Thompson, and after a two-week tour of the colony meeting with military, police, and civilian authorities, Briggs issued Directive No.1 on April 16, laying out the future direction of his proposed policy. Effective June 1, Briggs would form a Federal War Council, chaired by the director of operations and including in its membership the chief secretary, the GOC, the AOC, the commissioner of police, and the secretary of defense. The Federal War Council's role would be to produce policy. Each state was then required to form a State War Executive Committee (SWEC), chaired by the resident commissioner of that state and with a membership of the British advisor in state, the state's chief police officer, and the state's senior army commander. The SWEC's role was to implement the policy laid out by the Federal War Council. In each district within the state, the SWEC would form a District War Executive

Committee (DWEC), mirroring the composition of the SWEC only with lower-level officials. In addition to the SWECs and DWECs, Briggs established a Federal Joint Intelligence Advisory Committee, whose purpose was to examine "ways and means of strengthening the intelligence and Police Special Branch organisation to ensure that the mass of information which exists in the country becomes available and is sifted and disseminated quickly and at the right levels."[361] Briggs hoped that this "joint conception" would be "followed at all levels, with the Civil Administration, Police and Army working in the closest collaboration and using combined joint operations and intelligence rooms wherever practicable."[362] To assist in this coordination, Briggs would permit no ranking of army and police personnel within the SWECs and DWECs, with one claiming superiority over the other. He made this very clear in his second directive, issued on May 12, when he explicitly stated: "It is immaterial whether the local military commander is a Lieutenant-Colonel and the local Police Officer is a Sergeant or whether they are respectively a Major and a Superintendent; in each case they will establish a joint headquarters and will work in the closest co-operation also with the local Administrative Officer."[363]

Having established the administrative framework for his counterinsurgency campaign, Briggs next turned to strategy and tactics, issuing on May 24 the "Federation Plan for the Elimination of the Communist Organisation and Armed Forces in Malaya," referred to at the time and by historians since as the Briggs Plan.[364] Within this plan, Briggs stated his belief that the British government needed to demonstrate "effective administration and control of all populated areas." The government would do this by taking the initiative away from the communist insurgents and demonstrating to the Malay people that the Western way of life was superior to the communist way of life. Briggs intended to accomplish this through a six-step process. First, the police and British army would maintain security on the ground so that the government could demonstrate firmly its commitment to protecting Malaya against both external and internal attacks and disorder. Second, the government would resettle Malayan squatters into compact groups, where they could more easily be protected by the British security forces and given social welfare. Third, the government would strengthen local administration, so that it would become more effective and efficient than anything the communists could offer. Fourth, British military engineers would provide road communication in isolated areas to link all Malayan subjects to the British administrative structure. Fifth, the police force would set up posts in these isolated areas, both to protect the population and to show the flag. And finally, the government, police, and military would launch a concerted propaganda campaign to highlight the negatives of the communist insurgency and the positives of British governance.[365]

These six measures would coalesce within a twofold strategy: first, the British government and security forces would establish a "feeling of complete security" that would lead to a "steady and increasing flow of information from all sources"; second, the security forces would disrupt the communist insurgency and deny it access to general Malayan society. In particular, they would separate it from its food and information supply. Once such separation occurred, Briggs hoped that the insurgents would attack the British security forces on their own ground, having been left with no alternative, at which point the security forces could defeat them without inconveniencing the civilian population. The key point of Briggs' plan was that separation would be created between the insurgents and everyone else so that life could return to normal in Malaya as quickly as possible.[366] It was exactly what Creech Jones and Gurney had hoped to do in Palestine, but had been prohibited by Montgomery and the cabinet at large from doing.

To help implement the Briggs Plan and make it more effective, Gurney instructed the Malayan chief secretary, M. V. Del Tufo, to publish a broad definition of terrorism that could be used in legal proceedings against those convicted under emergency regulations. Del Tufo was happy to oblige, and on July

13, 1950, the Emergency (Amendment No. 12) Reg[ulation]s of 1950 declared that

> "terrorist" means any person who-
> (a) by the use of firearms, explosives or ammunition acts in a manner prejudicial to the public safety or to the maintenance of public order;
> (b) incites to violence or counsels disobedience to the law or to any lawful order by the use of firearms, explosives or ammunition;
> (c) carries or has in his possession or under his control any firearm, not being a firearm which he is duly licensed to possess under any written law for the time being in force;
> (d) carries or has in his possession or under his control any ammunition or explosives without lawful authority thereof;
> (e) demands, collects or receives any supplies for the use of any person who intends to or is about to act, or has recently acted, in a manner prejudicial to public safety for the maintenance of public order;
> And 'terrorism' shall have a corresponding meaning.[367]

Any "terrorist" was subject to charge and, if convicted, eligible for death by hanging. Del Tufo's definition therefore gave the government wide-ranging sentencing power over any guerilla or supporter of the insurgency. In reality, the government imposed the death penalty on just 226 of the thousands of insurgents it captured during the emergency. This does not detract from the hardening line the government was taking toward those who disturbed the king's peace in Malaya, however.[368] A terrorist was deserving of death, pure and simple, and those who qualified as a terrorist greatly expanded under the leadership of Briggs.

Although events were turning the government's way in Malaya, this was not the case in London. Because of its narrow majority in Parliament, the cabinet decided on February 25— just two days after the election—that "there could be no question of attempting to carry through any of the controversial legislation which had been promised in the Party's Election Manifesto."[369] Consequently, the king's speech—delivered by George VI on March 6—was a humdrum affair. Churchill later commented that it "might as well have read 'My Government will not introduce legislation in fulfilment of their election programme because the only mandate they have received from the country is not to do it.'"[370] In conservative circles, the stalemate in Parliament caused concern that Attlee might soon call a snap general election to shore up his majority. On April 23, Sir Alan Frederick "Tommy" Lascelles, keeper of the royal archives and private secretary to George VI, wrote to Oliver Lyttelton, offering him unsolicited advice about the king's role in a possible early dissolution of Parliament. Although it had been more than 100 years since the sovereign had refused a prime minister's request for a dissolution of Parliament, Lascelles believed that "The right to refuse a dissolution still exists." This action could be followed by the king if three basic conditions were met:

(a) a general election in the near future would be definitely harmful to the national interest (as distinct from being merely a nuisance)

(b) the existing Parliament was still vital, and capable of doing its duty in the country

(c) he could find somebody else, capable of forming a Ministry, backed by a working majority, which could effectively carry on the country's business, as distinct from merely "care-taking"; otherwise the Sovereign would only be postponing for a few weeks, or even days, an inevitable general election.

Lascelles cautioned, however, that when a dissolution was refused by the Canadian governor-general in 1926, "it left a legacy of bitterness against Crown Government in many Canadian hearts."[371] If an immediate general election could be shown to be "harmful to the national interest," the king was within his constitutional rights to refuse to dissolve Parliament.

But it was not a step any monarch should take lightly, nor one that the Conservative Party in opposition should recommend without carefully considering the potential consequences.

Lyttelton immediately sent the advice to Churchill, saying he believed he should "see this letter."[372] Churchill considered Lascelles' words for just over a week and then sent a reply to Lyttelton. He suggested Lyttelton forward his comments to Lascelles but recommended they arrive on Lyttelton's letterhead rather than his own due to the latter's "personal relationship" with Lascelles.[373] On May 4, therefore, Lyttelton wrote to Lascelles, cryptically informing him that he had discussed the matter with "the former Naval person." He then copied word for word the reply sent by Churchill. The conservative leader, through Lyttelton, informed Lascelles that "The prerogative is clearly a living and modern fact." Furthermore, Churchill insisted that if "a new political combination could be formed which gave a reasonable prospect of a working majority," the sovereign would be justified in forming a new government without a dissolution of Parliament.[374]

If the conservatives could ally themselves with the liberals and thus outnumber Labour with a working parliamentary majority, George VI could refuse any request from Attlee for a general election, instead inviting Churchill to form a new government. Attlee had only to lose his nerve and attempt to increase his majority by asking for a new general election and the top of Disraeli's greasy pole would be Churchill's once more. The former prime minister's wish was destined to be delayed however, for on June 24, 1950, the communist army of North Korea crossed the 38th Parallel in its invasion of South Korea. Suddenly, all talk of a general election evaporated.

IX.   The Special Air Service, the Briggs Plan, and progress in Malaya

On June 2, 1950—three weeks before the North Korean invasion of South Korea—the prime minister summoned together the

British chiefs of staff. He informed them that Robert Menzies, the Australian prime minister, had sent him a telegram suggesting that "there was scope in Malaya for an organisation of the type known as S.O.E. during the [Second World] war." Attlee hoped to hear the opinion of his service chiefs on the matter. He was no doubt surprised when Brigadier Pike, the army chief of staff, informed him that "The creation of a Special Force for the Malayan campaign working on the lines of the Prime Minister of Australia's suggestions [has] been under consideration for some little time and plans [are] well under way." Sir Stewart Menzies, director-general of MI6 since 1939, was also clearly in the know, noting that his organization had offered "help" in providing special equipment for this new force. Finally, Pike revealed that the war office had already identified Brigadier Michael Calvert to lead the force, that Calvert had accepted, and that he had been in Malaya for the previous five months for that very purpose.[375] Apparently unbeknownst to both the British and Australian prime ministers, the defense chiefs had already established a special forces unit in Malaya.

Brigadier "Mad Mike" Calvert had first risen to distinction as second in command of Orde Wingate's Chindits in Burma and thus had a shared experience with Briggs and Thompson of jungle warfare during the Second World War.[376] It was during this time that he received the nickname "Mad Mike," it being rumored that he had killed more Japanese by hand than any other British or American soldier.[377] Capitalizing on this experience, Calvert wrote a widely circulated paper titled *The Operations of Small Forces Behind Enemy Lines*, prompting the establishment of the Auxiliary Units.[378] In March 1945, the war office appointed Calvert commander of 1 Special Air Service (SAS) Brigade, and he spent the remainder of the European war in the Dutch-German theater.[379] Following Hitler's defeat, Calvert tried desperately to find a new role for the SAS, suggesting to the war office and—through SAS-founder David Stirling—to Churchill directly that a new brigade should be formed for service in the Far East. Churchill was supportive of the scheme but his electoral defeat in July, followed shortly thereafter by the dropping of the atomic bombs on Hiroshima and Nagasaki, put an end to the plan. With no apparent role for a special forces unit in peacetime, the British government officially disbanded the SAS on October 8, 1945.[380] Calvert, a professional soldier since 1933, could not stomach the prospect of civilian life, and so accepted a demotion to major on the disbandment of the SAS, immediately enrolling in a two-year course at the army's Staff College. Following this academic stint, he was posted to a staff position as a lieutenant colonel with the Allied Military Government in Trieste. Close to forty-five years of age and nearing the end of his military service, Calvert believed his fighting career was over.[381]

Meanwhile, following a report by the war office's Directorate of Technical Investigation that suggested the SAS had achieved "results out of all proportion to its size," on July 8, 1947, a Royal Warrant created the 21 SAS (Artists Rifles), a Territorial Army battalion within the Army Air Corps. Within a year, 200 men had volunteered for service—including 59 who had fought with the wartime SAS—and Lieutenant Colonel Brian Franks, its commanding officer, began to push for the war office to grant it corps status, separate from the Army Air Corps, which would give it the standing of a "specialist arm" within the British Army.[382]

As part of its assessment, the war office commissioned an investigation into the possible role a future SAS corps could play. The report, published on August 30, 1949, painted a picture of remarkable versatility. The role of the SAS, it noted, would be to "undertake small scale military operations of every type, from offensive to intelligence ... far from the main battle areas ... usually behind enemy lines." SAS troops would be trained to approach their targets "by land, sea or air transport." Because few men were used in any one operation, "many operations can be, and are, undertaken by SAS units simultaneously." These operations could be "of different types, in different areas, even against different enemies." Such was the uniqueness of the SAS, the report concluded, that "The SAS regiment is NOT organized and can NOT be employed as units; all operations undertaken by SAS troops are carried out by parties especially picked and equipped for the occasion. The strength, composition, equipment and method of employment of each party depends on the exact circumstances of each operation and are only decided when the operation is allotted and examined in detail."[383]

In October 1945, when the SAS was disbanded, such a formation of men seemed unnecessary. After all, the war was over. But by August 1949, with the Cold War heating up, the counterinsurgency campaign in Palestine a disaster, and the Malayan conflict escalating, the world suddenly seemed a more complex and dangerous environment in which to operate. In the midst of this new reality, the armed forces were in desperate need of adaptability. The report therefore recommended that Franks be granted his wish. Consequently, on May 22, 1950, the war office designated the Special Air Service Regiment its own corps within the regular army.[384]

While the SAS was becoming more established within the peacetime army, Calvert was growing increasingly frustrated, believing that he was becoming—in his words—"a true staff wallah."[385] He was relieved, therefore, to be posted to Hong Kong in January 1950. Shortly thereafter, General Harding (the commander in chief, Far East) summoned him to Singapore where, on the advice of Viscount Slim, he was sent to Malaya to advise the government on counterinsurgency strategy and tactics. On making this appointment, Harding informed Calvert that "Things are not going nearly as well as we had hoped. General Slim says you know all about guerilla warfare. I give you carte-blanche: go where you like, see who you like, and discover what is wrong."[386]

By the time the chiefs of staff met on June 2, 1950, Calvert had already been touring the federation for five months, travelling thirty-thousand miles, talking with civil, military, and police authorities, and undertaking patrols with army and police units. He was distinctly unimpressed with what he found, believing that British troops were "making a lot of noise and achieving very little."[387] Reporting his findings to Briggs in July, the director of operations authorized him to form a special forces unit. By the end of the month, the Malayan Scouts (SAS) had accepted its first volunteers.[388]

The Malayan Scouts was at once limited by certain stipulations placed upon it. Although Harding granted Calvert the right to pick his own officers (with the provision that they come only from Hong Kong or Malaya), the same was not true for other ranks, who were selected by battalion commanders. While some commanders subscribed to the SAS ethos and supplied their most suitable men, many others used it as an excuse to "off-load their unruly elements," with obvious consequences for unit cohesion and discipline.[389] Furthermore, the war office refused to provide the Malayan Scouts with adequate administrative support, so Calvert had to make do without an adjutant, quartermaster, or training officer, placing tremendous administrative pressure on himself.[390] Consequently, although Calvert had recruited enough officers and men by August 1950 to form 'A' Squadron, Malayan Scouts (SAS), the men were of varying quality, ranging from those who had served as Chindits during the Second World War to national service conscripts to a band of the French foreign legion who had deserted from a ship on route to Indochina.[391]

With this unlikely group of men, Calvert commenced training. He conducted it in an unconventional manner, sending his soldiers in pairs into the jungle, wearing fencing masks and armed with air rifles. Those who could not hide from their counterparts received painful reminders by way of a pellet that if the training operation had been live, they would be dead.[392] Despite the intensity of his training methods—or perhaps because of it—when his men were not on training missions, their behavior was boisterous and their discipline lax. By December 1950, the Malayan Scouts had gained a reputation for drunken and uncontrollable antics off duty.[393]

In an attempt to curb the excesses of 'A' Squadron, in January 1951, the war office dispatched men from 21 SAS regiment (Artists Rifles) of the Territorial Army to form 'B' Squadron Malayan Scouts (SAS). All of this new intake were volunteers rather than conscripts, most had combat experience from the Second World War, and as a whole they tended to be more mature than the young soldiers of 'A' squadron. Upon their arrival, Calvert left for an official visit to recruit a third squadron, 'C', from Rhodesia. In his absence, his intelligence officer, Captain John Woodhouse, ran 'A' Squadron and was able to mold it into a "fit, tough, and highly efficient unit."[394] So impressed was Calvert upon his return from Rhodesia that he petitioned the war office for a fourth squadron, 'D', which he placed under the command of Woodhouse.[395]

Calvert's initiative began to gain attention. On March 11, 1951, the *Bulawayo Chronicle*, Rhodesia's largest-circulating newspaper, reported:

> Small squads of hand-picked, highly trained men known as Malayan Scouts, are going to live with the Communists and the aborigines in the depths of the green hell. The scouts have undergone months of the most rigorous training and are now going into action. ... The Scouts will try to prevent the Communists from receiving help from the jungle people. Using guerilla tactics and operating from concealed bases, they aim either to kill the outlaws or to hunt them from the areas where they can make use of the aborigines. While stalking the guerillas they will use every opportunity of gaining the confidence of the aborigines.[396]

By the summer of 1951, the Malayan Scouts (SAS) was working as intended, engaged in deep penetration operations within the jungle where it combated communist insurgents and gathered intelligence on guerilla camps, which were later destroyed by RAF bombardment.

The strain of it all was too much for Calvert, however, and on June 9, 1951, he suffered a nervous breakdown following a meeting with Briggs. Never again to hold command of any significance, he immediately left Malaya for a two-month stay in a British military hospital. In a letter dated July 3, he wrote:

> I have been extremely busy in and out of the jungle and eventually cracked. I am now in hospital and on my way home. ... It has been a long grind raising, training, administering, operating and planning without much help, especially on the administration. However, successes are now coming through and at last we are paying a dividend. I may say that I broke down mentally due to overstrain. I am alright now, but I just had too much to do and think about.[397]

It was the end of an era for the Malayan Scouts. Despite Calvert's departure, the foundations had been laid for special operations units in Britain's counterinsurgency campaigns. They would form a crucial part of all such efforts in the future.[398]

While Calvert was actively launching his Malayan Scouts, Gurney and Briggs were equally busy with the larger aspects of emergency planning, particularly the implementation of the Briggs Plan. From the beginning of the emergency in June 1948 until the end of 1949, the British government had given free grants and loans to the administration in Malaya totaling £86 million pounds, including £5 million from the Colonial Development and Welfare fund and an investment of £3,750,000 from the Colonial Development Corporation that was specifically intended to improve the colony's electricity grid.[399] Gurney now wished to capitalize upon that investment to ensure that the Malay people, once protected from communist insurgency, would be given the benefits of good western governance. As such, he invited the newly promoted colonial secretary, James Griffiths, for a tour of the colony, where he might see first hand where new investment and support from the British government was needed. Along with John Strachey (the secretary of state for war), Griffiths arrived in Malaya in late May 1950, returning to the United Kingdom in the second week of June. He immediately prepared a preliminary report on his findings, which he circulated to the cabinet on June 13.

Griffiths began by assuring the cabinet that both he and Strachey were "completely satisfied" with the Briggs Plan, although acknowledged that its implementation would be a "lengthy task." In particular, the success of British efforts in Malaya hinged upon "the capacity of the civil administration to consolidate behind the military operations." That being the case, the police and civil service rather than the army and air force were the priority for resources, and the police force had a specific need for an additional 117 officers (superintendents and above) and 175 noncommissioned officers (sergeants and inspectors). Alongside these regular police officers, Briggs intended to form forty-five companies of police "jungle squads," which would fulfill a paramilitary role and would "relieve the military forces of internal security [duties]." These would not be composed solely of European policemen, though. If the Malays were to take control of their own security, Asian officers would have to be integrated into the force. Briggs therefore suggested that a police training college be opened in Kuala Lumpur—a recommendation Griffiths supported. Finally, alongside the police reinforcements, Gurney requested twenty-five administrative cadets from the civil service training program, fifteen of whom must be Chinese-speaking. He asked that these be sent out immediately without finishing their year of formal training. Gurney hoped these twenty-five would be joined by thirty more experienced civil servants over the course of the following year who could be transferred to Malaya as opportunity allowed.[400] Griffiths assured the cabinet that he agreed with each of these recommendations, and at a meeting on June 19 the ministers gave their assent to all suggestions.[401]

By the end of June 1950, the British were beginning to make progress in Malaya. In Briggs, Gurney had found a director of operations who agreed wholeheartedly with his approach toward counterinsurgency and who had the military credentials and force of personality to win the respect of the security forces. With the colonial and war secretaries fully on board and with the backing of the cabinet at large, Gurney had drafted a strategy that promised success. All he and Briggs needed now were time and resources. Unfortunately, with the North Korean invasion of South Korea on June 24—just four days after the cabinet had agreed to his requests—they were faced with the possibility that they might receive neither.

Upon North Korea's invasion, the American government immediately moved to support South Korea. Five-star general Douglas MacArthur, commander of US Forces in the Far East, dispatched arms and ammunition to the peninsula, and on June 25, President Truman ordered the American air force and navy to South Korea to assist in the evacuation of American civilians. When MacArthur informed Truman on June 26 that Seoul might fall, the president lifted all restrictions on American actions south of the 38th Parallel, essentially allowing his forces to engage the North Koreans. Finally, on June 30, with the North Korean armies still proceeding southwards, Truman ordered American ground troops into Korea.[402] Meanwhile, the UN Security Council adopted a resolution on June 25 calling for "the immediate cessation of hostilities" in Korea, followed by a second resolution on June 27 asking for "members of the United Nations to furnish such assistance to the Republic of Korea as may be necessary to repel the armed attack and to restore international peace and security in the area."[403]

It was on this date—four days after the invasion took place and two days after discussion began in the Security Council— that the American state department first contacted the British government, Secretary of State Dean Acheson apologizing profusely to Bevin for the delay. The American army, commanded by MacArthur, had been tasked to lead international efforts in support of South Korea, and Acheson wanted to know if the British government could, "as a matter of urgency," immediately commit forces to the United Nations' cause.[404] Even with the continuation of National Service, the British Army and RAF were stretched thin, with many thousands serving in Malaya. Nevertheless, by the end of the day the government had dispatched its Far East fleet—totaling five escorts, two cruisers, and a light fleet carrier—to join the American fleet in operations against North Korea.[405] By the end of July, these naval personnel were joined on the peninsula by a brigade of ground troops.[406]

In light of this new commitment, some within the government and among the loyal opposition began to place pressure on Griffiths and Strachey to divert troops from Malaya to Korea. In an attempt to quell such demands, Griffiths distributed two memoranda to the cabinet's Malaya committee, one giving general background on the emergency, the other looking at more specific considerations. In the first, Griffiths attempted to tie the emergency to the Cold War, thus asserting its importance alongside the Korean conflict. He insisted that "the disturbances caused by the Malayan Communist Party (M.C.P.) are part of the Kremlin's world-wide campaign against the Western Powers." He also noted that the MCP drew its support "largely from Chinese who have settled in the rural areas." Just like in Korea, the enemy in Malaya was supported by the Chinese communists, with Soviet aid.[407]

In his second memorandum, Griffiths provided more detail on his proposed way forward. He argued that "in handling the Chinese population [in Malaya] every effort must be made to distinguish the sheep from the goats." In particular, "Severe measures should be directed against the terrorists and their active and voluntary collaborators, while those who, but for fear and intimidation, would be good citizens must be given the conditions of protection and security which they need." This, he explained, was precisely what the Briggs Plan was designed to do, by producing "concrete successes by the security forces against the terrorists," by "the extension of effective civil administration, particularly police control and protection, over the country generally," and by the use of "resettlement" to "bring scattered populations within the orbit of administration." In each of these areas, the Briggs Plan—although only six weeks in operation—was making good progress. Already 20,000 Chinese squatters had been resettled and preparation had been made for far more than this number. Griffiths felt certain that the situation in Malaya would soon improve. This was contingent, however, upon being able to protect both the Malays and the resettled Chinese squatters. The security forces would be unable to do so if they were all transferred to Korea.[408]

Griffiths was not the only member of the government making the case for continued focus on Malaya. At a meeting of the Malaya committee on July 17, attended by the Australian Prime Minister Robert Menzies, Strachey confirmed that Malaya was the war office's primary concern. This did not necessarily require an increase of troops. As Strachey explained, "The essence of the Briggs Plan [is] to shift the emphasis [from jungle patrols] to using troops in a role which approximated more to that of the Police." Field Marshal Slim, the chief of the imperial general staff, supported Strachey's explanation, and Griffiths reiterated to the committee that this was a new kind of campaign, and that "it was necessary to try to establish loyal civilian organisations among the people … in order to consolidate our position as the military [moves] forward."[409] By the end of July, those calling for troop and resource reductions in Malaya were silenced by the overwhelming opposition to their pleas by the British prime minister, minister of defense, colonial secretary, war secretary, chief of the imperial general staff, and Australian prime minister.

As British support for UN efforts in Korea increased in August, it became clear that the war—rather than leading to a bust in resources for Malaya—might even be a boom. This was because the "heightening of international tension" that the Korean War engendered "catapulted the prices of raw materials, particularly rubber and tin to record heights."[410] Consequently, by March 1951, the price of rubber was four times what the average price had been in 1949, and the price of tin doubled. Such inflated prices continued throughout 1952, enabling the colonial government in Malaya to "reap a healthy harvest in revenue."[411]

In real terms, this meant that while the Malayan government had received $28.1 million in rubber duty and $31.1 million in tin duties in 1949, by 1950 this had risen to $89.3 million and $50.9 million, respectively, and by 1951, $214.1 million and $76.2 million, respectively.[412] As the total cost of defense, police, and administrative spending in the emergency rose from $82 million in 1948 to $296 million in 1953, this meant that the net increase could be met by the duties on rubber and tin alone, with other revenues freed up for the more social aspects of the Briggs Plan.[413] In the aggregate, the Korean War thus had a positive rather than negative effect on British efforts in Malaya, rapidly increasing revenue without diminishing in any way the number of security forces deployed.

Although these financial benefits were not yet completely clear to the British government in August 1950, a consensus nevertheless emerged that the emergency in Malaya could not be won on the cheap, nor could it take second place to the war in Korea in terms of governmental support and attention. This point the government made clear to its friends and allies. On August 9, the British defence coordination committee, Far East, recommended that cooperation on planning begin immediately with the armed forces of Australia and New Zealand in case the Chinese government gave widespread and overt support to the communist guerillas in Malaya, as it was doing in Korea. Furthermore, the committee recommended, "Discussions should be started now with the United States Government, followed, if the response is favourable, by discussions with the French Government, the Commonwealth Governments and with the other members of the United Nations concerned, with a view to determining whether there is a possibility of organising a collective scheme within the framework of the United Nations Organisation for the defence of South East Asia."[414] If the communist government of China, supported by the Soviet Union, was on the march, why would it stop in Korea and not move to British Malaya and French Indochina? In the event that such a move occurred, the British defense establishment believed a coordinated response, managed through the United Nations, would be more effective than any measure taken by individual powers.

Not all, of course, agreed with the Briggs Plan or with Gurney's approach to defeating communist insurgency. The leadership of the Royal Air Force held that a display of mass firepower would do more to win the fight than the resettlement of squatters and the provision of social welfare. Meeting on August 9, 1950, at the air headquarters in Malaya, four high-ranking RAF officers came together for the first time with nine army officers and two police commanders to discuss interagency cooperation in the counterinsurgency campaign. The RAF officers were disappointed by what they heard. Lieutenant Colonel A. K. Crookshank, commanding officer of the second battalion, 2 Gurkha Rifles, explained that under the Briggs Plan, the army's role was to "deny food, money, and information to the bandits." These denials would separate "the bandits" from the general population and in turn "force the bandits to meet the security forces, surrender, be captured or killed." Any firefights that did occur were at the platoon level, were "unexpected and [were] over in a matter of minutes." There was thus "no way in which the air could be alerted to help," preventing any real role for RAF air support. The police commanders present "unanimously supported the facts" as laid out by Crookshank. The main army and police recommendation was that the RAF could best be used to take aerial photographs that would "provide better maps for local operations."

Group Captain P. H. Dunn, the senior air staff officer in Malaya, thanked the army and police officers for their insights, but stated:

As the R.A.F. had hoped to show that its immense hitting power might, quite often, be used with better effect than the conventional ground operations or in close support of them, these conclusions are disappointing. ... The R.A.F. believe, though fully aware of the difficulties of pin-pointing and infrequent opportunities, that targets do exist, somewhere and sometimes, which would permit their independent action and produce substantial results. It is hoped that those responsible for conducting ground operations will still keep their minds open to this possibility.[415]

The army and police rejected his viewpoint. Unfortunately for the RAF, there was just no place for strategic bombing in the Briggs Plan. The civil administration believed it was far better to isolate the insurgents and have them attack ground troops than to risk killing a civilian with an aerial bomb, which in turn would only strengthen support for the insurgency.

By late September 1950, the Briggs Plan was beginning to bear fruit. In a report to the cabinet's Malaya committee on September 22, Griffiths revealed that the resettlement of squatters in South Johore was "more than half completed" and was "generally well received." In some cases, Chinese Malays were even "anxiously asking for admission to resettlement areas." Briggs expected South Johore to be completely pacified by November 1 and North Johore by the end of January 1951. Within the resettled areas, Briggs had initiated a Home Guards scheme based on the traditional Malay Kampong or Village Guards, whereby Chinese residents could begin to take control of their own security, thus relieving the burden on the British security forces and encouraging an ideological separation within the Chinese population from the communist guerillas. Griffiths concluded that "although no spectacular results have been achieved, considerable progress has been made in the preliminary measures necessary to implement the Briggs Plan. In particular enthusiasm abounds, the morale of all Forces deployed against the Communists is high, public support is just beginning to become active, and a feeling of achievement is already current."[416]

Griffiths' conclusions were supported by the Malaya committee, which met on September 25 with both Gurney and Malcolm MacDonald, the commissioner-general for Southeast Asia, in attendance. Emmanuel Shinwell, the minister of defense, suggested that the government ought to be given "some idea of when it might be expected that the campaign would be brought to an end and the British troops released." Gurney reassured him that British success in Malaya was highly likely but required patience. The "primary task" for the police, he told the committee, was to "protect the settled areas and prevent the bandits from infiltrating back into them. It was only by these means that public confidence could be restored and maintained." Until public confidence was restored, the police would be unable to obtain "the vitally necessary intelligence which could be provided by the inhabitants." The Briggs Plan was working, but it would take time. Lieutenant General N. C. D. Brownjohn, the vice-chief of the imperial general staff, agreed, explaining to Shinwell, "Until the Police [are] strong and experienced enough, with an adequate intelligence organisation, and until resettlement [keeps] up with military operations, there [are] bound to be setbacks." Such setbacks did not negate the essential soundness of the plan, however. If the British government was patient, it would be rewarded with victory.

Patience, however, began to wear thin as the pace of Briggs' resettlements slowed and the security forces encountered greater resistance from the insurgents. Internal critics began to find their voice. Perhaps the most damning of these was Sir William Jenkin, whom Briggs had brought to Malaya on June 20, 1950, to advice Malayan police intelligence and improve the quality of service it provided. Jenkin, a retired senior member of the Indian Police Service, found his advice consistently thwarted by the police commissioner, William Gray. On November 10, therefore, after less than five months in the colony, Jenkin offered his resignation, stating that "it is beyond my power to effect improvement in Malayan Police Intelligence so quickly as it is deemed necessary." In particular, Jenkin claimed that those employed in police intelligence had "defects" in character, which were impossible to overcome:

Important prerequisites of an efficient Police Intelligence organisation are a competent, well trained, Police Force drawn from important social levels of all communities and in constant and intimate touch with the public, an intelligence section staffed by men of all ranks carefully selected from such a Force and further trained in the specialised work they are required to do, and a control staff of able and experienced officers sincerely determined to make the organisation a success by all possible endeavour. In my judgment these essentials are not present.[417]

Gurney was alarmed by Jenkin's letter and immediately suggested to the Malayan attorney general, Stafford Foster Sutton, that "Jenkin should be offered appointment in charge of the C.I.D. on contract for two or three years with whatever title you may decide."[418] Foster Sutton invited Jenkin to an urgent meeting, where he informed him that it would be a "calamity" if he left Malaya. He then offered to appoint Jenkin on a two-year contract in a new position created for him with the title Director of Intelligence. In this position, he would have direct access to both Gurney and Briggs, and would hold executive control over the police special branch and the criminal investigation department. Although these departments would remain administratively within the regular police force, with Gray having the "final decision over personnel matters," Jenkin would bypass Gray on operational and tactical matters, reporting directly to Briggs. Jenkin immediately accepted Foster Sutton's offer and withdrew his letter of resignation.[419] From that moment forward, Jenkin served as Briggs' director of intelligence, fulfilling an essential role within the British security forces. So integral, in fact, did his position become that in May 1951 Briggs completely separated the special branch and CID from the regular police force, merging them into a single unit renamed the Intelligence Bureau that operated as an independent force alongside the army, air force, and police service.[420]

Yet in the late autumn of 1950, it was not only Jenkin who was concerned about the situation on the ground. Even Briggs admitted in a report sent to the cabinet's chiefs of staff committee on November 16 that "Progress of the plan has not been as quick as was hoped and is already seriously behind schedule." He qualified this somewhat by pointing out that in the areas "where resettlement has been completed an immediate improvement has been noticeable," but could not escape the conclusion that "unless the Federation Government is placed on a war footing and the gravity of the local situation in its relation to the present world situation is realised by H.M. Government, no quicker progress can be made and a still graver emergency will arise, straining the morale of Malaya beyond breaking point."[421] This finding alarmed the chiefs of staff to such an extent that they invited Briggs to discuss his conclusions at their committee meeting on November 23. When they gathered, Briggs offered them no comfort, nor did he in any way soften the blow of his written remarks. In contrast to his September report, indicating that Johore would be pacified by November, he now told them that progress had slowed to such an extent that this might not happen until mid-1951. He admitted that overall the results of his efforts had fallen "far short of requirements." Field Marshall Slim thanked him for his frankness, lamented that time was "not on our side," and remarked that it was "important to instill a sense of urgency into all aspects of the campaign against the bandits." He agreed to accompany Briggs when he met the prime minister the next day, so that he might impress upon him that despite its delays, the chiefs of staff still "strongly endorsed" the operational plan being followed by Briggs.[422]

When Briggs and Slim arrived at 10 Downing Street the following morning, they were joined by Sir Henry Gurney, Ernest Bevin, James Griffiths, John Strachey, Emmanuel Shinwell, and the Air Marshal Sir William Elliot. As promised, Slim publicly offered his full support to Briggs, who outlined for the prime minister the problems he was encountering in Malaya. He then explained that he and Gurney had decided to place the Malayan administration "on a war footing" with "full executive and financial control of Emergency matters" given to the Federal War Council. This council would take "ruthless action against the Malayan Communists." It would not, however, allow Malaya to develop into a "police state." The emergency measures, while harsh for the insurgents, were not designed to apply to all Malayan society. On the contrary, Briggs and Gurney hoped to shelter the general Malay and Chinese population from much of the violence. Their aim was that the British security forces would be the only persons who came into contact with communist insurgents, the rest of the society protected in sheltered villages where the administration could provide social welfare, education, and local governance. With the backing of his cabinet, Attlee agreed to give Gurney and Briggs more time to implement their plan.[423]

Having received a stay on their political execution, Briggs and Gurney returned to Malaya determined to hasten the pace of operations. In his next progress report, sent to the cabinet on February 15, 1951, Briggs noted that "there is a distinct apparent improvement in civil morale, some stiffening of anticommunist feeling among the Chinese, and a further increase in the flow of information and generally in Security Force results." As civil and military planners received feedback from those on the ground, it was becoming "daily more clear that our object must be to break down Communist morale while upholding that of the population." For Briggs, "The fact that bandits still do, and must maintain contact with the inhabitants confirms the correctness of our tactics." The role of the army was therefore "to prevent such contacts by interception in small parties on the jungle fringes." The role of the police was "to give local security to the population and to break up the Communist cells therein." As of February 1, 67,000 squatters from the priority areas had been resettled, with 52,500 remaining; in the nonpriority areas, 50,000 had been resettled, with 280,000 remaining. While this was a slower rate than originally projected, it was nevertheless impressive and Briggs believed that all priority area squatters would be resettled by May 1, 1951.[424]

On February 26, Briggs issued a directive addressing in detail the purpose and methods of the resettlement of squatters.

Beginning by stating that resettlement was a "means of bringing people who, at the present time, are not under effective administrative control into new settlements and so under State and Settlement administration," Briggs insisted that resettlement "affords only that measure of protection and concentration which makes good administration practicable." Those being resettled had been "exposed to Communist pressure." Upon resettlement, it was of utmost importance that they be "protected against Communist physical and intellectual attack and [be] helped to become contented communities." The district officers in each region had primary responsibility for this task. They were assisted by resettlement supervisors and resettlement officers, who were given the civil service rank of assistant district officer. Briggs spelled out their duties in fine detail:

(a) the establishment of a settlement Committee in each settlement;

(b) the organisation of village schools in conjunction with the State/Settlement education authorities;

(c) the provision of medical aid and supervision of public health requirements in conjunction with the State/Settlement medical authorities;

(d) the organisation of community centres, visits by Officers of other Departments, e.g. the Agricultural Department, community listening wireless sets, co-operative shops, visits by mobile cinema vans and Chinese community leaders, and the encouragement of welfare activities and such youth movements as Boy Scouts;

(e) the provision of Federation and State flags for each settlement;

(f) as soon as the people of the settlement are ready for it, the formation of a Home Guard to assist the Police in the security of the settlement, to ensure that no infiltration of Communist influence takes place and to deny food and contacts to active Communists. Once the Home Guard is trained and armed, its members should assist the settlement Police

Post, both in defence of the Post and in patrolling the area under the operational control of the Police Officer in charge. The strength of the Police Post can then be reduced.[425]

In this directive, Briggs made clear that the emergency was not primarily about the physical destruction of communist insurgents. Rather, it was about providing social welfare in the form of schools, medical attention, and cultural outlets, to win the battle for the minds of the Chinese population. Once this battle was won, this population could begin to defend itself against the guerillas.

In combination with this policy of providing social welfare in protected Chinese settlements, Briggs also introduced a more draconian program of food denial to the insurgents and collective fines on those who supported and supplied them. The food denial operations capitalized on the fact that "Malaya did not produce enough rice for its population, and the resettlement program ... allowed for strict supervision of the distribution of food and other essentials such as clothes and medicine."[426] Put simply, once the government removed Chinese residents from their squats, they became dependent on the government for all forms of sustenance. If the police or civil administration determined that a particular community was feeding the insurgency, its supply routes could easily be cut and the village punished with food denial. This same rationale applied to collective fines, and by February 27, three villages had suffered collective fines levied against them. Briggs did not want such fines to become the norm, however, but rather the exception in his execution of emergency measures: "[Collective fines] are only justifiable so far as they are balanced by constructive and progressive measures to assist the people who show signs of willingness to co-operate in the restoration of law and order. They are only the exceptions and emphasise by contrast the rewards which are available for co-operating with Government policy."[427]

The prime minister remained worried about the implementation of these measures. On February 26, he called a cabinet meeting to express his concern that "the Briggs Plan seem[s] to be progressing only very slowly." Slim could not deny that progress was slow, but again reminded Attlee that the government's main task "was not the purely military problem of killing bandits in the jungle; it [is] rather to re-establish law and order in the squatter districts and the settled areas and to break up the organisation which [is] sustaining the bandits, and this was a matter for the civilian authorities and the police."[428] Despite Slim's assurance, Attlee was losing his patience. He called cabinet meetings again on March 8 and 12 to discuss what he believed to be unacceptable progress in Malaya. At the latter meeting, General Sir John Harding, commander in chief Far East Land Forces, acknowledged the cabinet's "disappointment" at the "slow progress of the Briggs Plan," but suggested that "there was perhaps some misconception about the original intent of the Plan." He explained that Briggs had "spread a framework of security forces all over Malaya, which could contain the bandits and their supporters and prevent them from becoming even more troublesome." At its heart, though, the Briggs Plan was never about troop numbers and movement, and the progress of military operations was "closely tied up with that of the resettlement programme, the establishment of police posts and the improvement of communications," all of which took time. Briggs was not simply directing a military campaign. Rather, he and Gurney were effecting a social and ideological transformation. To be successful, they needed—and deserved—the government's full support.[429]

Such support was not immediately forthcoming. On March 19—just one week after the cabinet met—Gurney wrote to Sir Thomas Lloyd, permanent undersecretary of state at the colonial office, offering his resignation. In his letter, he remarked, "When officers are invited by Ministers to criticise my conduct of affairs, for which I am responsible, it seems right that I should be informed as to what takes place. From the fact of such consultations and from the absence of any information from London about them, I must be forgiven if I feel that there is in certain quarters a lack of confidence in myself." He also pointed to the fact that he had been "reluctant to take this on and only did so when pressed on grounds of public duty (as in Palestine). These grounds clearly no longer apply, and my reluctance to continue under present conditions is strengthened by the inability of my wife to join me here for reasons of health." Finally, he wrote: "The short fact is that when a man is entrusted with the job of finishing off Communist banditry in Malaya and appears unable to do it, there are bound to be demands that somebody else should be brought in. ... I hope therefore that the advocates of that course may be told that I shall be glad to facilitate their wishes and shall remain silent. I desire no further appointment."[430] After discussing Gurney's letter with Griffiths, Lloyd rejected his offer of resignation, sending a short but encouraging reply that assured him that he had the full support of the cabinet. He also related the colonial secretary's wishes that his work would "receive its due reward in an ever increasing measure of success in the anti-banditry campaign and in a realisation of the Briggs plan."[431]

His resignation refused, Gurney pressed on. In April he launched a vigorous propaganda campaign, during which the RAF dropped countless millions of leaflets into the jungle. Consisting of at least 474 different pamphlets by the summer of 1951, these leaflets had a variety of audiences. One leaflet, for example, showed a gruesome picture of a killed communist insurgent. Printed in Chinese, Malay, and Tamil, it was targeted toward the general population with the title "Bandit Murderer Shot Dead." It detailed how on March 7, 1951, guerillas had fired at the villagers of Kepong in Selangor while they were watching a film in a tent. Included among those killed were two 11-year-old Chinese boys and one 6-year-old Chinese boy, in addition to four young girls who were seriously wounded. An auxiliary police member—a Chinese volunteer from the village—had shot and killed the gang leader and consequently received $20,000 Malay as a reward. The leaflet closed by telling its audience: "Early information about the Bandits' movements would have saved the lives of Kepong workers. Early information saves innocent lives. Help to end the Communist Bandits' attack on the peaceful people's livelihood."

Other leaflets were targeted at the insurgents themselves, such as one that was headed with two gruesome pictures of dead insurgents and the title, "Two Bandits Shot (Surrender while you can)." Published in Chinese and Malay, the leaflet read:

Why suffer the horrible fate of these two foolish men? Why not take the opportunity to surrender given to you by the government before it is too late? Why endure unnecessary hardships and starvation; and face death in the jungle, when food and medical attention await you when you surrender? Many of your comrades have surrendered themselves. Those who have voluntarily surrendered have all been well treated. None of them have been sentenced to death for carrying arms. Do not be duped by your bandit leaders. Escape now from their clutches and get the protection of the security forces. Your situation is hopeless. Why die in the jungle? Surrender while you can!!!

Some leaflets were wordier, without pictures, and offered lengthy diatribes against communism, for example:

Communism seeks to destroy Society. Communism in Malaya is a new name for old crimes. Murder, arson, robbery, extortion, all these are carried on disguised under the name of Communism. A few evil men by telling attractive lies, by deceit, by terrorism have persuaded other simple ignorant men to do their evil work for them, so that they themselves may live in safety on the proceeds. Communism is like a rat, afraid to come out into the open. It hides in dark places, in the jungle, behind the iron curtain; it is a poison which evil men can use to capture the minds of ignorant people.

Other leaflets offered practical guidelines about the kinds of information the government sought, listing questions for

162

informers to answer, giving confidential PO boxes to deliver the information to, and promising rewards. Some included cartoons showing communist insurgents robbing farmers, with the words: "Communism means extortion from farmers. Communist-bandits prey on the workers' livelihood. They rob the honest labourers of their hard-earned money and attempt to destroy the industries which provide the people with employment and livelihood. There can be no peace until Communist banditry is ended." Some of these cartoons involved a cartoon strip, usually with three pictures showing Communist atrocities: the before, the attack, and the aftermath. Finally, there were leaflets with simple one-line, bold-print messages, from the very blunt ("Surrender or die") to the slightly more sophisticated ("You will be well treated unless you have committed a serious offense such as murder or some other violent crime").[432]

The government supplemented this leaflet-dropping campaign with the publication of fortnightly newspapers in Malay, Tamil, and Chinese. In all, in 1951, the Information Services Department printed five million weekly periodicals. Some newspapers, such as *New Path News*, had a circulation of 70,000 copies by the end of 1952.[433] The written word was not the only propaganda outlet utilized by the government. The Information Services Department also made great efforts to install radios throughout Malaya, so that government broadcasts could be heard. In 1949, there were only 35,000 listeners' licenses issued, but by 1953 this had grown to 110,800. Likewise, schools with radio receivers rose from 265 in 1949 to 1364 by 1953.[434] Finally, the government used newsreels shown before films in cinemas to reach their audience. In 1946, there were no cinemas in Malaya. By 1952, 155 had been opened. To supplement these, in 1951 the government launched mobile-film units that could travel to people in rural areas. Sixteen such units were immediately formed and by 1954 there were ninety units reaching one million rural residents.[435] The value of this combined propaganda campaign was immediately realized by insurgent leaders. By the end of 1951, the MCP had imposed the death penalty on any of its followers caught "reading or discussing the surrender leaflets dropped in the jungle by the RAF."[436]

Despite such efforts, officials in Whitehall and Westminster remained skeptical about the rate of progress in Malaya. On April 28, after more than 500,000 propaganda leaflets had been dropped and more than half of all squatters in priority areas had been resettled, Emmanuel Shinwell wrote to Attlee, providing him a copy of the Far East Land Forces Situation Report No. 142. This, he said, demonstrated that "the position in Malaya so far from improving is getting worse."[437] Shinwell met directly with the prime minister on May 2 to discuss his concerns. After this meeting, he informed Field Marshal Slim that Attlee had offered him no new information to assuage his fears and that the situation was "still very disturbing. We seem to be making little, if any, progress in the campaign against the bandits."[438] Slim agreed that "the situation in Malaya is still far from satisfactory." He nevertheless maintained that "we must be careful not to judge the position solely on the weekly returns of incidents and casualties." On the contrary, Slim had "always found in similar operations a better test of progress or otherwise is the freedom with which information comes in from local inhabitants. By this criterion we *are* making slow but real progress." He reminded Shinwell that "The real enemy are not the bandits in the jungle but the Min Yuen in the towns who finance, supply and direct them. It is against this side of the Communist organisation that the greatest efforts should be directed and the most lasting results achieved. This is a matter for intelligence, CID and the police and is largely a civil responsibility."[439] Unlike Viscount Montgomery, Slim was determined to offer his full support to the civil administration on the ground and would trust their judgment.

Shinwell took Slim's words to heart. On May 21, he wrote again to the prime minister, laying out the new conclusions he had reached based on consultations with Slim, the colonial secretary, and the war secretary. He repeated Slim's advice about the receipt of information being the ultimate indicator of progress, and stated that there was "general agreement that in the past month there has been a slight improvement in the overall situation." He noted that resettlement was now "complete in the main priority area and nearing completion in the remaining priority areas and there is evidence that the operation is seriously hampering the Communists." Finally, he related that "reorganization of the C.I.D. and Special Branch of the Police has been in progress for some months and the latest information indicates that the Police Intelligence Organization is better geared to cope with the increasing supply of information. A large proportion of contacts between the security forces and the bandits is now directly due to information supplied by the civil population."[440] There was only one conclusion that Attlee could reach from Shinwell's findings. The Briggs Plan—almost a year after its implementation—was working.

This conclusion was confirmed by Briggs and Gurney themselves in a "combined appreciation of the emergency situation" submitted to the cabinet Malaya committee on June 4, 1951. They began by stating that "There is a definite feeling among local Army, Police and Administrative officers, to which we subscribe, that the cumulative effects of our measures are bringing us, or have brought us, to the turning point of the campaign." Public opinion was "feeling more confident and secure," the flow of information was "increasing daily," and 240,000 people had been resettled. In general, although it could not "yet be said that the Chinese are no longer 'sitting on the fence,'" the government's strategy of "committing them to our side by getting them to join our Home Guard organisation, which they are doing in very great numbers, is bearing good fruit." In the past three months, insurgent surrenders had increased by 180 percent and insurgent casualties by 42 percent, compared with a security force casualty increase of less than 12 percent. Such security forces deaths that did occur (142 in these three months) were worth the sacrifice, as civilian deaths had been reduced by 3.5 percent and civilian injuries by 33.3 percent.[441] The strategy of separating the insurgents from the civilian population and thus drawing fire onto the security forces was working. The British were finally winning the battle for the minds of the Chinese and Malay peoples. In June 1951, it did indeed seem like a turning point had been reached in the Malayan emergency.

X. The end of the Attlee years

Just after lunch on Saturday, October 6, 1951, Sir Henry Gurney, along with his wife and private secretary, climbed into his government-issued Rolls-Royce and departed for the hill station at Fraser's Hill. Although just sixty-five miles north of Kuala Lumpur, Fraser's Hill was far cooler due to its elevation and Gurney was in desperate need of a short holiday following what had been his busiest summer in Malaya yet. As the convoy proceeded on its journey, the military escort encountered engine trouble and was forced to stop. The military commander advised Gurney to wait for reinforcements but the high commissioner insisted on pressing ahead with only a single Land Rover in tow, six Malayan policemen sitting in its open back. As the car entered a two-hundred yard S-bend at one of its narrowest points, a communist guerilla force of thirty-eight men opened fire with a burst from a machine gun. The chauffeur of the Rolls-Royce was instantly hit, as were five of the six Malay policemen, and both vehicles ground to a halt as the bullets slashed their tires. Gurney pushed his wife and private secretary into the footwell of the car and then, in an act of suicidal bravery, opened the door and stepped out. Hoping to draw the fire away from his wife, he began walking directly toward the ambush site at jungle's edge. His ploy worked and the guerillas turned their sights from the car to him. As bullets rained down upon him, he crumpled into the grass verge. The communist insurgents then withdrew. His wife and private secretary gingerly lifted their heads to confirm what they already knew to be true in their hearts. Sir Henry Gurney, the architect of British policy in Malaya, was dead.[442]

James Griffiths, the colonial secretary, received word of his death shortly after the assassination had occurred in a chillingly worded telegram.[443] Gurney's death was just one more piece of bad news to confront the Labour government that autumn. In Korea, the war was going from bad to worse. It had started well enough, with the Americans, British, and other allies stopping the North Korean advance before pushing north themselves, eventually crossing the 38th Parallel on October 7, 1950. On October 19, the American 1st Cavalry Division captured Pyongyang, the North Korean capital, and most presumed the war would soon be over. The government of the newly formed People's Republic of China decided to make good on its October 2 promise to aid the North Korean war effort, however, and the first Chinese troops clashed with American forces on November 1. By the end of November, the Chinese forces had retaken Pyongyang and pushed the UN forces back across the 38th Parallel, forcing American President Harry S. Truman to declare a national emergency on December 16.[444] The Chinese and North Korean armies continued their southward push, capturing Seoul before year's end and reaching Chipyong-ni by January 31, 1951.[445] In this retreat, British forces fought tenaciously but unsuccessfully, with the Ulster Rifles losing 157 killed or imprisoned on the night of January 3/4 alone.[446]

This Chinese advantage did not last long. In the face of a brutal winter, where tens of thousands of Chinese died—many of whom literally froze to death—the communist armies retreated north of the 38th Parallel again, ceding Seoul back to UN forces in March. On April 18, 1951, the North Koreans and Chinese renewed their offensive, however. It was during this offensive that the Battle of the Imjin River occurred, lasting from April 22 to 25, a battle that came to epitomize British efforts on the Korean peninsula. Taking up position on the western flank of the main UN armies, the British 29th Independent Infantry Brigade was tasked with protecting a twelve-mile stretch along the Imjin River with its four battalions. One of these battalions—the 1st Battalion, the Gloucestershire Regiment

(1 Glosters)—was separated from the remaining three battalions by the Kumak-san hill. When the Chinese forces attacked on April 22, the communications and supply routes between 1 Glosters and the rest of the brigade were cut, as was the Glosters' line of retreat. For three nights, the Glosters doggedly fought while heavily outnumbered, until finally surrounded and captured. In all, during the battle, the 29th Brigade lost 1091 men, half of whom came from 1 Glosters.[447] The Glosters had done all and more than could be asked of them, but they were simply outnumbered and without resupply.

Watching from London, Aneurin Bevan, the minister of health, voiced grave reservations about Britain's military strategy in Korea. In a cabinet meeting, the previous August, he had told his colleagues, "Our foreign policy [has] hitherto been based on the view that the best method of defence against Russian imperialism [is] to improve the social and economic conditions of the countries now threatened by Communist encroachment. The United States government seem[s] now to be abandoning this social and political defence in favour of a military defence." Bevan believed that "this change of policy was misjudged and that we should be ill-advised to follow it."[448] Bevan, however, was overruled in the cabinet and British involvement in Korea continued for another three years, with British soldiers facing what was largely a stalemated situation. In October 1951—when Gurney was assassinated in Malaya—the British were in the midst of this quagmire.

Yet Korea was not the government's only concern. In the winter of 1950–1951, economic crisis once again reared its ugly head as the nation faced coal shortages to rival those of 1947. On January 1, 1951, the government issued advice to "Use Less Coal." Seeing that this was impractical in the middle of a cold snap, Attlee amended this after only a week to instead encourage the miners to work a little harder. Conservative opinion, already appalled by the Labour government's programs of nationalization, was aghast at this debacle. As the Conservative MP Sir Cuthbert Headlam commented on January 7, "What a sorry mess 'the planners' have made of things."[449] In an opinion poll of voting intention taken at the end of that month, the Conservative Party led by 13 percent.[450] In February, the government faced another challenge, as the National Union of Railwaymen, together with the train drivers union, threatened a strike if they did not immediately receive a 7.5 percent pay increase. This was an increase the government simply could not afford, and the British Railways executives offered a compromise figure of 5 percent. When this was rejected, the government caved, granting the 7.5 percent raise at a cost to British Railways of £12 million.[451] It was a decision that did little to renew the nation's confidence in Labour's ability to steer Britain through its economic woes, and one which only furthered the budget crisis facing the government.

Sensing its moment, in March 1951, the Conservative Party launched a political strategy that was best articulated by Robert Boothby, the member of parliament for East Aberdeenshire, who stated in a speech on March 13: "We shall harry the life out of them. … We shall make them sit up day and night, and grind away until they get absolutely hysterical, and say 'We can't stand it any more.'"[452] The Conservatives did this by using an archaic parliamentary practice of moving prayers to annul statutory orders, resulting in the House of Commons sitting until the early hours of the morning and, on occasion, for so long that the speaker of the House was forced to cancel the next day's business.[453] The exertions of such governance took their toll on the Labour Party. In October 1950, Stafford Cripps had been forced to resign as chancellor of the exchequer under doctor's orders. On March 10, 1951, Ernest Bevin was likewise forced to leave his job as foreign secretary due to his deteriorating health, instead moving to the less arduous position of lord privy seal. At Easter time, Attlee himself was forced into hospital for several weeks for treatment of a duodenal ulcer.[454] In his memoirs, Attlee commented: "We had a number of Members whose health was not too good, so that our nominal majority was seldom reached."[455] The cabinet was literally growing too ill to govern.

While Attlee was in hospital, the new chancellor of the exchequer, Hugh Gaitskell, presented his first budget to the Commons. Within it—facing increased defense costs both in Korea and Malaya—he suggested that National Health Service (NHS) patients pay for half the cost of their dentures and spectacles. Aneurin Bevan, the new minister of labour who had been minister of health during the founding of the NHS and who was a fervent opponent of the Korean War, immediately resigned from the cabinet in protest. He was joined in his resignation by Harold Wilson, president of the board of trade, and John Freeman, parliamentary secretary at the ministry of supply. Four days later, Ernest Bevin—so central a part of Labour's cabinet throughout its six years in power—died.[456] His death was a "great shock" to the prime minister, who considered him "a most dear friend and loyal comrade."[457] To fill these lost positions, Attlee was forced to turn to the second tier of a party that had already lost its shine in the eyes of the voting public.[458] Sensing that the support of the nation was slipping away, the prime minister began to consider an October general election in the hopes of shoring up his parliamentary numbers. In June, Hugh Dalton—who although only minister of local government and planning still held the ear of the prime minister—argued that as many as four Liberal MPs might cross the floor to join the Labour Party in the event of a general election, thus increasing their majority. This was enough to convince Attlee of the rightness of this course of action and at the Labour Party's annual conference in September he announced that the general election would be held on October 25.[459]

The Labour Party that went to the polls that October was one much diminished from its soaring heights in the late 1940s. Attlee was battling recurrent illnesses; Ernest Bevin was dead; Arthur Creech Jones had been ousted at the previous election; and both Hugh Dalton and Stafford Cripps had been forced out of the Treasury. Sir Henry Gurney was also now dead and Malaya was left leaderless at a crucial stage of its fight against communism. Yet in both domestic and colonial affairs, the party had much to be proud of, from the founding of the NHS to the successful grant of self-government to the Indian people. On balance, Malaya too could be considered a success, albeit in a qualified way. With the clear thinking of both Creech Jones and Gurney and the operational expertise of Briggs, the government had pioneered a new imperial strategy for those colonies embroiled in uprisings and insurgencies. Predicated on the inherently political nature of such conflicts, this strategy hinged on the notion of separating the greater part of colonial society from those involved in the insurgency. For the former, the government would provide health care, education, and other forms of social welfare to ensure that British influence remained in the region and to preempt the temptation of turning to the Soviet Union for aid. Against the insurgents, the security forces would pursue a ruthless military campaign, in which guerillas would be baited by the police force and then destroyed by the army and air force. Once the insurgency was defeated, the British government could devolve power to indigenous leaders, moving toward an independent and self-governing polity under the umbrella of the Commonwealth. By October 1951, there were convincing signs that this strategy was beginning to work.

Although the electorate had been trending away from the Labour Party since its narrow victory in February 1950, there was therefore no reason for its members to be overly pessimistic on entering the campaign. They believed they could simply stand on their record in office. However, unlike the electoral campaigns of 1945 and 1950, the campaign of 1951 was characterized not by polite political discourse and rational debate but by intense partisan rancor. Although each party launched its manifesto in a spirit of moderation, in the closing days of the campaign, Labour's Herbert Morrison, joined by Shinwell, Aneurin Bevan, and Strachey, began to paint Churchill as a warmonger who would deploy British troops to Iran and Egypt. Churchill snapped back that it was a "cruel and ungrateful accusation." From that moment forward, the temperature in the campaign increased dramatically.[460]

When polling day finally arrived on October 25, 1951, 82.6 percent of the voting public turned out to have their say. The Labour Party won the largest number of votes of any political party in British history (almost 14 million), but due to the 1950 redistricting of parliamentary constituencies it lost the election, seeing twenty-one of its constituencies fall to the Conservative Party and ending up with 295 seats to the Conservatives 321.[461] When it became clear in the early evening of October 26 that his government had lost power, Attlee travelled to Buckingham Palace to offer his resignation as prime minister. King George VI immediately invited Churchill to the palace and asked him to form the next government.[462] Six years and three months after the British public had so ingloriously voted their great war leader out of office, Winston Churchill was British prime minister once again.

Plate 1 The explosion of a second bomb at the King David Hotel in Jerusalem, Palestine, 22 July 1946. © Imperial War Museum.

Plate 2 Damage done by terrorist bombs to a police station in Jaffa, Palestine, 1946. © Imperial War Museum.

Plate 3 A derailed mail train in Johore, Malaya, c. 1950. © Imperial War Museum.

Plate 4 A New Village in Malaya, c. 1952. © Imperial War Museum.

Plate 5 Members of the Malayan Home Guard receiving hand grenade training, c. 1950. © Imperial War Museum.

Plate 6 A Dyak tracker being instructed in Malaya, c. 1949. © Imperial War Museum.

Plate 7 A suspected Mau Mau insurgent being taken for interrogation, 1955.
© Imperial War Museum.

Plate 8 Sir Evelyn Baring inspecting the King's African Rifles in Kenya, 1957.
© Imperial War Museum.

Plate 9 A British Army lorry burnt out by EOKA in Cyprus, 1955.
© Imperial War Museum.

Plate 10 The British Army on patrol in the Western Aden Protectorate, July 1955. © Imperial War Museum.

2

The Churchill Years

October 26, 1951, to April 7, 1955

I. A new government, a new approach

Winston Churchill rose slowly from the green leather benches
of the House of Commons to place his hands lightly on the dispatch box. It was more than six years since he last stood in the
chamber as prime minister and now he faced a distinctly different crowd. Rather than a national coalition government with
Clement Attlee sitting at his right hand as deputy prime minister and Socialists as well as Liberals and Conservatives placed
solidly behind him, he stared across the aisle at a hostile and
partisan Labour Party, many of whom had never served under
him or with him through the shared experience of World War.
They were thus more concerned with what Churchill believed to
be cheap party tricks than with the national interest. More than
anything else, this new parliamentary intake demonstrated that
the political landscape of postwar Britain had changed forever.

Churchill, in his tumultuous parliamentary career, had weath-
ered such storms before. Born the son of the acclaimed par-
liamentarian Lord Randolph Churchill in 1874, Winston first
entered Parliament in 1900 as a member of the Conservative
Party. Although just twenty-six years of age when elected, he
had already served with the 4th Hussars in India, with Spanish
forces in their guerilla war against rebels in Cuba in 1895, with
Sir Bindon Blood's punitive expedition against rebel Pathan
tribesmen in the Swat Valley on the Afghan frontier in 1897,

and in the fateful Battle of Omdurman in the Sudan in 1898, and had been held in and then escaped from a Boer prison in South Africa in 1899. He had also published an 85,000-word book on the Malakand field force in 1898, a 250,000-word, two-volume opus on the reconquest of Sudan in 1899, and his first novel in 1900.

Upon entering Parliament, Churchill initially gravitated toward the so-called Hughligan faction of the Conservative Party under Lord Hugh Cecil, but in 1904 he switched to the Liberal Party in disgust at the Tories' adoption of protectionism over free trade. As a Liberal, Churchill prospered politically. In 1906, he served under Sir Henry Campbell-Bannerman as undersecretary of state for the colonies, and in 1908 Asquith brought Churchill into the cabinet as president of the Board of Trade at the age of thirty-one. He was promoted home secretary in 1910 and first lord of the Admiralty in 1911, a position he held during the first months of the First World War. Following the failed Dardanelles campaign in 1915, he was demoted from the Admiralty to the chancellor of the Duchy of Lancaster, a position he immediately resigned, choosing instead to command a battalion of the Royal Scots Fusiliers on the western front. He was recalled by Lloyd George in 1916 to become minister of munitions, and from 1918 to 1920 served as secretary of state for war and air. In 1921, he was transferred to the colonial office, but lost his parliamentary seat in 1922, thus turning to work on his five-volume history of the First World War.

Churchill was reelected to the Commons in 1924, at which point he was persuaded to return to the Conservative Party as chancellor of the exchequer under Stanley Baldwin. Following the fall of Baldwin's government in 1929, Churchill became somewhat of a recluse within his party, remaining in the political wilderness as an outspoken and lonely critic of appeasement until the outbreak of the Second World War in 1939. At this time he was brought back into the cabinet as first lord of the Admiralty. Following Chamberlain's resignation in May 1940, Churchill reached the pinnacle of his parliamentary career as wartime prime minister of a national coalition government, holding this position until the breakdown of the coalition and the defeat of the Conservative Party in July 1945. He remained leader of the Conservative opposition throughout Attlee's years in power until the election of October 1951 when he was duly asked by King George VI to form a new Conservative government. Already seventy-seven years old and the sufferer of two strokes, Churchill willingly accepted this charge, confident that he could restore Britain to its former greatness and overcome the increasingly bitter tone that had entered the House of Commons.[1]

Now, confronted in the chamber by the cynical stares of a recently defeated party, Churchill attempted magnanimity. "A hard task lies before His Majesty's Government and grave responsibilities weigh upon the new Parliament," his deep voice projected to the House. "The nation is deeply and painfully divided, and the opposing forces are more or less evenly balanced. ... We meet together here with an apparent gulf between us as great as I have known in fifty years of House of Commons life." Offering a hand of reconciliation to the Labour Party, he suggested that the nation needed "several years of quiet, steady administration, if only to allow Socialist legislation to reach its full fruition." Although he believed it was "indispensable to the general welfare" of the nation to repeal the nationalization of the iron and steel industry, other aspects of the British welfare state pioneered by Attlee would be left intact. The main priority of the new government would be to overcome a deficit crisis worse than the one experienced in 1947; it would not be to once again remake the British economy. Turning to foreign affairs, Churchill uttered a final word of caution: "The realities which confront us are numerous, adverse and stubborn." He believed they could be overcome, but implored the House to "move forward together in our united fight as faithful servants of our common country, and as unwearying guardians of the peace and freedom of the world."[2]

The men tasked with implementing this foreign policy were Anthony Eden (the foreign secretary), Oliver Lyttelton (the colonial secretary), and Churchill himself (who in addition to being prime minister had also taken the job of minister of defense). Of these, it was Lyttelton, a close friend of Churchill's since their service together in the First World War, who had the surest hold on the prime minister's ear. In many ways, Lyttelton was perfectly suited to be colonial secretary at this moment in British history. He confessed in his memoirs that "high political office" was "only attractive to me in war or times of crisis,"[3] and the colonial office was facing these in spades in 1951, above all in Malaya, where Gurney was dead just twenty-two days when Lyttelton was appointed on October 28. Upon arriving at the colonial office, he was met by James Griffiths, the outgoing secretary, who presented Malaya as the government's most pressing dilemma, admitted that the Labour Party had been "baffled" by the territory, and lamented that "At this stage it has become a military problem to which we have not been able to find the answer."[4] Given the recent progress made by Gurney and Briggs, this seemed a somewhat incongruous remark for Griffiths to make.

Nevertheless, Lyttelton took his words to heart and spent the first two days in his office reading and talking with officials about the conflict in Malaya, a situation made worse by the September 1 retirement of Sir William Jenkin, the Malayan director of intelligence, and the announcement that Briggs would be retiring due to ill health on November 6 to be replaced by General Sir Robert Lockhart (a retirement date that was subsequently delayed until November 27).[5] With the loss of both Gurney and Briggs, all continuity of government and strategy was broken in Malaya, and the colonial secretary feared that the government was "on the way to losing control of the country."[6] On October 30—six days before Churchill spoke to the House of Commons—Lyttelton sent a memorandum to the prime minister, noting that the "Malayan problem" was the colonial office's "first priority." Due to the gravity of the situation, he felt he should personally visit Malaya "as soon as possible" so that he might "see and judge for myself."[7] Together with his parliamentary private secretary Hugh Fraser, his private secretary Angus MacKintosh, and his undersecretary of Far East affairs Sir John Paskin, Lyttelton flew from Heathrow on November 26, almost a month to the day after he had become colonial secretary and the day before Briggs officially retired.[8]

Before he could depart, Lyttelton had much to do in London, though. First and foremost, he had to articulate to the nation the new Conservative government's vision of the empire and Commonwealth. From Lyttelton's perspective, Labour's colonial policy had been muddled, vacillating between quick and short-sighted withdrawal from India on the one hand and continued engagement in Africa and the Far East on the other, from a failed and half-hearted counterinsurgency campaign in Palestine to increased involvement in Malaya. The Labour government, Lyttelton believed, had stumbled from one crisis to another without any "overall strategic concept" to guide statesmen, soldiers, and civil servants alike. Without such a "master plan," he doubted whether success in any individual colony or territory was possible. As October passed into November, Lyttelton formulated a simple goal, which he articulated to the government in cabinet, to his fellow parliamentarians in the Commons, and to the civil servants working in the colonial office: "First, we all aim at helping the Colonial Territories to attain self-government within the British Commonwealth. To that end we are seeking as rapidly as possible to build up in each territory the institutions which its circumstances require. Second, we are all determined to pursue the economic and social development of the Colonial Territories so that it keeps pace with their political development."[9] While not noticeably different from the policy articulated by Creech Jones in 1948, Lyttelton felt Labour's actions had more often than not shown an irresponsible disregard for steady devolution of power, preferring to cut colonies loose with little transition period. He believed the policy he had articulated was now the "only practical course" for the British government to follow.[10]

With this philosophy in mind, Lyttelton received his first telegram from the Malayan government on November 1. It informed him that Briggs had submitted a proposal for "full executive authority" to be devolved from the high commissioner to the director of operations "in all emergency matters falling within the sphere of the federal government." The rationale behind this move was that it would "put the director in direct chain of command on emergency (repeat emergency) matters in substitution for chief secretary and [would] give him policy control over the police force as a whole in addition to limited control for operational purposes only, which he now exercises."[11] Lyttelton immediately granted this request and within an hour the Malayan government sent him a second telegram confirming that "Full executive authority in all emergency matters falling within the sphere of the federal government has been delegated to the director ... He will consequently be responsible for deciding all important questions of policy relating to [the] emergency, including those matters which fall within the sphere of the defence branch, such as police, home guard, and civil defence."[12] Unlike his predecessors Griffiths and Creech Jones, Lyttelton would defer to the proverbial man on the spot when reaching his decisions, and would do so without hesitation or delay.

It was not only Briggs who wished to see a consolidation of power in the emergency hierarchy. On November 5, less than a week after Lyttelton transferred power from the chief secretary to the director of operations, Malcolm MacDonald—still commissioner-general of British territories in Southeast Asia—sent a telegram to Sir Thomas Lloyd, permanent undersecretary of state at the colonial office, to discuss the possibility of appointing a soldier to fill the vacated high commissioner's spot following Gurney's assassination. This question had previously been raised with MacDonald in conversation and although open to the idea in principle, he was concerned that a soldier would be unlikely to "understand adequately the need to continue Gurney's political and social policy."[13] Nevertheless, if a soldier with the requisite political and social understanding could be found, he might be just what Malaya needed, particularly as the war office was refusing even to contemplate the withdrawal of any British troops from the territory before the end of 1952. MacDonald would certainly not reject outright the idea of appointing a soldier.[14]

Having listened carefully to advice on Malaya from all angles, Lyttelton drafted his first memorandum for the cabinet on November 20. His priorities, he suggested, were sixfold. First, he needed to "reassure the planters and miners of our determination and ability to support them by all means in our power, and to bring the anti-Communist campaign to a successful conclusion"; second, he sought to "secure the active co-operation of the Chinese, if necessary by a more forceful policy towards those who fail to 'come off the fence'"; third, he needed to "settle disagreements between the military and police authorities," possibly by replacing Gray as police commissioner; fourth, he hoped to "improve the organisation and training of the police force"; fifth, he needed to find a replacement for Sir Henry Gurney as high commissioner; and finally, the "division of responsibilities between the various authorities" needed to be improved.[15]

He attached to his memorandum three annexes. The first was a telegram dated November 15 giving the conclusions of the British defence coordination committee (Far East), which noted that "The crux of the problem is winning the confidence and loyalty of the bulk of the Chinese population to an extent that they are willing to join with us actively in the fight against Communist terrorism." It suggested the best way to do this was by making the Chinese "feel safe from internal Communist pressure and external Chinese attack," which could only be accomplished by improving police efficiency and introducing a Chinese contingent to the Malayan police force.[16] The second annex, an undated memorandum from the colonial office, also stressed the importance of winning the support of the Chinese population, noting that their help was "essential not only to bring the campaign to a more rapid conclusion but also to avoid serious communal disorders which would place a further and grievous strain on the British forces." The memo concluded that "if the emergency were to end without the active co-operation of the Chinese, the hope of building a single Malayan people might never be realised."[17] The final annex listed the fighting forces currently engaged in Malaya as seven British infantry battalions, eight Gurkha battalions, three colonial battalions, two Royal Armoured Corps regiments, four battalions of the Malay Regiment (with a fifth being raised), four squadrons of the Malayan Scouts (Special Air Service, SAS), ten RAF squadrons (comprising 114 aircraft), two Royal Australian Air Force squadrons (fourteen aircraft), a Royal Naval contingent of one frigate, six minesweepers, and two motor launches, and Malay police forces consisting of 23,000 regular constables and officers, 38,000 special constables, and 175,000 part-time auxiliary and Home Guard constables.[18] The government certainly had the forces to wage a military campaign in Malaya, but without the support and cooperation of the Chinese population it would all be for naught.

The cabinet gathered to discuss Lyttelton's memorandum and its annexes on November 22. At this meeting, the colonial secretary floated an idea that he had not yet made public: to concentrate the powers of both the high commissioner and the director of operations into a single supremo. With the death of Gurney and the imminent department of Briggs, now was the time to make such a change. He suggested that he would not ask for a vote in cabinet until he had seen "the conditions on the spot," but believed this might be the way forward for an effective and efficient counterinsurgency campaign. Field Marshal Sir William Slim, the chief of the imperial general staff, agreed, stating that he would favor "more radical measures" for a unified civil and military command.[19] With such encouragement, Lyttelton boarded his plane in Heathrow on November 26, touching down in Singapore on the morning of November 29. He did not return to London until December 21. His task, as he saw it, was to conduct "an intensive study of the whole situation, political, military and para-military, police, administrative, legal."[20] It was unlike anything undertaken by a colonial secretary in British history, both in its depth of study and in the secretary's duration in a single territory examining just one problem.

On the day Lyttelton left England, Sir Robert Lockhart—the new director of operations in Malaya—composed his first report on the situation. His analysis did not differ greatly from Briggs, although there were some noteworthy elements that demanded fresh attention. Focusing more on what he termed the "racial problem" than Briggs ever had, Lockhart wrote, "Whilst the problem of creating a united Malayan nation is obviously a political matter and so perhaps without my province, there is no doubt that the main division of the population between Malays and Chinese closely affects the Emergency." He could "offer no solution to the problem of securing the active support of the Chinese population," but believed that the government should make a concerted effort to do so "by intensive propaganda, by people who are prepared to show an active and friendly interest in the Chinese; by assuring the Chinese of a real stake in the future of Malaya; and by stern and rapid retribution (such as deportation, sequestration of land, detention of the families of men who are known or suspected to be bandits, and so forth) against those who refuse to cooperate with Government." Even with such measures, Lockhart questioned "whether this is enough."[21]

When the colonial secretary arrived on the morning of November 29, he quickly came to share Lockhart's concerns. Indeed, Lyttelton was dismayed by what he found, believing the situation to be "far worse than I had imagined."[22] Following deputations from Malays, Chinese, Tamils, Indians, Britons, and Europeans; meetings with the commissioner of police, the head of the special branch, and the army commander in chief; site visits to Pahang, Perak, Kelantan, and Johore; interviews with members of the Malayan civil service; conversations with soldiers, airmen, and police constables; and observation of security force patrols leaving their base areas, Lyttelton determined what needed to be done. He immediately sought the resignation of the chief secretary, the police commissioner, and the head of the special branch, all of whom reluctantly agreed to go, giving him a clean slate to work with.[23] Then, on December 8, he sent his initial recommendations to Churchill. He proposed the appointment of a single individual to be called "the High Commissioner and Director of Operations," who would "assume entire responsibility for both military operations and civil administration." This position would be supported by a deputy director of operations and a deputy high commissioner, the former specializing in military matters, the latter in political. He recommended that Lockhart be retained as deputy director of operations and Sir Donald MacGillivray, currently serving as colonial secretary in Jamaica, be appointed deputy high commissioner. He promised a full report upon his return to the United Kingdom.[24]

Lyttelton did not dither when he arrived back in London and circulated his memorandum—together with fifteen appendixes—to the cabinet before day's end on December 21. Providing perhaps the fullest governmental examination of the situation since the emergency's beginning in 1948, Lyttelton's report and recommendations made fascinating reading for his colleagues. Summing up the situation in a single sentence, he wrote: "You cannot win the war without the help of the population, and the Chinese population in particular, and you cannot get the support of the population without at least beginning to win the war." For this reason, his primary recommendation was that the government "organise a much heavier and more concentrated impact upon the enemy and key up the machine at once." To achieve this, he repeated his recommendation for the appointment of a single high commissioner and director of operations, under whom a deputy high commissioner and a deputy director of operations would serve. The system of SWECs and DWECs established by Briggs should be kept in place, but the Federal War Council (chaired by the director of operations) and the Federal Executive Council (chaired by the high commissioner) should be merged, with a war cabinet existing within the Executive Council and the War Council ceasing to survive. In Lyttelton's view, there had to be complete integration of the civil and military elements of the conflict, with each controlled by a single authority figure.

Turning next to the police, Lyttelton noted that "The Emergency is in essence a Police rather than a military task." This was problematic because "the Police is in utter disorder and even the Regular Force is inefficient." He was convinced that the firing of the police commissioner would go a long way in combating this problem. The Home Guard was having greater success but it—like the police—was overwhelmingly Malay, and it was not the Malay population that the British had to win over. For this reason, Lyttelton suggested the establishment of a Chinese Home Guard, which could be used as a first step in the recruitment of Chinese members into the wider security force community. Equally important were the ideological aspects of the conflict. In this area there was nothing more central than education. Lyttelton therefore recommended the establishment of compulsory primary education in Malaya, at the cost of £2,140,000 per annum. This was not a purely altruistic venture, however. As Lyttelton explained:

> Children coming back from school convert their parents to our way of thinking ... and provide some answer to the [communist] propaganda being whispered to them from the jungle. ... [A] most important feature of primary education is to bring the races together while they are children and to teach them a common language. ... In the long-term war of ideas, which we must win if we are to see a peaceful country and one which can some day be entrusted with self-government within the British Commonwealth, it is obvious that education and the impartial administration of the law must take first place.

In summing up his conclusions, Lyttelton argued that "the objective of one day building a united Malayan nation within the British Commonwealth and Empire should not be abandoned." With the "ever-increasing communications of our century," it was "impossible to hold any other policy than the creation of new Dominions, self-Governing but part of the Commonwealth owing allegiance to the Crown." The circumstances of the twentieth century demanded such: "Fifty million islanders shorn of so much of their economic power can no longer by themselves expect to hold dominion over palm and pine on the nineteenth century model of power and paternalism which made us the greatest nation in the world. We may regain our pinnacle of fame and power by the pursuit of this new policy." This required patience, though. If the government rushed the transition to self-government, it would "condemn the whole country to confusion, and almost certainly to civil war." The government had to "adopt the old saw of one of the wisest political peoples of their day: *'Festina lente'* [Make Haste Slowly]".[25] The cabinet met seven days later, on December 28, to discuss Lyttelton's report. It expressed "general support for the Colonial Secretary's approach to the problems of restoring order in Malaya."[26] Lyttelton had been given the green light for his plans.

In expectation of this cabinet approval, the colonial secretary lunched with Churchill at Chequers on December 23, together with Field Marshal Montgomery, who at that time was serving as deputy supreme allied commander of Europe. The press wrongly inferred from this gathering that Montgomery was to be selected the new high commissioner and director of operations, but as Lyttelton explained in his memoirs, the guests at the meeting were dictated by a simple oversight on Churchill's part—he had invited Lyttelton to lunch without remembering that he had already invited Montgomery.[27] At this meeting, Lyttelton summarized his report for the prime minister and repeated his recommendation that a single man be placed in charge of the emergency. Once this change was accomplished, and once the Chinese population was engaged, "the improvement would be at an increasing rate."[28] Churchill pledged his support to Lyttelton's position without providing further feedback.

Montgomery, as always, felt obliged to contribute more, and on December 27, he laid out in a letter to Lyttelton his thoughts on Malaya and Southeast Asia as a whole. He began by stating that he was "disturbed about the whole situation in our Colonial Empire," which he believed had "drifted down hill since the war, chiefly because of two useless Secretaries of State for the Colonies: Creech-Jones and Griffiths." He supported Lyttelton's plan to replace both Gurney and Briggs with a single individual, but held that this was only the first necessary step on the road to creating a "Master Plan for South-East Asia." In particular, Montgomery believed that the "contrast between the East and West, between Communism and Democracy, between evil and Christianity, is approaching its climax." Stalin, he claimed, had Asia as his main objective for the expansion of communism. If the southeastern portion of the continent were to fall, "the West will be in grave danger." He recommended that the entire area, including Malaya, Singapore, Burma, Hong Kong, and Indochina, be placed under the responsibility of a single high commissioner, with a single commander in chief placed over all fighting forces in that region. Malaya would be only one part of this much larger jigsaw puzzle.[29]

Lyttelton duly noted Montgomery's opinion but kept his focus on Malaya. Of foremost importance was selecting the man who would serve as high commissioner and director of operations. Although Lockhart had done well in his three-month tenure in the latter position, he was not considered suitable for the higher profile job of high commissioner.[30] Lyttelton's initial thoughts turned to General Sir Brian Robertson, the commander in chief, Middle East Land Forces, but Robertson refused. Having spent twenty-eight of the past thirty-one years overseas, he was ready to return to the United Kingdom and settle down. Lyttelton therefore invited Lord Portal, Lieutenant General G. C. Bourne, Lieutenant General Sir Robert Scobie, and General Sir Gerald Templer for short interviews. He spent an hour with each of the first three and three hours with the last, after which he was convinced that Templer was the man for the job. Fifty-three years old and currently general officer commanding Eastern Command, Templer had previously served as vice-chief of the imperial general staff under Montgomery and as director of military intelligence before that. Having made up his mind, Lyttelton sent a telegram to Churchill on January 4, 1952, asking that Templer be appointed.[31] Churchill received this request on board the *Queen Mary*, which had docked in New York, ahead of talks first with American president Harry Truman and next with Lord Alexander, the governor-general of Canada. Churchill immediately requested that Templer fly to Ottawa on January 10 for discussions in person. This he did, meeting with the prime minister for two hours on the eleventh.[32]

Churchill was as impressed with Templer as Lyttelton had been and indicated there and then that he intended to recommend his appointment to the king, a mere formality. To all intents and purposes, Templer's job was to begin immediately, even before the royal assent was given.[33] Churchill also asked that the general prepare for him a note outlining how he perceived the new position. This Templer provided him the following day. He stated that he was clear about what must happen from a "purely military point of view" but was "not at all clear" what the political objectives were. For that reason, he requested that he be given a directive from the government laying down in plain terms Britain's purpose in Malaya. Templer felt that this should "state plainly that the British are not going to be kicked out of Malaya; and that there is still a great future for the British in that country."[34] The colonial office began at once to compose such a document, consulting with officials from the war office, the prime minister's office, and with Templer himself over several drafts. The final draft was completed and approved by Lyttelton on January 31, 1952, and by Churchill on February 1. Following agreement by the cabinet, it was sent to Templer on February 4. With the text in hand, he boarded a plane for

Malaya, arriving on February 7 as the new high commissioner and director of operations.[35]

Lockhart, sensing that change was in the air, sent to Field Marshal Slim an assessment of the emergency on January 14. He wrote: "My opinion is that this campaign is something different from anything we've been faced with before; although there are obvious similarities to Palestine, and perhaps to Ireland, and even India in 1947. Theoretically the fighting services are 'in aid to the civil power'. Actually I should say this campaign is a combined operation of the civil authorities, the fighting services (mainly the army) and the Police, who are in effect another fighting service." He then graciously offered to remain in Malaya with a demotion to deputy director of operations, serving under whoever was appointed to replace him as full director.[36] Following the announcement of Templer's selection and confirmation that he would retain Lockhart as his deputy, Lochart wrote to his new boss on January 27 giving him his best advice: "I feel that leadership is not nearly personal enough. Civil servants should be assembled periodically and spoken to en masse. I have arranged for Secretaries of Departments to attend [the] monthly (this is too seldom and shows the tempo which Government thinks sufficient) briefing of the Federal War Council so that they are at least somewhat in the picture. I strongly recommend that when you have had time to take stock you should assemble all civil servants in Kuala Lumpur and address them." He closed his letter saying, "I have I think given you enough to chew on for the time being. The sad part of the whole thing is that while the number of problems remains vast none of them are new: they have been frequently raised and debated for at least two years."[37]

With Lockhart's advice on his mind, Templer arrived in Malaya on February 7, 1952. The day before, King George VI had passed away and his daughter, Elizabeth, was proclaimed Queen Elizabeth II. The directive Templer read out at his official installation ceremony was therefore one of the first to carry the new sovereign's name. Its message could not have been clearer. "The policy of Her Majesty's Government in the United Kingdom," it declared, "is that Malaya should in due course become a fully self-governing nation. Her Majesty's Government confidently hope that that nation will be within the British Commonwealth." It stated that Templer's primary duty was to "guide the peoples of Malaya towards the attainment of these objectives and to promote such political progress of the country as will, without prejudicing the campaign against the terrorists, further our democratic aims in Malaya." It noted that "Communist terrorism is retarding the political advancement and economic development of the country and the welfare of its peoples." Templer's main task, therefore, was "the restoration of law and order, so that this barrier to progress may be removed. Without victory and the state of law and order which it alone can bring, there can be no freedom from fear, which is the first human liberty." Finally, the directive proclaimed that "Her Majesty's Government will not lay aside their responsibilities in Malaya until they are satisfied that Communist terrorism has been defeated and that the partnership of all communities, which alone can lead to true and stable self-government, has been firmly established."[38]

Following delivery of this declaration, Templer distributed to those present and to communities throughout Malaya a leaflet containing the declaration, together with a special "Message to the People of the Federation of Malaya." It stated:

I have not come here with any ready-made, clear-cut solution to Malaya's present problems. That is not possible. The solution lies not in the hands of any one man, nor alone in the hands of the government of the United Kingdom. It is in the hands of all of us, the peoples of Malaya and the governments which serve them. I have the assurance of all possible help from His [sic] Majesty's Government in the United Kingdom. I demand the same from all the peoples of Malaya and in particular from the younger men and women of every race with whom the responsibilities of the future must largely rest.[39]

From the moment his plane touched the ground, Templer made it abundantly clear that unlike in Palestine, the British in Malaya would not tuck tail and run. Both he and Lyttelton were convinced of this, if nothing else.

II. The carrot and the stick

On the night of March 24, 1952, communist guerillas cut the water pipeline between Tanjong Malim—a rubber-tapping town fifty-one miles north of Kuala Lumpur—and its reservoir. Such sabotage was not unusual for the spring of 1952 in Malaya. What did make it stand out was the fact that the pipeline had already been cut five times since the start of the year and in the vicinity of the town seven civilians, eight policemen, and seven soldiers had been killed. Determined not to allow the guerillas to disturb normal town life, Assistant District Officer Michael Codnor, just thirty-two years old, assembled a party of fifteen policemen, the executive engineer of public works in the area, and the necessary repair technicians. The twenty-one men set out early on the morning of March 25 and reached the sabotaged spot by 7:00 a.m. As they approached the pipeline to examine the extent of the damage, a carefully planned communist ambush opened fire on them. Codnor, the engineer, seven policemen, and three repairmen were shot dead, eight policemen were wounded, and only one repairman escaped unharmed. Following the attack, the guerillas stripped the dead and dying of their weaponry before melting back into the jungle.[40]

General Sir Gerald Templer had been in the country almost eight weeks when he heard the news from Tanjong Malim. In those eight weeks, he had begun to put his own stamp of authority on the emergency situation, bringing to it a personality quite different from Gurney's and Briggs' before him.

On February 9, two days after arriving in Malaya, Templer gathered together all division one officers and left them with no doubt that he would not tolerate any incompetence, inefficiency, or cowardly behavior, telling them that if mistakes were made, he would "do something very rude to the individual concerned" and that "If someone below me fails to take action because he has not got the guts to take it, then I will take far more serious action against him."[41] One civil servant who was present commented that Templer "[gave] us a jolly good rousing pep talk. No words were minced. We were told to get off our bottoms and get cracking, but not make any mistakes, and if we all pulled together we could deal with the situation."[42] Following this pep talk, Templer pursued a hands-on leadership style, completing 45 two- to three-day tours of new villages, mines, estates, and security force units in his first twelve months alone, and 122 such tours in the twenty-eight months he served as high commissioner and director of operations.[43]

At the heart of Templer's approach was his belief that the counterinsurgency campaign would not be won by defeating the guerillas militarily, but rather by demonstrating the superiority of Western over communist ideology. As he himself put it shortly after arriving in the colony, "The answer lies not in pouring more troops into the jungle, but in the hearts and minds of the people."[44] He expanded this sentiment in a statement to the Malaya Federal Legislative Council on March 19, arguing that the job of both civil and military authorities in Malaya was to persuade those in the country "that there is another and far preferable way of life and system of beliefs than that expressed in the rule of force and the law of the jungle. This way of life is not the American way of life. It is not the British way of life. It must be the Malayan way of life."[45]

Such an approach necessarily required a determined effort not to marginalize the civilian population in Malaya. Consequently, Templer was convinced that policing action must hold a higher prominence than army operations, a conclusion Gurney had reached before his death. This viewpoint was also shared by the colonial office in London and was laid out in detail by Hugh Fraser, Lyttelton's parliamentary private secretary, just days after Templer was appointed high commissioner but prior to his arriving in Malaya. In a report presented to the colonial secretary—and copied to Templer—on January 16, Fraser wrote:

> Assuming all goes well with [police] reorganisation one can envisage an overall picture of the regular police doing police work, the Home Guard being responsible for resettlement areas, the gendarmerie for local patrolling, at the risk of abandoning some static guards, and of the Army proper being sometimes deployed to platoon formation based on police stations and sometimes concentrated into large formations to cooperate with the deeper jungle penetration of the [Police] Jungle Co[mpan]ys and Malay Scouts.[46]

Significantly, in Fraser's vision, the army was to play a supporting role to the police force, not the other way around. Joining Templer in implementing this vision was the newly appointed commissioner of police, the forty-four-year-old Arthur Young, who had been commissioner of the City of London Police when Lyttelton asked him to go to Malaya.[47] Similar to Templer in outlook and energy, Young accompanied the general on many of his tours around the country and "not only exuded confidence but also managed to inspire everyone around him with that confidence."[48]

The police force, of course, was only as good as the intelligence it was able to collect and act upon, and in this regard the security forces in Malaya were performing dismally. On January 31, Templer met with the cabinet Malaya committee, informing them that after spending the previous two weeks meeting with various officials in London, he had come to the conclusion that "there was an urgent need for the various intelligence agencies in the Federation to be coordinated." He believed this could best be done by appointing a single director of intelligence who would exercise general authority over all intelligence collection in the territory through the chairmanship of an all-encompassing intelligence committee. This man, Templer thought, should be a civilian, as he was "anxious not to introduce more Service officers."[49] Upon arriving in Malaya, Templer's suspicions about the lack of intelligence coordination were confirmed. For this reason, on February 13 he sent a telegram to Lyttelton requesting that MI5's Dick White be appointed director of intelligence, a position that "would have the right of direct access at any moment to [the] High Commissioner."[50] White, however, hoped to succeed Sir Percy Sillitoe as director-general of MI5 and thus refused. Templer therefore turned to another MI5 officer, Jack Morton, who gladly accepted the job, anxious to join Templer and Young at the top of the security force hierarchy.[51]

On the same day Templer invited White to join him as director of intelligence, he also circulated to the deputy high commissioner, the deputy director of operations, the army's GOC in Malaya, the permanent secretary of defense, and the commissioner of police a memorandum specifically addressing the topic of intelligence. Writing that "It is obvious that the first priority in the solving of the problem today is the collection, collation, evaluation and presentation of intelligence," Templer suggested that "the really important parts of all the various intelligence agencies must be grouped together physically." He recommended that "there should be an inner keep, so to speak, in the present Police Headquarters," where "certain portions of the Intelligence set-up at Headquarters Malaya District," the "sharp end" of the Special Branch, the "sharp end" of the deputy director of operations headquarters, and the intelligence elements of the secretary of defense's office would be grouped together. This would mean that "the Deputy Director of Operations, the Secretary of Defence, the Commissioner of Police, and the Director of Intelligence will all be sitting alongside each other, beside the Police Operations Rooms and beside all the really important Police intelligence agencies."[52] Templer hoped this setup would provide flawless integration of all intelligence and security efforts in Malaya. He would no longer allow any excuse for a failure to communicate or share information.

In addition to a more focused intelligence establishment, Templer also felt there was greater scope for special forces operations led by the Malayan Scouts (SAS), as he indicated to the cabinet committee in his January 31 meeting with them.[53] The Malayan Scouts had come a long way since their initial formation under Mike Calvert in the summer of 1950. By 1952, the regiment was composed of four squadrons (three British, one Rhodesian), totaling 26 British and 6 Rhodesian officers, and 322 British and 68 Rhodesian other ranks. An army report from December 22, 1951, noted that the regiment was operating in "deep jungle areas not already covered by other Security Forces." As a result, it was "becoming a 'Corps d'Elite' in deep jungle operations."[54] Templer was determined to see this success continue. So convinced of the unit's greater utility to the army was the high commissioner that his first order changed its name from Malayan Scouts (SAS) to 22 Regiment, SAS (22 SAS). By removing the "Malayan" designation, he hoped to indicate to the war office that the operations currently undertaken by the SAS in Malaya could be performed elsewhere. In doing so, he saved the regiment from potential disbandment at the close of the emergency, providing it with a permanent role in the regular army.[55]

Templer also sought to use the SAS more aggressively. Up until 1952, individual SAS troops (16 men) had carried out limited operations to find and destroy insurgent camps and supply routes, with little coordination between troops or squadrons. In February 1952—in his first operational order—Templer authorized a three-squadron offensive to break the communist base area. The plan was for C and D squadrons to march in across the mountainous jungle while B squadron parachuted into the rice paddies. C and D squadrons set out early in February, prior to Templer arriving in country. B Squadron dropped onto the selected target area on February 9, two days after Templer was officially installed. The operation, code-named Helsby, was a disaster. C and D squadrons encountered swollen rivers throughout their march, which significantly delayed their progress, and all but four of B Squadron missed their drop zone, landing instead in the tree canopies. The regiment engaged some communist guerillas but did not find the base area it had hoped. Within a week, the SAS decided to cut its losses and withdraw.[56] Despite this failure, it demonstrated to all in Malaya that Templer would not shy from risky operations in pursuit of a successful completion to the emergency, and it set the tone for operations to come.

Beyond increasing the quality and efficiency of intelligence-gathering and supporting special forces operations, Templer's most pressing need was to reorganize the administration in Malaya, which he believed to be wasteful of resources and in general cumbersome. He had hinted at these proposed changes prior to leaving the United Kingdom, but in a telegram to Lyttelton on February 28—three weeks to the day after arriving in Kuala Lumpur—he documented his reorganization. Beginning on March 1, 1952, the Federal War Council and Federal Executive Council would be merged into a single Executive Council. Complementing this council would be a director of operations committee with Templer in the chair, meeting at least three times a week with the deputy director of operations, the chief secretary, the secretary of defense, the director of intelligence, the army general officer commanding, the air officer commanding, and the commissioner of police. This committee would "undertake direction of all those controls and activities which are necessitated solely on account of the emergency, and which would not form part of the functions of the government in normal times." The larger Executive Council would no longer have any say in such matters. The SWECs and DWECs would remain in place but would report directly to the director of operations committee rather than the council. Taken as a whole, Templer's reorganization streamlined the management of the emergency, separating it from the normal functions of government and placing all power and responsibility for the emergency in the hands of a select few at the top of a rigidly hierarchical structure.[57]

It was shortly after this autocratic system was put into place that the communist attack at Tanjong Malim occurred on March 25, providing Templer with his first real test as high commissioner and director of operations. After considering his options, Templer traveled personally to Tanjong Malim on March 28. He immediately ordered 350 village leaders to gather in the hall of the Sultan Idris Training College. Once there, he spoke quickly with an unrestrained "savage anger." Recorded verbatim by a number of sources and translated into Malay, Chinese, and Tamil, Templer said: "It doesn't amuse me to punish innocent people, but many of you are not innocent. You have information which you are too cowardly to give. You are all aware of the savage outrage that took place here forty-eight hours ago. It could only have taken place with the knowledge of certain of the local inhabitants. Of that I am certain." He then announced that he would be imposing a collective punishment for "the crime of silence." There would be a 22-hour-a-day curfew enacted on the town, with its residents only able to leave their homes between 12 noon and 2:00 p.m. Even then, no villagers would be allowed to leave the town. Schools and places of employment would be closed and all public transportation would be stopped. Furthermore, the rice ration for the town would be halved.

Templer did not wish to be entirely punitive, however. He also arranged for a questionnaire to be delivered to every head of house in the village, requesting information about the insurgency. Every questionnaire had to be returned, whether or not it contained information, and Templer promised confidentiality. After three days, British army soldiers—not Malays or Chinese—collected the first batch of questionnaires in a sealed box. They then brought with them six community leaders from the town to King's House. In their presence, Templer opened the boxes, read the questionnaires, took notes, and then destroyed the questionnaires. Once all questionnaires had been read and destroyed, the leaders were permitted to return to Tanjong Malim, with the instructions from Templer, "Go back and tell them how their letters were brought straight to me." Templer then sent out a second batch of questionnaires to the town, with the same guarantee of confidentiality, and again had them collected under the watchful eyes of community leaders three days later. Such was the intelligence contained in these documents that on April 9—less than two weeks after the collective punishment had been imposed—the police were able to descend on Tanjong Malim and make thirty-eight arrests. Later that day, Templer lifted the curfew and removed all other restrictions. There were no more guerilla attacks in the Tanjong Malim area that year, and having removed the threat of communist intimidation, within a few months more than 3500 residents of the village volunteered for the Home Guard. Tanjong Malim remained one of the more peaceful villages for the remainder of the emergency.[58]

Buoyed by this success, Templer continued to use the tactic of collective punishment. In addition to the curfews and rice ration reductions, he also imposed collective fines on communities said to be supporting the enemy. On one occasion, at Permantang Tinggi in August 1952, he even sent all sixty-two residents to detention camps and destroyed their village after they refused to provide any information.[59] Yet alongside this coercion, Templer continued to offer an opportunity for redemption. In particular, he was determined to expand Gurney and Briggs' resettlement program, making it a permanent structure for social betterment. Immediately after becoming high commissioner and director of operations, he announced that resettlement areas would henceforth be known as "New Villages," the provision of services would be referred to as "development" rather than "after-care," and a new senior post would be created, the New Village Liaison Officer, whose responsibility it would be to coordinate all activities in the new villages.[60]

In explaining the rationale for these changes, Templer wrote to a United Nations select committee, relating that by the end of March 1952—a month after he had arrived in the country—423,000 men, women, and children had been resettled into 410 new villages. Nevertheless, a great deal of work remained to develop these villages into "well balanced and useful communities." In particular, the government held to the principle that "long-term titles to land should be given to the villagers in appropriate cases." It was also committed to giving three acres per family to those entirely dependent on agriculture for their livelihoods, to providing elected local councils "wherever the villagers are ready for them," and for developing schools, medical facilities, and community centers.[61] Templer put his money where his mouth was in implementing this policy, providing new village schools with $1400 (Malay dollars) for the construction of each classroom, $1500 for each teacher's quarters, and a grant of $10 per pupil for books and supplies. By the end of 1952, close to 250 new villages had such schools, and by 1954, the government was able to claim that "no New Village with a population of more than 400 was beyond easy walking distance of a school."[62]

Even so, in the spring of 1952, the government's focus was as much on security as social rebuilding, a point Templer made clear in his General Circular No. 5, issued on March 31, 1952:

1. Our primary task in Malaya is the restoration of law and order, so that barriers may be removed.

2. It is our duty to guide the peoples of Malaya towards the objective of a united Malayan nation.

3. It is our duty to promote such political progress in the country as will, without prejudice to the campaign against the terrorists, further our proper democratic aims.

4. It is our duty to ensure that these ideals do not involve the sacrifice by any community of its traditions and culture and customs.

5. It is our duty to encourage and assist the Malays to play a full part in the economic life of the country, so that the present uneven economic balance may be redressed.[63]

While collective punishments and rewards for cooperation might encourage the population to cease their support of communist insurgents, they did not target the guerillas themselves. The restoration of law and order and the elimination of the insurgency had to be the first priority.

The army's GOC in Malaya, Major General R. E. Urquhart (of Arnhem fame), could not agree more. On April 7, one week after Templer issued his circular, Urquhart wrote to Templer, telling him, "As you know I feel desperately strongly that the easiest and quickest way of increasing our successes against the bandits is to increase the ratio of kills per contact."[64] Templer gave Urquhart great leeway to do so. Yet the high commissioner also decided to supplement his conventional military patrols and policing operations with a more scientific approach, combining the chemical destruction of roadside vegetation with a concerted campaign of food denial to the insurgents, including the obliteration of their crops. Although food control operations had been in effect since June 1951, it was not until January 14, 1952—three days after Churchill asked Templer to take up his position—that food destruction was first contemplated.[65] This occurred when London-based civil servants and military staff met to discuss what they called "the chemical defoliation of roadside jungle." The military representative, Colonel Yeldham, contacted Imperial Chemical Industries (ICI) and discovered that they had available 1500 tons of sodium trichloroacetate at £350 a ton (£450,000 total). C. B. Synes of the colonial office suggested that instead of using the RAF, the government could employ Auger aircraft operated by commercial pilots who were trained to spray chemicals, although noted that spray rigs for such aircraft would be available only by February or March. The six men present unanimously agreed to place a purchase order both for the chemicals and for the spray rigs, and to inform the Malay government that they had done so.[66]

When the chemicals arrived in Malaya in March, they proved so successful at clearing roadside vegetation that Templer authorized their use against insurgent food crops also. Before the Auger pilots could implement such spraying, however, rumors of the impending defoliation reached the British press, which without exception reported with negative connotation that the "Royal Air Force" was seeking to "poison" terrorist food supplies. The colonial office rushed to limit the damage of these stories, playing on semantics to claim that the Royal Air Force had no intention of spraying chemicals (it was, after all, a private firm that was conducting the spraying) and that the government would not "poison" the terrorists (they were instead causing crops to "wither"). A confidential memorandum sent from Templer to Lyttelton suggested that it was "desirable to play down the story" and that any references to ICI should be censored from news columns lest the company's equipment "engaged in these experiments" become a terrorist target.[67] Consequently, on April 9 the colonial office released the following statement:

> No poisonous chemicals have been sprayed from R.A.F. planes on terrorist food crops, nor has any such action even been contemplated. Experiments are, however, being carried out in connection with non-toxic forms of weed-killer, both for the destruction of undergrowth and other vegetation which afford terrorist cover and for the destruction of terrorist food crops, whether by ground forces or from the air. These chemical weed-killers are not dangerous to animals.[68]

There was nothing in the statement that was an outright lie, for the RAF had indeed played no part in the scheme, yet the words were nevertheless meant to deceive, suggesting perhaps that in Templer's battle for hearts and minds, the truth could on occasion become a liability.

Despite Templer's denials, opposition to the program continued to gain traction in the British press, forcing the RAF to release its own statement admitting the use of chemical defoliation but denying poison. Explaining that the chemicals in question were "Hormone killers," the statement noted:

> In a greatly over-simplified form, Hormone plant killers work like this. Hormones are complex organic substances, now made artificially, whose proportions in any form of life regulate orderly and normal growth. By isolating the Hormones peculiar to vegetation and embodying them in a spraying solution which can easily be absorbed by plants, it is possible to give the plants an overdose of their essential growth substances. This overdose sends the plant's whole mechanism crazy, and distorts its growth so that it becomes useless for human consumption, although in no way poisonous.[69]

The statement failed to note that the sodium trichloroacetate purchased from ICI, which lay at the heart of the controversy, was not a hormone plant killer. Although the RAF had indeed employed hormone plant killers, their use was a completely separate issue from the experiments with sodium tricholoroacetate. As with the colonial office statement, the RAF's was true but deliberately misleading.

The issue reached Parliament on April 23, when Labour MP William Field asked the minister of state for colonial affairs, Alan Lennox-Boyd, when he would stop "the mass destruction of village crops which is being used as a punishment in Malaya." Having received the question several days in advance (as was standard parliamentary practice), Lyttelton sought Templer's advice, which the general gave on April 21. He told the secretary that there was "no question" of crop destruction being used as a punishment "in the sense of their use to law abiding persons who might otherwise enjoy them." However, crop destruction had taken place under two circumstances: first, when villagers had been moved for resettlement to "safer places," where crops that were left "would have benefited no-one but the bandits"; and second, where crops in the jungle had been cultivated "solely for the bandits either by themselves or by aborigines intimidated into working for them." As such planting on uncultivated land was "illegal by the ordinary law of the land," it was a criminal matter and therefore the destruction could in no way be construed as "mass destruction of village crops" or as "collective punishment."[70]

Using the advice Templer gave to Lyttelton, Lennox-Boyd informed the House of Commons that "Village crops in Malaya are not destroyed as a punishment. It is sometimes necessary to destroy crops which have been grown by terrorists or might fall into their hands." Thomas Driberg, another Labour MP, asked if this reply did not mean that "the method now used to get two-thirds of the people of Malaya on our side is the method of starving villagers, women and children?" Lennox-Boyd simply replied: "It appears to the Government and to the High Commissioner in Malaya, in whom we have entire and growing confidence, that a measure of this kind may well help to bring the present intolerable war in Malaya to a speedier end. We believe that these experiments, which, we hope, will be successful, may play a major part in helping to bring this calamitous war to a conclusion."[71]

It was not only for his food destruction operations that Templer was beginning to come under parliamentary scrutiny, but also for his policy of collective punishments in general, which William Field labeled "contrary to the principles of British justice and calculated to make more recruits to Communism than the reverse."[72] On April 30, Labour MP Stanley Awbery raised with Lyttelton the matter of the collective punishment against Tanjong Malim, asking if he was aware that "this form of collective punishment is very repugnant to right-thinking people and that this method is causing hostility against the Government among the people of Malaya?" Before Lyttelton could reply, Emmanuel Shinwell—the former minister of defense—jumped in: "While it is undesirable to cause embarrassment to General Templer, who has been appointed to undertake this difficult task, will the right honorable Gentleman [Lyttelton] not agree that it is desirable, on the other hand, that

General Templer should proceed with the utmost caution in enforcing collective punishment, which may not be at all efficacious?" Shinwell was supported by Sydney Silverman, another Labour MP, who asked, "Is the right honourable Gentleman aware that repressive measures on a collective scale of this kind have always had the effect, not of reducing resistance to them, but of increasing it? Is he also aware that there is no war crime in history that has not been justified by the doctrine of giving unquestioning, blind support to the commander in the field?" Lyttelton gave his response curtly: "I can accept neither suggestion of the honourable Member. I am afraid each is founded on ignorance of the circumstances."[73]

The colonial secretary's retort was not mere political grandstanding. In the weeks leading up to the parliamentary question, he had given much thought to Templer's use of collective punishment. Besides receiving in-depth reports on the events in Tanjong Malim, Lyttelton had also received reports on a collective punishment in Selangor, spelling out in detail the rationale for such action. His attention had first been drawn to the incident on April 10, when Templer issued a press release announcing that sanctions had been imposed on the 4000 people living in the old and new villages of Sungei Pelek for "continually supplying food to Communist terrorists and because they did not give information to the authorities." The sanctions included all free rice, with the exception of a two weeks' supply, being removed from the villages and sold, with the money raised given to its owners; the rice ration for the area being halved for a period of two weeks; three of the five grocery shops being permanently closed; a perimeter curfew being imposed from 2:00 p.m. to 10 a.m., and a house curfew from 6:00 p.m. to 6:00 a.m.; and the entire area being surrounded with a chain-link fence 22 yards beyond the existing barbed wire fence.[74] Templer issued a second statement on April 22 confirming that each of these measures had been enacted and were ongoing.[75]

Somewhat concerned by these measures, Lyttelton requested further information from Templer. On April 25, the high commissioner explained that Sungei Pelek was known to have "harboured bandits from the early days of the emergency." Since May 30, 1951, thirty-two incidents had occurred (eighteen since January 1, 1952), including murder, attempted murder, and armed robbery. The government had established a new village in 1951, but on April 5, 1952, the police received information that residents of this village were supplying food to the insurgents. Consequently, on April 6, Templer dispatched a section of Royal Marine Commandos to patrol the perimeter. That night, they came into contact with an insurgent party, suffering one casualty. The following day, one of the insurgents surrendered to the police and, in exchange for clemency, offered to lead the security forces to the area's main insurgent base. The deal was struck and on April 9 the surrendered man led a troop of commandos to the camp where a firefight broke out, causing the serious wounding of a Royal Marine sergeant. Due to the resistance offered and the surrendered insurgent's statement, which "showed that there were inhabitants of Sungei Pelek who were consorting with armed bandits and were helping them with supplies," Templer felt compelled to impose the measures he did. He pointed out to Lyttelton, however, that "no collective punishment in the sense of collective fine" had been issued, and that the action taken "was preventive (i.e. to prevent food supplies reaching terrorists) and not punitive." Under the circumstances, Templer believed this was perfectly reasonable.[76] Lyttelton apparently agreed, hence his somewhat brusque reply to Silverman in Parliament five days later.

In any case, the food denial operations were only one part of Templer's strategy. On April 30—the same day his methods came under question in Parliament—Templer announced that the government had "decided to increase the amounts of rewards offered for bringing in alive or for information leading to the capture or to the killing of the leading members of the Malayan Communist Party who are directing the armed terrorist activities in Malaya." These rewards were classified on an eleven-point scale, ranging from 1A to 3C. At the top end of the scale, 1A was for the secretary of the communist central executive committee. A reward of $250,000 (Malay) would be provided to any person who brought him in alive or provided information leading to his capture and $125,000 would be provided for information leading to his death. At the bottom end of the scale, 3C was for any general Malayan Communist Party member. It provided $2500 for information leading to his capture alive, or $2000 for information leading to his killing.[77] Laying out in chilling precision the price of a man's head, the government nevertheless provided a monetary incentive for capture rather than death.

Meanwhile, the government's experiments with sodium trichloroacetate continued. The Institute for Medical Research in Kuala Lumpur issued a report in early May titled "Precautions to be Taken During the Handling of Sodium Trichloroacetate [*sic*] (S.T.C.A.)". It noted that the substance was "caustic and, either in the solid form or as a strong solution, may cause burns if it comes in contact with the skin. It also appears to corrode metal surfaces, such as iron shovels, containers, etc." The report did note that "the strength of the solution actually used for spraying is about 3 per cent. I have tested a 10 per cent solution on my arm and this did not appear to have any harmful effect on the skin." Nevertheless, it also cautioned that "it would seem undesirable for anyone to expose himself, unnecessarily, to the spray. For instance, it would seem to be advisable to keep the windows of the driving cab of the 'spraying lorry' tightly closed during the actual spraying operation." Furthermore:

> While, generally speaking, weak solutions of STCA may not have any harmful effect on the skin, it is possible that some individuals may be more sensitive than others. ... [I]rritation of the skin and the formation of a painful rash may occur generally if the dilute solution is allowed to dry out on the skin. In every case, therefore, where this solution has come in contact with the skin, it will be washed off with plenty of clear water as soon as possible after contact. The weak solution must on no account be allowed to dry off on the

skin surface. Goggles will also be worn at all times during spraying operations.[78]

It was this solution that the government intended to drop on insurgent food crops from Auger airplanes flying at low level.

Templer was determined not only to use the stick, though. On May 10, he launched Operation Question, an initiative he himself designed, which was intended to "enable the public to give information about terrorist activities with complete security." The operation began with a house curfew imposed from 5:00 p.m. on May 10 (a Saturday) through noon on May 11 (a Sunday) in the villages of Broga in Selangor, Terap in South Kedah, Triang in Central Pahang, Cha'ha in Central Johore, and Layang Layang in South Johore. Government information officers with loudspeakers stressed in the local languages that "this was not a punishment but only a method used for asking them to give information concerning Communist terrorist activities in their area." Boxes were given to each household, as had happened in Tanjong Malim, where information could be placed. British soldiers in the presence of village representatives picked up the boxes at the end of the curfew and took them directly to Templer, where they were read, noted, and destroyed in the presence of the representatives. Templer then announced that once the insurgency in those areas was destroyed with the help of the information provided, "the money now being spent in beating the terrorists would be used on building more schools, hospitals, roads and many other works for their benefit."[79] The British government would invest in Malaya one way or the other. Templer provided the choice to the villagers whether that investment would be spent on security force operations or the betterment of their villages and communities. If villagers would cooperate with the government and security forces, they would reap the benefits. This he made crystal clear.

Behind the scenes, Templer sought to make good on the promises he had issued to the Malay people. He wrote to Field Marshal Sir William Slim on May 15, lamenting that he needed eighty-two doctors but had only sixty-one, giving a deficiency of 25%. Furthermore, since January 1, 1952, nineteen of these doctors (30%) had been "admitted to hospital on account of strain and overwork. Of these, four have been admitted twice and two of them have died." If Templer was to truly win the hearts and minds of those in Malaya, he needed also to be able to care for the bodies of those who were protecting and governing them, and at present he was desperately short-staffed.[80] Slim immediately sent a note to his military assistant, Lieutenant Colonel C. H. P. Harrington, asking him, "What can be done about this? These Far East countries should have some priority in doctors, don't you think?"[81] Harrington agreed, and on May 26 sent a letter to Ernest Hall, the Deputy Director-General of the Army Medical Service (DGAMS), forwarding Slim's concerns.[82] Hall replied on the twenty-eighth, explaining that he was aware of the problem and that he had instructed reinforcements to be sent to the headquarters of Far East Land Forces in Singapore, where they could be directed to Malaya.[83] Slim wrote to Templer, reassuring him that "The D.G.A.M.S. is very alive to the problems confronting the medical service in Malaya and gives priority to it over other theatres in the provision of medical personnel. ... There is, as you are aware, a serious shortage of medical doctors in the army which is a constant problem. Despite this fact every effort is and will be made to keep the number of doctors in FARELF up to requirements."[84]

Slim's remarks were no doubt encouraging to Templer. It was one less concern for him to worry about. He next turned his attention to the propaganda campaign, which was central to his theory of counterinsurgency. On May 17, the Executive Council noted that there was "no official designation of the Communist Guerilla Forces and various terms have been in use in English such as 'bandits,' 'terrorists,' etc. Furthermore, in referring to the component units of the Communist Forces, it has been customary to employ the title which they have given themselves for the armed units in the jungle, i.e., the Malayan Races Liberation Army, and the Min Yuen for the supporting organisation."

The council felt that this multitude of different designations was confusing. Furthermore, it believed that by using the terms designated by the insurgents themselves, the government went some way to legitimizing them as an opposing army rather than a criminal menace. For that reason, the council proposed that henceforth "the term 'Communist terrorist' will be the general designation for all members of these organisations, and in the particular context 'Communist Terrorist Army' for the words 'Malayan Races Liberation Army', 'Communist Terrorist Organisation' for the 'Min Yuen.' The designation 'bandit' will not be used in future in official reports and Press releases emanating from the Government."[85] Templer agreed to this revision and on May 20 ordered that the changes take place with immediate effect. From that date forward, all communist insurgents would be referred to as Communist Terrorists (CTs).[86]

Despite the controversy that Templer's approach generated in the press and in Parliament, Lyttelton was impressed. In a speech given at the Corona Club Dinner on June 17, 1952, he remarked, "I feel that very often the best telegram that can be sent from the Colonial Office to those far flung territories ... is 'Make up your own damned mind, and if you do it upon good principles we will support you. If you don't, we shall want to know why.'" He continued with his philosophy of colonial governance:

The modern habit of trying to think for the other man leads to some astonishing results, and most of them are bad. It is unlikely that a member of the Colonial Service will have reached the position of Governor without being aware of some of the simplest facts of life. I deprecate telegrams and despatches to the Colonies which contain this sort of phrase "If the supply of groundnuts should fall and the demand should continue at its present level it may well be that we shall witness even higher prices." This is the sort of fluff that Governors may have been expected to know almost in their infancy. Nor is it in the main the role of the Secretary of State of the Colonial Office to warn Governors about what political results are likely to follow from many of their actions. The truth is that the man on the spot either knows what they are likely to be, or if he does not know them then he is clearly unfit to hold his job and should be removed. [87]

Lyttelton was determined as colonial secretary to trust "the man on the spot" and delegate to him as much responsibility and room for initiative as possible. In the person of General Templer, he was convinced he had found the right man on the spot for Malaya.

III. The challenge of Mau Mau

On May 15, 1952—the same day Templer wrote to Slim requesting more doctors for Malaya and only days after he launched Operation Question—a passerby found two bodies floating in the Kirichwa River in Nyeri, Kenya, tangled in the reeds by its banks. The passerby alerted the police to the incident who, when they removed the bodies, found that they had been shot and mutilated. By the end of June, the passerby had also been murdered along with two police informants, and by early September eighteen others had joined their fate. All had been brutally mutilated following a death by strangling or gunfire. The violent campaign of Mau Mau had begun.[88]

Mau Mau was not a new development in Kenya and its roots could in some ways be traced all the way back to the origins of British involvement in that region of the world. British influence came late to East Africa, at least when compared to Britain's long-standing control of territories such as India, the Caribbean, and even Malaya. Although West Africa had been an important center of British involvement in the Atlantic slave trade since the seventeenth century, with serious attempts to survey the western interior made by British explorers in the 1830s and 1840s, East Africa had traditionally held little interest for the British government, explorers, or private entrepreneurs. Beginning in the 1850s, however, the acclaimed explorer David Livingstone changed British perceptions forever. His expeditions from 1853 to 1856 and 1858 to 1864 caught the attention of the Royal Geographical Society, which undertook its own expeditions from East Africa to Lakes Tanganyika and Victoria from 1857 to 1858, from East Africa to Cairo via Lake Victoria, Bugando, and Bunyoro from 1860 to 1863, and from Cairo to Lake Albert via Khartoum, Lake Victoria, and Bunyoro from 1862 to 1865. The society then turned to Livingstone himself, commissioning the explorer to undertake a special expedition that lasted from 1866 to 1871, culminating in his famous meeting with American journalist Henry Stanley ("Dr Livingstone, I presume?").[89]

It was not long after that the first Briton, Joseph Thomson, penetrated the Maasai-dominated territory of the Kenyan Highlands in 1883, confirming the earlier discovery in 1848 of Mounts Kilimanjaro and Kenya by a German missionary.[90] William Mackinnon chartered the Imperial East Africa Company in 1889[91] and the British government declared a protectorate—the East African Protectorate—upon the company's collapse in 1895.[92] The following year, the government did as it had always done in colonies over the previous half-century: it laid railway tracks to allow access, 582 miles by 1901, stretching from the seaport of Mombasa to Lake Victoria and into Uganda. To assist it in this project, the government encouraged the immigration of more than thirty thousand Indians for labor purposes, as well as select Britons to help settle the land, three thousand of whom had arrived by 1905. Once in country, these Britons established large farming estates where they experienced a quality of life far superior to what they could in Britain, complete with domestic servants, game hunting, and a hedonistic lifestyle centered around the Muthaiga Club in Nairobi.[93]

The tribe first affected by this British expansion was the Nandi, who were outraged at the railway's intrusion upon their traditional grazing grounds in the Nyando Valley. To "punish" these recalcitrants for their insubordination, the protectorate government dispatched five military expeditions between 1895 and 1905, culminating with the Nandi Field Force that finally forced them to the negotiating table. At these negotiations, a British army officer shot dead their tribal leader, following which the Nandi agreed to be confined to a reservation. The government also sent punitive expeditions against the Kager in 1896, the Sakwa, Seme, and Uyoma in 1899, the Vugusu (Kitosh) in 1895, 1907, and 1908, the Kipsigis between 1902 and 1905, the Gusii from 1904 to 1905 and again in 1908, the Elgeyo and Marakwet in 1911, and the Elegyo again in 1919.[94] In each of these cases, the African resisters fought with as much courage as the British did brutality and ultimately the Africans were defeated not by British skill at arms but by technology. They fell under the newly invented Maxim gun.[95]

East Africa's largest tribe, the Kikuyu, presented a different story. While the government still faced raids from the Nandi as late as 1923, the Kikuyu largely submitted to British rule by 1901, with the last expedition against them coming in 1906. For this reason, the tribe as a whole was far less damaged than other East African tribes and was viewed by the British as more amenable to their plans for white settlement.[96] Consequently, it was to Kikuyu lands that both missionaries and settlers flocked, a process that was accelerated following the First World War when the British government encouraged demobilized army officers to resettle in East Africa. Within half a decade, over five hundred of these captains, majors, colonels, and above had arrived on Africa's shores, many establishing estates on lands that once belonged to the Kikuyu.[97] Writing about the state of the East African Protectorate in 1912 (a state not much changed after the war), historian G. H. Mungean gives a fair summation of the effects of British rule on the Kikuyu:

> Around Nairobi, in Kiambu and its environs, the Kikuyu were becoming more and more conscious of European demands. They had lost some of their land; they were going out to work on local European farms; they were travelling to the coast in search of work, and they were being swallowed up

by the growing township of Nairobi. The Kikuyu, more than any other tribe, were beginning to experience what [Sub Commissioner J. D.] Ainsworth and [Assistant Deputy Commissioner C. W.] Hobley had called "the blessings of civilisation". But they were experiencing also, in greater measure, what [Governor Sir Percy] Girouard described as "denationalisation". The old tribal society was beginning to crack under the strains of a new way of life. It was small wonder that, some months after Girouard's resignation [in 1912], a District Officer at Kiambu described the Kikuyu reaction to the new order as "a sulky acquiescence in our rule." Administration might have been established in the Protectorate. It had still to be fully accepted.[98]

Eight years after Girouard's resignation, the East African Protectorate officially became a British colony, renamed Kenya in 1920.[99] By this stage in its development, the territory had become divided by race, with white settlers dominating both land and religion. In 1915, the Crown Land Ordinance recognized "native rights" in land reserved solely for the use of Africans, a policy that inevitably led to the creation of African Reserves in 1926.[100] All Kikuyu men resident on these reserves were required by law to carry a pass when leaving the reserve, detailing their name and address, ethnic group, finger print, employment history, and current employer's signature.[101] This land segregation was accompanied by the establishment of Christian missions and church schools throughout Kenya, which by the 1920s had created "their own literate Christian elite, a small but rapidly growing body of African men and (rather fewer) women, filled with ambition for 'progress and modernity.'"[102] These missionaries and white church leaders encouraged the African Christian elite to become engaged in politics. To facilitate such, they established the Kikuyu Association (KA) in 1921, the purpose of which was to lobby the European representatives who sat on the Kenyan Legislative Council on issues affecting the Kikuyu people.[103]

Later in 1921, a rival organization—not tied to the churches—was also established with the express intent of challenging the KA for leadership of the African people. The East African Association (EAA) sought to do this by more aggressively opposing European governance and settlement, becoming particularly vocal on the issue of working conditions for urban Kikuyu. Sensing the potential threat from this new association, the colonial government attempted to quell any dissent by bringing together African leadership in the Local Native Councils (LNC), which were loosely allied with the KA and were intended to speak with authority for all Africans. In response, Harry Thuku—the leader of the EAA—founded the Kikuyu Central Association (KCA) in 1924. While there was some overlap between the two (several members of the KCA served on the LNC), it was clear that the government viewed the LNC as the spokesperson of African society and the KCA as mere "agitators." By the 1930s, these divisions had cemented within Kenyan society and the Kikuyu population was firmly split into two camps: those who were loyal to the British government, closely associated with the Church missionary societies and schools, and active in the LNC; and those who were radically opposed to European settlement and government, who largely spurned European Christianity, and were represented by the KCA.[104]

One of those involved in the latter organization was a young Johnstone (later Jomo) Kenyatta, who in 1929 traveled to London to represent the KCA directly to the colonial office. With the exception of a brief period from September 1930 to April 1931, Kenyatta remained in London until 1946.[105] When he returned to Kenya after the Second World War, he found a very different colony from that which he left in 1931. Since the arrival of Europeans in Kenya at the turn of the twentieth century, Africans had squatted on newly designated British land, providing the white farmers with a cheap labor source as well as cattle manure for their crops and a means of controlling their vast acreage of land. By the 1910s, the number of squatters far outnumbered the land that could support them and thus the Kikuyu began a vast migration westward into the Rift Valley. With the onset of the economic depression in the early 1930s, squatters began to cultivate more and more European-owned land so that by 1931, 1,850,000 acres of the total 6,847,000 acres of the so-called White Highlands were occupied by squatters. With the prosperity that the Second World War brought, European settlers were in a position to claim back this land. When the war ended, the settlers became resolved to use their newfound wealth to modernize Kenyan agriculture, leading to a determined policy of clearing the squatters from their land. When Kenyatta returned to the colony, the existence of the Kikuyu squatter population was at its most perilous since 1905.[106]

To make matters worse, in 1940 the colonial government proscribed the KCA, removing any legitimate form of address for the discontented elements of the Kikuyu population.[107] When in 1945 the first settler district in the Rift Valley imposed limits on the number of livestock a squatter could hold, there was no means for the Kikuyu to remonstrate.[108] Such limits became more widespread and, in combination with other restrictions, meant that few squatters could feasibly remain on their land. Between 1946 and 1952, at least 100,000 Kikuyu were consequently "repatriated" from the Rift Valley and White Highlands to the Kikuyu Reserves.[109] This new influx into the reserves placed intolerable pressure on those already there, leading to a fresh land crisis that resulted in the peasant uprising in Murang'a in July 1947.[110]

Into this deteriorating situation, Jomo Kenyatta attempted to assert new leadership. In 1944, Kikuyu politicians had formed the Kenya African Union (KAU) to replace the banned KCA. On June 1, 1947—nine months after he returned from Europe—Kenyatta assumed the presidency of the KAU.[111] Yet in many ways he was too late. By 1947, many of those in Kikuyu society who were not loyalists were already beyond the point of constitutional political engagement with the colonial government. In 1943, Kikuyu residents in Olenguruone restored the old Kikuyu tradition of oathing in times of war or other crisis. Rather than administering these oaths just to men (as was traditional practice), those in Olenguruone gave the oath to men, women, and children, pledging to collectively fight what they claimed to be British injustice. By 1945, this oathing had spread beyond Olenguruone. By 1948 it had become a movement known as Mau Mau.[112]

In addition to expanding the oath from men to women and children, Mau Mau also administered the oath at night (in violation of Kikuyu custom), by force (when all previous oaths were voluntary), and in multiple stages or grades. As historian Caroline Elkins has pointed out, because of the secretive nature of the oathing ceremonies it is difficult to paint a complete picture of them.[113] Nevertheless, a British Army document produced in early 1953 details some of their elements. The first oath, in its original 1947 wording, read:

(a) If I ever reveal the secrets of this organisation, may this oath kill me.
(b) If I ever sell or dispose of any Kikuyu land to a foreigner, may this oath kill me.
(c) If I ever fail to follow our great leader, Kenyatta, may this oath kill me.
(d) If I ever inform against any member of this organisation or against any member who steals from the European, may this oath kill me.
(e) If I ever fail to pay the fees of this organisation, may this oath kill me.

In 1950 or 1951, the oath was amended to the following wording:

(a) If I am sent to bring in the head of my enemy and I fail to do so, may this oath kill me.
(b) If I fail to steal anything I can from the European may this oath kill me.
(c) If I know of an enemy to our organisation and I fail to report him to my leader, may this oath kill me.

(d) If I ever receive any money from a European as a bribe for information may this oath kill me.

(e) If I am ever sent by a leader to do something big for the house of Kikuyu, and I refuse, may this oath kill me.

(f) If I refuse to help in driving the Europeans from this country, may this oath kill me.

(g) If I worship any leader but Jomo, may this oath kill me.

In addition to this general oath, a second grade oath was introduced in the late spring of 1952 at the onset of Mau Mau's violent campaign, given to those in leadership positions within the movement. It read:

(a) If I fail to lead the children of Mumbi in a proper manner, may I die.

(b) If I fail to support the Independent School movement, may I die.

(c) If I betray the leaders of the Kenya African Union, may I die.

(d) If I fail to support this organisation until the day of independence, may I die.

(e) I must sacrifice my blood and the blood of the Kikuyu for freedom.

The general and second stage oaths were supplemented by oaths in an additional five stages given to those who were committed to actively fighting British rule in Kenya. These oaths were each accompanied by certain rituals, also detailed in the army document, involving the eating of animal flesh or blood, often the genitalia, and contact between the animal's flesh and the initiate's genitals. Many of the rituals also included elements of sexual intercourse, both with Kikuyu women and with animals. Based on these practices, the army report concluded:

The only possible deduction to be drawn from the details of the bestiality and perversion connected with the ceremonies is the horrible one that we are now faced in Kenya with a terrorist organisation composed not of ordinary humans fighting for a cause but of primitive beasts who have forsaken all moral codes in order to achieve the subjugation of the Kikuyu tribe and the ultimate massacre of the European population of the Colony.[114]

From the beginning, the British believed that the disturbances in Kenya were of a very different nature than those in either Palestine or Malaya, and they would treat them accordingly. An interview given by Oliver Lyttelton in 1970 perhaps best sums up the government's view at the time: "[T]he Labour Party thought that the Mau Mau was primarily due to economic reasons. But it wasn't you know, this is plain African witchcraft."[115] This belief led to a greater level of brutality in the Kenyan emergency than in any of Britain's other dirty wars of the twentieth century, with violent coercion increasingly overshadowing the liberal mission the government claimed to be engaged in.

Mau Mau first began to obey their oaths in 1949, violently intimidating African workers who voluntarily served on British estates and farms. Consequently, in August 1950, the colonial administration declared Mau Mau an illegal organization.[116] Nevertheless, intimidation and oathing continued, and in 1951 members of the Kikuyu tribe who had taken the oath started to destroy farm property. In response, loyalist Kikuyu led protests against Mau Mau, leading to retributive attacks. In January 1952 alone, there were eleven cases of arson on the homes of Kikuyu who stood with the government against Mau Mau. The following month, fifty-eight unexplained grass fires combusted on European estates, and in March the number of attacks against Kikuyu loyalists rose dramatically. When the police attempted to investigate these attacks, they were met with an "impregnable wall of secrecy" and told that "the events had so terrified the local chiefs, headmen and church leaders that they were no longer prepared to cooperate with the government in any way."[117] In an attempt to penetrate this silence, on April 4 the government enacted the Collective Punishments Ordinance, allowing "collective fines to be charged against communities who refused to cooperate with police investigations."[118] The first such fine was levied four days later for £2500.[119] Just one month after this, the two bodies were found in the Kirichwa River, marking the first killings of the Mau Mau campaign.

It was an inconvenient time for the British government to be faced with a colonial revolt in East Africa. Not only was it engaged with the ongoing emergency in Malaya and the Korean War, it was also managing a transition of leadership within Kenya itself. Sir Philip Mitchell had become governor in 1944, following tours as high commissioner in the Western Pacific, governor of Fiji, deputy chairman of the East African Governors' Conference, governor of Uganda, and chief secretary in Tanganyika. It was Mitchell who oversaw the clampdown on squatters and the vast migration of the Kikuyu population into the reserves. Despite this movement, based on his experiences in Fiji—where Polynesians, Europeans, and Indians intermixed without conflict—he was convinced that in Kenya the government could pursue a "multiracial strategy," where the white settler population would provide a "steel-frame" in which Africans could slowly progress toward modernity and equality.[120] Because of this belief, Mitchell refused to accept reports of increasing hostility on British farms and he intentionally downplayed the threat in his reports to the colonial office. When he tendered his resignation in April 1952, he informed Lyttelton that he "had the satisfaction of handing over to his successor a colony at the height of prosperity and lapped in peace."[121]

The job of finding this successor fell to Lyttelton, who in April 1952 had no idea of the extent of discontent among Kenya's Kikuyu population. After consultation with officials at the colonial office, Lyttelton turned to Sir Evelyn Baring. Born in 1904 to Lord Cromer (consul general in Egypt from 1883 to 1907 and known to history as "the Maker of Modern Egypt"), Baring received a First Class Honors degree in history from Oxford University before entering the Indian Civil Service in 1926.

A damaged liver forced him to retire in 1933 and he returned to Britain to work at the family's banking firm in London. Upon the outbreak of the Second World War, however, he took up government service once more, this time with the foreign office. Immediately impressing his superiors, in 1942 he was appointed governor of South Rhodesia at just thirty-eight years of age. Two years later, he was appointed high commissioner to the Union of South Africa, a position he held until 1951. He had been back in the United Kingdom just a few months when Lyttelton turned to him about going to Kenya. Both men believed this would be a considerably easier post to handle than the racially charged atmosphere of South Africa's apartheid state.[122]

However, Lyttelton's invitation was problematic in its timing. Baring, just a few days before Lyttelton contacted him, had "nearly chopped off his hand with an axe, while felling a tree."[123] He accepted the position contingent on being given three or four months off to first recover. Mitchell agreed to remain in Kenya until June 21, 1952. Up until the day he left he remained convinced that the colony was peaceful.[124] Feeling buoyed by Mitchell's reassurance, Baring looked forward immensely to his new posting. As he confessed to his friend Paul Emrys Evans on April 14, "I am very ignorant of East African affairs and I expect I shall soon be fighting violently with everyone. All the same I think that much of it should be fun."[125] Sadly for Baring (and the rest of Kenya), there was far less "fun" than he hoped for, and quite a bit more "fighting violently"!

Baring's hand took longer to heal than anticipated, so in late June Lyttelton appointed Henry Potter as the colony's acting governor, with Baring's arrival date pushed back to September 1952. Far less experienced in executive leadership than Baring, Potter had most recently served as chief secretary in Uganda from 1948 to 1952, before which he held positions as financial secretary in Uganda and district officer in Kenya.[126] Having received a sunny assessment from Mitchell at the handover, Potter was shocked upon taking up his position to be given a report by the Kenyan commissioner of police, Michael O'Rorke, which suggested that "a general revolt was afoot among the Kikuyu."[127] Michael Blundell, the leader of the white settler contingent in the Legislative Council, also received a copy of this report and he immediately instigated a debate, demanding a declaration of emergency and the immediate proscribing of the KAU.[128] John Whyatt, the Kenyan attorney general and member for law and order, was present on August 8 when the settlers delivered their request to the governor. In a letter to the colonial office written several weeks later, he described the atmosphere:

All the European Elected Members (with two exceptions) rolled up at Government House in their cars and seated themselves at the long table in the Executive Council room facing Potter, the Commissioner of Police and myself. They then proceeded to state their views, Blundell acting, for the most part, as spokesman though the others joined in from time to time. When I say that they put forward their views, that is an understatement; it would be more correct to describe them as being in the nature of "demands"; and as I sat there listening to them the thought flashed through my mind, "This must be what it is like to be present at a coup d'etat."[129]

Ultimately, Potter was able to persuade the council against immediate action but it was clear to him that the white population was on edge.[130]

On August 17, Potter wrote to Philip Rogers, assistant undersecretary of state at the colonial office, providing the government in London with its first intimation that anything was wrong in Kenya. He stated, quite bluntly, that "there has been a progressive deterioration in the state of law and order in the areas of the Colony where the Kikuyu tribe preponderate." He explained that "The main overt Kikuyu political organisation is the Kenya African Union which, while purporting to represent all Africans, does not do so but is in fact Kikuyu controlled under the leadership of Jomo Kenyatta. ... The covert organisation is the proscribed Mau Mau secret society, the terms of whose illegal oath include the killing of Europeans 'when the war-horn blows' and the rescue of Kenyatta should he ever be arrested." Potter stated that "The activities of both these bodies have greatly increased in the past two or three months," and that wherever meetings by the KAU were held they were "followed by a great increase in lawlessness, sullenness towards Europeans, and Mau Mau activities." More alarmingly, "responsible people" among the Kikuyu tribe described Mau Mau activities as "no less than a reign of terror over decent Africans." This was evidenced by a number of attacks: "Tribal Police constables and others have been murdered in so-called 'Mau Mau executions', there have been cases of arson in which the houses of Government supporters have been destroyed, and some Chiefs are either reluctant or unable effectively to carry out their duties." He concluded that "the public opinion of all races is greatly disturbed and the Kikuyu are sullen, mutinous and organising for mischief. It is because I fear that we are in for a difficult and very troublesome time that I thought it well to give you informally this brief personal appreciation."[131]

Taken aback by Potter's report—so different from those Mitchell had sent—the colonial office requested that Whyatt draft legislation for measures to quell Mau Mau.[132] This Whyatt sent to Rogers on September 2, admitting that "some of them are of a very unusual character" and suggesting that the legislation would be introduced at a special session of the council on September 25. The bills included provisions, among others, to allow for government control of the printing presses, for traffic curfews after dark, and for changes in the evidence rules that would allow a senior policeman to attest a prisoner's confession, which could then be accepted as court evidence. Taken together, Whyatt believed these measures would give the colonial administration "greater control over the thug element which is still, I regret to say, intimidating and terrorising large numbers of peaceful and respectable Africans in Nairobi, the Kikuyu Reserves and in part of the Rift Valley Province."[133]

Upon receiving Whyatt's report, the colonial office requested that he and Eric Davies, the chief native commissioner, come to London to explain more fully the consequences of their proposed legislation and to present their recommendations to Parliament, which they did during the third week of September.[134] Many in Parliament, particularly in the Labour Party, were aghast at what they heard. Following Whyatt's presentation on September 19, Fenner Brockway—soon to become chairman of the parliamentary Movement for Colonial Freedom—wrote to Oliver Lyttelton, expressing his "dismay" at the proposed legislation that he believed "denies the most essential features of the Declaration of Human Rights of the United Nations." He felt that the bills "read more like the regime of a totalitarian state, the other side of the Iron Curtain, than a society moving towards democratic freedom," and hoped that Kenya might become "an inspiring example of racial equality, democracy, and co-operation." Brockway urged Lyttelton to have "second thoughts" before allowing the Kenyan Legislative Council to proceed in its course of action.[135] His plea was in vain. On September 25, the council passed all of its proposed bills.[136]

Meanwhile, on September 12, the Criminal Investigation Department (CID) of the Kenyan police prepared a memorandum for Potter and the Executive Council detailing the incidents of Mau Mau activity thus far. It described Mau Mau as "basically anti-European, anti-Christian, and anti-Government," an organization that "does not hesitate to employ the most brutal methods of intimidation towards the enlistment of adherents to its ranks, nor to exploit the ignorance and superstition of the African to ensure subsequent loyalty to its illegal purposes and aims." The report illustrated the widespread nature of forcible oathing and provided an example of a Roman Catholic Kikuyu who had refused to take the oath:

> This unfortunate woman was lured to the house of a Mau Mau adherent, together with a number of others, and informed

shortly after her arrival that the oath was to be administered to her. She courageously refused and was thereupon informed that, if she would not consent to the oath being administered, she would be killed and those present would drink her blood. Some of the male officials were armed with native cutting weapons and flourished these in a most threatening way. When she persisted in her refusal a rope was obtained, thrown over a rafter and a noose placed around her neck. She was then hoisted off the floor at the end of the rope until she lost consciousness. When she partially regained her sense she was compelled to drink some blood from a bottle and to perform the other disgusting rites constituting the Mau Mau Oath-taking ceremony.

The CID revealed that it had investigated six other cases where the same method was used to induce oath-taking. In addition to forcible oath-taking, between January and September 1952, the police had documented forty cases of arson against property belonging to Kikuyu African headmen or other African government supporters, and twenty-three murders of African loyalists. Such intimidation had led to "charges against over one hundred persons for administering or participating in the administration of illegal oaths [being] withdrawn because of witnesses turning hostile or disappearing." Put simply, the CID believed that Kenya's system of law and order was beginning to collapse.[137]

It was into this rapidly deteriorating situation that Sir Evelyn Baring descended on September 29, 1952, being officially sworn in as governor the very next day. After briefings with the police commissioner O'Rorke, the attorney general John Whyatt, the leader of the settler community Michael Blundell, and other government and community officials, Baring set out on a tour of the Central Province, meeting with Europeans and Africans, officials and laypeople. On October 7, the day before he was to return to Nairobi, he received some disheartening news. Chief Waruhiu wa Kungu, the government's paramount chief for Central Province and the most senior African official in the administration's hierarchy, had been assassinated that afternoon while on his way home from a native tribunal hearing. His car had been flagged down by two men wearing colonial police uniforms, who shot him once in the mouth and three times in the torso after he had identified himself. It was by far the most high profile Mau Mau incident to date.[138]

Baring arrived back in Nairobi on October 8. Early the next morning, he sent a lengthy letter to Lyttelton. From his extensive ten-day tour of the colony, he had grasped the complexity of the issue, explaining to the colonial secretary that, "The [Mau Mau] Movement has many heads and we are dealing with a hydra. There is the exploitation of grievances concerning land, housing, wages; and many of them have much force." Despite the validity of Mau Mau grievances, Baring had no illusions as to the threat it posed:

> There is the attempt to gain control over the whole Kikuyu tribe by attacks on those who refuse to take the Mau Mau oath. There is the determination to destroy all sources of authority other than Mau Mau, hence the attacks first on headmen and now on chiefs. There is a strong anti-Christian and particularly anti-Christian education side to the Movement. There is intimidation of children going to Mission schools and of parents attending church services.

Baring was greatly concerned about the situation—much more so than he had been on reading Potter's accounts. He believed that if Mau Mau could not be quelled, "first there will be an administrative breakdown and next a great deal of bloodshed amounting, possibly, even to something approaching civil war."

The new governor was worried not only about a civil war within the Kikuyu population but also one involving the Europeans. Thus far, he had found them "very reasonable" but worried that "there would come a moment when the more hot-headed would undoubtedly take the law into their own hands." For this reason, he felt compelled to recommend that a state of emergency be declared. He fully realized that "the strong action I recommend will cause you much political trouble, for which I am very sorry," but nevertheless had to stick to his convictions. He closed his letter telling Lyttelton, "[W]e are faced with a formidable organisation of violence and if we wait the trouble will become much worse and probably lead to the loss of so many lives that in the future bitter memories of bloodshed will bedevil all race relations. I have in South Africa seen too much of the effect of these memories to take any risk of letting Kenya go the same way."[139] For Baring, fresh off a posting where he had unsuccessfully tried to quell the rolling tide of apartheid, the disturbances in Kenya were very personal. He would not allow another British territory to become beset with intractable racial strife.

Following Baring's letter, events in Kenya moved rapidly toward his requested declaration of emergency. At nine o'clock on October 9, Whyatt chaired a committee meeting to draw up a list of key Mau Mau adherents who would be arrested immediately upon the declaration. At the top of the list was Jomo Kenyatta, who Baring believed was at the center of the conspiracy. The following day, at a meeting presided over by the chief secretary, the arrest operation was given its code name: Operation Jock Scott. Four days later, on October 14, Lyttelton sent a telegram to Baring granting him permission to declare an emergency in Kenya, with a provisional date of October 20.[140]

With less than a week to prepare for the emergency, Baring got started immediately. His first task was to ensure that there were sufficient security forces to cope with Operation Jock Scott. Part of the groundwork for this decision had already been completed. On September 29, a London-based committee composed of the chiefs of staff, representatives from the ministry of defense, and representatives from the colonial office had discussed whether a small British force could be sent from Egypt to Kenya to assist the civil government there in preserving law and order. At the time, Major General McLeod, sitting in for the vice-chief of the imperial general staff, noted that with eight battalions of the King's African Rifles already in Kenya, Tanganyika, Southern Rhodesia, and Mauritius, there was little need to move troops from Egypt. Rogers of the colonial office agreed, stating that the disturbances in Kenya were "primarily a policing problem and, with the new powers that they had been given, it was anticipated that the situation could be dealt with satisfactorily."[141] This viewpoint was confirmed by the minister of defense, Earl Alexander, on October 1,[142] and on October 8 Lyttelton reaffirmed that it was "unnecessary" to bring any troops from Egypt to Kenya.[143] However, that was before Baring's letter of October 9 and his request for a declaration of emergency, which changed everything. On October 13, Sir Edward Jacob, Alexander's chief staff officer and deputy military secretary, wrote to the minister of defense informing him that the situation in Kenya had now "deteriorated" and the colonial secretary was "strongly in favour of having available in the country a British battalion when the arrests of the leaders of the trouble are made." This battalion, he suggested, should come from Egypt.[144] Alexander agreed to the transfer of troops and notified Lyttelton and Baring on October 16 that they would get their men.[145]

On October 17, at 7:30 a.m., Baring wrote to Lyttelton, outlining the plan in a telegram. He proposed to fly the British battalion from Egypt to Nairobi in four stages, beginning on October 20 and continuing until October 23. Kenyatta and his most prominent supporters would be arrested during the night of the twentieth and immediately flown to the Northern Frontier Province.[146] Baring wrote again ten hours later, at 5:00 p.m., providing a list of the 138 people who would be arrested. He confessed that this was "much longer than I had anticipated" and apologized for any "political embarrassment" it might cause, but excused it by the "widespread nature of violence." Those on the list fell into one of four categories:

(a) Planners of outrages, whether at the centre or in the districts;

(b) Habitual oath administrators or intimidators of loyal Africans or of children at mission schools or of members of mission congregations;

(c) Emissaries going from or to the central command of the Movement and links in the chain of command;

(d) Persons whose previous activities have shown they are seeking to establish bridge-heads for a campaign of violence in new areas. They are likely to become more dangerous once drastic steps are taken in "Kikuyuland."

Baring was certain that once such individuals were arrested, Mau Mau would collapse.[147] Everything was now in place. The plan was set. The colonial secretary, governor, and security forces had only to wait three more days and the first step to restoring law and order in Kenya would be upon them.

IV. The General's stamp in Malaya

While conditions deteriorated rapidly in Kenya, elsewhere in the empire things seemed to be looking up. On September 22, 1952—seven days before Baring arrived in Nairobi—the war office published an appreciation of the situation in Malaya. It noted that in the six months from March to August, the number of insurgent attacks in the federation had "steadily decreased," with August 1952 as the month with the lowest number of attacks since April 1950. At the same time, the security forces were tightening their noose around the insurgency's neck, slowly choking it of life. August 1952 recorded the second highest number of insurgent casualties since the emergency began in 1948. It was clear that the government's strategy was working: "Acts of terrorism against civilians have decreased, and Communist attention has been directed to causing economic damage and attacks against the Security Forces." The insurgents were engaging the army and police rather than the civilian population, allowing normal life to resume in most areas of Malaya, just as Briggs had intended.

The war office attributed these changes directly to the appointment of Templer as high commissioner and director of operations:

> By using the powers of this dual appointment and a strong personality, General Templer has given [a] tremendous lift to morale throughout the Federation, and imbued the Security Forces and civil administration with a new spirit and the will to win. The foundation for the recent improvement is the Briggs plan, which is aimed at Resettling half a million Chinese squatters away from direct Communist influence. But it is General Templer who, by his tremendous energy and drive, is pushing this plan and attendant measures to their logical conclusion.

The report also drew attention to the reorganization of the police force, the improvement of the intelligence services, the strengthening of security and social programs in the new villages, and better government propaganda as reasons for improvement. It concluded: "Provided that the present circumstances do not radically change, the rate of progress is maintained and measures now in force are carried to their logical conclusion, there are reasonable prospects that within a year or eighteen months the Emergency will be well under control and militant Communist forces reduced to very small proportions." If the government remained committed, the war office believed that with Templer in command and the Briggs plan at hand, the emergency in Malaya could be nearing its conclusion by March 1954.[148]

This did not mean, of course, that in September 1952 Templer could dispense with the stick entirely and feed only carrots to the Malay people. On the contrary, the use of collective punishment and other draconian measures increased as the summer turned into autumn. In August, Templer imposed a four-day curfew on the people of Permatang Tinggi following the assassination of a Chinese government contractor, telling its inhabitants, "It is villages like yours that make it possible for the bandits to continue their operations." As he spoke, he noticed several men in the crowd slipping away. He interrupted his speech to address them directly: "It is no use thinking that you men can run away and escape the issue. You must face it now. As I am talking your village is being surrounded and a wire fence is being erected at this moment round you. No one will be allowed to escape through it."[149] The villagers failed to heed his words. Having received no information on the murder after four days of curfew, Templer arrested all eighteen families (sixty-two persons) and sent them to the Ipoh detention camp, where they stayed for the remainder of the emergency.[150] Following their imprisonment, Templer issued a press statement assuring the people of Malaya that "people who have been blackmailed into giving help to the Communist terrorists will not be punished by Government, unless they withhold from the Police information of the help they have given." If the villagers refused to provide such information when presented with the opportunity, they could expect to suffer the fate of Permatang Tinggi.[151]

As Templer continued to harass the insurgency and sought to instill greater discipline in the new villages, he also attempted to reform the SWEC and DWEC system. Beginning in August and continuing through September, Templer organized four 3-day courses at the police depot in Kuala Lumpur for members of DWECs, providing them with a mixture of lectures and hands-on exercises on topics ranging from intelligence, air support, and the army in Malaya, to social services in the new villages and joint planning. At the beginning of each course, Templer opened the proceedings by telling those who had gathered:

Now is the time to improve our ideas—I believe we are beginning to bring pressure to bear on the enemy—they are suffering ever-increasing casualties which cannot be easy to replace—even a bandit has to be trained, armed, and equipped—Special Branch is really getting us the information and giving it to us in a form which we can use—the Police retraining programme is having its intended effect—the

Army is going over to Company retraining which leaves a unit in one place for long enough to get to know it—all these factors are working up now, and it is in the next six months that I hope to see results—we've got to turn the heat on, and when we do we must be ready to develop the full current.[152]

Templer followed this series of workshops with a conference in November for all members of the SWECs. In a memorandum sent prior to the conference, he explained that "with the steadily increasing diminution in terrorist overt activity, that is in 'the shooting war', and the growing importance of administrative action to win the hearts and minds of the people, that is 'the other 75% of the battle against communism,'" the time had come to reevaluate British methods. He therefore provided a list of questions for the SWECs to consider at this conference:

(a) What subjects should be taken over from SWECS by State/Settlement Governments?
(b) On what date, or dates, would this best be done?
(c) What steps should be taken to enable State/Settlement Governments to take over these subjects smoothly and efficiently, and to handle them satisfactorily when taken over?
(d) What changes will be required:
    (i) in State/Settlement Staffs
    (ii) in SWEC staffs
(e) What the responsibilities of SWECS and their Executives Secretaries should be after certain responsibilities have been handed over to State/Settlement Governments.
(f) What kind of officer is required for Executive Secretary.[153]

Templer had been in Malaya just nine months when the SWEC leaders met to consider these questions. After less than a year in charge, he believed the time had come to undo some of the emergency establishment and procedures laid out by Briggs in his plan.

The reports Templer received from his intelligence staff confirmed this judgment. On September 30, the combined intelligence staff reported that "there has been a vast improvement in the situation in Malaya during the last six months." The number of attacks on rubber estates and tin mines had fallen from 138 in February, to seventy-three in July, to just twenty-one in September, with the number of rubber trees slashed reduced from 70,000 in February, to 46,000 in July, to 9000 in September. In January, twenty-seven buses were destroyed; since February, on average only nine buses a month met that fate. From January to May, the monthly average of railway sabotage was ten attacks; from June to September, it fell to just three per month. Casualties suffered by the security forces likewise dropped, from thirty-nine in January to thirteen in July to seven in September, while insurgent casualties exceeded the 1951 monthly average in each month of 1952 thus far. From whichever angle the emergency was viewed, the British were winning the fight.[154]

With success in the "shooting war" seemingly assured, it was time for Templer to turn his attention more fully to the problems of governance and the winning of the hearts and minds of the Malayan people. This could best be done, he felt, by encouraging the indigenous people to take increasing responsibility for all elements of the emergency. The first step in doing so was to increase trust between villagers and the government. The police, as the most immediate face of government for many Malayans, would necessarily hold the chief responsibility. This concerned Templer, who believed that the relationship between the police and the civilian population was "appalling." He worried that this problem was insurmountable, as such animosity surely stemmed from the fact that the police in Malaya were in essence acting as a supplementary part of the armed forces rather than as a civilian organization in the British tradition.[155]

Templer's deputy, General Sir Robert Lockhart, saw the problem differently, placing the blame not on the emergency situation but squarely at the feet of the European officers who led the force: "In my opinion the attitudes of many of them to their job, their men and the public leaves much to be desired." He explained that many of the younger officers considered that in their positions as police officers they were "the masters rather than the servants of the public," displaying "signs of superiority and impatience with ordinary folk." He suggested that "a drive should be made to inculcate in all officers a realization of the fact that they are first public servants, with a duty to treat law abiding citizens with courtesy and consideration."[156] Following discussion with police commissioner Arthur Young, Templer decided that the root of this police attitude lay in a lack of training due to the rapid expansion of the force (its numbers had risen from 11,177 in 1948 to 52,662 in 1950 to 74,417 in 1952[157]). In December, therefore, Templer announced that the force would undergo an annual reduction of 10,000 of its ranks until its number had dropped from 75,000 to just 30,000 within four years. Those who left the force voluntarily would be provided with vocational training and a small grant of land. Those who remained would be more thoroughly integrated with appropriate training and supervision. No longer would it be acceptable for the European officers not to speak the language or know the names of the men who served under them.[158]

Having addressed the problem of sound policing, Templer next returned to the question of food denial operations. Since May 1952, the Malayan government had used private contractors to spray sodium trichloroacetate from the air on roadside vegetation, as well as on crop fields that were believed to feed the insurgents. The effectiveness of this tactic was not as hoped for, however, as it was difficult to dispense with any accuracy and was not as efficient in destroying crops as early experiments had suggested.[159] On December 8, the RAF headquarters in Malaya suggested that it could solve the problem simply by bombing the crop areas with conventional munitions, but this was dismissed by the army chief of staff as too indiscriminate and inflicting too much damage on civilians.[160] The government therefore turned once again to the scientists, meeting on December 11 with Drs E. K. Woodford and G. H. Kearns of Oxford University's Department of Agriculture, who "revealed that a chemical called CMU had been produced recently by Duponts in the USA which would be particularly suitable for crop destruction." Two pounds of this chemical dispersed in small pellets could completely destroy all seedlings within an acre radius. If cost were not an issue, it had the added advantage of making the ground "completely sterile" for at least a year if applied at the greater density of forty pounds per acre. Following this meeting, the army chief of staff recommended that the government obtain a supply of CMU as quickly as possible, "as it seems to be the most promising weapon for dealing with bandit cultivation."[161]

General Sir Robert Lockhart, the deputy director of operations, accepted the chief of staff's recommendations and instructed Woodford and Kearns to contact H. A. Sargeaunt, the scientific adviser to the army council, upon their return to the United Kingdom. This they did and together the three men agreed to prepare a report for Templer.[162] On January 21, 1953, Sargeaunt chaired a meeting with Kearns, Woodford, C. E. Blackman (also of Oxford University), R. E. Hadden, and F. B. Uffelmann of the ministry of supply, and D. F. Bayly-Pike and R. W. Brittain of the war office's science section. Those gathered concluded that CMU was "extremely toxic and would probably be very successful."[163] It was exactly what Templer was looking for. On January 29, Sargeaunt wrote to the high commissioner to inform him of the good news.[164] Within weeks, CMU had replaced sodium trichloroacetate as the government's chemical of choice.[165]

As 1953 began, the government in Malaya felt more comfortable with its situation than it had for many years, a fact that was outlined in a memorandum by the Police Operations Information Branch on January 2. Comparing statistics from 1951 to 1952, the information branch provided a stark comparison. In 1951, the security forces had killed 1066 insurgents. This had increased to 1462 in 1952. Insurgent captures had remained the same at 121 in each year, but insurgent surrenders had increased from 201 in 1951 to 253 in 1952. At the same time, the number of security forces killed had fallen from 504 in 1951 to 263 in 1952, and those wounded from 691 in 1951 to 401 in 1952. More importantly, civilian deaths had fallen from 533 to 341, with those wounded dropping from 356 to 158. Insurgent attacks on estates and mines had been reduced from forty-five in 1951 to eighteen in 1952, with the number of rubber trees slashed dropping from 88,000 to 38,000. The destruction of buses had fallen from eighteen to ten, the cutting of telewire from seventy incidents to forty-four, and attacks on railways from eight to three.[166] Many of Templer's policies had been draconian in nature and had created great controversy in Parliament. Yet, despite their moral ambiguity, they were working, and working in a far more concrete way than had been the case in the years 1948 to 1951, or in Palestine before that.

V.   "The Horned Shadow of the Devil Himself"

On the afternoon of October 20, 1952, Sir Evelyn Baring—governor of Kenya for less than two weeks—summoned to his office Michael Blundell, the leader of the European contingent in the Legislative Council. Baring cut to the chase: "I think I ought to tell you that the Lancashire Fusiliers are flying in and will be landing tonight. And I've declared a state of emergency, and Jomo Kenyatta is being arrested."[167] Just hours after Baring spoke, twelve aircraft landed at Nairobi's Eastleigh airfield, carrying the soldiers of the First Battalion, Lancashire Fusiliers, who began patrolling the streets in armored cars the very next morning.[168] Meanwhile, at midnight the Kenyan police spread out across Nairobi in Operation Jock Scott to arrest 150 individuals whose names had been placed on a list provided by the special branch. These included Kenyatta, members of the Koinange family (who worked closely with Kenyatta), and other senior figures of the KAU, along with those suspected of serious involvement with Mau Mau. By daybreak, 106 of the 150 suspects were in British custody, ready to be tried under the

Emergency Powers Act passed by the Legislative Council only days before.[169]

The response of Mau Mau was swift. On October 22, a mob hacked to pieces a prominent Kikuyu chief, Senior Chief Nderi, when he attempted to break up an oathing ceremony. When the police arrived, supported by a platoon of Lancashire Fusiliers, they found the crowd to be "uncooperative and hostile."[170] Five days later, Mau Mau killed its first white victim. Eric Bowyer, who had fought under the British flag in both world wars before retiring to a farm in the Rift Valley, was hacked to death as he relaxed in his bathtub. Mau Mau murdered his two house servants, both of the Kikuyu tribe, in like fashion, before raiding Bowyer's farm store.[171] Oliver Lyttelton, the colonial secretary, read with increasing discomfort the incoming reports from Baring and found that from London, "the whole situation appeared confused, and worsening."[172] For that reason, he boarded a plane for Kenya so that he could "judge for myself," landing in Nairobi on October 29.[173] Just as he had done in Malaya, Lyttelton hoped a personal visit would bring clarity to an otherwise murky situation.

The very next day, Lyttelton met with the European representatives of the Legislative Council, where he found a pervasive spirit of fear and aggression. Blundell, who had gained a reputation as a moderate voice in the council, told the colonial secretary that "drastic action" was needed against the "80% to 90% of Kikuyu [who had] no mental or moral fibre." Major Keyser suggested that a shoot-to-kill policy be enacted against Mau Mau and Humphrey Slade proclaimed that "these Mau Mau men are rebels who work by terrorism. They are fighting a war against this country's Government. ... the only way of dealing with those men is to treat them as men with whom you are at war. And if you cannot arrest them, as you cannot, the only alternative is to kill them."[174] Lyttelton cautioned restraint, lecturing those gathered that "Sixty thousand Europeans cannot expect to hold all the political power and to exclude Africans from the legislature and from the Government. The end of that will be to build up pressures which will burst into rebellion and bloodshed." He added, "The security of your homes, the security of your money, hard work and skill which you have lavished upon your farms, and upon the industries which you have begun to build, cannot rest upon battalions of British troops; it can only rest upon the building of a multiracial society."[175]

Nevertheless, and despite his words, Lyttelton felt greater unease over Kenya than he ever had over Malaya, even though the violence and casualties were so much lower. The reason for this was that the colonial secretary believed something more was at work in Kenya than simple political discontent and insurgency. As he later wrote in his memoirs, "I can recall no instance when I have felt the forces of evil to be so near and so strong. As I wrote memoranda or instructions, I would suddenly see a shadow fall across the page—the horned shadow of the Devil himself."[176] It was a feeling held not only by Lyttelton but also by the white settlers in Kenya and, to a certain extent, by Baring. Consequently, from the very first days of the emergency, British actions in Kenya followed a different path than they had in Malaya. Immediately upon his return to London, Lyttelton placed photographs of Mau Mau atrocities, including the slaughtered body of Bowyer, in the House of Commons library.[177] He then informed those in the chamber that Mau Mau was in no way "the child of economic conditions" but rather "the unholy union of dark and ancient superstitions with the apparatus of modern gangsterism."[178]

It was not only in rhetoric that the British government drew some distinction between the communist insurgency in Malaya and Mau Mau's violence in Kenya. In action, also, Baring was encouraged to act in ways different than Templer. Whereas Templer had used collective punishment on a restricted and limited basis, with the intent being to receive intelligence quickly and then lift the punishment as soon as possible, in Kenya, Baring instituted the practice for purely punitive reasons. On November 10, he reported to Lyttelton that in the Nyeri district where Senior Chief Nderi had been murdered, a combined police and army operation had seized 3775 cattle and 6098 sheep and goats. Unlike in Malaya, no attempt was made to collect information from those on whom the punishment was inflicted, nor was any indication given as to when (if ever) the animals might be returned. As Baring clarified in his telegram to Lyttelton, "Impression has been given by local press (which may be repeated in the U.K.) that purpose of seizure of stock was to extract evidence against return of stock, but this gives a wrong emphasis to the operation, the primary object of which was punitive."[179]

Yet Baring went further than simply meting out collective punishment upon the Kikuyu people. Following the murder of Bowyer, he also instituted a process by which the Kikuyu population was "screened" en masse. For those found guilty of Mau Mau involvement, arrest and internment soon followed. Even for those who were eventually released, screening involved several hours or even days of intense interrogation, causing much disruption to lives and occupations. By November 15, the security forces had screened 31,450 Kikuyu, arresting 8500. Of those arrested, 2871 were released for lack of evidence, 1258 were charged, and the remainder was indefinitely imprisoned while investigations were completed. Because of the fluid nature of the screening process, Baring reported that "Figures of persons in custody naturally fluctuate from hour to hour."[180] In all, in the first four weeks of the Kenyan emergency, the British security forces arrested more people than they had done in all three years of the Palestine insurgency, or in the first four years of the Malayan emergency, with the numbers screened surpassing both Palestine and Malaya combined. No thought was given to the winning of hearts and minds in Kenya.

Baring had mixed feelings about these operations. Almost a month to the day after he had proclaimed the emergency, the governor wrote to the colonial secretary offering qualified support, informing Lyttelton that the situation was "in some ways hopeful, in other ways unsatisfactory." He was pleased that in Nyeri, Kikuyu Home Guards—modeled on the system of Home Guards pioneered in Malaya—were being successfully formed and beginning to take part in the breaking up of oathing ceremonies. However, he expressed concern at the screening process, suggesting that it was "not very effective" as the Kikuyu were "becoming used to the sight of large numbers of troops and police, and many innocent Africans are caught up in a large scale operation in which control of individual police or troops is difficult." He therefore suggested that the mass screening process be abandoned, to be replaced instead with a more discriminate focus on areas where "a serious crime or a Mau Mau meeting occurs." In these areas, communal punishment would be used without reservation. His hope was that the punishment of guilty communities would "drive home the lesson that Government as well as Mau Mau is to be feared." This, he believed, would help nip Mau Mau in the bud.[181]

The events of November 22, 1952, challenged Baring's assumptions. That evening, Ian Meiklejohn—a retired naval officer—and his wife were sitting down for an after-dinner coffee when several members of Mau Mau burst into their sitting room in the Thompson's Falls district. Baring had issued orders for all white settlers to arm themselves following the Bowyer murder, and both Meiklejohns had handguns close by, but Mrs Meiklejohn's wrist was cut as she reached for hers and Ian Meiklejohn's shoulder and scalp were slashed before he could leave his chair. He was then further cut on his head and body, while she was mutilated on her breasts and torso. When they lost consciousness, their attackers left the house taking with them clothing, the handguns, and ammunition. Sometime later, Mrs Meiklejohn regained consciousness and drove to the police station at Thompson's Falls, eight miles away. When she returned with police support, she found Ian in an upstairs room, deep in shock, trying to load a shotgun he had hidden. Both Meiklejohns were driven to the nearest hospital in Nakuru, but Ian died of his injuries two days later.[182]

Baring immediately requested from Lyttelton a change to the emergency regulations, asking for any district officer to be given permission to "direct male inhabitants over 18 ... to perform for police, or a Military force within that area, or for the Government, such works or services as may be specified, provided that no such inhabitant works more than eight hours a day in the aggregate." He felt this would be "an effective punishment for the young men in the area who have been the main troublemakers."[183] The colonial secretary immediately agreed and granted the change. Baring followed this brief request with a longer telegram on November 24—two days after the Thompson's Falls attacks, and the day Ian Meiklejohn died—stating that "the situation has now changed." Mau Mau, he believed, had obtained firearms and were "hiding in the dense forests." The government could expect their campaign of terror to be intensified, with "armed resistance in the forests" and "attacks by armed gangs on farm houses with the intent to kill the Europeans in them." He could only conclude that "we are in the process of moving in some areas from a police operation to a small scale guerilla war." He therefore recommended a "change of organisation," with "one man in charge of all sides of the campaign," and asked for "a Director of Operations who is a soldier, possibly of Major General rank, with experience of guerilla war." If Kenya was becoming Malaya, then the Kenyan administration needed a General Templer.[184]

Lyttelton rejected Baring's request, reluctant to add to the security forces already in Kenya. However, he did authorize a large-scale sweep in Thompson's Falls, carried out by the Lancashire Fusiliers, in which 750 men and 2200 women and children were interned without trial, with 5000 cattle seized.[185] In retaliation, there was extensive rioting in Nairobi, and on November 26, Tom Mbotela, a member of the city council and a critic of Mau Mau, was murdered while shopping at the Burma market. His body was left on the road throughout the morning hours until a European discovered it and reported it to the police.[186] Just days earlier, a crowd of 2000 members of the Kikuyu tribe armed with pangas (a long knife carried by Kikuyu farmers) had gathered in a marketplace at Kirawara to witness a young boy who had apparently been miraculously cured of dumbness. Seeing the numerous pangas, the lone European police constable called for backup and twenty-four other officers arrived (two European, twenty-two African), attempting to disperse the crowd. When this was unsuccessful, the inspector in charge ordered his men to open fire, fearing that the crowd would turn on them. In all, the police killed sixteen Kikuyu and wounded seventeen.[187] Lyttelton showed little remorse for this turn of events, telling Parliament: "I know of no other way in which they could have acted when set upon by 2,000 armed with knives. I have other responsibilities in this matter, and if these 25 policemen had been hacked to pieces—which is what would have happened if they had not opened fire—then another series of equally disastrous events would have ensued."[188]

Despite his defiance in Parliament, the colonial secretary was clearly shocked by the events in the marketplace. In the aftermath of the Meiklejohn and Mbotela murders and the tragedy at Kirawara, Lyttelton became unwilling to risk any more needless slaughter. Consequently, he suggested to Baring that in the event of more rioting the police should be authorized to use shot guns loaded with buckshot rather than rifles.[189] This was not for purely humanitarian reasons, however, as he made quite clear in an internal colonial office memorandum: "It is generally more painful to be wounded than killed outright. At 20 yards fatal wounds, if fire is low, are rare with buckshot (No. 2 & 3), whereas a rifle bullet goes through two men quite often. Few mobs would face buckshot at 20 yards."[190] Lyttelton's aim was to create injuries rather than fatalities because he correctly reasoned that pain was a greater deterrent than death. In a return telegram on December 1, Baring confirmed that he had ordered his police officers to use No. 3 buckshot rather than rifles wherever possible.[191]

Yet Baring's anti–Mau Mau strategy did not rest on sweeps, screenings, and riot control alone, and Oliver Lyttelton was not the only visitor he received that autumn. Upon Baring's declaration of emergency, Sir Percy Sillitoe, the director-general of MI5, wrote to the colonial office offering the services of his organization. His advances were initially spurned by Sir Thomas Lloyd, the permanent undersecretary of state, but following the murders of Bowyer and Senior Chief Nderi, Baring himself requested a delegation from MI5. On November 20, Sillitoe touched down in Nairobi, together with MI5 officers A. M. MacDonald and Alex Kellar, the latter of whom had served in Palestine as head of Security Intelligence Middle East (SIME) from 1946–1948 before transferring to Malaya as head of Security Intelligence Far East (SIFE). After several days of meeting with members of the security forces in Kenya, Sillitoe presented his recommendations to Baring on November 24 (the day Ian Meiklejohn died).[192] He suggested that the number of special branch officers in Nairobi be doubled, that an interrogation center be established, that "technical aids" be used, that intelligence centers be formed in each province and district, that informers be properly protected, and that intelligence information be centrally sifted.[193] He also agreed to leave MacDonald in Kenya for a period of one year to act as security adviser, where his role would be to "concert all measures to secure the intelligence Government requires" and to "co-ordinate the activities of all intelligence agencies operating in the Colony and to promote collaboration with Special Branches in adjacent territories."[194] Baring immediately accepted all of Sillitoe's recommendations, informing the colonial secretary of his decision on November 28.[195]

However, not all Britons who arrived in Kenya in the wake of Baring's emergency declaration were as supportive as Lyttelton and Sillitoe. On October 28, the day before the colonial secretary traveled to the colony, two opposition members of Parliament arrived, coming not at the invitation of the Kenyan government but at that of the KAU. Fenner Brockway had visited Kenya before in 1950, when he stayed with Chief Koinange, and Kenyatta served as his guide. Leslie Hale had never been to Kenya before. They now came to investigate the arrests and imprisonment of Kenyatta and Koinange as part of Operation Jock Scott.[196] Upon viewing the situation and returning to London, Brockway offered to the House of Commons an ominous warning: "We are at a moment of the parting of the ways in Africa. It is racial conflict or racial co-operation, and it depends upon the policy which this Government and the Government of Kenya now pursue in which of those two directions we shall be moving in the coming years."[197]

Lyttelton, knowing from his experience with Malaya that more parliamentary questioning would be forthcoming, arranged for Baring to provide him with information that could be used in response to parliamentary inquiries. On December 3, Baring replied with a sunny report. Livestock seized were treated well, he informed the colonial secretary. Although some of the animals were in "poor condition" when taken so had to be killed, the remainder were receiving daily inspections by veterinary officers, were grazed on 300 acres of pasture land during the day, and were kept in secure paddocks at night, where their grazing food supply was supplemented by thirty tons of hand-cut fodder, 180 bales of lucerne, twenty tons of starry grass hay, and mineralized salt bricks. Furthermore, a piped water supply was connected to each paddock and "local residents took charge of the lambs for bottle feeding." The governor's message was clear: this livestock was better off with the British than with the Kikuyu. He also stressed that collective punishment had been imposed in just two areas since the declaration of emergency, neither of which could be called villages or towns "in the English sense." It was true that gallows had been erected in H.M. Prison in Thompson's Falls to "hang those found guilty by the Supreme Court of murder in the Thompson's Falls area," but all executions would take place in the presence "only of official witnesses"—there would be no public spectacle. Finally, he insisted that there were "no concentration camps in Kenya." Those residents who were being detained were kept "in conditions similar to those laid down for judgment debtors, except that rations are free."[198] Baring's report was exactly what Lyttelton needed. It cataloged British actions, but painted them in the best possible light.

Even so, the British government had other difficulties in Kenya. On December 3, the trial of Jomo Kenyatta began. Unlike the others who were arrested and charged as part of Operation Jock Scott, each of whom was tried and sentenced quietly in magistrates' courts, Baring decided that Kenyatta would be given a show trial. There were logistical problems with this, however. One was location. Baring judged Nairobi too close to Mau Mau's epicenter and thus had the trial moved to the remote northern town of Kapenguria. Because Kapenguria was in a declared "closed district" under the emergency regulations, nobody except those holding a government permit would be allowed to enter or even come close to the location of the courthouse. Then there was the fear that witnesses to Mau Mau crimes might be intimidated, a not unreasonable concern considering that twenty-seven crown witnesses had been murdered in September and October alone. To combat this problem, the attorney general—John Whyatt—altered the witness protection rules. Henceforth, all subpoenaed witnesses would be given police protection. If this protection failed and the witnesses came to any harm, their home communities would be blamed and collective punishment would be leveled against them. If, alternately, the witnesses refused to testify, all police protection would be removed, leaving them at the mercy of Mau Mau. In all, the government gave police protection to twenty witnesses during Kenyatta's trial. Prosecuting lawyers and police officials provided each with expert coaching on their statements, and in the aftermath of the trial the government paid the witnesses over £10,000 in "compensation" and "rewards" for their loyalty.[199]

Once location and witness protection were assured, Baring next had to determine who would preside over the trial. For this role he selected Ransley Thacker, a retired High Court judge who had served on the Kenyan High Court since 1938 and was attorney general in Fiji before that. Thacker, who had settled in Nairobi since retirement, demanded "special payments" to cover relocation back to the United Kingdom following the trial's end, claiming that it would no longer be safe for him to remain in Kenya. Baring agreed and once sentence was passed he had Thacker driven by armored car directly to the airport, where he was presented with £20,000 in compensation and placed on a flight to London.[200] The trial dragged on for five months, but the witnesses were well coached, KAU supporters were denied access to Kenyatta or the site of the trial, and Thacker—as a member of Kenya's white settler community for the past fourteen years—shared the same fears of Mau Mau and Kenyatta as they did. Although the prosecution could produce no evidence to suggest that either the KAU or Kenyatta himself were involved with Mau Mau, on April 8, 1953, Thacker found Kenyatta guilty of "managing Mau Mau and being a member of that society" and sentenced him to the maximum seven years of hard labor, with lifetime restrictions to follow.[201]

Meanwhile, the removal of Kenyatta and other senior members of the KAU from Kikuyu society had little effect on Mau Mau. Following the start of Kenyatta's trial in December 1952, Baring returned to London to brief the colonial secretary and other members of the cabinet on progress made during the emergency. In a meeting held at the colonial office on the fifteenth of that month, he deferred to Lyttelton (against his better judgment) in not recommending the appointment of a director of operations, instead simply suggesting that a colonel be appointed "Staff Officer to the Governor." Unlike in Malaya, no steps to coordinate operations would be attempted in Kenya. There would, however, be coordination in intelligence efforts, as recommended by Sillitoe. Baring reported that the Special Branch would "run an interrogation centre and would form a central registry for documents and reports of intelligence and security interest. ... Information from the districts [would] come to the centre in a single stream, not a divided one." MI5's A. M. MacDonald would oversee all these efforts.

Beyond intelligence collection, Baring suggested that it was of "great importance" to impose a special tax of twenty shillings per annum for two years on each member of the Kikuyu tribe. The reason for this was that "everybody in the Colony would have to pay something towards the cost of the emergency but that the Kikuyu would have to pay a bit more." Baring also felt that although collective punishment was a practice he "disliked," it was a "lesser evil than the method which had been adopted at first in areas where crimes took place, when the police and military forces made sweeps through the area detaining large numbers for screening." During such operations, "numbers of Africans were manhandled and the sympathies of loyal Kikuyu alienated." Finally, and with respect to deteriorating support from the House of Commons, Baring announced that he had abandoned a proposal to extend the number of crimes for which corporal punishment could be inflicted, as well as one intended to make administering an illegal oath a capital crime. He would instead continue to rely upon collective punishment and the internment of those found guilty of Mau Mau associa-tion as his primary methods for controlling the emergency.[202]

The ineffectiveness of this approach was made evident on Christmas Eve 1952 when Mau Mau struck again. Five separate homesteads in south Nyeri, all housing African elders who were senior members of the Church of Scotland, were simultaneously attacked at dinnertime. At the first, Richard Muhogo, a relative of his, and his daughter, were speared to death. At the second, Ndegwa Mugo was chased and slaughtered in his bedroom, while his wife was murdered in the kitchen, witnessed by her nine-year-old daughter. Two guests in their house, Douglas Kagorani and Stephen Ngahu, were likewise slashed to death. Mau Mau found the final three houses unoccupied, their resi-dents dining elsewhere, and thus simply looted and ransacked them without injury to anyone. Although the victims of these Christmas Eve atrocities were African rather than European, their standing in the Christian church seemed to confirm for the settler community the inherently "evil" nature of Mau Mau.[203]

A week later, on January 1, 1953, Mau Mau claimed more European victims. That evening at a farm in the Rift Valley, two neighbors—Charles Fergusson and Dick Bingley—were sitting down together to share an evening meal in Fergusson's dining room when fifteen attackers burst in and slew them where they sat, before looting both farms for food and supplies. Neither Fergusson nor Bingley survived the attack, each dead before the security forces found them. The following evening, Mau Mau again attacked a settler farm, this one in Nyeri. Instead of two men, this time they faced two women, Kitty Hesselberger and Raynes Simpson, each of whom had armed themselves at the advice of the police. As the first Mau Mau attacker burst into their living room, Hesselberger shot him dead before firing at the second attacker. Simpson then fired her shotgun at the doorway, forcing the attackers from the living room into the kitchen. Before they could pursue them, the two women heard noises from the bathroom next door and began to fire shots through the thin wall. At this point, the remaining attackers fled. When Hesselberger and Simpson ventured into the bathroom, they found two more dead Kikuyu, bringing their confirmed total up to three. In the aftermath of their defense, they were lauded in the British and Kenyan press for their bravery and willingness to stand up to Mau Mau.[204]

Yet Hesselberger and Simpson had been lucky to survive. The European members of the Legislative Assembly knew that not all who were attacked would be so fortunate, and it was the deaths of Fergusson and Bingley that more clearly resonated than the actions of Hesselberger and Simpson. Consequently, on January 15 they petitioned Baring for tougher sanctions, informing him that on January 16 they planned to introduce a resolution in the Legislative Council mandating the death penalty for Mau Mau oath administrators whose oaths included a "clause with a promise to kill." Baring wrote to Lyttelton asking for advice, informing him that the European members would outvote the African members and that if the government defied the democratic wish of the council it would be placed in a "difficult position."[205] Lyttelton replied immediately, agreeing to "the imposition of the death penalty for Mau Mau oath administrators should the oath contain clause with promise to kill." He did, however, add the caveat, "I do not (repeat not) consider that imposition of the death penalty should be left to the discretion of the Courts. It should be left to the Governor to decide whether or not to commute the death sentence, in the exercise of the prerogative vested in him in regard to the execution of sentences."[206]

The following day, the Legislative Assembly did as promised and oath administration became a capital crime in Kenya. By the close of the emergency seven years later, the government had hanged 1090 members of the Kikuyu tribe for Mau Mau–related crimes, had sentenced to death another 240 whose sentences were subsequently commuted, had convicted another 160 who were released on appeal, and had sentenced to death another 7 who died in custody before their executions could be carried out.[207] It was a grisly total and one that was unparalleled in the history of the British Empire. In contrast, throughout the Malayan emergency, the government executed just 226 insurgents.[208] In Palestine, the number was even less, with only twelve hanged for anti-government activities between 1938 and 1947.[209] More British civilians and soldiers lost their lives in each of these territories than in Kenya. The difference was that in Kenya, Mau Mau's victims were killed by blade rather than bullet and Mau Mau as a movement was considered by the British government to be superstitious, primitive, and even wicked, compared with the more rational and—to the Western mind—understandable danger of Zionist terrorism or communist insurgency. Fear of the unexplainable drove British actions in Kenya, and what was viewed as a premodern threat was dealt with in premodern ways.

Baring's grant of capital punishment did little to quell the bloodlust of the white settler community in Kenya. On January 16, following their passage of the capital punishment law, the European members of the Legislative Council met with the governor to push him further. In addition to the increase in the use of the death penalty, they laid down six demands. First, they wished to see the establishment of a "Defence Council of all races," which would "help to bring the public of all races more into the picture." Second, they wanted several European members to be "brought into smaller and more secret organisations connected with the emergency," which would not have the inclusiveness or transparency of the Defense Council. Third, they demanded the appointment of a single director of operations, with powers similar to those held by Templer in Malaya. Fourth, they felt that Mau Mau should be declared a terrorist organization, and that "District Commissioners should be given powers of summary jurisdiction in Mau Mau offences, with apparently no appeal." Fifth, they argued that Kikuyu on farms who were "known to be in the Mau Mau movement, but against whom nothing could be proved," should be forcibly removed to reserves. And finally, they demanded that the single position of member for law and order and attorney general (at that time held by Whyatt) be split into two positions, with a European member of the council appointed to the former, which would have direct control of the police force. Baring immediately agreed to the first two demands, wavered on the third, rejected the fourth and the sixth, and acknowledged that he was "contemplating" something similar to the fifth demand for a mass removal to reservations.[210] For the white settlers, it was a successful meeting.

The hand of those who wished to see vengeance against the Kikuyu population was further strengthened eight days later, when Mau Mau descended upon the Ruck farm in Kinangop on the evening of January 24. Roger and Esme Ruck, together with their six-year-old son Michael, had just finished dinner and dismissed their domestic servants for the evening when one of Roger's farmhands called from outside, claiming to have caught a Mau Mau attacker. Little did Roger know that many of his workers had already been oathed and had been planning to attack his family for some weeks. As he emerged from the farmhouse with a Beretta pistol in hand, he was grabbed from behind. A second attacker then slashed his legs with a panga and as he collapsed more attackers hacked at his body and head. Esme, hearing Roger's screams, ran out with a shotgun in hand, but she too was slaughtered, as was a loyal farmhand—Muthura Nagahu—who came to assist them. The attackers then entered the house, where they broke into the locked upstairs room that Michael was sleeping in and slew him in his bed. One of those involved in the attack had been Michael's domestic servant and just days earlier had carried the six-year-old home when he fell from his pony. The attack sent shockwaves through the white settler community, particularly as the newspapers widely published gruesome photographs of the slaughtered Michael, along with his blood-stained teddy bears, lying where he died.[211]

The following day, January 25, over 1500 settlers marched onto Government House, demanding that Baring act more aggressively against Mau Mau. One even suggested that the way to fix the problem was to "put the troops into the villages and ... shoot 50,000 of them, men, women, and children."[212] The governor refused to go so far but did request permission from Lyttelton to replace the Kenya Police as lead security agency with the British Army, asking that a new commander be sent to the colony to take overall control of the security forces. The war office dispatched Major General W. R. N. "Looney" Hinde as director of military operations.[213] Hinde, who had gained his nickname for his reckless courage displayed in battle, had served as one of Montgomery's famous Desert Rats during the Second World War desert campaign before becoming commander of the 22nd Armoured Brigade in Normandy. Upon arriving in Kenya, he embarked upon a month-long tour of the colony during which time he became immediately sympathetic to the white settler community, particularly after the February 5 murder of yet another European, Anthony Gibson. Gibson's death was particularly meaningful for Hinde as he was a British war veteran who had been taken prisoner in the North African campaign in which Hinde had participated.[214] Within days of his arrival in the territory, Mau Mau's violence had become deeply personal for Hinde.

On March 5, the new military commander sent his first appreciation to the war office. He reported that since Baring's declaration of emergency in October, Mau Mau had murdered 8 Europeans and 106 Africans, with the result that "Every loyal citizen feels the danger despite precautions he takes and the efforts of the forces of law and order to protect." Nevertheless, Hinde was cautiously optimistic. Contrasting the situation with the emergency in Malaya, he noted that although in Malaya the insurgents were "strongly supported" by external communists, in Kenya Mau Mau was "fighting without such formidable assistance." This fact in and of itself lessened the potential danger of Mau Mau and separated it—operationally speaking—from Malaya. Of course, that did not mean the lessons of Malaya could be ignored altogether. Templer had decided that "social measures for the betterment of the inhabitants must go hand in hand with military and police measures for the restoration of law and order," and Hinde intended to follow his lead: "We must heed the example of Malaya and ensure that repressive measures do NOT result in an unbridgeable gap of bitterness between us and the Kikuyu."

It was not only in its outside aid that Mau Mau differed from the communist insurgency in Malaya. When Hinde listed the capabilities of Mau Mau, it bordered on the pathetic when compared with the MRLA. Hinde estimated that there were thirteen gangs operating, armed primarily with pangas and spears, with just fifty-five firearms between them. The "hard-core" element of Mau Mau numbered no more than 100 men, although they could "draw reinforcements from Kikuyu in almost any area where they operate." To combat this threat, the government had at its disposal 8251 Kenyan policemen, 6484 part-time and 1645 full-time members of the Kenya Police Reserve (KPR), 459 soldiers of the Kenya Regiment, 3900 British Army soldiers (excluding the Kenya Regiment), and 368 tribal police. These ground forces were supported by the Air Wing of the KPR, composed of ninety-eight part-time men and three aircraft. Although the police force was still not strong enough numerically to protect all settlements, Hinde believed that "a patrol composed of Europeans, police/KPR askaris, irregular trackers, and Kikuyu Home Guard, approximate strength 15, acting on good information is more than a match for the gangs."

In his recommendations, Hinde did not differ dramatically from the advice given by Gurney, Briggs, and Templer in Malaya. He suggested that "If we are to stamp out Mau Mau we must have Kikuyu support. ... We shall have to give the Kikuyu hope for a good life under our administration. I do not propose to examine now what is to be done to that end, but I would give priority to, for example, higher agricultural wages." Hinde, like Briggs and Templer, believed that a battle for the hearts and minds of the Kikuyu population would make or break the government's counterinsurgency efforts. As in Malaya, Hinde also argued that the effectiveness of the campaign depended on cooperation between the various elements of the security forces, and between the security forces and the government, with the police taking the lead role: "This whole Operation is basically a Police one." Within the policing apparatus, "a high priority must be given to the development of the Special Branch," as it was intelligence that enabled successful operations against Mau Mau. In his conclusions, Hinde stressed that "There is really only one sensible course to take at present and I do not propose to examine any other." It was:

(a) to deny by close policing the Reserves and settled areas to Mau Mau;
(b) to hunt down the gangs in the forest by light military forces;
(c) to prevent the trouble spreading;
(d) to get the Kikuyu on our side.

To do this, he planned to focus on four areas:

(a) *The firm base* where law and order is maintained by the Police with some military backing.

(b) *The Killing ground* in the Prohibited Areas to which the gangs are driven. They are hunted and annihilated by the Army in a sustained and ruthless offensive.

(c) *The provision of useful constructive work* to occupy the unemployed and likely to starve, thereby easing the position in the prisons and Reserve and turning the Emergency to good account.

(d) *The Carrot*, in the shape of a good life for the Kikuyu in the future, satisfying his reasonable demands and ensuring him a better standard of living alongside the British community, thereby bringing the hesitant majority of the tribe firmly to our side. This inducement NOT to be held out in the form of any positive inducements until the application of (a), (b) and (c) above have demonstrated that we are masters of the situation, nor must it be too little and too late.[215]

The plan of action detailed by Hinde, based on the previous four years' experience in Malaya, was sound. The problem came not in its theory but in its practice, for as was already becoming clear, the British in Kenya would act very differently from how they acted in Malaya.

VI. Dirty wars, dirty deeds

At around eight o'clock on the evening of March 26, 1953, the hundred or so members of the Lari Home Guard received word that a body had been found on the perimeter of the settlement, three miles from the main village, in the vicinity of Headman Wainaini's residence. Fearing for the loyalist elder's life, the patrol set off immediately, walking east for almost an hour until they came across the exposed and mutilated body of a local Kikuyu, nailed to a tree in full view of the busy footpath. Puzzled by this scene, which was clearly meant to be discovered, the Home Guard cast furtive glances back toward the village of Lari, now an hour's walk away. Curiosity turned to fear as they saw fires breaking out in their undefended homes. Mau Mau had deliberately led them from their posts and was now attacking their families with impunity.

By the time they arrived back at the village, the fifteen homesteads had all been burnt to the ground and 120 bodies lay smoldering and mutilated. The few who survived described how at nine o'clock, five or six gangs of Mau Mau descended on the village, their faces shielded by linens, armed with pangas, spears, knives, and axes. The gangs immediately tied the doors of the village huts to prevent them from being opened, after which they set light to the thatched roofs. As the terrified occupants struggled to climb through the windows, they were cut down without mercy. Mau Mau quickly threw those who did make it out back into the blaze. The majority of the victims were women and children, the men having joined the Home Guard patrol. The Lari massacre lasted for almost an hour, until the returning men chased the attackers away.[216]

As the Home Guard sought to make sense of the carnage, Anthony Swann—the district commissioner for Kenya's Kiambu district—received a wireless call from the police station at Tigoni claiming that "something was going savagely wrong." Concerned that a company of the King's African Rifles (KAR) had been withdrawn just forty-eight hours earlier, Swann radioed for all police in the district to make their way to the village as quickly as possible. He then collected the tribal police in Kiambu and went "to find out exactly what was going on." The sight that awaited him took his breath away, as he later recalled: "When I got there, there was the most dreadful scene I've ever seen in my life. There were huts in flames, a man called ex-Chief Luca and his family were burnt to death, small children had been crucified. Bodies of other families had been mutilated."[217] It was indeed an atrocity to rival any other the British had witnessed in the postwar era.

Yet the massacre at Lari was not Mau Mau's only mischief on that March evening. At just after ten o'clock—right as the Lari attackers were fleeing the scene—another Mau Mau gang arrived in several lorries at the Naivasha police station in the

Rift Valley. No European officers were present and the highest ranking African—a subinspector—was sleeping in the duty officer's room. Other constables waited in the watchtower, patrolled the perimeter, slept in the bunkhouse, or watched over the 150 prisoners housed near the charge room. None were particularly alert as all had been told that Mau Mau only attacked isolated, country posts. Furthermore, the sight of lorries entering the compound was nothing out of the ordinary. By the time those in the watchtowers and perimeter posts realized that anything was afoot, it was too late: many of those within the compound had been slain from behind and the Mau Mau attackers had broken down the doors of the armory. Within minutes, it was all over. Six African constables lay dead, 47 precision weapons and 4000 rounds of ammunition had been stolen, and all 150 prisoners had been released. While the death toll was much lower than at Lari, the brazen nature of the attack was much greater and the surprise the government felt all the more for that reason.[218]

Yet if Anthony Swann was shocked by the events of March 26, the Home Guard, police, and members of the KAR were even more so and were determined to take their revenge on Kikuyu suspected of oathing. By dawn the next morning, when the Lancashire Fusiliers arrived to assist in capturing the Mau Mau suspects, 200 bodies from Lari had already arrived at the mortuary, far more than had been killed in the village itself, and many others lay slaughtered in the surrounding forest. In an April 5 article written ten days after the massacre, the *East African Standard* suggested that "the security forces had killed 150 people alleged to have been involved in the massacre."[219] Most of those killed had died at the hands of the Home Guard—Kikuyu killing Kikuyu—and the summary justice ended with the arrival of the fusiliers. However, the killings did not stop, as in the coming weeks the police arrested some 300 suspects who all made "extra-judicial statements that amounted to confessions of guilt."[220] All told, the British held nineteen trials where 309 suspects were accused of murder. In all 136 were convicted and 71 eventually hanged. Baring was said to be disappointed with this result, as he had hoped for far more executions.[221]

The capture and killing of Lari suspects was not Baring's only response to the massacre. He also reintroduced the mass screening of the Kikuyu population that had first characterized the emergency, and on April 24 reported to Lyttelton that thus far, "82,840 persons have been arrested in Kenya in connection with the disturbances. Of this total 73,865 have been screened and the remainder released after preliminary questioning." Of those who had been screened, 28,912 were tried and sentenced, 38,947 were released without charge, and the remaining 6006 had been charged but were awaiting trial.[222] Beyond these arrests and screenings, Baring also sought to reform the emergency command structure. With permission from Lyttelton, he promoted Major General Hinde from director of military operations to overall director of operations, a new position modeled on that created for Briggs in Malaya.

Using his new powers, Hinde issued his first directive (Emergency Directive No. 1) on April 12—a little over two weeks after the Lari massacre had taken place. He made clear that the "aim of all operations" in Kenya was to "restore law and order." This would be done in three ways: "(a) preventing the spread of Mau Mau; (b) putting a stop to terrorist attacks; (c) stamping out Mau Mau and the ideology behind it." Gone was any mention of the winning of hearts and minds that had so dominated his March 5 assessment. In terms of command structure, Hinde stated that Baring would retain executive control in a constitutional sense but claimed that "Directions on his behalf will be issued by me." Under Hinde would sit layers of emergency committees at both the provincial and district levels, which would also "receive direction from me." Finally, the general warned that "Time is NOT on our side. The longer we take to destroy Mau Mau, the more formidable it will become and the greater will be the danger of the infection spreading."[223]

Baring was unimpressed with Hinde's directive, particularly with those parts that seemed to usurp power from the governor.

On April 20, he reminded Hinde of the existence of the Colony Emergency Committee and clarified in a telegram to Lyttelton the command structure: "The Colony Emergency Committee, under my Chairmanship, formulates policies governing all measures necessary to restore law and order. In the light of the advice of the Committee, I then issue the policy instructions for the conduct of operations, ensuring that the activities of all Government Departments are directed to the re-establishment of law and order, and delegate authority to the Director of Operations to take such decisions as are necessary in the pursuance of approved policies."[224] Baring made it clear that while Hinde had some discretion with the implementation of operational decisions, ultimate authority and responsibility remained with the governor.

Even the use of such limited authority by Hinde concerned Baring. Since the events at Lari, the general had increasingly gravitated toward the white settler community, to the extent that he seemed willing to overlook the cavalier behavior of some of the security forces toward the Kikuyu people. Between October 1952 and the end of April 1953, 430 Mau Mau suspects had been "shot while attempting to escape or while resisting arrest," the majority of these deaths coming since Hinde's appointment.[225] The final straw for Baring came in May, when Hinde was reported widely in the press as having remarked to a group of European settlers that "100,000 Kikuyu should be put to work in a vast swill-tub."[226] Baring summoned General Sir Brian Robertson, the British commander in chief, Middle East, and asked that he immediately relieve Hinde of his post.[227]

Hinde was replaced by Lieutenant General Sir George "Bobbie" Erskine, who arrived in Nairobi in early June.[228] He was, however, given the title "commander in chief," as Baring had decided to eliminate the position of director of operations after his brief experience with Hinde. Erskine seemed readymade to command a counterinsurgency campaign. Having passed out from the Royal Military Academy, Sandhurst, in April 1918, his first taste of battle came in 1919 when he was posted for two years to Ireland as a young lieutenant, just as the Irish War of Independence was erupting. He quickly progressed through the officer ranks, serving in India from 1922 to 1926 and again from 1931 to 1937, before taking command of the Second Battalion, King's Royal Rifle Corps, following its evacuation from Dunkirk in 1940. He won the Distinguished Service Order as brigadier general staff officer with the 13th Corps at El Alamein, and commanded the 7th Armored Division in its capture of Tunis in 1943. Following the Second World War, Erskine served briefly as deputy to the British military governor in Germany, before commanding first the Hong Kong garrison and then the Territorial Army. He moved to command British forces in Egypt in 1949, where he oversaw the evacuation of British families in October and November 1951 and controversially ordered the destruction of a village to protect a water filtration plant. When he was approached in May 1953 to become commander in chief of British forces in Kenya, Erskine had just been appointed general officer commanding-in-chief eastern command, located in England. As a man of action, he jumped at the chance to return to an operational command.[229]

Upon his appointment, Baring composed a memorandum for the colonial secretary to give to the new military commander. He wrote that after visiting two of the most disturbed areas, "my conclusions are that the situation is better and the machine to deal with rebellion greatly improved." He was particularly encouraged by the fact that "there has been no significant spreading of Mau Mau into other tribes and, secondly, that Kikuyu are now coming into the open in increasing numbers in support of the Government." There had been a "flood of confessions, [a] greatly increased flow of information to the police and [a] rapid buildup of Kikuyu Home Guard." He concluded: "We want more punch and we want it now. Unless we can stimulate it there is a danger of present favourable trend being halted or reversed. ... Nevertheless, I remain convinced that if we can now press home our advantage we might finish them off quickly."[230] Lyttelton, who had visited Kenya a second time in

May to see personally the Lari village site and meet some of the massacre's survivors, agreed with Baring and was likewise determined to finish Mau Mau off quickly.[231]

Erskine did not share the optimism of his two superiors. Within weeks of landing in Kenya, the general became distressed at what he perceived to be a lack of military discipline among the security forces and their tendency toward "indiscriminate shooting." He was particularly sickened by the habit that some units had begun of keeping scorecards for those they had killed and of some commanders paying £5 rewards for each kill.[232] Consequently, Erskine sent to all units—police, army, and Home Guard—an order "reminding them that they represented the British government and the forces of civilization" and instructing them to stop "'beating up' the inhabitants of this country just because they are the inhabitants."[233] He then sent a second order to all commanders, instructing them to "stamp out at once any conduct which he would be ashamed to see used against his own people."[234] When problems continued with the KAR, Erskine dismissed the brigade commander and had a KAR officer, Captain G. S. L. Griffiths, court-martialed for murder after killing two Kikuyu prisoners at close range with a Sten gun. When Griffiths was acquitted for murder due to a technicality (the prosecution could not prove the victim's identity), Erskine had him tried a second time for torture (evidence suggested he had beaten and cut off the ear of his victims before shooting them). This conviction Erskine secured and Griffiths served the next five years in a London prison.[235]

Yet it was not only the abuses of the security forces that disturbed Erskine but the emergency itself, as he felt a natural sympathy for the grievances of Mau Mau, if not for their methods: "[The Africans] hate the police and absolutely loathe the settlers. It is not difficult to realize how much the settler is loathed and the settler does not realize it himself. ... [Mau Mau was rooted in] nothing but rotten administration. ... [I]n my opinion they want a new set of civil servants and some decent police."[236] Such sympathy did not extent to the white settler community, as Erskine confessed in a letter to his wife shortly after arriving in the colony: "I hate the guts of them all, they are all middle-class sluts. I never want to see another Kenyan man or woman and I dislike them all with few exceptions."[237] His comments were clearly grounded in an upper class disdain for "new money." Nevertheless, for Erskine the conflict was simple: a privileged settler community had for generations exploited the land and labor of an indigenous people who were finally striking back—Mau Mau was certainly not witchcraft. As the commander in chief of the security forces Erskine would do his duty and do all he could to quell the militant aspects of Mau Mau, but he would not partake in the larger white hysteria that Lyttelton, Hinde, and even Baring had succumbed to.

The deteriorating situation in Kenya began to place a heavy strain on Lyttelton. At a Buckingham Palace reception preceding the Commonwealth prime ministers' luncheon on June 1, 1953, he approached Edwina Mountbatten, Countess Mountbatten, the last vicereine of India and wife of Louis Mountbatten, first earl Mountbatten of Burma, the last viceroy of India, informing her that he wished to meet Jawaharlal Nehru, the prime minister of India, as he had not yet had a chance to do so. Mountbatten, as one of Nehru's closest friends, obliged, but was immediately filled with regret for doing so:

> A few seconds after [the meeting had taken place] Oliver plunged into the most violent attack on the cruelty and viciousness of *the Africa*. He then recounted in some detail the horrors of the Nyeri [Lari] Massacres. These both Nehru and I naturally deplored as deeply as anyone else, and agreed as to their shocking nature. I remarked, however, that what disturbed me more than anything was the bitterness and mounting hatred on all sides and the subsequent danger of continued killings and excesses. Oliver immediately rounded on me, and with a violent outburst of temper, asked if by my remarks I was accusing his police and officials. I immediately

replied that nothing was further from my mind and that I was accusing no one. I was merely stating what I felt must be true, that when violence was met with violence, bitterness and hatred were likely to be perpetuated and consequently a peaceful solution rendered almost impossible. Oliver said that there were cases of police brutality (two or three I think he mentioned) being investigated, but all but one had already been cleared. As I knew nothing of these it seemed strange that I should learn of these "investigations" on this occasion, and from him personally.

Lyttelton's "outburst" was noticed by several visiting dignitaries, including one of the Commonwealth's "very outspoken representatives from one of our oldest Dominions," who asked her "who that indolent and arrogant Person was." She could provide no excuse for him. Indeed, so exasperated by Lyttelton's behavior was Mountbatten that she committed the encounter to paper that evening so that she might remember exactly what was said.[238]

Mountbatten was not the only person writing about the incident, however. Lyttelton himself documented it. Rather than keeping his words private as Mountbatten had, he put them in a letter to Churchill on June 4:

Edwina Mountbatten introduced me to Pandit Nehru whom I did not know and after some rather frigid exchanges she said "Oliver has just been to Kenya." I said something to the effect that "I have been looking into things there and the ferocity of some of the attacks beggars description. The savagery is terrible." Edwina said, "On both sides." I could not conceal my anger and said, "What do you mean, 'On both sides'? These are murders of Africans by Africans." I had already said that if any of the Police were guilty of any brutality they would be visited with the severity of the law. Practically no evidence had come forward but one case was under investigation. Nehru afterwards said to me that

Africans were being shot down and that we should not solve anything by these means. He was barely civil and turned on his heel.[239]

Lyttelton also wrote to Mountbatten that day, sending her photographs of the Lari massacre and telling her, "It is of course true that there have been allegations that the Police have acted with brutality, beaten up witnesses and so forth. So far no evidence has been brought to prove any of these cases, although one is under investigation. You should know that the atrocities to which I referred are of quite a different character altogether, as the enclosed photographs with which I fear I must affront you will show." He concluded by saying, "I do suggest that no one in possession of the facts could be other than angry when it is suggested that the British Troops or Police in a struggle which is at present almost entirely confined to one African against another should have been accused of similar atrocities. To accuse them of such crimes upon no evidence whatever in front of Pandit Nehru does not serve the cause of the loyal Africans who are subjected to these horrors or for that matter of the Europeans whose lives and safety are so constantly in danger."[240] For Lyttelton, Mountbatten's comments had placed British excesses in the same category as the slaughter at Lari, a comparison he found offensive. To make such a comparison in front of a Commonwealth prime minister was all the more unforgivable.

Mountbatten refused to see Lyttelton's perspective. Having heard that he related their conversation to Churchill, as well as to other members of the cabinet, she wrote to him again on July 7, telling him, "I am afraid I am quite unable to agree with your version of our conversation. ... I was so shocked by the quite uncalled for remarks which you levelled at me on that occasion, that I took a course I have seldom done before, namely to write down in my own handwriting, that same evening, a full account of what actually occurred. ... I have now had this typed out, and attach it so that you may see what my immediate recollection of that particular incident was."[241] Lyttelton read her account in good humor, saying that he would not be "drawn into defending myself against charges" and that he took her comments "in good part and like to see the spirit with which you seize any weapon at hand, or not at hand, with which to belabor me." He would, however, have the last word:

> But one misunderstanding or inaccuracy I must correct. You say I attacked the cruelty of Africans. This of course arises from the opinion, alas so widely held, that the struggle in Kenya is between black and white, an opinion which I have done everything I can to dispel, and which I wanted to dispel from Nehru's mind also. Seventeen Europeans have been killed by Mau Mau and over 400 Africans. The African has never been attacked by me: that would have made complete nonsense. It is a natural misunderstanding to confuse remarks about Mau Mau, because they happen to be Africans, with attacks on Africans as such, but it is the latter who have suffered and I am determined to see them protected.[242]

Even though Lyttelton believed that Mau Mau as a movement was "evil," he continued to take a positive, if paternalistic, view of the Kikuyu people as a whole, and would do all in his power to see that they continued to live with the benefits of British governance.[243]

If Kenya was causing the colonial secretary loss of sleep, the same could not be said of Malaya, which was continuing to show steady improvement. Indeed, if success was judged by an increasing number of insurgents "eliminated," then British triumph was beyond the shadow of doubt: from May 1950 through April 1951, the security forces killed 1038 insurgents; from May 1951 through April 1952, 1350; and from May 1952 through April 1953, 1426. At the same time, there was a "marked decline" in security force casualties, with only 41 soldiers and 116 policemen killed in the year May 1952 to April 1953.[244] Nevertheless, Templer continued to use controversial and, at times, morally ambiguous methods to deal with his opponents. On June 17, 1953—as Lyttelton was embroiled in his spat with Mountbatten—the high commissioner issued orders for the formation of the Special Operational Volunteer Force, an armed unit of 180 surrendered insurgents organized into twelve platoons of fifteen men each, which would be deployed into the jungle to hunt down and kill its former comrades. Although the police commissioner rather than the army commander was its ostensible commanding officer, it had no powers of arrest and could not perform in an auxiliary role to the regular police.[245] Templer was, quite literally, using the enemy to kill the enemy.

Templer also decided to use artillery for the first time in his operations against the communists, deploying "O" Field Troop of the 1st Singapore Regiment, Royal Artillery, on July 27. Captain Peter Head, troop commander of "O" Troop, described how their "first round in anger was fired on August 4." By the close of that day, they had fired 128 rounds at reported communist camps and lines of communication, and on February 26, 1954, they fired their 10,000th round, "indicating the amount of activity in the first seven months." Head reported that HQ Malaya Command had designated five main roles for artillery in the emergency:

Flushing: the application of pressure on CTs in areas where they were known to be operating, and where their presence had been established, to drive them into prepared ground where they could be engaged and killed.

Harassing Fire: keeping CTs constantly on the move, especially at night, preventing rest and food gathering, and to lower their morale. Denying their use of camp sites in cooperating with AOP fire observation.

Blocking escape routes: preventing CT movement away from our own troops, and driving them into ground of our own choosing.

Deception: lulling CTs into a false sense of security through intense activity elsewhere and relax their vigilance while they were the real targets of ground troops.

Illumination: the use of flares for night illumination when required.

Head also noted that there was one additional role, not specified by HQ Malaya but certainly expected: "to 'show the flag,' as it had been established that the presence of artillery in action had a marked effect on civilian morale with a strong deterrent effect on CT supporters."[246] If nothing else, the constant shelling of the jungle provided a comforting firework display for the government's allies while demonstrating to the insurgents the superiority of Western weaponry.

Such artillery bombardment, combined with the continued chemical destruction of insurgent crops and roadside vegetation, the aggressive patrolling by army platoons and police jungle squadrons, and the provision of social welfare, education, and employment in the new villages, had the desired effect. On August 28, 1953, Templer informed the colonial secretary that on September 3 he intended to proclaim parts of Malacca a "white area." He explained in his telegram that it had "long been my feeling that it would give a great fillip to morale if I could raise some of these irksome restrictions on the liberty of individuals in areas where, in the opinion of the local authorities it could safely be done. Such an area I call a WHITE area." He continued: "A scheme of this sort might have considerable results. Apart from its repercussions on public opinion outside Malaya, it might well have a great affect for good on the local population here, encouraging those people in areas where restrictions are still, of necessity, imposed, to co-operate more freely with Government to remove the CTs so that they also could reap the benefits of greater freedom." In Malacca, the British government would lift all curfews, impose no food controls, remove all restrictions on shopkeepers, and search no one for food at village gates. In doing so, Templer hoped to restore trust between the government and the residents of Malaya.[247]

Lyttelton gave his blessing in a one-line telegram: "Congratulations. These risks are worth taking. I hope the experiment comes off."[248] The white areas—representing a devolution of power and responsibility to the local population once loyalty was assured—encapsulated the colonial secretary's vision for the empire. They seemed to suggest that for all the criticism that had emanated from Parliament and elsewhere, he had been right to stick to his guns.

VII.   A fresh start in Kenya?

In the early morning hours of June 24, 1953, soldiers of 39 Infantry Brigade, together with the 1st Battalion, King's African Rifles and members of the Kenya Regiment, the police, and the Kikuyu Home Guard, panned out into the forest and across the Kikuyu Reserve of Kenya's Fort Hall district as part of Operation Buttercup, the largest offensive attempted since Baring's declaration of emergency the previous October. General Bobbie Erskine had been in command of emergency operations for less than two weeks but had already determined that a change in direction was necessary, with a far more aggressive stance taken against the insurgency. After intensive questioning of the Special Branch, he had discovered that Hinde's projections of Mau Mau strength were grossly underestimated; the police informed him that there were actually 2500 to 3000 forest fighters, 600 of whom could be described as "hard core." Historians have since shown that in the summer of 1953, there were in fact 5000 Mau Mau on Mount Kenya, 6000 in the Aberdares forests, with several thousand more in the Rift Valley.[249] With such numbers stacked against him, Erskine realized that a more protracted and organized counterinsurgency campaign was needed than had thus far been attempted.

Operation Buttercup lasted from June 24 until July 8. It was divided into three stages—penetration of the forests, control of the forest fringes, and reclamation of the Kikuyu Reserves—and had mixed results. In the Ruathia Reserve, which had been in a "state of anarchy" since the start of the emergency, the security forces enacted a "well executed" operation, with "excellent co-operation between British and African troops," in which ninety-five Mau Mau fighters were killed, British administration was restored, communal labor was established, and a Kikuyu Guard post was formed. In Reserve Locations 12 and 13, the results were "less spectacular." Although a number of Mau Mau were killed and administration was restored, the security forces could encourage no Kikuyu to form a Home Guard and the majority of the residents remained disengaged, if not outwardly hostile. On the forest fringes, the security forces were more successful than in Reserve Locations 12 and 13, although there was still "some movement" of Mau Mau from the forests to the villages. The operation was least successful in the forest itself, where although many Mau Mau camps were found and destroyed, the security forces had no major contact with an actual Mau Mau gang.

In an appreciation written shortly after the operation, the executive officer of the district emergency committee listed seven lessons learnt. First, the operation confirmed the large number of Mau Mau residing in the forests and proved beyond a shadow of doubt that the government had a major problem on its hands. Second, the RAF aerial bombardment that accompanied the army and police patrols had caused great "terror," and it more than anything else encouraged those who deserted and surrendered to do so. Third, the operations showed that Mau Mau's sentry system was far more advanced than previously thought, and necessitated the army to use "smaller patrols and greater cunning" in future operations. Fourth, the Kikuyu Guard could not be trusted. The appreciation suggested that the guard be given "a very simple role and must not be informed where they are going until they arrive on the scene." It further recommended that "When used on operations, [the Kikuyu Guard] must wear brightly coloured headbands, issued specially for a particular operation and then withdrawn." Fifth, the operational area had been far too large and it would be better in future operations to form a tighter cordon around a smaller space. Sixth, the operation showed the importance of cooperation between the army, police, and civil administration, and warned that "The partial failure of one small unit operation, planned and carried out without liaison with either police or administration, emphasised the absolute necessity for co-operation at all levels." Finally, all prisoners should be immediately questioned by trained interrogators—the average soldier and policeman should play no role in the gathering of crucial intelligence.[250] Two similar operations launched in July and August, Operations Carnation and Primrose, experienced similar mixed results and demonstrated parallel lessons.[251]

Consequently, Erskine wrote to Lieutenant General Sir Harold Redman, the vice-chief of the imperial general staff, on July 28, expressing some of his concerns. At the heart of the matter, he believed, was the weakness of the police, which necessitated the deployment of numerous soldiers in a policing role simply to make up for their inadequacies. If the police could be strengthened, the role of the army could be lessened and the situation could return to normalcy more quickly. He suggested that the static police force be increased "very considerably" so that the army could be relieved of "placing posts in certain vulnerable areas to protect and reassure the population," and requested the establishment of a "striking force of mobile police in each District," with 3 European officers and 60 African other ranks per district, totaling 44 officers and 875 other ranks. Because such recruitment and training could not be completed until the end of the year, he recommended a further deployment of army forces to bring the troop strength up to five British battalions from its current three battalions.[252] On August 17, Antony Head, the war secretary, agreed to Erskine's request,[253] and in September the 1st Battalion, Northumberland Fusiliers, and the 1st Battalion, Royal Inniskilling Fusiliers, landed in Nairobi as part of 49 Infantry Brigade. At the same time, the Lancashire Fusiliers were replaced by the 1st Battalion, The Black Watch Regiment, and a battalion of the King's African Rifles was recalled from Malaya, bringing the net gain of troops in Kenya up to three battalions, or about 1800 soldiers.[254]

With these extra troops arriving in September, Erskine began to finesse the government's surrender policy in anticipation of his next major operation. In his Emergency Directive No. 9, issued on July 28, Erskine noted the success of the Malayan surrender policy and stated that "The time has come to have ready plans for similar action here." In contrast to Malaya, however, he intended to keep the public in the dark about the surrender policy to avoid "heated public controversy" and ordered that all "'surrender' propaganda be directed to reach the terrorists themselves with a minimum of general publicity." He made it clear that his surrender policy was not a general amnesty:

> The policy is to encourage surrender by telling the terrorists that if they surrender voluntarily they will not be prosecuted for a capital offence merely in respect of their adherence to terrorism, e.g. carrying arms. It is not proposed, however, to offer them immunity against prosecution in respect of murders or other atrocities (whether capital or non-capital) which can be proved against them.

He warned that the Kikuyu Home Guard would have to be briefed on the policy "in case those wishing to surrender should fall into their hands and be dealt with in such a way as to discourage other surrenders," but suggested that the guard be told only the bare minimum. In general, it would be far better for the surrenders to be taken by the army, civil administration, or regular police units. He reiterated that "When they do surrender, terrorists should not be ill-treated. They may subsequently be our main propaganda weapon in encouraging further surrenders." He finished by again drawing attention to the benefits of the surrender policy in Malaya:

> In Malaya, surrendered terrorists were a very reliable source of operational intelligence, and, when well treated by the

Security Forces, were subsequently used successfully to identify other terrorists, food-suppliers, couriers and other terrorist supporters; they were also used as guides to operational patrols, on screening teams, etc., and in some cases they were even used as members of patrols of the Security Forces against terrorists gangs in areas in which they knew the paths, hideouts, arms and food caches, etc., used by the terrorists. Sometimes a surrendered terrorist would be reluctant to give any information at first; such men were not beaten or ill-treated in any way to extract information from them— that is an unprofitable way of dealing with them. The procedure was much more subtle and rewarding: in such cases, the man (or woman) was just put in amongst previous surrendered terrorists who had "talked" and had assisted the Security Forces, and it was found that in a very short time he would be "spilling the beans" like the rest of them. This psychological "softening-up" process was found to be most effective, and it did not prejudice the policy of good treatment, and subsequent propaganda based thereon, as beatings and rough treatment would have done.[255]

Erskine was determined to rid the emergency operations of some of the brutality that had characterized them under Hinde, particularly after the Lari massacre.[256]

Immediately following the issuance of Erskine's directive, Henry Potter—who had become chief secretary following his replacement as governor by Baring in October—composed a memorandum providing further details on how the surrender policy would actually work. No surrendered insurgents would be prosecuted at the police interrogation centers. However, case files would be opened on all who surrendered voluntarily. If evidence suggested that the insurgent had been involved in a noncapital crime, his file would be forwarded to the assistant commissioner of police (CID), who in turn would forward the file to the assistant commissioner of police (Special Branch).

The Special Branch would then request from the governor a detention order under Emergency Regulation No. 2 and the surrendered insurgent would be interned in a special camp for others in his situation where he could be rehabilitated and eventually returned to Kikuyu society as a free man. If, however, evidence suggested that the surrendered insurgent had been involved in a murder or other "grave atrocity," his case file would be sent from the CID to the attorney general, who would decide on prosecution. For optimal propaganda purposes, "Prosecutions will not be undertaken until the time is decided to be opportune," no matter what the offence committed.[257] In these important cases, Kenya's criminal justice system would be co-opted for the needs of the emergency. Justice would certainly not be blind but would see with a very calculating eye.

On August 20, three days after the war secretary agreed to the dispatch of an additional two infantry battalions to Kenya, Baring announced that he would implement Erskine's surrender policy beginning August 24.[258] On August 21, Lyttelton gave it his blessing.[259] When the appointed day arrived, the RAF dropped propaganda leaflets over the Kenyan forest, while army and police patrols posted them on trees along known Mau Mau supply routes and paths. The leaflets, signed by both Baring and Erskine, carried a mixture of threat and promise:

Many Mau Mau gangsters have been killed so far. The Government has now put in more police and troops to hunt and kill the Mau Mau. The loyal Kikuyu, Embu and Meru Guard grow stronger every day. Only starvation or death awaits you if you continue to fight. ... Many of you have been forced by Mau Mau to join their gangs and assist them in their acts of violence. The Government now gives you an opportunity to save your life. Come in and surrender yourself. If you do, Government will understand your position and will not execute you for having carried arms or consorted with the Mau Mau terrorists. This especially applies to you if you have not committed murder. For all those there is NOW an opportunity to save your lives. Make up your mind quickly and surrender. YOU HAVE NOT MUCH TIME. But you have a chance now, so decide quickly, for operations against the Mau Mau will be ruthlessly continued against those who do not surrender.[260]

By January 17, 1955, over 800 Kikuyu had surrendered under these terms. Surrendered Mau Mau insurgents subsequently became a vital source of intelligence for the British security forces and played a critical role in continued operations against Mau Mau.[261]

Yet as Erskine had noted in his directives, the surrender policy could only succeed if all those who surrendered were treated well and, despite his best efforts in this regard, the commander was still running into problems. On September 21, the trial of Jack Lionel Ruben of the Kenya Regiment and Richard Geoffrey Keates of the Kenya Police Reserve began in Nairobi. Each was accused of beating to death Elijah Gideon Njeru under questioning. The jury's decision to acquit them of manslaughter and instead find them guilty of the much lesser charge of "assault occasioning bodily harm," with just a fifty and one hundred pound fine, respectively, contradicted Erskine's emphasis on the fair treatment of suspects. He was further undermined by the judge's statement of sympathy with the jury and his claim that "I do not think I would have imposed a very much greater sentence even if the conviction of them had been of manslaughter."[262]

More troubling for Erskine was the case of Brian Haywood. On September 4, Erskine, along with Sir Frederick Crawford, the deputy governor of Kenya, met with a delegation from the British government in Tanganyika to discuss the repatriation of 8000 Kikuyu in the Northern Province back to Kenya. Crawford and Erskine agreed that "in the interests of East Africa generally," it was preferable to have all Kikuyu confined to Kenya in order to limit the spread of Mau Mau. However, "for political and military reasons," Erskine could not agree to the immediate repatriation of all these Kikuyu. He suggested instead that the Kenyan government take back only those who were proven supporters of Mau Mau, with more loyal Kikuyu being repatriated at a later date. To ascertain who were Mau Mau and who were not, Erskine offered to send screening teams to Tanganyika. At meetings on September 28 and 30, the Kenyan government decided to send Brian Haywood to lead the screening teams. Haywood, the son of a British settler in Kenya and a temporary district officer, had experience of leading screening teams on the Kikuyu Reserves, and volunteered to accompany more screening teams in the Rift Valley to gain additional exposure before leaving.

On October 8, Haywood and two screening teams arrived in Tanganyika. They began screening the Kikuyu population on October 12 and continued until October 17, during which time six Kikuyu were found to be Mau Mau supporters. On that morning, however, the provincial commissioner in the northern part of the colony heard rumors that "the screening teams were being very rough with the Kikuyu." He checked with a local European farmer, Colonel Minnery, who confirmed that excessive violence was being used as part of the process, after which the provincial commissioner ordered an immediate stop to the screening. Two days later, on October 19, a crown counsel and the Tanganyikan assistant commissioner of police (CID) flew from Dar-es-Salaam to the Northern Province to investigate the allegations. Their report revealed a shocking truth:

[V]iolence, in the form of whipping on the soles of the feet, burning with lighted cigarettes and tying leather thongs round the neck and dragging the victims along the ground, had been used on those interrogated. Between 170 and 200 were interrogated of whom at least 32 were badly injured and others received some injury. Hayward himself took an active part in the chastisement of the Africans and is said to have threatened to shoot one man after pointing his revolver at him.[263]

Subsequent investigations revealed that Kikuyu had also been whipped and beaten with sticks and soaked with water before being made to spend the night without bedding on the floors of huts soaked with water. One of those who had been beaten on the feet to the extent that he had difficulty walking committed suicide within days of the assault.[264]

The British government immediately condemned the screenings and charged and tried Hayward and ten African members of his screening team, who were all found guilty on November 10. Nevertheless, Hayward was sentenced to just three months' imprisonment without hard labor for each victim, to run concurrently, and was fined 100 pounds. Subsequently, he was permitted to perform "extra-mural labour instead of undergoing imprisonment," which he fulfilled with three months' clerical work in a hotel.[265] Despite the finding of guilt, the Haywood case proved intensely embarrassing to Erskine, who had made a point of emphasizing the humane methods employed by the security forces in Kenya and who had hand-selected Haywood to lead the screening teams in Tanganyika.

The commander's embarrassment was heightened by a decision taken by Baring on November 28 to reinstate Haywood as district officer in Kenya once his sentence was complete, based on "his youth [he was just nineteen years old], the lack of supervision of his activities in Tanganyika, [and] his previous good record."[266] Incensed by this undermining of his authority, on November 30, Erskine again issued a special message addressing abuse of prisoners to all army officers and policemen:

I must remind all Members of the Security Forces of the instructions I gave them on the 23rd June. It is absolutely imperative to the success of the operations and to the honour of the Forces operating under my command that every single member of these forces—Army and Police—should carry out their duties strictly in accordance with the letter and spirit of my instructions. ... Since I issued this instruction there has been a satisfactory General Standard of Conduct. There have however been some complaints which lead me to think there are still a few individuals who are taking the law into their own hands and acting outside my orders—I am out to catch and punish such people—there must be no ground for complaint—even one act of indiscipline can tarnish our reputation.[267]

Not content with this statement, Erskine continued to badger Baring and, with the support of the attorney general, finally convinced the governor on December 15 to overturn his previous decision and terminate Haywood's employment as district officer.[268]

Yet allegations of abuse by the British security forces—particularly the police—continued to haunt Erskine. On December 17, Baring wrote to Lyttelton informing him that "a case is coming before the Resident Magistrate at Nakuru on 21st December which has an unpleasant similarity to the Hayward case." Three European Kenya Police Reserve officers—Sawyer, Pharazyn, and Hvass—along with six Africans were charged with assault causing bodily harm, having carried out interrogations at a police post near Naivasha, which involved severe beatings with whips. Additionally, Sawyer and Pharazyn (though not Hvass) were charged with picking up an elderly Kikuyu by his hands and feet and holding him horizontally over a fire until his clothing caught fire and he was badly burned. A European farmer reported the incident to the regular police, who immediately suspended the reserve officers. The attorney general believed that "the regular police at Naivasha investigated the case thoroughly and conscientiously [and] there is no question of covering up." All Africans involved pleaded guilty on December 3, but Baring did not know how the Europeans would plead when they came to trial on December 21.[269]

At the trial, Hvass immediately pleaded guilty and was fined fifty pounds sterling for his abuses. Sawyer and Pharazyn, however, pleaded not guilty and elected to be tried by jury.[270] Their plea proved a wise one and the jury—composed largely of white settlers—found them not guilty.[271] Meanwhile, on December 10 the war secretary announced in Parliament that Erskine had recommended a court of inquiry be set up to investigate British abuses, as the general "conceived it to be his duty to uncover everything and to force into court even the most unpleasant crimes and that it should be his aim to clean up rather than cover up." Consequently, he dispatched Lieutenant General Sir Kenneth McLean to establish such a court.[272]

McLean arrived in Kenya within a week. He presented his findings to Erskine at the end of the month, and the commander in chief sent his report to the war office on January 1, 1954. Unfortunately, the court—and Erskine—chose to focus solely on the British army and thus the police and police reserve (who were responsible for the vast majority of reported abuses) were not examined. Consequently, the report had a whitewashed feel to it, however unintentional. Erskine wrote:

> The troops under my command have shown a high sense of responsibility and application to duty. There are no grounds for accusing them of indiscriminate shooting, irresponsible conduct or inhuman practices. There have been individual lapses from the general high standard of conduct but these have been dealt with as a matter of discipline and certain other cases are pending disciplinary action. The fact that such cases are dealt with is an indication of the determination of all ranks to do their duty in the best traditions of the British Army.

He did suggest that the practice of paying rewards for Mau Mau kills was "stupid and it may be childish," but found it to be "not vicious." Finally, with regard to the cutting off of Mau Mau hands, he stated that he had now forbidden the practice although allowed that it "was not done in a spirit of sadism but for the practical reasons that identification was necessary and it was impossible to carry bodies any distance."[273] In his public comments, Erskine acknowledged there had been abuses but claimed these had been dealt with appropriately and were not reflective of British Army practices as a whole.

In a private memorandum to the individual commanders of his regiments, he took a harsher tone:

(a) There will be no mutilation of bodies for identification or any other purposes. If it is impossible to finger print a dead terrorist, or if it is impossible to move his body to a place where identification can be carried out, I am prepared to accept the loss of identification.

(b) It is obviously necessary to keep a record of operations and of the casualties arising out of such operations but these records must be kept in proper surroundings (offices, Intelligence Rooms, etc). On no account will they be displayed in public or used to foster a spirit of competition or to induce soldiers to go beyond the bounds of their duty. Pride of Regiment is in every way desirable but this should not extend to soldiers boasting in public of the numbers of men killed in operations by their units.

(c) No financial or other rewards should be necessary to induce a soldier to do this duty. This practice will cease.[274]

To outsiders, Erskine was determined to defend the honor of the British Army and downplay the scope of mistreatment and degrading practices that had occurred. In private, however, he put his officers and soldiers on notice. There would be no abuse. Any such behavior would be punished. Regardless of what had occurred prior to his arrival in June, Erskine made it clear he was attempting a fresh start in Kenya. The problem, however, was that the police and the Kikuyu Home Guard did not receive this message.

VIII. The end of the Churchill years

On July 27, 1954, Oliver Lyttelton tendered his resignation to Sir Winston Churchill. He admitted that there was "probably no wholly opportune moment for a Secretary of State for the Colonies to resign," but suggested that although, "[m]any colonial problems remain, and others will follow," by and large "the main tasks with which this Government was faced when they took office are now well in hand."[275] In a letter written two days later, he praised his chief civil servant, telling him, "We have had to face many difficulties and obdurate problems, and the experience, wisdom and good humour with which the office has dealt with them have more than compensated me for the rather tempestuous seas which I have had to navigate in the House of Commons."[276] Reflecting on his years at the colonial office, Lyttelton was proud of his accomplishments:

I can hardly think that colonial conditions will be other than fairly troublesome for the next decade. Western ideas of democracy are heady wine for these peoples, and they are only too anxious to do in a fortnight what it has taken us seven hundred years to build up. But I think things are steadier, and that we have a reasonable prospect of so gaining the confidence of the colonial people as to be able to share the responsibilities for government and guide them along the right road.[277]

Churchill was "grieved" to see Lyttelton go, a man whose "personal friendship" he had "treasured" through "forty stormy years."[278] He could not have been surprised, though. The colonial secretary wrote as early as December 3, 1953, warning that "The time is drawing near when I must resign my office, leave politics, and reseek my fortunes in the narrower world of industry and commerce." His reason for going was clear: "I can only finance myself for a few months more. ... I am nearly 61 and shall start from a capital point of view where I was when I was about 30. Moreover, if I were to die with the red box [that carries cabinet papers] still in the house my family would be very hard up indeed. The moment I go back to industry they are adequately provided for."[279] As devoted as Lyttelton was to the advancement of colonial peoples, those closer to home now had to take priority.

The six months preceding Lyttelton's resignation were ones of great change in the empire, particularly in Malaya and Kenya. For Templer, they spelled the end of his tour as high commissioner and director of operations. As with Lyttelton's, his departure was not a shock. When he accepted the position in January 1952, he received a written assurance from the colonial secretary that it would be for no more than two years. A year later, in April 1953, Viscount Montgomery wrote to him, advising him to "leave Malaya in the Spring of 1954, have six months leave, and succeed Gale in BAOR [British Army of the Rhine] in November 1954 and succeed Harding in November 1955 [as chief of the imperial general staff]."[280] On a visit to London in November 1953, Templer confirmed this plan. He intended to remain high commissioner until June 1954, when he would be succeeded by Sir Donald MacGillivray, his deputy high commissioner since 1952. MacGillivray, however, would not also take the position of director of operations. Instead, the roles of high commissioner and director of operations would once again be separated. From June 1954, the army's GOC, Malaya, would become director of operations, with control over all security forces. In 1953, that man was General Hugh Stockwell, but Stockwell was due to be replaced in April 1954 by Lieutenant General Geoffrey Bourne, who himself had interviewed for Templer's position in January 1952. When Templer officially resigned, MacGillivray became high commissioner and Bourne director of operations.[281] As promised, after a period of leave, Templer was appointed commander in chief of the British Army of the Rhine, later becoming chief of the imperial general staff.

Templer's final months in Malaya witnessed a continued improvement of the situation. Following success in the Malacca "White Area," the general extended the white areas to also cover northern Trengganu, Perlis, northern Kedah, and Kelantan. By the beginning of April 1954, there were 800,000 people living without restrictions in white areas. Templer was so pleased with this rate of progress that on April 21 he wrote to Lyttelton, informing him, "We have not had a single incident in any of the White Areas. Before the middle of May I shall be declaring the whole of Mersing District, which is most of the East Coast of Johore, a white area and I am hoping that this will have a considerable psychological effect in that very difficult State."[282] Mersing District extended the white areas to more than a million people. In his final letter to Lyttelton, written on May 24, Templer boasted, "The White Area conception still goes ahead. The declaration of Mersing District white had a very good effect in Johore. Today eight out of the eleven States and Settlements contain white areas and just about a quarter of the whole population of Malaya is living in them. ... More White Areas are on the way."[283] True to his word, when Templer departed Malaya in early June 1954 there were 1,300,000 people living and working within white areas.[284]

In Kenya, change was no less dramatic. From January 8 to 26, 1954, a cross-party parliamentary delegation visited the colony. Its conclusions were damning. Based on the evidence it gathered, it believed "the influence of Mau Mau in the Kikuyu area, except in certain localities, has not declined; it has, on the contrary, increased; in this respect the situation has deteriorated and the danger of infection outside where the Kikuyu are is greater, not less, than it was at the beginning of the State of Emergency." It pointed the finger of blame for this worsening situation at the police force, which it claimed was undermining any potential hearts and minds campaign:

> [B]rutality and malpractices by the Police have occurred on a scale which constitutes a threat to public confidence in the forces of law and order. Official records with which we were provided show that there have been 130 prosecutions for brutality among the Police forces, ending in 73 convictions. Forty cases are pending. There have also been 29 prosecutions

for corruption of which there were 12 convictions; 13 are pending. These are significant figures, representing much larger numbers of complaints received by the authorities, investigated and not proceeded with because they could not be proved or were disproved by investigation.

The delegation suggested it was "useless to expect the general public to respect, and collaborate with, the Police if the Police Force is gravely implicated in brutality and corruption."[285]

Baring responded to this criticism. Immediately following publication of the report, he formed a war council, chaired by Erskine, which had the responsibility of managing a swift end to the emergency. In Malaya, the police was at the heart of the counterinsurgency campaign. In Kenya, Baring decided to place more emphasis on the army.[286] This decision was prompted not only by parliamentary censure but also by a feeling by all involved that "During the months of January and February 1954 there was a distinct change in the situation and it was soon possible to identify and locate enemy gangs throughout the Rift [Valley]."[287] From the British perspective, the time had finally come to finish Mau Mau off.

The war council determined that the best way to do this was by an aggressive army offensive into the forest, followed by surrender offers targeted at Mau Mau's leaders, which would go beyond the surrender offers of the previous September. This military thrust met with immediate success and on January 15, 1954, the security forces captured Waruhiu Itote—also known as General China and one of Mau Mau's most senior commanders. Itote, fearing torture, was surprised to be taken to hospital for treatment of his wounds, after which he was interrogated in his own language and without physical violence by assistant superintendent Ian Henderson of the Kenya Police. In an extraordinary turn of events, Itote agreed to cooperate with the government and take the British surrender terms to his former comrades in return for clemency. This the British immediately agreed to and on March 4 Baring announced that Itote had been pardoned.[288] It was a remarkable vindication of Erskine's insistence on the humane treatment of captured enemy suspects.

Elsewhere, British operations were equally successful, if more violent. The 1st Battalion, Devonshire Regiment, revived its nickname "The Bloody Eleventh" during these months, a moniker its hometown newspaper *The Western Morning News* delighted in.[289] Rex Charles Mace of the 156 (East Africa) Independent Heavy Anti-Aircraft Battery of the East Africa Artillery—the only artillery unit engaged in operations in Kenya during the emergency—reported that on February 16, "the Battery fought its biggest action since the start of the Emergency, when the sections commanded by Lts R H Young and D J Budd engaged a gang which was attacking a police post near Kandar. In the ensuing running battle 40 Mau Mau were killed, 8 of them personally by Lt. Budd, who was subsequently awarded the MBE for his brave conduct."[290]

Two days before this action, Henderson and Itote flew from Nairobi to Nyeri, where they established a Special Branch operational headquarters. They code-named their operation "Operation Wedgwood," playing on Itote's *nom de guerre* General China (Wedgwood being an expensive brand of fine bone china). Unfortunately for the British, Wedgwood was a failure. Itote met with several top Mau Mau leaders between March 6 and March 27, and by April 6 over 1000 Mau Mau fighters, with another 600 on their way, were encamped at Konyu with the expectation of a surrender offer. On April 7, however, they were set upon by the 7th Battalion, the King's African Rifles, who claimed to be unaware of Wedgwood. Twenty-five Mau Mau were killed, seven captured, and the remainder fled. The action prematurely ended the surrender negotiations.[291] Nevertheless, despite its failure to secure a mass surrender, Wedgwood did succeed in provoking suspicion of their leadership within Mau Mau ranks and forcing a divide between the leaders themselves. Mau Mau would never again mount a serious offensive.

Furthermore, Wedgwood was not the only operation mounted by the British security forces in Kenya that spring. In the early morning hours of April 24, Erskine launched Operation Anvil in Nairobi. Holding a strong resemblance to Operation Agatha—the action against the Jewish Agency in Palestine on June 29, 1946—British army soldiers and members of the Kikuyu Home Guard surrounded the city at 4:30 a.m., blocking every road and path and preventing any African from entering or leaving. All buses and trains were stopped and African taxis were prohibited from operating. At 6:00 a.m., the soldiers and Home Guard were joined by police officers and members of the Kenya Police Reserve. By sunrise, there were 20,000 members of the British security forces in Nairobi. These forces set about a four-week operation, during which the city was declared a "closed district" and the roadblocks remained in place.

The purpose of Operation Anvil was to screen every African, to separate the Kikuyu from members of other tribes, and to subject the separated Kikuyu to more intensive screening. The operation was without precedent in its scope. Within forty-eight hours, the security forces had screened 11,600 Kikuyu, of whom 8300 were detained. By the end of the operation—on May 26—more than 50,000 Kikuyu had been screened. Of these, 24,100 were detained, with an additional 6150 "repatriated" back to reserves in Central Province.[292] By the end of May, the Kikuyu population detained without trial by the British surpassed 70,000 and Nairobi was quiet for the first time since the emergency began. Erskine later remarked that Operation Anvil was "the turning point in the Emergency."[293] In a sense he was correct. Mau Mau lost its urban base. Without it, the movement was pushed deeper and deeper into the forest where it was engaged by the security forces with minimal effect on the civilian population. Militarily, Anvil was a success. In the larger campaign for the hearts and minds of the Kikuyu population, however, it was a disaster. As historian David Anderson has written:

In its pervasive, all-encompassing magnitude, Operation Anvil had been both a bureaucratic triumph and a political disaster. The British had pilloried friend and foe alike. ... Anvil broke the back of Mau Mau's organization in Nairobi, but at what cost? For the respectable Kikuyu middle classes, many of whom lived in fear and dread of Mau Mau intimidation, Anvil had been nothing less than a betrayal. Already threatened by Mau Mau, they had now been the victims of a state-sponsored raid.[294]

In his last months at the colonial office, Kenya was a headache for Oliver Lyttelton in a way that Malaya had never been. But it was not his only headache. In January 1954—while the cross-parliamentary delegation was in the midst of its visit to Kenya—the colonial secretary appointed Sir Robert Armitage as governor to Cyprus. The British Crown had first seized Cyprus from the Ottoman Turks in 1878 during the premiership of Benjamin Disraeli, when the government concluded that it needed a solid supply line to the eastern Mediterranean in the face of increased traffic on the newly opened Suez Canal.[295] The Greek government immediately requested that Cyprus be turned over to them, claiming that the Turks had stolen the territory some 300 years earlier. Disraeli dismissed the request, choosing instead to keep ostensible Ottoman rule in place while also establishing a British protectorate. Within both Greek and Greek-Cypriot society, a protest movement known as *Enosis* began, holding the belief that Cyprus should become one of the Greek islands based on "a consciousness of belonging to Greek culture and civilization."[296] This sentiment was expressed more widely following the establishment of a local Legislative Assembly in 1882, where Greek-Cypriot representatives openly called for *Enosis*. It was heightened with the Greco-Turkish war of 1896. With the British declaration of war against the Ottoman Empire in November 1914, the British government officially annexed Cyprus into its empire, ending any fiction of Ottoman control. Those in favor of *Enosis* celebrated, believing the British would now turn over the island to the Greeks. Their hopes were dashed, however, when the pro-German government in Athens refused Herbert Asquith's offer to give Greece Cyprus in return for Greek entry into the war on the British side.[297]

Following the war and the complete breakup of the Ottoman Empire, Britain confirmed in the 1923 Treaty of Lausanne that Cyprus was now a Crown Colony, a sovereignty the leader of the new Turkish Republic, Kemal Ataturk, reluctantly recognized. As part of this arrangement, the Legislative Assembly was closed, with all power transferring to the British colonial government. The Greek-Cypriots were not as keen as the Turks to accept their British masters and in October 1931—following eight years of uneasy relations with the colonial administration—they revolted, rioting in the cities of Nicosia, Larnaca, Famagusta, Lyrenia, Paphos, and Limassol, the latter of which suffered the burning of the district commissioner's residence. The colonial governor, Sir Ronald Storrs, immediately declared a curfew and dispatched the Cyprus police, but this having failed to quell the riots, he requested help from the United Kingdom. Within two days, HMS *London* appeared off the coast of Larnaca, followed two days later by HMS *Colombo*, which landed marines at Famagusta. These naval ships and marines were supported by RAF air detachments from Egypt, which flew squadrons of bombers over Cypriot villages in a show of force. The security forces quieted the situation by November 5, but the damage had been done. The marines killed six Greek-Cypriots and injured another thirty. Furthermore, the police arrested over 2000 Greek-Cypriots, magistrates levied collective fines totaling £34,315 against Cypriot villages, and the government deported the Greek Orthodox bishops of Kition and Kyrenia for the role they had played in the uprising.[298]

The events of 1931 encouraged the British colonial administration to pursue a more illiberal style of governance in Cyprus. It passed laws limiting the ringing of church bells (which had been used to trigger the uprising), took control over elections to the archiepiscopacy, and directly intervened in secondary education, in essence taking it out of ecclesiastical hands. In so doing, it inadvertently gave more power to the

283

Turkish-Cypriot community at the expense of the Greek-Cypriots, placing each on a level playing field when previously the Greeks had been privileged.[299] The Second World War highlighted the importance of Cyprus to Britain's strategic defense in the Mediterranean, particularly following the fall of Crete and the Italian invasion of Greece. The latter of these ironically served to bridge some of the divide that had emerged between the British administration and the Greek-Cypriots, as Greece and Britain now became united in a common struggle against fascism. Thirty-seven thousand Cypriots volunteered for the Cyprus Regiment, one-third of whom were Turks, and their loyalty in the fight against Germany and Italy encouraged the wartime governor, Sir Charles Wooley, to allow municipal elections in 1943 for the first time since the 1920s. The first act of the newly elected Greek-Cypriot representatives, however, was to send a letter to London, bypassing Wooley, demanding *Enosis*.[300]

Following the war and the election of Clement Attlee's Labour government, those in favor of *Enosis* hoped their demands would finally be met. In October 1946, Creech Jones introduced to the House of Commons a bill that repealed the law giving Britain control of the archiepiscopal elections, and instructed the governor to provide amnesty for the bishop exiles of 1931, accelerate economic development on the island, and establish a Consultative Assembly to look in more detail at the constitutional question. There would be no *Enosis*, though, and the Consultative Assembly came to naught. In April 1948—with the loss of India fresh on their mind and the withdrawal from Palestine imminent—the members of the cabinet rejected any suggestion of a transfer of power to Greece.[301] They were no doubt influenced in their decision by a colonial office memorandum published on November 14, 1947, which stated that withdrawal from Palestine would "leave Cyprus as the only remaining territory in the Near and Middle East under direct British administration." It recommended a continuation of Creech Jones' policy of accommodation but stressed that the island should remain within the empire: "A self-governing Cyprus [within the British Empire], on the lines of Malta, which was in close contact with the rest of the Middle East might make a useful contribution to the maintenance of British influence in that region."[302] If Cyprus were lost, all hope of British authority in the Middle East would be lost along with it. This the cabinet could not allow.

From 1948 to 1950—as the British government struggled in Malaya prior to the appointment of Sir Harold Briggs—the movement for *Enosis* gathered speed, culminating in a plebiscite organized by the Greek Orthodox Church. Condemned by the colonial administration and without official sanction, the voting was held openly in Orthodox churches between January 15 and 22, 1950. Without the participation of the Turkish population, the Greek-Cypriots turned out in droves and under the watchful eyes of their clerics, 96.5 percent cast votes in favor of *Enosis*. The British government immediately rejected the results. The governor, Sir Andrew Wright, went even further. He sent to the colonial office a dispatch requesting "the grant of special powers to curb the press, prosecute sedition, and, through a change to the Deportation (British Subjects) Law, to act decisively against troublemakers."[303] The new colonial secretary— James Griffiths—turned down his request and a senior legal advisor in the colonial office described it as "far and away the most extreme demand put up by any territory so far as my experience ... extends."[304] Nevertheless, it served to put the British government on notice that in Cyprus—as in Palestine and Malaya—all was not well. Consequently, Griffiths instructed the chiefs of staff to prepare an assessment of the strategic value of Cyprus. This they did in April 1950, arguing that the island held "a positive and increasingly strategic role as an air base and a garrison" and that "only access to the whole island under conditions of sovereignty could serve the resulting British needs."[305]

For the next four years, the British government held the Greek-Cypriot population at arm's length, denying their requests for *Enosis* and maintaining the strategic significance of Cyprus to the empire. Following the election of the Conservative government in October 1951, Oliver Lyttelton suggested that Cyprus should "be left undisturbed [for] as long as possible."[306] He was able to maintain this position throughout 1952 and 1953, but on February 23, 1954, the Greek government unexpectedly announced that unless the British government immediately started talks on the future of Cyprus, it would refer the question to the United Nations at its autumn session.[307] Sir Robert Armitage had been governor less than a month when this demand was made. His background was not unlike Sir Henry Gurney's. Like Gurney, he had received his degree from Oxford before entering the colonial service, receiving his first posting to Kenya where between 1929 and 1939 he served in district administration in Kakamega, Kericho, Kisumu, Wajir, Isiolo, and Tambach. In 1939, he moved from district administration to the secretariat in Nairobi, where he served as assistant secretary, clerk of the legislative and executive councils, secretary to the member for agriculture, and administrative secretary. In 1948, after nineteen years in Kenya, he was posted to the Gold Coast (missing Gurney by just two years), where he first served as financial secretary and then minister of finance. He was in this latter position when Lyttelton turned to him and asked that he go to Cyprus as governor.[308]

Armitage, along with the British government as a whole, at first ignored the Greek's February demand for talks, believing it to be mere bombast and bluster, but on April 20, 1954, the Greek government again made its call for talks, this time setting a deadline of August 20, 1954. Anthony Eden, foreign secretary since Churchill's election in 1951, immediately called for a major review of what he termed "the Cyprus issue." On June 29, 1954, Selwyn Lloyd, the foreign office minister of state, chaired talks to determine future British policy. The meeting concluded that "any British statement of policy for Cyprus should declare self-government and not self-determination to be the ultimate goal. Cyprus should remain a Commonwealth fortress."[309] Just days later, the war office announced that British

Middle East Headquarters for Land and Air Forces would be permanently moving from its Suez base to Cyprus, bringing with it thousands of additional soldiers and airmen.[310] With this announcement, the British government publicly indicated that they intended to spurn the Greek demand for talks. In preparation for the expected Greek petition to the United Nations, the cabinet instructed the colonial office to prepare a parliamentary statement on the future of Cyprus.[311]

The drafting of this statement was Lyttelton's last act as colonial secretary. Due to be delivered on July 28, the day he resigned, he deferred the responsibility for presenting it to his junior minister at the colonial office, Henry Hopkinson, while he remained at his desk writing some final telegrams. After announcing that the government would shortly introduce a new constitution to create an executive and Legislative Assembly in Cyprus, Hopkinson stated:

> British administration in Cyprus, besides bringing much prosperity to the island and safeguarding the rights of all sections of the population, has maintained and still maintains stable conditions in this vital strategic area. Her Majesty's Government are resolved to continue their vigorous policy of economic development in Cyprus. The efficient administration in the island, in which a large number of Cypriots play a most effective part, has brought about vast improvements in health, agriculture, communications and many other fields. ... Her Majesty's Government fully recognise that the Greek-speaking and Turkish-speaking parts of the population have close cultural links with Greece and Turkey. Without sacrifice of those traditions, Cypriots have before them the prospect of expanding opportunities in economic, social and constitutional development.[312]

Hopkinson, expecting his statement to be the final word on the matter, was surprised when James Griffiths, the opposition spokesman for colonial affairs, questioned the extent of the constitutional reforms. Without a prepared answer at hand, Hopkinson blurted out, "it has always been understood and agreed that there are certain territories in the Commonwealth which, owing to their particular circumstances, can never expect to be fully independent. ... I am not going as far as that this afternoon, but I have said that the question of the abrogation of British sovereignty cannot arise—that British sovereignty will remain."[313]

Hopkinson's use of the word "never" set off a firestorm among the parliamentary opposition, so much so that the Conservative chief whip summoned Lyttelton by telephone to return immediately to the House to make an intervention in the debate.[314] Lyttelton did little to help the matter. In his final statement as colonial secretary, he repeated the government's assertion that "Eastern Mediterranean security demands that we maintain sovereign power in Cyprus." Then, damningly, he described Greece as a "friendly but unstable ally."[315] In the words of one historian, Hopkinson's assertion of "never," together with Lyttelton's suggestion that Greece was "unstable," were "directly responsible for the later bloodshed in the island."[316] It was an ominous sign of things to come in the colony.

Following Lyttelton's resignation, Churchill selected Alan Lennox-Boyd as Britain's new colonial secretary. Prior to coming to the colonial office, Lennox-Boyd served as minister of state at the Ministry of Transport and Civil Aviation for three years, having been part of a highly vocal group of back-bench Conservative MPs before that. Yet it was the empire rather than transport and civil aviation that truly caught his imagination, as evidenced by his winning of the Beit essay prize for colonial history in 1926 while an undergraduate at Christ Church, Oxford.[317] When in 1954 he finally took the reins of his beloved empire, it was one very much on the run. And despite the political upheaval in Cyprus, Malaya and Kenya still dominated the colonial office's concerns. Consequently, it was to these territories that Lennox-Boyd first turned his attention.

On July 17, just weeks prior to his taking office, the new Malayan director of operations, General Geoffrey Bourne, sent his first appreciation to Field Marshal Sir John Harding, who had succeeded William Slim as chief of the imperial general staff in November 1952. He reported that the actions of Gurney, Briggs, and Templer over the previous four years had done much to stabilize the situation, and noted that "A million and a quarter people are now living in White Areas. We have done well to reduce murder and banditry to its present 'bearable' level." However, the insurgency had recently moved from the more populated areas to communist strongholds in the deep jungle, which would require a different approach from the "hearts and minds" emphasis of his predecessors. "This deep jungle task," he wrote, "is specialized work, often best started by a parachute drop and certainly best continued by British regular soldiers who are fit to stay in the deep jungle for months on end. The normal British battalion, with its National Servicemen, cannot do this work. Nor are the Gurkhas and Malays so suited to it." What Bourne needed was a different kind of soldier, a particularly committed soldier. He therefore requested "two British SAS Regiments," giving him the ability to do two or three deep-penetration operations simultaneously "in order to kick the higher CT organisations off the central spinal ridge and so to smash their at present very comfortable direction of the war."[318] Briggs and Templer had secured the civilian population. Now it was time to use special forces to eliminate the insurgency once and for all.

Bourne followed up his appreciation with a planning directive sent to the war office on August 11. In it, he repeated the analysis he had already given to Harding, writing: "The Briggs-Templer 'steady squeeze' plan carried out over the last 4 years has made real progress. It has resulted in a reduction of the monthly incident rate from about 500 to about 100 and aggressive incidents are now relatively infrequent. But monthly eliminations have dropped in the past year from about 120 to the present 70–80 and monthly surrenders from 30 to only a few." The reason for this, he suggested, was that the communist insurgents had adjusted to British strategy, migrating from the populated areas and jungle fringes into the deep jungle—they had voluntarily moved from the white areas to places more distant from British control. In such areas, SWECs, DWECS, police companies, and regular British battalions were of no use. Much more, he argued, could be achieved "by a company (or squadron) of SAS getting to know a jungle area and remaining there to dominate it, than by a drive through the same area by several [regular] battalions." This was not to say that the regular security forces were no longer of any use in Malaya, only that a new approach to operations was needed.

Bourne therefore laid out a "new plan," which would be "more offensive in character" and would have three objects:

A. *SAS type units*: Along the spinal mountain range to win over all the remaining unfriendly aborigines to our side, and so to unseat the high CT organisations from their comfortable and hitherto safe jungle bases. This will involve establishing more Jungle Forts.

B. *Army and Field Force*: To employ the Army more offensively by descending on to known bandit areas, remaining in them, dominating them and disrupting the District and Branch Committee organisations.

C. *Police cum Civil*: To continue to keep the MCP short of food and other supplies by all possible means including cutting their supply lines between villages, estates etc, and the jungle; progressively to hand over more relatively "easy" areas to the Police and as soon as possible to place responsibility for strict food control on the Civil authorities and Police; to employ only the minimum of army units in future on food control work or on ambush and patrol in the vicinity of villages.[319]

The security forces had pacified most areas of Malaya. It was now time to turn these areas over to the police and allow the army to concentrate on eliminating the communist insurgency where it remained. Lennox-Boyd, as committed to deferring to the man on the spot as Lyttelton, agreed to this change in tactics.

If the security forces were close to victory over the insurgency in Malaya, the same could not be said in Kenya, where the army struggled to convincingly defeat Mau Mau. In August 1954, B Company of the 1st Battalion, Devonshire Regiment, moved from the Kikuyu Reserve to Embu, where it was tasked with patrolling a "huge and difficult" area on the fringes of the forest. While there, it operated in a reactive fashion, waiting for intelligence on particular Mau Mau gangs to be distributed before attempting to intercept and destroy them, rather than seeking to actively win the hearts and minds of the Kikuyu people and, in time, create white areas. Major M. C. Hastings led one such patrol on August 27. His account describes the somewhat haphazard nature of army operations at this time:

> We had just recrossed a rather open steam when a dog came up to investigate us, but it would not come close. We kept quietly on our way along the track, the dog keeping in front of us. My tracker whispered "Mau Mau" and pointed to the right. I could just make out some figures behind trees some distance away. I ordered the assault group to turn right and in line abreast, we charged about 30 yards firing from the hip with our automatics. Just before I got to one man behind a tree, something knocked me off my balance and I toppled over to my right and realised that I had been hit. ... It was all over pretty quickly and the patrol killed two gangsters armed with rifles. I realised that we were in a pretty pickle as I found I was not in a fit state to stand and walk, and as it was now about 1530 hrs, some fast work would have to be done if we were to get out of the forest that day.[320]

Major P. Burdick of the same company and battalion described a similar scene:

At river's edge we parked our transport and spread out into sweep formation with our right flank resting on the river bank. The noise was most warlike. Firing seemed to come from every direction and, with some doubt in my mind, I ordered the party to advance towards an area of flat stunted bush which I hoped would, by now, be infested with trapped and demoralised Mau Mau. Sure enough small parties of black-faced figures were darting in and out of the scrub a long way ahead of us. ... We pushed on and meanwhile saw and killed two Mau Mau. ... [A]t the river bend men were moving about like figures at some grotesque fairground shooting booth. We broke into a double, and firing as we went, reached the river bank to see a mass of bubbles and whirling legs as the gangs took to the fast moving water. As the same moment we saw a party of farmers and Home Guard on the opposite Bank. The result of a quick conference over the water was that we flung ourselves to the ground, unpinned our grenades and threw one each into the swirling water while our friends on the other side shot at everything they could see until the water became calm. A few unpleasant bits and pieces drifted away while we scoured the thick bush at water's edge—but, swimmers and non-swimmers, they had all gone.[321]

As in Malaya, the army, police, and Home Guard were not the only forces involved in the fight. The RAF also desperately sought a role for itself. In a memorandum on the use and value of heavy bombing operations written in September 1954, it claimed that the RAF's job was to "drive the terrorists out of the forests." This would be achieved "not only by killing terrorists, but by imposing on them such intolerable conditions that they will elect to come out of the prohibited areas. ... It is more in the sapping of terrorists' morale than in the infliction of casualties that the value of bombing lies."[322] A report written by Air Vice Marshal S. O. Bufton suggested that the RAF should "increase our Lincoln [bomber] effort to the maximum in order to have the greatest possible effect upon the hard-core terrorists in Mt. Kenya, and to this end I have set the target as 200 sorties during the month."[323] Nevertheless, when on November 27 General Erskine published his 167-page handbook on anti-Mau Mau operations, he made no mention of the RAF.[324] Furthermore, in a December 6 report to the war office he noted that army responsibilities in 1955 would be to "seek out and destroy terrorists in the prohibited areas and in the Settled Areas" while police responsibilities would be to "maintain law and order in the native reserves." He again did not hold RAF operations important enough to warrant discussion.[325] The RAF was simply not well-suited for counterinsurgency operations.

Having inadvertently dismissed the RAF's role, Erskine kept his focus on the army and police. In January 1955, he launched a three-month operation known as Operation Hammer, which was designed to "attack and break up terrorist gangs in the Aberdares and Mount Kenya Forests."[326] The operation was the largest to date in Kenya, costing more than £10,000 for every Mau Mau killed or captured. While Erskine received criticism at the time for its price tag, Mau Mau fighters in the forest increasingly became "hunted men on the run, kept short of food and supplies by their pursuers, and unsure whether a former friend was still one or had been converted to the cause of the government."[327] Operation First Flute followed Operation Hammer in February and was equally successful. By May 1955 when Erskine's time in Kenya came to an end, the security forces had driven Mau Mau not only from Nairobi but also largely from the forests.[328] General G. W. Lathbury, Erkskine's successor, had some remaining "mopping-up operations" to complete, but for all intents and purposes Mau Mau was beaten.[329]

Sir Evelyn Baring was ecstatic at this sudden reversal of fortunes in Kenya. As he told Paul Emrys Evans in a letter on January 10, "We are having plenty of lively trouble, but at bottom things are really getting much better."[330] In recognition of this success, he proposed to Lennox-Boyd that the government introduce a policy of "lifting the sanctions against the civil population in the co-operative areas of the Kikuyu Reserve, so as to produce a contrasting effect and to bring home to the population the advantages of compliance with Government orders and the penalties of opposition."[331] Although he did not use the term, Baring was essentially proposing the adoption of General Templer's system of white areas—something unfeasible in the Kenya of only six months earlier. Oliver Lyttelton, out of public office for half a year, was even more optimistic. Addressing the annual city meeting of the Royal Institute of International Affairs on January 17, he stated bluntly, "the Pax Britannica has banished tribal warfare from the Kenya scene. ... [T]ribal warfare was the principal occupation and the standard career for the young men of many of these tribes. It is no longer allowed."[332] While certainly an exaggeration—the British government in Kenya had neither the resources nor the reach to "disallow" warfare, and Mau Mau's attacks continued for a further two years, albeit in an ever decreasing number—Lyttelton nevertheless articulated a common belief among British officials in the early months of 1955: the back of the Mau Mau uprising had been broken.

Throughout these years, Winston Churchill gave his unqualified, if distant, support to the colonial office, but his health was increasingly failing him. His principal private secretary, John Colville, noted as early as November 9, 1952, that the prime minister was "getting tired and visibly ageing. He finds it hard work to compose a speech and ideas no longer flow. He has made two strangely simple errors in the H. of C. lately."[333] The situation did not improve and on June 23, 1953, Churchill suffered a stroke.[334] He continued as prime minister but confessed to Colville in October that he could not "make up his mind whether or not to go on as P.M."[335] In addition to his ill health, Churchill increasingly showed little interest in the job. The highlights of his second premiership were four transatlantic trips, the first in January 1952, the second in January 1953, the third in December 1953, and the fourth in June and July 1954.

Although air travel was widely available by this time, Churchill nevertheless chose to make four of the eight crossings on luxury ocean liners, leading to yet more time away from 10 Downing Street.[336]

Beyond his visits to the United States, Churchill's attention was monopolized by a budgetary crisis in the autumn of 1951, by the death of George VI and the coronation of Queen Elizabeth II in 1952, and by the end of the Korean War in 1953.[337] His later years in power, overshadowed by stroke, were dominated by questions of his own succession. In April 1954, he promised his foreign secretary Anthony Eden that he would resign to make way for him on September 20, 1954. He changed his mind in August, however, and went on to lead a successful Conservative Party conference in October. In early March 1955, though, he recognized that the job had become too much for an elderly man and he wrote to Eden to inform him that he would shortly be going. Colville recorded in his diary the consequences of this decision:

> The ensuing days were painful. W. began to form a cold hatred of Eden who, he repeatedly said, had done more to thwart him and prevent him pursuing the policy he thought right than anybody else. But he also admitted to me on several occasions that the prospect of giving everything up, after nearly sixty years in public life, was a terrible wrench. He saw no reason why he should go: he was only doing it for Anthony. He sought to persuade his intimate friends, and himself, that he was being hounded from office.[338]

Churchill held a final farewell party attended not only by cabinet members but also by Queen Elizabeth II and Prince Phillip on April 4, after which he admitted to Colville, "I don't believe Anthony can do it."[339] The following afternoon, he dressed in his top hat and frock coat and went to Buckingham Palace to resign. The Queen immediately offered him a dukedom and elevation to the House of Lords but Churchill refused, telling her that he preferred to remain in the House of Commons until the day he died.[340] At eighty years of age, he left the palace for the last time, still a commanding figure but no longer head of government. The following day, April 6, the Queen summoned Anthony Eden to the palace and asked him to serve as prime minister.[341] The empire was now his.

3
The Eden Years

April 7, 1955, to January 10, 1957

I. Problems in paradise

Lieutenant Colonel George Grivas, a retired Cypriot officer who had served in the Greek Army during both the First and Second World Wars, could not have been more pleased with his handiwork. At just after one o'clock in the morning on April 1, 1955, his organization—the Ethniki Organosis Kyprion Agoniston (EOKA, the National Organization of Cypriot Fighters)—detonated a series of bombs in government buildings in Nicosia, Limassol, and Larnaca, causing damage to the exteriors of each and completely destroying the new transmitters of the Cyprus Broadcasting Service. Following the explosions, Grivas and his men distributed pamphlets in the vicinity of the attacks, calling on the Greek-Cypriot people to rise in support of *Enosis*. Each of the pamphlets was signed with the initials EOKA and Grivas's *nom de guerre*, Dighenis. Before sunrise that morning, Grivas also dropped pamphlets in Turkish-Cypriot neighborhoods, assuring their residents that EOKA wished the Turks no harm but warning them against supporting the "British colonialists" in the coming struggle.[1] Seemingly without warning, insurgency had come to Cyprus.

The Cypriot police were as surprised by these actions as the British government. Neither had heard of EOKA before and the name Dighenis meant nothing to them. Later that morning, a hastily erected checkpoint on the road from Famagusta to Larnaca stopped a car and the police found nine hand grenades, three packets of explosives, and two sticks of dynamite. On April 3 the police also discovered an illegal armory in Limassol with 300 pounds of gelignite, twenty-four smoke grenades, several detonators, and a stash of ammunition for a light machine gun.[2] Beyond that, however, they gathered no intelligence on the movement. They were unaware that Grivas had returned to Cyprus from Greece in 1951 to test the waters for possible backing of a paramilitary organization in support of *Enosis*, nor that on July 2, 1952, he had taken a "Holy Sacred Oath" with the archbishop of Cyprus, Makarios (Mihail Christdoulou Mouskos), binding each to the "sacred cause" of *Enosis*. The government did not know that beginning in October 1952, Grivas had started to clandestinely organize men and weapons in Cyprus in preparation for an armed struggle against British rule, nor that by November 1954 he had persuaded Makarios of the need for physical force in the movement for *Enosis*.[3] When the explosions erupted on the morning of April 1, 1955, the uprising had been almost four years in the making. The bombs were not a mere flash in the pan set off by disillusioned and ultimately incompetent youths who had neither the resources nor the will to strike again. They were signs of a much more serious insurgency to come. Yet the British knew nothing.

Anthony Eden, foreign secretary when Grivas began his campaign of violence, was invited to Buckingham Palace and asked by the Queen to form a new government just seven days after EOKA detonated its first bombs. As his driver transported him from the palace to 10 Downing Street for the first time, Cyprus was the furthest thing from his mind, though. Three months shy of his fifty-eighth birthday, on the morning of April 7, Eden's ascent to the premiership had been a long time coming. He had first entered the House of Commons as Conservative member for Warwick and Leamington in 1923 at the tender age of twenty-six. For the next seven years, Eden remained on the parliamentary backbenches, staying respectful of party leadership while beginning to develop for himself a niche of expertise in foreign affairs and defense issues. His diligence paid off following the formation of the national government in August 1931 with a promotion to parliamentary undersecretary at the foreign office. He remained a junior minister until 1935, when prime minister Stanley Baldwin invited him to become the youngest foreign secretary since the second Earl Granville in 1851, at just thirty-eight years of age.

With the situation on the European continent becoming more volatile, it was an important time to lead the foreign office; and Eden quickly gained a reputation for solid competence. He remained foreign secretary when Neville Chamberlain succeeded Baldwin as prime minister, but on February 20, 1938, resigned in opposition to the policy of appeasement. His convictions were sadly vindicated by the start of the Second World War, at which point Chamberlain brought him back to ministerial office as head of the dominions office, although without a seat in the war cabinet. Following Chamberlain's resignation and Churchill's elevation in May 1940, Eden was moved from the dominions office to be secretary of state for war, although still without membership in the war cabinet (Churchill had taken for himself the position of minister of defense and chairman of the defense committee, which largely overshadowed the war office at this time in British history). Eden remained at the war office until December 1940 when Churchill moved him once again to become foreign secretary, this time with full membership in the war cabinet. He soon added to this position the role of leader of the House of Commons, which he kept throughout the war. Following the Labour Party victory in July 1945, Eden became deputy leader of the Conservative Party in opposition, although due to Churchill's prolonged absences he in essence functioned as party leader. Consequently, many supposed Churchill would soon give way to allow Eden to take full control. These hopes were dashed by the Conservative victory in October 1951 and Churchill's return to 10 Downing Street. Eden dutifully agreed to serve as foreign secretary for the third time, a post he remained in until Churchill finally gave way in April 1955. For many in the party and country, he had become

Conservative leader ten years too late and prime minister three and a half years after he should have.[4]

Eden's most immediate task was to pick his new cabinet. He chose a path of minimal disruption to the government, keeping Rab Butler as chancellor of the exchequer and Lennox-Boyd as colonial secretary. He did promote Harold Macmillan from the position of minister of defense to become his new foreign secretary, and brought Selwyn Lloyd into the cabinet as minister of defense.[5] Once the cabinet was in place, Eden's next priority was to set the date for a general election, which would have to be called by October 1956 at the latest. He decided to go earlier rather than later, and on April 9—just two days after assuming the premiership—announced that the election would be held on May 26, 1955. His first weeks at No. 10 Downing Street were consequently spent politicking rather than attending to great matters of state.[6] He was lucky, therefore, to have appointed Macmillan as foreign secretary, for as minister of defense Macmillan had taken a special interest in the Cyprus question and in imperial security in general.

Macmillan had first spoken with Churchill about the island on November 10, 1954, although he found their conversation to be "very rough going" with a clearly distracted prime minister.[7] He persevered and in early December sent to Churchill a memorandum by the Joint Intelligence Committee, Middle East, which assessed the security threat in Cyprus. In an attached letter, Macmillan informed the prime minister that it was his intention to arrange an investigation into "the intelligence, security, police and armed forces of the Colonial Empire, with a view to the Cold War struggle and to preventing such breakdowns as have led to the necessity for large-scale armed intervention as in Kenya and Malaya." He recommended that General Templer be tasked to lead the investigation and advised that Templer begin in Cyprus, where he would "attract no particular attention."[8] As a big supporter of Templer's career, Churchill immediately agreed, suggesting that Macmillan present the idea to him as a prerequisite before being appointed chief of the imperial general staff. Macmillan did so and on January 18, 1955, informed Antony Head, the war secretary, that Templer had accepted.[9] In early February, Macmillan, Head, and Lennox-Boyd met to finalize arrangements and shortly thereafter Churchill issued a statement announcing that Templer would serve as the next chief of the imperial general staff, before which he would conduct an investigation into colonial security.[10]

The explosions of April 1, 1955, propelled Cyprus to the forefront of Macmillan's mind. This was all the more so after his appointment as foreign secretary one week later, for although the island was a colony and therefore officially within the domain of Lennox-Boyd and the colonial office, the Greek and Turkish dimension ensured the foreign office would be heavily involved. On April 1, just hours after the explosions, Anthony Nutting, minister of state for foreign affairs, wrote to Eden (still foreign secretary) to suggest that Templer's proposed visit to Cyprus be moved forward, as his advice was urgently needed to ascertain what was required to "ginger up … what is patently an inadequate security force."[11] In the commotion surrounding Churchill's resignation, this request was put aside, but upon moving to the foreign office Macmillan instructed Templer to travel to Cyprus as soon as possible. The general did so immediately and reported that the numbers and morale of the Cypriot police were dangerously low, that there was no special branch and consequently no real intelligence-gathering organization, and that Governor Armitage seemed thoroughly unsuited to rule in an insurgency situation.[12]

Templer was not the only person offering advice to Macmillan on the Cyprus question. On April 18, Lord Halifax, who had served as viceroy in India from 1926 to 1931, as foreign secretary from 1938 to December 1940, and as British ambassador to the United States from 1941 to 1946, sent a letter to Macmillan suggesting that senior Greek officials believed that the Cyprus problem could be easily resolved if the British government would "only show understanding of Greek feelings and not slam doors."[13] Macmillan sent his reply on April 26, reminding

Halifax that "the responsibility for the recent outbreak of terrorism in Cyprus lies largely with the inflammatory broadcasts from the government-controlled Athens station, and the Greek Press, including papers friendly to the government, has been publishing a spate of violently anti-British articles." In these circumstances, it would be "very difficult" for the foreign secretary to "make friendly gestures, or saying soothing things."[14]

Meanwhile, in Cyprus itself the government turned its attention to the necessary security measures, forming a new committee on April 27 termed the Cyprus Internal Security Committee, chaired by Armitage and with a membership of the colonial secretary in Cyprus, the army commander in Cyprus, the air officer commanding Cyprus, the naval flag office Middle East, the deputy colonial secretary in Cyprus, the commissioner of police, and the director of intelligence (a new position recommended by Templer and first held by MI5's Donald Stephens).[15] The formation of this committee was accompanied by the deployment of army units to mount static guards outside government installations and by the creation of an MI5 interrogation center in May.[16] Nevertheless, EOKA attacks continued. On June 19, the organization detonated explosives at police stations in Nicosia and Kyrenia, after which Lennox-Boyd urged the government in Cyprus not to overreact: "I must ask that no preparations of any kind for the declaration of an emergency be made."[17] His pleas were harder to sympathize with after June 21, when EOKA destroyed the front of the police headquarters in Ataturk Square, killing one person and injuring five—the first time it had targeted a building in the Turkish quarter. The following day, EOKA brazenly attacked the police station in Amiandos with machine guns and assassinated a Greek-Cypriot sergeant of the newly formed special branch.[18]

In response to the intensity and frequency of this violence, Selwyn Lloyd, the minister of defense, instructed the foreign and colonial offices to draft a combined paper on Cyprus setting out their recommendations. This they did and submitted their report to the cabinet on June 25. It began by describing

the United Kingdom as a "world power with primary responsibility for the defence of the Middle East" and as a "Colonial
power with a reputation for sagacious and disinterested administration." Taking these as the underlying assumptions of the
paper, it stated that Britain's needs and aims in Cyprus were the
following:

(a) Secure bases for the deployment and supply of troops in
the Middle East.
(b) The maintenance of a physical symbol of British power in
the Eastern Mediterranean and Middle East.
(c) The preservation of good relations with Greece and
Turkey.
(d) The maintenance of order and good government in
Cyprus itself, and the insurance of its steady progression
to full internal self-government, and, if defence needs and
needs of good government permit, self-determination.

With its pledge to secure "good relations" with both Greece
and Turkey, as well as its determination to maintain British
sovereignty over Cyprus, the colonial and foreign offices recognized that their paper was trying to have its cake and eat it too.
After all, maintaining sovereignty almost inevitably strained
relations with Greece. The paper therefore suggested three possible options for Cyprus. First, the government could announce
that there would "ultimately [be] a right of self determination
for Cyprus, provided that meantime there has been orderly constitutional development." Second, the government could offer
to the Greek and Turkish governments "some form of association with the Cyprus Government in the administration of the
island, and the immediate introduction of a liberal constitution for Cyprus, while sovereignty is indefinitely maintained by
Her Majesty's Government." Or finally, the government could
"conclude a defence agreement with the Greek and Turkish
Governments by which they would undertake that whatever the
ultimate disposition of the island, Her Majesty's Government

would retain all the defence rights which the British forces might require."

The paper advised that the first option would be preferable for the British government, as it gave no concrete timeline to self-determination. It would, however, be met with opposition from both Greeks and Turks for that very reason. The second would require much discussion and compromise and was therefore likely to fail, but would at least give the impression that the British government was reaching out to all parties involved. The third option seemed less than desirable for a variety of reasons. The paper therefore recommended that the government call a tripartite conference between Britain, Greece, and Turkey in an apparent attempt to secure the second option. When this failed (as they knew it would), the government could then unilaterally impose the first option without reference to Greece and Turkey, and without sacrificing world opinion.[19]

With this recommendation in hand, Lennox-Boyd contacted Armitage to ascertain his impression of what effect a tripartite conference might have on the Cypriot people. Armitage replied on June 28 that "The effect on Greek Cypriots could hardly be anything but good, except for extreme Nationalists and EOKA, both of whom could support nothing but *Enosis*. ... Turks should welcome any easing of tension, but are fearful of any action leading to self-government." The governor warned, however, that, "Whatever statement may be made about future policy, EOKA must be crushed. It cannot be left, able to erupt whenever it chooses." He therefore asked for permission to declare a state of emergency, following which he would instigate an island-wide operation to arrest all individuals involved with the militant wing of the *Enosis* movement. The advantages of such a declaration were fourfold. First, it would boost morale, both of the public and of the police force—they would feel like something was being done. Second, it would restore confidence that the government could act resolutely and thus protect the public. Third, it would provide powers to detain suspects without hard evidence, thus allowing the police to move more quickly against EOKA's operations. Finally, it would provide powers to the police to arrest without warning, enter and search properties without warrants, detain and search persons upon suspicion, stop and search vehicles without cause, and restrict the power of movement within Cyprus, all of which would help quell the violence.[20] Lennox-Boyd promptly dismissed Armitage's request, telling him that a declaration of emergency would undermine the tripartite conference before it had even begun.[21] Behind closed doors, colonial office civil servants described Armitage's "proposed razzia against EOKA" as "ill-timed and capable of prejudicing the Greek government."[22]

On June 30, Lennox-Boyd confirmed the direction of government policy by formally announcing Britain's intention to hold a tripartite conference and publicly issuing invitations to the Greek and Turkish governments.[23] Armitage immediately wrote to the colonial office, asking that Lennox-Boyd reconsider his decision. He also requested permission to, at the very least, carry out planning for an emergency "in strictest secret" so that measures might be implemented as soon as a state of emergency was declared.[24] This the colonial secretary allowed, although he kept his focus squarely on the proposed conference, even though he expected it to collapse. Others in the government likewise prepared for the implementation of "Plan B" once "Plan A" failed. On July 1, Eden wrote to Lennox-Boyd, telling him:

I think it is very important that if our plans for a Conference with the Greeks and Turks on Cyprus turn out as we hope, we should be prepared to formulate as soon as possible a long-term development plan for the Colony. This would give the Cypriots something to look forward to and might even have some effect over the years on their attitude towards the British connection. ... Education, it seems to me, is particularly important. There might be much gained by the provision of an institution of University status, linked with our own Universities, which would help to wean the Cypriots away from the cultural attraction of Athens.[25]

A brief prepared on July 2 for the foreign secretary made it clear that the government had no intention of serious compromise with either the Greeks or the Turks at the conference.[26] The cabinet hoped to be able to go it alone on Cyprus.

While the foreign and colonial offices began to prepare for the conference, Lennox-Boyd wrote to the prime minister bringing him up to date on the situation. He revealed that although the government had denied Armitage's request for a declaration of emergency, the colonial secretary had proposed that the governor enact a special law—something less than an emergency regulation—which would be directed solely at EOKA. The governor agreed and submitted a draft of the new law on July 6. This was the information Lennox-Boyd provided to Eden.[27] The following day, the cabinet authorized the passage of the measure, to be enacted beginning July 8.[28] It also granted permission for Lennox-Boyd to travel immediately to Cyprus to assess the situation firsthand. When he landed in Nicosia on July 9, Lennox-Boyd became the first colonial secretary to ever set foot on the island.[29]

His schedule while in Cyprus was demanding. Driven straight from the airport to a meeting with the governor and the executive council, he traveled from there to meet directly with Archbishop Makarios, who by now had become the mouthpiece of the *Enosis* movement. Armitage was also present at this meeting and the colonial secretary reported in a telegram to Eden that it had been "relaxed and illuminating, though entirely non-committal. ... I am sure that this was [an] essential and helpful part of the general ice breaking. Until last night no Governor and Archbishop had met since 1931."[30] The meeting was, however, overshadowed by violence, as EOKA exploded two bombs—one on the day of Lennox-Boyd's arrival and a second, within the Secretariat, the following day. The colonial secretary suggested to Eden that "We have been incredibly fortunate so far in that only one person has been killed by bombs: but one serious incident involving police or service families would create a highly combustible situation. ... I consider we must now take limited but decisive action to neutralize terrorism without waiting to be forced into this action by further loss of life."[31] Lennox-Boyd was further confirmed in this judgment by EOKA's detonation of a third bomb before he boarded his plane to return home.[32]

Upon Lennox-Boyd's return, all attention shifted to the upcoming tripartite conference, which was scheduled to begin on August 29. The cabinet determined on August 7 that there could be no discussion of self-determination for the Cypriots and thus the conference became more of a foreign office issue than a colonial one. Consequently, it was Macmillan rather than Lennox-Boyd who took the lead in its planning and preparation.[33] In the meantime, Field Marshal Sir John Harding, the chief of the imperial general staff, visited Cyprus in late July and suggested that in addition to strengthening the police and special branch, the security forces on the island ought to be led by an all-powerful supremo.[34] Selwyn Lloyd took Harding's suggestion to the cabinet on August 8 and Macmillan also offered his support for the idea, telling Lloyd that he "entirely agree[d] with ... the co-ordination of security operations in Cyprus by a single authority."[35] Macmillan went further, however, informing Eden on August 16 that he was "really worried about Cyprus" and asking, "Could we not have a new Governor?" He suggested there would be "a lot of trouble after the Conference," and felt that "we must have somebody with guts and imagination."[36] Armitage clearly did not fit that bill.

Macmillan continued to press his point. On August 16, the day he wrote to the prime minister, Armitage imposed a curfew on the Cypriot town of Agros, where a shot had been fired at a policeman. The government cut off all electricity to the village, one hundred British army soldiers ensured that all residents were housebound between seven in the morning and seven in the evening, and searchlights continually lit up the night sky throughout the curfew period. Yet it did not have the desired effect. A British journalist who had been present both at this curfew and at the one imposed by General Templer upon

Tanjong Malim in Malaya reported a major difference between the two: while the Chinese had been "sullen" and clearly affected by the curfew, in Agros, villagers "seemed to enjoy the break from the hard routine of minding their flocks, and in daytime were often found to be chatting to British troops over their tea."[37] Artimage, it seemed, could not even organize an effective curfew. Macmillan wrote in exasperation to Eden again on August 19, asking him, "Do you not think that we ought to have a man at the top in Cyprus who radiates the impression that he knows what he wants and can get it?"[38] Eden assured Macmillan that he "shared" his "worry about Cyprus," but believed that any change at the top had to wait until after the conference.[39]

The twenty-ninth of August 1955—the day of the conference—got off to an ominous start. That morning, just hours before Harold Macmillan opened proceedings with an intentionally "dull and pompous" speech, EOKA murdered another Greek constable in Nicosia, casting an immediate shadow over its deliberations.[40] Macmillan, fully expecting the conference to fail, recommended to the prime minister that seven British officers from Malaya and Kenya be immediately sent to Cyprus to bring necessary experience to the police force there.[41] The foreign secretary was not disappointed on either count. The seven officers were transferred within a week and the conference duly failed. Lasting until September 7, it became clear early on that no resolution was possible. The Greek government insisted on full self-determination for the Cypriot people, the Turkish government campaigned for the status quo or, failing that, a return of Cyprus to Turkey, and the British government portrayed itself as above the fray by offering a proposal for fairly extensive self-government but remaining intentionally quiet on self-determination. The final straw came on September 6, the day before the conference collapsed, when anti-Greek riots swept through the Turkish cities of Istanbul and Izmir, resulting in the destruction of 4500 shops, 1000 houses, 73 churches, and 26 schools, at an estimated cost of $300 million. The Turkish government apologized and promptly offered compensation, but the damage had been done. There could be no agreement.[42]

While the Greeks and Turks contested Cyprus at the conference, Macmillan finally persuaded the prime minister to replace Armitage as governor of the island. On August 30, Eden told the foreign secretary: "I agree with all you write ... as to the type of man we need as Governor. I have not met Armitage myself but can quite believe from the telegrams that we could do better."[43] This was not enough to justify the governor's removal, however. Macmillan needed positive evidence that Armitage was failing in his position. This the governor provided aplenty in the coming weeks. On September 8, a police checkpoint stopped Archbishop Makarios' car. When the police constables realized who was standing before them, they radioed to police headquarters for advice. Headquarters in turn checked with the secretariat. As a crowd of more than 2000 people gathered, the police decided to frisk the archbishop's fellow passengers but not to approach him, eventually allowing his car to proceed. When this event was reported on the BBC, Lennox-Boyd angrily informed Armitage that the car should either have been allowed to proceed freely without delay or, if stopped, all occupants, including the archbishop, should have been frisked. By singling out Makarios for special treatment the security forces played into the hands of EOKA, recognizing him as the leader of the *Enosis* movement and thus giving it legitimacy.[44]

Armitage responded on August 10, asking that the government grant him the power to deport clerics. This the cabinet discussed on August 15. Its members agreed in principle that it was a good idea but also felt that Armitage was not the man to implement such drastic measures. Two days later, on August 17, their opinion of Armitage soured further, as a mob of Greek-Cypriot youths overturned a British Army jeep, set it alight, and rioted, culminating in the burning of the British Institute in Nicosia. London's newspaper *The Daily Mail* immediately began a campaign to dismiss the governor, claiming these events had brought shame on the British government. The cabinet met in emergency session on September 24 to discuss the matter and finally decided that Armitage would cease to be governor. His service would end at midnight on October 3. In an unprecedented move, the cabinet members then asked Harding to step down as chief of the imperial general staff and instead take up the position in Cyprus. Eden informed him: "I have been profoundly unhappy about Cyprus for some time past. ... What we would now hope to do is to show the Cypriots steadily and firmly rather than harshly that we mean to carry out our responsibility."[45] Without hesitation, Harding agreed to take up the position, arriving in Cyprus on the morning of October 4, 1955. For the first time in its troubled history, the island had a military governor.[46]

II. Templer's return

With the resignation of Field Marshal Sir John Harding as chief of the imperial general staff, the prime minister appointed General (soon to be Field Marshal) Sir Gerald Templer to fill the newly vacated position. One of the first letters Templer received as chief of the imperial general staff was from General Sir Geoffrey Bourne, director of operations in Malaya, sent on October 3—the day before Harding arrived in Cyprus. Bourne informed him that beginning on September 9, the Malayan government had launched an amnesty campaign aimed at bringing the insurgency to a quick end with generous surrender terms for those who had fought against the security forces. In the first three weeks, the government had received twenty high-profile surrenders, which had largely resulted from "hunger and military pressure." While this amnesty campaign was directed at the insurgents, Malayan society in general was "displaying a [greater] interest in ending the Emergency than ever before." This was evidenced in part by marches and processions, some numbering upwards of 1000 people, protesting the insurgency. The Special Air Service (SAS) was still operating deep in the jungle "killing ... the old hands," but in general the security forces now had the luxury of being more interested in the Federal Football Final than in counterinsurgency techniques, the former of which had been "an extremely fast and clean battle."[47]

In Kenya, also, Templer was greeted with an improved situation. In May, General Lathbury wrote to the war office recommending that the Mau Mau surrender terms that had been in place since January be withdrawn, as it was "clear that they will not by themselves achieve an early end to this emergency." Lathbury instead suggested that "From the operational point of view some form of shock treatment is required to destroy the Terrorists' will to resist. The first step is to hit them hard and to keep up the pressure. ... The second step is to convince them of the futility of continuing to fight."[48] Antony Head, the war secretary, consulted Alan Lennox-Boyd, who requested a summary of the surrender operation from Sir Evelyn Baring. This Baring provided on June 3, explaining that since January 18, 1955, as many as 570 Mau Mau had surrendered, including 43 leaders, who collectively had "given information of great value to the Government and Security Forces." Military operations continued throughout these surrenders, and in the same time period the security forces killed 1351 Mau Mau. Baring informed Lennox-Boyd that there was a "split" in the ranks of Mau Mau, with "a great number of the rank and file, and some leaders" holding "an expressed desire to come in and cease fighting." He therefore suggested that the surrender offer be kept in place until July 10, but that after this date those who failed to surrender be hit with ever-increasing intensity.[49] The cabinet agreed to his recommendation on June 8.[50]

With the imminent expiration of the surrender offer, Lathbury turned to devising his methods of "shock treatment" for those Mau Mau who remained in the forest. In an appreciation written in early July, he stated that "the aim of the War Council must be to finish the Emergency as rapidly as possible by killing or capturing the remaining terrorists." The way to do this, he suggested, was to add a "fourth Emergency winning factor." The first three winning factors were a "policy of closer administration based on villages," "perfecting the intelligence machine," and "improved training for the soldiers." The fourth factor he hoped to introduce was "the use of surrendered and captured terrorists in guerilla units."[51]

This idea was crystallized in a report by R. C. Catling, the commissioner of police, on July 4. Catling stated that these guerilla units would have four main roles:

(a) Pseudo-gang operations to seek out and kill terrorists in specific areas cleared of, or in conjunction with, Security Forces.

(b) As above, but operations directed at selected targets upon Special Branch indication.

(c) Reconnaissance of specific areas to gain intelligence as a prelude to planned operations by Security Forces.

(d) Verification of vague information and intelligence reports in defined areas.

The report envisioned that this force would be composed of five teams, each led by two European officers with ten surrendered Africans. The Europeans would be armed with a sterling submachine gun, three regular grenades, three phosphorous grenades, and a silenced .300 carbine. The Africans would be armed with 12-bore shot guns, with two acting as scouts who would also hold a .45 revolver. The African personnel would be eligible for "published rewards payable for terrorists killed or captured."[52] In essence, Catling was suggesting that the government pay surrendered Mau Mau to return to the forest from whence they came to assassinate their former comrades. Baring agreed to the recommended course of action, and by the time Templer became chief of the imperial general staff in October 1955, these gangs were already operating in the forest.

Kenya was not Templer's only concern. He also had to confront trouble in a territory that until only very recently had been considered a calm and loyal part of the empire. That territory was Aden. The British first acquired Aden in 1839, when the famed East India Company seized the port town following a slight from the local sultan. It was the first European colony taken in Arabia, and the first British colony acquired in the reign of Queen Victoria. Having begun its colonial existence as part of the East Indian Company, Aden remained governed by the Indian administration until 1937, when it received Crown Colony status.[53] Consequently, at that time it came under the orbit of the colonial office rather than the Indian office. During the Second World War, Aden assumed a new position as a strategic fortress that could protect the Red Sea, the eastern Mediterranean, and the Indian Ocean. With the end of the war and the beginning of the insurgency in Palestine, trouble came to Aden. On the night of December 2, 1947, an Arab strike against British policy in Palestine escalated into a full-blown riot and assault on the city's Jewish quarter. When the violence was finally quelled two days later, seventy-five Jews and thirty-four Arabs lay dead. Following the British withdrawal from Palestine six months later, 900 Adenese Jews left the colony for the new state of Israel.[54]

The future of Aden was further complicated by the loss of India. Now that the British government no longer looked to the East, the strategic necessity of the outpost came into doubt. Nevertheless, in 1954 the government opened a British Petroleum (BP) oil refinery in the wake of the 1951 oil crisis in Iran. Lacking manpower to staff this refinery, the Aden administration relied largely on Yemini migrant workers who had a strong sense of Arab nationalism and militant trade unionism. By 1959, these Yeminis outnumbered Adenis by 48,000 to 37,000, and in that year alone there were eighty-four strikes.[55] These Yeminis increasingly sought to undermine British control of the colony and to disrupt the economic productivity of British industry there, particularly the BP oil refinery. On May 11, 1955—at about the same time that MI5's Donald Stephens arrived in Cyprus as director of intelligence—members of the Lower Aulaki Sultanate in the Western Aden Protectorate (sitting adjacent to Aden Colony) ambushed a government convoy on the road to Said, the principal town of the Aulaki Shiekdom. In this attack, they killed one civilian and three government guards, seriously wounding a fourth. Rumor circulated that they had received money and arms from Yemen. The governor, Sir Tom Hickinbotham, immediately ordered the tribe to pay a fine and to give up fifty of their rifles. When they refused to do so, he ordered the RAF to destroy the tribe's villages and forts in retaliation.[56]

Such drastic action came at a time when the Conservative government was already under scrutiny for its imperial strategy. Within weeks, the Labour Party tabled a question in parliament relating to the bombings and Lennox-Boyd was forced to do as Lyttelton had done countless times before him. He requested further justification from one of his governors. This Hickinbotham provided on June 13, revealing that the tribal leaders had fled to Yemen where they were each given $2000 and 4000 rounds of ammunition from the Yemini government. They were not merely a criminal menace but potentially something more subversive. With regard to the RAF bombing, Hickinbotham assured Lennox-Boyd that the government had prewarned all villages of the target and the timing of the bombing and consequently, although one village, five hamlets, and two forts were destroyed, there had been no casualties. This, he hoped, would suffice in parliament.[57]

The same day that Hickinbotham provided his justification, the colonial office requested from the air ministry details of all RAF operations in the Aden Colony and Protectorate from 1946 to 1951. When the report arrived on June 18, it listed sixteen operations, almost all of which were retaliation bombings of a similar kind to those ordered by Hickinbotham.[58] Should the Labour Party question Lennox-Boyd's methods in the Commons, he knew he had evidence to suggest that his policy was in fact one of continuation from Labour's rather than a dramatic shift away from it. For Labour MPs to criticize it now that they were in the opposition would smack of rank hypocrisy.

The question came on July 13, asked by Labour MP Peter Freeman who challenged Lennox-Boyd to "prohibit such forms of collective punishment which impose indiscriminate hardship; and ensure that punishments are imposed only upon persons proved guilty of lawbreaking and violence." Lennox-Boyd refused to do so. Freeman pressed him again, asking, "Is not this method entirely contrary to all sense of British justice—this indiscriminate bombing of innocent people who have done no harm and no wrong?" This was the question the colonial secretary had been waiting for and he was ready for it. Describing Freeman's words as "a gross travesty of the facts," Lennox-Boyd pointed out that "Collective punishment is imposed only when collective tribal responsibility for the crime can be ascertained. It is the only practical method of dealing with offences of this kind in the Protectorate." Labour MP Richard Stokes then reminded Lennox-Boyd that the government had strongly protested when the Germans had bombed the French city of Lidice as a collective punishment during the Second World War, but the colonial secretary refused to be moved. Collective bombing of tribal areas in Aden would continue, with or without Labour Party support.[59]

On July 1, J. C. Morgan of the colonial office wrote to General Cecil Llewelyn Firbank, director of infantry at the war office, providing a summary of the colonial office attitude to the developing situation in Aden. Morgan stated that "the whole revolt has been primarily instigated by the Yemenis to such an extent that if we wish to make it so there will be a *casus belli*." He then listed four conclusions the colonial office had reached, all of which were supported by the cabinet. First, there would be no bombing of Yemen itself, although this would "of course do the trick if allowed." Second, the government in Aden would increase the Aden Protectorate Levies (APL) by three squadrons and would immediately raise one armored car squadron. The APL had first been established by the RAF in 1928 and was a local defense militia armed and officered by the British. As there were few regular army soldiers on the ground, it was essential that the numbers of the APL be raised to provide sufficient follow-up to RAF bombing runs. Third, the Aden government should be granted "special administrative subsidies, including some private bribery," up to a maximum of £76,000 each year for the use of "winning over" hostile tribes. Finally, there needed to be a "general review of the whole state of the security forces," with the possibility of moving away from an RAF-dominated strategy to one that relied more heavily on British soldiers on the ground.[60] By addressing these issues early on, the colonial office hoped to prevent the disturbances in Aden developing into a full-blown insurgency on the scale of those in Malaya, Kenya, or Cyprus.

Meanwhile, parliamentary questions continued. On July 15, Hickinbotham provided further explanation of the bombings to Lennox-Boyd: "Notice was given by leaflets dropped from aircraft 48 to 24 hours before the attack. On day of attack, attack was preceded by the dropping of half-hour delay action bombs as further warning that attack was imminent. Leaflets were also distributed in the area by hand, and instructions were given that no dwellings were to be attacked until the political officer had given a specific assurance that the inhabitants had been given 24 hours warning of the attack." The aim of the bombings was to punish the tribe by destroying its property, not to maim and kill. In that regard, the warnings had proved sufficient as there were no casualties.[61] Three days later, Morgan informed Lennox-Boyd that "The general principles on which punitive air action can be used in the Aden Protectorate were laid down in 1943, and were confirmed in 1947 by the then Secretary of State, who authorised the Governor of Aden to use air action or the threat of it to maintain order within the Aden Protectorate."[62] With this information on hand, Lennox-Boyd again rejected any suggestion for him to put a stop to the bombings. As he bluntly told the House of Commons on July 20, "This form of collective punishment has proved exceedingly successful over a great many years."[63]

Despite the confidence of Lennox-Boyd's performance in the Commons, not all in the government were as buoyant.

On July 29, Foreign Secretary Harold Macmillan wrote to the minister of defense Selwyn Lloyd, admitting that he was "disturbed about Aden." He believed that the intelligence system in the colony was "inadequate," and that there had "not been good use of the Security Forces." Macmillan acknowledged that other cabinet members were quick to point the blame at Yemen but felt that "we must look very closely at our own arrangements before we assume that the trouble is primarily due to the Yemen."[64] If any British counterinsurgency campaign were to succeed in Aden, it was imperative that the government knew exactly what was causing the problem in the first place. In the summer of 1955, this was not at all clear.

When Eden appointed Templer chief of the imperial general staff in October, the general clearly had his hands full, with insurgencies still raging in Malaya and Kenya and trouble just beginning in Aden. Yet it was with Cyprus that Templer was most concerned. With Harding's appointment as governor, Templer had a man on the ground upon whom he could rely. Prior to serving as chief of the imperial general staff, Harding had interviewed for the position of high commissioner and director of operations in Malaya (the government had instead chosen Templer). Before that, he had undergone a long and varied army career, beginning with service as an officer during the First World War, where he fought in the Dardanelles campaign and then in the third battle of Gaza. In 1917, he received the Military Cross for his actions as an acting major at just twenty-one years of age. After the war, Harding served in India before attending the Staff College at Camberley. He received his first battalion command in 1939. Harding fought in North Africa and Italy during the Second World War, reaching the rank of lieutenant general by 1945. He then acted as military governor of the free city of Trieste from 1945 to 1947, before joining southern command in 1948 and becoming commander in chief, Far East, in 1949, where he had responsibility for all British Army troops in the Malayan emergency. In 1951, Harding left the Far East command to instead take control of the British Army of the Rhine, remaining until his appointment as chief of the imperial general staff in 1952. In the three years he held that position he oversaw all army operations, including those in Malaya and Kenya. There were few men alive in Britain in 1955 who could match the depth of experience dealing with emergencies and civil strife of Harding, which he now brought to the Cyprus government.[65]

Harding's first action upon arrival in Cyprus was to call a meeting with Archbishop Makarios, which he did his very first evening. Their conversation, although "frank and cordial," resulted in a stalemate. Makarios insisted that discussion could not move forward without British willingness to consider Cypriot self-determination; Harding replied that this was not possible due to British strategic constraints and the government's commitment to NATO. The two men parted without resolution, although pledged to meet again soon.[66] This they did three days later, on October 7. Harding offered Makarios eventual self-government within the empire but stopped short of full self-determination. Markarios, disappointed by what he considered a refusal to compromise by the British government, agreed to put the offer before the other leaders in the *Enosis* movement but warned that it would almost certainly be rejected.[67] Eden carefully read Harding's reports of these first two meetings and wrote to him on October 8, congratulating him on "the skill and vigour with which you pressed on him, in your second talk, the case for accepting our proposals for the development of self-government. Even if in the end he deliberately shuts the door, your initiative and efforts can have done nothing but good."[68]

Encouraged by Eden's letter, Harding wrote to Lennox-Boyd, arguing that he could "carry the Archbishop with me" if the colonial office would allow him to agree to the possibility of self-determination at some point in the future, contingent upon self-government within the British Commonwealth proving successful. It was an approach similar to that taken in Malaya and Kenya, and one with which Harding was very familiar. Lennox-Boyd, however, refused to grant Harding this leeway, arguing that the cabinet would never permit self-determination for Cyprus. Consequently, when the archbishop and field marshal met again on October 11, they reached no agreement. Makarios hinted that he might be able to accept something similar to what Harding had proposed to Lennox-Boyd, but Harding—forbidden from discussing it—could only restate his original offer of self-government. Makarios thus declared that he was "very unhappy" and the meeting ended without resolution. Unlike after the first two sessions, there was no promise of further discussions.[69]

Harding realized that with the collapse of their talks, there would be no quick end to the conflict. Makarios had refused to accept anything less than self-determination yet Lennox-Boyd had forbidden Harding from even discussing that. Immediately after the failed meeting he sent a telegraph to Eden, informing him that "discussions with the Archbishop broke down this evening. ... I am as certain as I can be that break did not (repeat not) come as a misunderstanding."[70] He then released a statement to the print media and radio, expressing his "deep regret" that the talks had failed but pledging that "the life of the people of Cyprus must go on and that can only happen under peaceful conditions." He ended his statement with a plea and a warning:

It is my duty as Governor to maintain law and order and that I intend to do, but I would call on law abiding citizens of Cyprus to exercise restraint and to carry out their duty by doing all in their power to prevent disorders and disturbances, terrorism and intimidation. The police and troops have direct orders from me to exercise proper restraint, but law and order must and will be maintained.[71]

In a second telegram to the prime minister, Harding wrote: "I do not propose to declare a state of emergency unless there are widespread disorders but in that event I shall not hesitate to do so. I hope you will agree." He added, "Also if any high ranking cleric makes any seditious statement or gives me any other reasonable excuse from now on I consider he or they must be deported at once."[72] With a clear understanding of the need for political engagement in counterinsurgency campaigns, Harding had been willing to negotiate with Makarios. Now that negotiations had failed, however, it was time once again to do battle as a general. In that war, the *Enosis* movement was his enemy with the archbishop its standard bearer.

Eden immediately drafted a telegram granting Harding permission to deport bishops but requesting notification before any deportation of the archbishop himself took place. Before he could send it, Macmillan intervened, asking, "Do you think that it is right to draw this distinction between these holy men? I would feel happier if the Governor had to seek authority to deport any bishop; for then we would know what were the grounds and be ready to defend our action abroad."[73] Eden had made up his mind, however, and on October 13 granted Harding a military aircraft on twenty-four hours' notice to deport any bishop. Eden also gave Harding the authority to declare a state of emergency without prior approval from London if it seemed "imperatively necessary," on the condition that he seek approval from London before any move against the archbishop.[74] Little did Eden realize how quickly Harding would act on this new authority.

The same day Eden defied Macmillan, he also clashed with Lennox-Boyd, arguing for a reappraisal of the hard position the government had taken against Cypriot self-determination and calling instead for a more nuanced understanding. He wrote to Sir Thomas Lloyd, permanent undersecretary of state for colonial affairs, telling him, "It is not our position that we will never grant self-determination to Cyprus. It is our position that we cannot grant it now, both on account of the present strategic importance of the island and because of the consequences that any such move must have on relations between NATO Powers and the Eastern Mediterranean." He then repeated almost word for word the compromise Harding had suggested but Lennox-Boyd had spurned: "We have offered a wide measure of self-government now. If the Cypriots will come in and work this then, at some later date unspecified, when self-government has proved itself a workable proposition, we are prepared to discuss with them stages in the island's political future. These stages would not exclude self-determination."[75] Tragically, had Eden communicated this message to the colonial office just three days earlier, the governor's negotiations with Makarios would no doubt have been very different. It was a missed opportunity that would cost the government dearly in the years to come.

While Eden chastised Lennox-Boyd in London, on the island Harding had already begun to make the transition from diplomat to soldier. On October 10, he had informed Eden that whatever the outcome of the talks, he would need more troops to ensure stability, and asked that an infantry battalion be placed on notice to be dispatched immediately.[76] On October 14, following the breakdown of negotiations, he confirmed this request, telling Eden, "I need one more infantry battalion and one more infantry brigade headquarters."[77] Four days later, the Cyprus intelligence committee, which had been set up by MI5's Donald Stephens issued a report concluding that EOKA was a "clandestine nationalist terrorist organisation which aims at leading the struggle for *Enosis*," composed largely of middle class youth and basically anti-Communist in nature.[78] The report confirmed Harding's opinion that the time had come to forego diplomacy and instead act. On October 24, he wrote to Lennox-Boyd, telling him, "It is my firm belief that to turn a blind eye to any breach of laws affecting security is fatal to respect for Government."[79] That same day, the first trial of an EOKA suspect began—twenty-two-year-old Michael Karolis who was accused of the August 29 murder of Constable Poullis. The trial lasted for just five days and on October 29 Karolis was found guilty of murder and sentenced to death by hanging.[80] The day before, EOKA had seized a cargo of arms and ammunition being off-loaded in Famagusta.[81] In response, Harding enacted a law allowing British Army forces to have "all the powers, privileges and protection conferred upon a member of the Cyprus

Police Force under the provisions of the law in force."[82] From October 28 onward, soldiers could act as policemen.

To assist them in understanding these new duties, the war office provided British soldiers with a "Red Card" to be carried with them at all times laying down "Instructions to individuals for opening fire in Cyprus." It informed them that although it was their duty to assess the situation before opening fire, if they were sure there was "no alternative but to open fire" they would be doing their duty and "acting lawfully whatever the consequences." The occasions on which they were entitled to open fire were to defend themselves, their comrades, their families, and other "peaceable inhabitants"; to protect government property against serious damage; to disperse a riotous mob that they "honestly believed" would "cause injury to life and property"; and to prevent suspects from escaping when under arrest.[83] Although billed as police powers, the red card allowed soldiers far more opportunities to open fire than were afforded to their civilian comrades.

With such measures in place, it was only a matter of time before Harding declared an official state of emergency. Riots on November 12, provoked by the refusal of the Cypriot Supreme Court to consider the appeal of Karaolis' death sentence, led Harding to close schools in Nicosia and Larnaca as a punitive measure, claiming that most of the rioters were pupils at these institutions. EOKA responded with a bombing offensive on November 18, exploding fifty devices throughout the island, which killed one British army sergeant and fatally injured another two while inflicting much damage on government property.[84] That evening, Harding wrote to Lennox-Boyd informing him that he would make one last attempt at accommodation with Makarios. If he failed again this time, however, he would bring the full weight of the sedition laws against the archbishop.[85]

When the meeting occurred on November 21, Harding was in no mood for small talk. Before even sitting, he passed to Makarios a piece of paper from his pocket, saying, "Your

Beatitude, I have very good news for you." The document reflected the language used earlier by Eden, reading: "It is not the position of Her Majesty's Government that the principle of self-determination can never be applicable to Cyprus. It is their position that it is not now a practical proposition both on account of the present strategical situation and on account of the consequences of the relations between North Atlantic Treaty Organization Powers and the Eastern Mediterranean." The document then revealed that the British government would provide a "wide measure of self-government" to Cyprus. If this proved successful, it would move forward with discussions on self-determination. The Cypriot people first had to prove they could govern within the empire, but if they could do that, they would be allowed to do so without it. It was certainly a paternalistic policy but nevertheless offered the chance of eventual independence or even *Enosis* if the Greek Cypriots so chose. They only had to play by Britain's rules in the immediate future and independence would be theirs. Makarios read the document carefully, declared that there was "a difference between the substance of the proposals and the phraseology," and suggested that it was in fact "the negation of self-determination." He promised to put it before the other leaders of the *Enosis* movement but was not hopeful.

It was now the archbishop's turn to be intransigent. On November 23, he notified Harding that he and his colleagues had decided to reject the offer, instead holding out for a full grant of self-determination. Makarios's notification was followed by an announcement from the Greek-Cypriot trade unions that they would stage a general strike in protest of British rule. The next day, EOKA assassinated a British Army sergeant going home for lunch at his suburban house in Nicosia. Harding immediately requested permission from Eden and his cabinet colleagues to declare a state of emergency. This he was granted, and at five o'clock in the evening on Saturday, November 26, the governor appeared on the Cypriot radio service to announce that there now existed a state of emergency on the island. Anthony Eden had not yet been prime minister for eight months and already the British government was combating insurgencies in Malaya, Kenya, and Cyprus, with a fourth brewing in Aden. Little did he know how much more trouble 1956 would bring.

III. The Dirty wars become even dirtier

On December 21, 1955, the army's general headquarters, East Africa, circulated its thirty-fifth "instruction" since Sir Evelyn Baring's declaration of emergency in Kenya three years earlier. It proclaimed that "As long as the top grade Mau Mau leaders remain alive their existence will constitute a major threat to security." Consequently, the new mission of the security forces was to "eliminate one or more top grade Mau Mau leaders." This mission, it revealed, would be carried out by the "Special Force" units of surrendered Mau Mau formed by General Lathbury in July. From December 21, these Special Force teams would have as their "primary task" the killing of Mau Mau leaders. Of the six Special Force teams in existence at that time, one would be tasked to kill Dedan Kimathi, one to kill Stanley Mathenge, three to kill lesser leaders within specified districts, and one to be kept in reserve to assist the other teams as and where needed. The teams would be deployed by January 1, 1956, at the latest and would work in conjunction with local special branch officers, army officers, and police commanders.[86] For the first time in its dirty wars of empire, the British government was ordering the assassination of named individuals.

That is not to say that the Special Force teams had not killed before. On the contrary, killing Mau Mau had always been one of their primary tasks. In July 1955, they killed thirteen Mau Mau (including one leader); in August, twenty-seven (including two leaders); in September, twenty-three (including four leaders); in November, fourteen (including four leaders); and in December, eight (including one leader). Indeed, the only month they did not kill was October. Throughout these six months, they managed to capture only two Mau Mau alive.[87]

The difference with these previous killings, however, was that the individuals targeted were unnamed and the deaths of the leaders were completely coincidental—the Special Force teams had been looking for any Mau Mau and had merely happened upon leaders.[88] With Instruction No. 35, the British now gave Special Force teams specific, named individuals to target—and that made all the difference in the legality and morality of the operations.

The increased deployment of Special Force teams was not the only change introduced in Kenya during the autumn of 1955. On October 26, general headquarters, East Africa, also published a new policy concerning the handling of surrendered or captured terrorists. Effective immediately, army and police units involved in the capture of Mau Mau suspects could keep those suspects for up to forty-eight hours for "immediate operational use," including the elimination of Mau Mau known to the suspect and the recovery of weapons that might otherwise be lost. After the forty-eight hours passed, the suspect was to be dispatched to the Police Divisional Special Branch unit for "deliberate interrogation" for an unspecified period. Once such interrogation was complete, the suspect could be returned to the operational unit at the discretion of Special Branch for a further forty-eight hours or, "in exceptional circumstances," up to sixty hours. The suspect's ordeal did not end there, however. He was then kept in a divisional detention center for "as long as required by the Administration for the purpose of encouraging surrenders or for use by the Information Services," before being sent to a place of "permanent detention." There was no mention of a trial.[89]

This latter omission caught the eye of John Whyatt, the Kenyan minister of legal affairs and attorney general, who published his own memorandum on captured and surrendered terrorists on November 5. In this document, he made clear that although he recognized the need for immediate interrogation for operational purposes, he nevertheless had "an inescapable constitutional responsibility for the due administration of criminal justice." He therefore laid down new guidelines that would supersede those of the army headquarters. He hoped these guidelines would maintain "a reasonable balance between operational desiderate on the one hand and the requirements of justice on the other." Suspects could be held for up to four days from capture for "operational exploitation" before being turned over to Special Branch for "deliberate interrogation." Following interrogation by Special Branch, which could last no longer than twenty-eight days from capture, the suspect had to be turned over to the police criminal investigation department (CID) for "charging, caution, and trial." At the time of his writing, the law dictated that no prisoner could be detained for more than fifteen days without reference to a court, a law that had been openly breached for some time. To remedy this, Whyatt promised to increase the number of days a prisoner could be detained without charge to thirty, to allow twenty-eight days with Special Branch and two with CID. In contrast to the army memorandum, he insisted that "no single [Mau Mau suspect] be exempted from prosecution without my authority."[90] Whyatt's regulations were more draconian than any used in the United Kingdom or elsewhere in the empire at that time but, at least, introduced some semblance of legality to the process.

In light of this debate, commissioner of police R. C. Catling began work on a War Council Instruction to clarify who exactly a "terrorist suspect" was, what the difference between capture and surrender was, and how suspects in each case should be treated.[91] The instruction was issued on November 23, stating that a "terrorist" was "any person who in any way participates actively in the Mau Mau terrorist campaign," including but not limited to members and followers of Mau Mau, splinter groups from Mau Mau, armed or unarmed persons supplying Mau Mau (including supplying with food), and persons in a prohibited area without proper authority. A "surrendered" terrorist was anyone fitting the above description who voluntarily surrendered to government forces during an official surrender offer. Any person who came into government hands at

a time other than during an official surrender offer was designated a "captured terrorist," even if he or she had in fact surrendered. Surrendered terrorists would be treated in the manner
outlined by Whyatt, with an additional step added: "rehabilitation." If successful, rehabilitation would lead to eventual release
and placement into a protected village. Captured terrorists, in
contrast, would have no chance of "rehabilitation" and would
instead end their journey in indefinite detention.[92]

Such surrenders and captures continued into the New Year,
with the British security forces launching two new operations
in the southwestern and eastern areas of the Mount Kenya
forest. On the night of January 19–20, 1956, the 3rd, 5th, and
23rd (Kenya) Battalions of the King's African Rifles (KAR), the
26th (Tanganyika) Battalion of the same regiment, the 1st
(Independent) East African Reconnaissance Squadron, and
several Kenya police, tribal police, and Kikuyu Guard units
moved into the eastern part of the forest in Operation Hannibal,
where they remained for twenty-six days. On January 25, the
7th (Kenya) Battalion KAR, a company of the 23rd (Kenya)
Battalion KAR, and Kenya police and tribal police moved into
the southwestern part of the forest in Operation Schemozzle II
(Schemozzle I was launched in November 1955). By the time
the two operations came to a close on February 15, British
forces had killed thirty-eight Mau Mau, captured fourteen, and
accepted the surrenders of a further twenty-three. In subsid-
iary operations launched in nearby areas of the forest, another
thirteen surrendered. In all, these operations accounted for 30
percent of all remaining Mau Mau in the Kenya forest, leading
General Lathbury to declare them "a great success."[93]

Elsewhere, the British government used no less brutal tactics
to achieve similar results. In Malaya, in 1955 alone, the RAF flew
1730 sorties and launched 570 attacks, dropping 5089 1000-lb
bombs, 5712 500-lb bombs, 2660 20-lb fragmentation bombs,
and 3096 rocket projectiles.[94] In Aden, the colonial administration of Sir Tom Hickinbotham busily prepared itself for an
expected emergency. In August 1954, upon the recommendation

of MI5's A. M. MacDonald, the Aden Colony police formed a Special Branch for the first time in its history, with a section of Special Branch attached to the Aden Protectorate police (as distinct from the colony police) in December 1955. In an attempt to coordinate intelligence between the two territories, on January 1, 1956, Hickinbotham ordered a joint intelligence center to be opened, effective immediately. Its responsibilities were broad, ranging from exploiting and developing current intelligence leads, to identifying and exploiting new sources, to recording information of a "general nature" about all Arab countries and Arab affairs relevant to Aden.[95] Unlike in Malaya and Kenya, Hickinbotham did not establish an interrogation center at that time but the implication of his founding of the intelligence center was clear: the information it produced would soon be needed by the security forces.

It was in Cyprus that the government introduced the greatest number of new coercive measures, though. On December 4, 1955—eight days after he declared a state of emergency— Harding informed Lennox-Boyd that he intended to impose his first collective fine under the emergency regulations, which would be levied against the people of Lefkonico. The post office in that village had been burnt to the ground in protest of governmental actions, and Harding was imposing a £2000 fine for its rebuilding.[96] Pressed by the colonial secretary for further detail, Harding explained that the fines would be progressively assessed based on people's ability to pay, ranging from a few shillings for the poorest villagers to £45 for the richest.[97] The governor put into place a curfew with immediate effect until the fines could be paid. With this restriction enacted, and with the fines set by income rather than a single, across-the-board figure, the villagers quickly relented and the security forces collected all fines by ten o'clock on the morning of December 7. Once the last shilling had come in, Harding lifted the curfew. The rebuilding of the post office began immediately, a visible testament to the purpose of the money and a lesson that if government property was destroyed, Cypriots would pay for its resurrection.[98] The contrast between Harding's actions and the curfew imposed by Armitage only a few months earlier could not have been greater.

The curfew and collective fine were not the only aggressive operations launched by Harding that week. On December 5, EOKA ambushed and killed a Royal Marine, a Cypriot police-man, and a Greek civilian who were walking together at Amiandos. In response, on December 8, Harding ordered British soldiers, accompanied by army chaplains, to search for arms in twenty-four of the island's monasteries. This action was largely symbolic—to indicate that just because Makarios was an arch-bishop and the church was in favor of *Enosis*, he and it could not shelter EOKA with impunity—and soldiers recovered only a few hunting rifles, two pistols, some sticks of dynamite, and several EOKA pamphlets. Nevertheless, in Harding's view it demonstrated the resolve of the government to quickly quell the insurgency.[99] Three days after the soldiers searched these churches, Harding furthered this resolve by imposing a "strict traffic system" on the most troubled areas of the island, under which all nonoperational traffic was confined to movement in convoys along certain roads. He wrote to Lennox-Boyd on December 11 requesting that an armored car regiment be sent to Cyprus immediately to act as close escort for the convoys and to patrol the prohibited roads.[100] As with almost all of his requests, this Lennox-Boyd granted him.

Meanwhile, on December 22, A. M. MacDonald, who had been seconded from MI5 to the colonial office to act as its secu-rity intelligence advisor, submitted a report to Harding on the state of the intelligence organization in the colony. He noted that the morale of Special Branch had been badly weakened since it became a primary target of EOKA attacks, but argued that with proper leadership and guidance it could rally and become as effective as its counterparts in Malaya and Kenya. In particular, he recommended more military intelligence and special branch officers be brought from other territories to Cyprus to add an additional layer of expertise. Several such officers had already arrived and had "effected a considerable improvement in morale."[101] MacDonald's wish was granted and by the end of the year an additional cadre of special branch officers arrived in Cyprus from other troubled colonies, including Malaya and Kenya.[102]

On January 7, 1956, Harding sent to the colonial secretary a review of the security situation. He claimed that "additional units and personnel are urgently required to destroy Eoka and reestablish law and order with the minimum delay," and then outlined three main areas where these forces were needed:

(a) The destruction of the Eoka mountain groups, which consist of a hard core of trained guerilla fighters who terrorise the local villagers and exert an influence out of all proportion to their numbers. This is of first priority. Once these groups have been eliminated the clearing up of the remainder of the countryside should not present a great problem.

(b) To prevent the smuggling of arms and equipment into the Island from the sea and from the air.

(c) To eliminate the assassins in the towns.

To meet these needs, Harding asked for an additional battalion of infantry soldiers (to combat the mountain guerillas); two naval destroyers, four coastal minesweepers, and sufficient army radar equipment to establish two new radar substations (to protect against smuggling at sea and by air); ninety additional police and fifteen police jeeps (to implement urban anti-assassination measures); an RAF helicopter flight (for internal security operations and mountain reconnaissance); three assistant commissioners of police (one for each of the three main towns); at least sixteen specially trained police or army interrogators (at his time of writing, there were only five for the whole island); four additional customs officers; and at least three prison officers and twenty-two warders (to man the two detention camps Harding had set up upon his declaration of emergency). His request was not unreasonable and he believed that even this modest rise would make a tremendous difference in the campaign.[103]

While the cabinet in London considered this request, EOKA struck again, killing its first Turkish-Cypriot policeman on January 13. This prompted the governor to announce that it was time to "take off the gloves." On January 20, he boarded a plane for London to make his argument heard more loudly with the government there. He remained in London for a week, by the end of which he had extracted from the cabinet a new statement on Cypriot self-determination. This pledged the government to consider self-determination following a period of successful self-government, but was contingent upon Makarios first signing a statement that denounced all violence in the cause of *Enosis*. If Makarios refused to sign this state-ment, Harding had the cabinet's permission to deport him from Cyprus without delay.[104]

Upon his return to the island on January 27, Harding imme-diately sent to Makarios the government's new statement and asked for discussions. Makarios stalled, claiming that he first had to meet with the leadership of the *Enosis* movement before pro-ceeding further. On January 28, the archbishop consulted Grivas, who demanded that in return for ending EOKA's campaign he would need a firm commitment from the British government to establish a Legislative Assembly with a Greek majority and to grant a general amnesty for all EOKA attacks committed since April 1, 1955. Grivas agreed to suspend all EOKA attacks until April 1, 1956, to give the archbishop time to secure these condi-tions. On February 2, Makarios wrote to Harding, telling him that he could "provisionally" accept the government's state-ment although there were some aspects that required further discussion. When the two finally met on February 24, their conversation was as unsuccessful as on previous occasions. Makarios refused to issue a statement of nonviolence until an amnesty was agreed. The British government would do no such thing until Makarios denounced EOKA. Harding, unwilling to allow the talks to immediately collapse, sent a telegram to

Lennox-Boyd asking him to come urgently to Cyprus to take part in the discussions himself. This the colonial secretary did, and on February 29 the three men sat down together.[105]

It was to no avail. By the time they met, each side had become further entrenched. On the morning Lennox-Boyd arrived, EOKA detonated several bombs in Nicosia in violation of its cease-fire, explosions that were heard by Harding and Lennox-Boyd as they drove to the meeting. Just days earlier, Harding had confirmed the death sentences of a further two EOKA suspects, Andreas Zakos and Charilaos Michael, who joined Michael Karaolis and Andreou Demetriou on death row. Consequently, each side was suspicious of the other as they sat down. Makarios began by asking about the amnesty, acknowledging that violence resulting in death could not be included but protesting against the death penalties given to those who were merely carrying explosives. Lennox-Boyd replied that the blind eye of British justice could not "draw a distinction between violence which succeeded in its purposes and those which did not." Had the carried explosives been planted and detonated, deaths would surely have resulted. The colonial secretary then offered to Makarios a "normal, liberal constitutional doctrine" for Cypriot self-government. The archbishop claimed that this "did not really meet the point," which was ultimate self-determination. The meeting ended then, with Lennox-Boyd saying to Makarios, "God save your people," and Makarios politely thanking the colonial secretary for his time. For his part, Harding said goodbye to the archbishop for the last time. The two would never meet again.[106]

Harding considered his position for several days and then on March 3 sent a telegram to Lennox-Boyd requesting the immediate deportation of Makarios. He warned that this would lead to "immediate and violent reactions" followed by "mobs of villagers" hoping to disrupt all island services, intent on bringing about the total "breakdown of the administration and essential services." Despite these risks, he believed the *Enosis* movement could never be defeated with Makarios at liberty on the island.

His deportation was therefore worth the trouble it would bring.[107] Harding explained his reasoning further in a letter to his son, John Charles, on March 4, writing: "By his persistent refusal to denounce violence the Archbishop forces me to the conclusion that he believes in violence as a political weapon and would not hesitate to use it again—a curious attitude for a so-called Christian leader. Having failed to get his cooperation in restoring law and order and in eliminating the terrorists I shall have to resort to other methods to create conditions in which we can approach self-government with some hope of success." He ended his letter ominously stating, "Up to date I have had to pursue two divergent policies—agreement by negotiation and restoration of law and order—which has compelled me to refrain from some security measures while negotiations were still in progress. Now I can give the restoration of law and order, and the elimination of the terrorists, overriding priority."[108] The gloves were indeed coming off.

The government, upon receiving Harding's request, was understandably squeamish, one member claiming that the deportation of a Christian leader was "reminiscent of Henry VIII."[109] On March 6, therefore, the cabinet instructed Lennox-Boyd to see if he could change Harding's mind. When the colonial secretary failed to do so, the government reluctantly authorized an RAF transport plane to be deployed to Cyprus, where it landed on the morning of March 7. As the Cypriot police authorities made their final preparations for the archbishop's arrest, Harding discovered that Makarios was planning to travel to Athens on March 9. He therefore suspended the arrest operation and allowed the archbishop to arrive at the airport unaware of what awaited him. When Makarios stepped onto the tarmac to board his plane to Greece, he was surrounded by British army soldiers and instead escorted to the RAF transport plane, which promptly flew him to "indefinite detention" on the Seychelles Islands.[110] The *Enosis* movement no longer had its spiritual leader, but for Harding and the British government as a whole the trouble was just beginning.

The extent of the reaction to Makarios' deportation became clear that evening, as the Greek-Cypriot community declared a three-day general strike in protest and immediately shuttered all shops and restaurants. The situation worsened on April 14 when the Privy Council in London dismissed the final appeal against the death sentence imposed on Karaolis. Harding was now the only individual who could offer him clemency. This he was not prepared to do. On the morning of May 10, 1956, both Karaolis and Demetriou were executed in Nicosia Central Prison. Just hours later, EOKA announced that in retaliation it had executed two British army hostages: Corporal Gordon Hill, held since November 1955, and Corporal Ronnie Shilton, held since April 1956, both of the Royal Leicestershire Regiment. As had occurred in Palestine when the IZL murdered two British police sergeants in retaliation for the execution of two of their own in 1947, in Cyprus any sympathy the government or public may have felt toward the *Enosis* movement rapidly melted away. From that point forward, Harding had the full support of the cabinet for more repressive action.[111]

The governor was not shy to implement such measures. In the late spring of 1956, he had just over 20,000 British army troops at his disposal, supported by many more police constables, RAF personnel, and sailors. To these he added two squadrons of reconnaissance helicopters in mid-May, as well as a pack of tracker dogs flown in from Kenya where they had been hunting Mau Mau. Confronting him, EOKA had approximately 200 active and committed members.[112] On May 25, Harding authorized the chairman of the Famagusta District Security Committee (modeled on the Malayan DWECs) to invoke Emergency Regulation 44, which allowed for destruction of crops as a form of collective punishment. As Harding explained in a telegram to Lennox-Boyd, in proportion to its size and population, Famagusta had a higher incident of bomb attacks than any other Cypriot village—since April 1955, the security forces had suffered 104 bomb attacks and 17 firearms attacks, resulting in nine deaths and fifty-five woundings. The reason, he claimed, was EOKA was able to hide in the orange groves that lined the roads. Consequently, using Emergency Regulation 44 Harding ordered the committee chairman to take control of all orange groves and to "render bomb throwing impracticable." This necessitated the destruction of 5000 orange trees valued at £60,000. The 200 owners of these trees received compensation for their losses, but this compensation was not all paid from the government coffers. Instead, Harding levied a collective fine of £25,000 against the people of Famagusta, varying from £1 for the poorest resident to £300 for the richest. Government emergency funds would then make up the remaining £35,000 of compensation.[113] As at Leftonico, Harding insisted that the residents pay for the damage they caused. Only by enforcing such could the government reasonably expect the attacks to cease.

Harding clarified his position on collective fines in a June memorandum. He noted that the primary purpose of such fines was to pay compensation to "persons suffering injury, loss, or damage in the area" as a consequence of government actions. If the fines exceeded the need for compensation, the balance would be paid into a "special account" held by the district commissioner, which would be frozen until a suitable purpose for the money could be identified by the governor. All such funds would be used for betterment projects in Cypriot society. Finally, Harding made clear that all fines would be levied on a progressive basis, with the poor and rich each only paying as much as they could afford.[114] In addition to these collective fines, Harding also articulated a policy on evictions. Thus far, these had been used on only two occasions. On March 16, the security forces had evicted ten households and eighteen shopkeepers from their properties in Nicosia for a period of three months for giving material support to EOKA. On May 24, seventeen households and thirty-five shopkeepers had been evicted for three months for the same reason. Harding intended to continue the use of this tactic, although he made clear in a telegram to Lennox-Boyd that homelessness would be avoided: "All cases of eviction were investigated, and although inconvenience was caused all had alternative places of residence either with relatives or in a second property."[115] As with the collective fines, Harding wished the evictions to be painful but not excessively so, inconvenient but not crippling. Just as he was unwilling to bankrupt the poorest of Cypriots with unreasonable collective fines, so too he would not throw people out into the street if they had nowhere else to go.

Harding was also careful not to allow the type of aggressive RAF air operations that were being used in Malaya and Kenya, in part because of the more complex international dynamics of the Cyprus emergency (Cypriot civilians were being carefully watched by two British allies, the Greeks and Turks—in contrast, Mau Mau had no defenders and the Malayan Communists were in alliance with the Chinese, a British enemy). For that reason, on June 18 he ordered the commander in chief, Middle East Land Forces, to send to the air ministry in London certain stipulations on the use of offensive air operations in Cyprus. These included the following:

(A) To be used in limited areas in the mountains which will have been declared danger areas. Intensive publicity both on the ground and using sky hailing aircraft will precede this use.
(B) 20 pound bombs from Austers may be used at an ambush site. But only if it is quite certain no innocent person will be harmed.
(C) Safety precautions will be carefully applied. Our experiments show 20 pound bombs can be used from Austers with a very small margin of error, these are the largest weapons we propose. Use of rockets or SA fire would be limited to hill areas only.

The RAF could perhaps be useful for the "lowering of morale of terrorists," but ultimately because of "very important political considerations," this would be a war fought primarily by police constables and soldiers.[116]

The problem with this was that in June 1956 there were simply not enough troops in the empire to meet all of the problems the British government faced. A report given to the cabinet on June 20 warned that while the situation in Malaya was looking more promising day by day, in Kenya the Mau Mau outbreak continued, representing "a reversion to primitive tribalism and a violently hostile reaction to Western civilization." More worrying was the situation in Aden, the "last Arab area under European control," which was succumbing to ever greater risk of subversion "through the Yemen and Saudi Arabia, both of which countries have been increasingly running arms."[117] The consequence was that there were no soldiers to spare. In Cyprus, this raised great concern. On July 6, the chiefs of staff notified the minister of defense, Sir Walter Monckton, that the Parachute Regiment battalions that had been on the island since January were slated to leave at the end of the year. They suggested that they be replaced by battalions of infantry. Monckton passed on these recommendations to the colonial secretary, who in turn notified Field Marshal (newly promoted) Templer, the chief of the imperial general staff.[118]

On July 26, Templer rejected the colonial secretary's request. He explained that the parachute battalions would in fact be replaced by two light artillery regiments rather than infantry. This was not due to the changing dynamics of the conflict in Cyprus, nor to any apparent need for more heavy weaponry, but because the British infantry battalions had finally succumbed to the burden placed upon them since the end of the Second World War. Templer revealed that at the time of his writing, there were only nine infantry battalions remaining in the United Kingdom that had been resident there for a period of more than twelve months, three of which were already earmarked for internal security operations in Somaliland. With a reserve of only six battalions that were not pledged elsewhere, the chief of the imperial general staff simply could not afford to send more infantry to Cyprus.[119] In July 1956, Templer had real concerns about imperial security. Yet, for the first time since

1948 these did not stem primarily from Malaya, Kenya, Aden, or even Cyprus. Rather Templer's attention was increasingly drawn to Egypt, and in particular to the Suez Canal zone, where simmering tensions were about to rapidly come to a boil.

IV. Suez

On July 26, 1956—the same day Templer informed Lennox-Boyd that he would be unable to replace the parachute battalions in Cyprus with infantry battalions—Egyptian colonel Gamal Abdel Nasser delivered a speech in Alexandria announcing the nationalization of the Suez Canal. Using stirring words, he declared that Egypt had waged "a battle against imperialism and the methods and tactics of imperialism"; that "Arab nationalism progresses. Arab nationalism triumphs. Arab nationalism marches forward"; and that "today, when we build the High Dam, we are also building the dam of dignity, freedom, and grandeur. We are eliminating the dams of humiliation, and servility. We, the whole of Egypt in one front, a united national block, announce that the whole of Egypt will fight until the last drop of her blood." Finally, he informed his listeners: "The Suez Canal was one of the façades of oppression, extortion, and humiliation. Today, O citizens, the Suez Canal has been nationalized. ... Today, O citizens, we declare that our property has been returned to us."[120]

The very next day, Anthony Eden wrote to his "dear friend," the American president Dwight D. Eisenhower, bluntly informing him that "we cannot afford to allow Nasser to seize control of the Canal in this way, in defiance of international agreements," and warning that "we must be ready, in the last resort, to use force to bring Nasser to his senses."[121] This was not a surprising stance for a British prime minister to take. After all, the British government had used force to seize the Suez Canal in the first place, some seventy-four years earlier. The canal was built in 1869 on the orders of the Egyptian khedive, carved out

338

using Egyptian labor but with British locomotives and steam shovels.[122] British interests in Egypt went back further, however, to the period after 1815 when the city of Manchester's need for raw cotton led investors there. Officially part of the Ottoman Empire, Egypt was forced to move to a free trade system of economics following Britain's imposition of such upon the Ottomans in 1838. By 1880, Britain received 80 percent of Egypt's exports and provided 40 percent of its imports.

It was with this foreign investment in mind that the khedive began raising state bonds in 1862 to fund the construction of the canal. By 1873, British investors held more than half of this Egyptian public debt.[123] Two years later, in November 1875, the British government became an owner as the khedive put his shares up for sale to pay off substantial personal debt. Conservative prime minister Benjamin Disraeli immediately borrowed money from his friend Lionel de Rothschild to make the purchase, giving the British state part ownership of the canal.[124] When Egypt fell into bankruptcy in 1876, it was the British government and British investors who stood to lose the most. Consequently, Disraeli employed the banker George Goschen to negotiate dual (Anglo-French) control over all Egyptian finances, insisting on the imposition of a balanced budget and a scheduled debt service. When as a result of these economically austere measures the Egyptian people deposed the khedive in 1880, the British government tightened the system of dual control and passed the Law of Liquidation, which consolidated Egyptian public debt and rescheduled debt payments.[125]

It was not only the British government and investors who were committed to the success of the Suez Canal, however. British merchants and industrialists, likewise, had a great stake there. In 1870, a year after the canal opened, 300,000 tons of British merchandise and materials passed through its waters. By 1875, this had risen to 2,000,000 tons and by 1880 to 3,500,000 tons. In the short time it had been in service, British companies had become completely dependent on the canal.[126] These merchants, the government, and investors were all alarmed when in 1881 the nationalist leader Urabi led protests against foreign involvement in Egyptian finances and the Egyptian Chamber of Notables (newly reestablished) challenged European control of its debt. When riots erupted in the city of Alexandria in July 1882, the British government ordered Admiral Seymour to bombard the city, Royal Marines landed, and the British occupation of Egypt began.[127]

From that time until 1914, Egypt held a unique position on the world stage. It was both part of the Ottoman Empire and an unofficial British protectorate, with a British-installed khedive who was ostensibly loyal to the Ottoman sultan but who in fact did the bidding of the British government with British soldiers stationed in his land. Upon the outbreak of the First World War, the khedive sided with the sultan rather than the king. Consequently, Britain made official what had up until that point been left unstated—with the troops it had stationed in Egypt, it formalized its occupation and proclaimed Egypt a British protectorate. Following rioting in the years 1919–1922, the government declared Egypt an "independent, sovereign state." In reality, however, it simply reverted to the position it held in the years 1882 to 1914, with British advisors dictating policy to the British-installed sultan who himself was protected by British soldiers. In 1936, Anthony Eden—then foreign secretary—negotiated the Anglo-Egyptian Treaty, which formally ended the British military occupation but also stipulated that until an Egyptian army could be formed to properly safeguard the Suez Canal, British forces would remain, never to number more than 10,000 soldiers, 400 airmen, and the necessary supporting staff. There was a further proviso that in time of war, the Egyptian government would make its entire territory and resources available for the use of Britain.[128]

With the outbreak of the Second World War, the British government took full advantage of this final clause, flooding the territory with troops. At the end of the war, these inflated forces remained. In 1949, Clement Attlee's Labour government agreed to withdraw from the country so long as the Egyptian government promised full use again in the event of future war. This time the Egyptians refused. Consequently, although the government pulled its troops from the Egyptian delta, 80,000 remained in the Canal Zone.[129] Following the coming to power of Winston Churchill's government in 1951, the situation in Egypt deteriorated rapidly. In July 1952, Colonel Nasser seized power from the Egyptian king Farouk I in the first Arab nationalist coup of its kind.[130] King Farouk, who was also king of the Sudan and a graduate of the Royal Military Academy, Woolwich, fully expected British support. He was thus surprised when in February 1953 the British government signed the Anglo-Egyptian agreement guaranteeing self-determination to the Sudanese people (the government did this in a misguided attempt to curry favor with Nasser). From that point forward, Sudanese officials gradually replaced Britons until on January 1, 1956, the government officially transferred power to an independent Sudan.[131]

Meanwhile, in Egypt, Nasser was determined to throw off what he saw as the imperialist yoke of Britain. Thus, although Churchill announced in 1954 that the British government planned to withdraw its base from Suez and relocate it to Cyprus, Nasser still felt under threat from the West. In 1955, he turned to the Soviet Union, by way of Czechoslovakia, for military assistance, including the importation of arms.[132] This caused Eden, newly appointed prime minister, a great deal of consternation, and he warned Eisenhower on January 16, 1956, that there was a danger of "the whole of the Middle East fall[ing] into Communist hands."[133] Three days later, Eden instructed Sir Walter Monckton, the minister of defense, to "slow down" the British withdrawal from the Canal Zone.[134] In early March, he asked foreign secretary Selwyn Lloyd to discuss with American secretary of state John Foster Dulles the situation in Egypt.[135] This Lloyd did and on March 7 informed the prime minister that he had "repeated our views on the seriousness of the situation and that you felt no reliance could be placed on Nasser."[136]

Throughout the spring and early summer of 1956, the energies of Eden, Selwyn Lloyd, and Lennox-Boyd were largely monopolized by the ongoing drama in Cyprus. Nasser's announcement of the nationalization of the Suez Canal caught them somewhat by surprise. On July 28, two days after Nasser's speech, Eden wrote to the prime ministers of Canada, Australia, New Zealand, and South Africa, telling them, "We cannot allow him [Nasser] to get away with this act of expropriation and we must take a firm stand. If we do not, the oil supplies of the free world will be at his mercy and Commonwealth communications and trade will be gravely jeopardised." He revealed that his hope was to "seize this opportunity" to put the canal under international control on a permanent basis. If this was not possible through diplomacy, he warned that "force may have to be used to secure Egyptian agreement."[137] He communicated this message also to Eisenhower, who on July 31 told the prime minister, "From the moment that Nasser announced nationalization of the Suez Canal Company, my thoughts have been constantly with you." Nevertheless, the president stressed the "unwisdom even of contemplating the use of military force at this moment," and urged Eden to explore "every peaceful means of protecting the rights and the livelihood of great portions of the world."[138]

The prime minister was undeterred. On August 5, he told Eisenhower, "In the light of our long friendship I will not conceal from you that the present situation causes me the deepest concern." He stated that British and American aims were the same, which were to "undo what Nasser has done and to set up an International Regime for the Canal." The difference came in their respective attitude toward Nasser. The Americans believed him to be a mere pest, an irritant but ultimately harmless; Eden was convinced he was something altogether more sinister: "I have never thought Nasser a Hitler; he has no warlike people behind him. But the parallel with Mussolini is close. Neither of us can forget the lives and treasure he cost us before he was finally dealt with." Eden informed Eisenhower that he was "grimly determined that Nasser shall not get away with it this time."[139]

The government set this determination into motion even before Eden wrote to the president. On August 3, the joint intelligence committee circulated to the chiefs of staff a report describing Nasser as "a demagogue" who was likely to "be carried away by the violence of the passions he himself has whipped up." The report warned that Nasser might break off diplomatic relations with the British and French governments, withdraw all air transit facilities, nationalize all British assets in Egypt, cancel the residence permits that were required for all British citizens living in Egypt, persuade other Arab states to take similar "anti-Western measures" including the denial of military facilities, and "incite feeling against British and French nationals in Egypt so as to make their position precarious." Although the report admitted he would be unlikely to resort to any of these measures without further provocation, it could not rule them out entirely due to the "considerable element of emotion in Nasser's actions."[140] The following day Eden wrote to Sidney Holland, prime minister of New Zealand, asking for the use of the New Zealand naval ship *The Royalist* "if military action should ultimately prove necessary."[141]

On August 7, the joint intelligence committee circulated another report assessing the capabilities of the Egyptian armed forces. It noted that "At the moment, about 80% of the regular Egyptian Army and by far the greater part of Egyptian armour, together with associated maintenance units and stockpiles, are in Sinai." The report suggested that "If Egypt were to lose control of the canal crossings, these forces would be isolated, without prospect of reinforcement and useless except against Israel." The committee's clear insinuation was that if there was a war with Egypt, all British forces need do was seize the canal crossings and 80 percent of Egypt's power would be negated. Britain could easily win such a war in a matter of days, if not hours.[142] This the committee confirmed to the cabinet in a memorandum written on August 17, concluding that if the British government waged war on Egypt, the Soviet Union would abstain, operations in Egypt would be "short and decisive," the Western position in the Middle East would be "greatly strengthened," and "favourable conditions" would be created for "a settlement of the Arab/ Israel dispute." If, in contrast, the government accepted a "bad compromise," its "whole position in the Middle East [might] very soon be in complete jeopardy."[143] The case for war was hardening. Eden indicated this to Eisenhower on August 27 when he described the situation in Egypt as "the most hazardous that our country has known since 1940."[144]

Events moved more rapidly in September. On the seventh of that month, Lennox-Boyd confidently asserted that if the internationalization of the canal was secured by force, "the traditional Arab respect for strength would come into play and, although there might be some legacy of resentment, the situation would probably be accepted by the great majority of the population."[145] Following a conference in London that was attended by representatives of eighteen nations making up 90 percent of the canal users, Eden wrote to Selwyn Lloyd: "We are agreed that the Canal must remain international and cannot therefore be left to the unrestricted control of one nation or one man."[146] He then dispatched the foreign secretary to Washington, DC, to solicit American support for any British use of force in Egypt. Selwyn Lloyd reported back on October 8 that John Foster Dulles, the American secretary of state, was "in full agreement with us on every point except the wisdom of the ultimate use of force. Even on that he thought that we had been absolutely right to make our preparations and that we were right to maintain the threat." He added, "He did not himself rule out force at a later stage."[147] Eisenhower seemed to confirm this message on October 11 when he wrote to Eden stating: "I know that Foster is working there [in New York] closely with Selwyn Lloyd, and I deeply deplore the suggestions of the press both here and abroad that you and we are at cross purposes."[148]

With the leading British cabinet members in agreement on the necessity of force against Nasser and with apparent American concurrence if not outright support for such action, Eden set into motion the plans that would bring about a British invasion of Egypt. He had already met with representatives from the French and Israeli governments on August 1. He now formalized the alliance with the Protocol of Sèvres, signed on October 24 following two days of clandestine negotiations between the three governments. This secret protocol pledged each government to take immediate action against Egypt. More specifically, Israeli forces would invade Sinai, where the bulk of Nasser's forces were located, followed a few days later by a British and French "intervention," purportedly to separate the warring Egyptian and Israeli armies but in fact to secure an international zone around the Suez Canal.[149]

Once the plan was in place, war came quickly. On October 29—just five days after Selwyn Lloyd returned from Sèvres—an Israeli parachute battalion dropped onto the Sinai Peninsula, followed by a ground invasion led by two infantry brigades. These brigades linked up with the airborne contingent on October 30.[150] This invasion allowed the British and French governments to execute their plan and immediately issue a demand to the Egyptian and Israeli governments (with clandestine Israeli support) that each withdraw their troops and allow the temporary occupation of the Suez Canal zone by British and French forces. If this demand was not met within twelve hours, the British and French governments threatened to "intervene in whatever strength may be necessary to secure compliance."[151]

The plan having gone so smoothly in its initial stages, Eden was surprised not to immediately receive the support he expected from outside parties. The first indication of this came in a telegram from Eisenhower on October 30, just hours after the government issued its ultimatum. The president relayed his "deep concern at the prospect of this drastic action" and repeated his belief that "peaceful processes can and should prevail."[152] Eden was determined to press forward with his plan, however, and when the 12-hour ultimatum expired on the morning of October 31, he ordered Operation Musketeer to begin with an air offensive on Egypt. The RAF dropped its first bombs at 6:15 p.m. local time. By the end of the following night, it had flown eighteen sorties and unloaded 1962 bombs.[153] With the bombs came more opposition. Sidney Holland, prime minister of New Zealand, sent a telegram to Eden on November 1, withdrawing the use of the ship *Royalist* for operations against Egypt. In explanation, he wrote, "The fact that the United Kingdom and France have taken direct action without the approval of the [UN] Security Council is of special significance to New Zealand, which has always paid the utmost attention to its United Nations Charter obligations."[154] Having supported the position of the British government in Palestine, Malaya, Korea, Kenya, and Cyprus, the New Zealand government was no longer able to do so.

Fearing that other Commonwealth countries might soon follow suit, Eden instructed Lennox-Boyd to send a telegram to the governments of twenty-seven Commonwealth nations and other British territories, which he did on November 2, explaining, "Once Israeli troops entered Sinai we became vitally concerned at threat to the Canal. Our military appreciation was that her troops were capable of advancing to Canal quickly. ... Had Israeli troops reached Canal it would have been dividing line between warring forces and would probably have been destroyed." The government, the telegram claimed, had considered UN action but "[e]xperience has convinced us that we could not have hoped for swift and effective action by the Security Council in such a situation." Consequently, and with purported regret, the British and French governments had no choice but to act. The telegram closed by assuring its recipients that "Anglo-French occupation of key positions on Canal will be temporary."[155] It was one of the more disingenuous telegrams sent by the British government during its dirty wars and the Commonwealth countries did not buy it. The Australian and Canadian prime ministers immediately issued public statements condemning British actions, followed shortly thereafter by the prime ministers of India and Pakistan. The government, it appeared, had lost the support of the Commonwealth.[156]

Yet with the air offensive already launched, Eden felt it would be foolish to back down. In the face of international opposition, he was determined to push on. At 7:15 a.m. local time on November 5, the 3rd Battalion, Parachute Regiment, dropped onto Gamil airfield four miles west of Port Said. This was followed by an amphibious assault by 40 Commando, 42 Commando, and 45 Commando Royal Marines, supported by a squadron of tanks from the 6th Battalion, Royal Tank Regiment. By mid-morning on November 6, British forces—together with French units—had achieved their objectives.[157] The true battle was not to take place on the banks of the canal, however. In Britain, public and parliamentary support was quickly beginning to sour. The parliamentary legislation authorizing the operation was only passed by 270 to 218 votes, with the Labour and Liberal parties united in opposition. The dissenting voices now began to make themselves heard. At Oxford University, 335 members of the Senior Common Rooms, including ten heads of colleges, issued a statement reading: "We consider this action is morally wrong, that it endangers the solidarity of the Commonwealth, that it constitutes a grave strain on the Atlantic alliances and that it is a flagrant violation of the principles of the UN Charter."[158] Oxford dons were not the only Britons who felt this way.

Britain's rapidly deteriorating relationship with the United States worried the cabinet the most. Having spurned Eisenhower's request for a peaceful solution, Eden now risked feeling the full force of American opposition. On November 2, Saudi Arabia closed its oil supplies to Great Britain, necessitating British reliance on American oil. Yet following the landing of British troops in Egypt, the American government announced an oil embargo on Britain. NATO countries soon followed suit, pledging they would not sell any oil to Britain that had first come from either the Arab countries or the United States. Without oil, Britain's postwar nationalized state was simply not viable.[159] Oil was not the government's only concern, though. Harold Macmillan, chancellor of the exchequer since December 20, 1955, informed the cabinet on November 6 that the sterling area's currency was "hemorrhaging" as it became clear how isolated Britain was. Reserves had fallen by £20.3 million in September and £30 million in October. Macmillan now announced that in the first five days of November, they had dropped an astonishing £100 million more as the markets rapidly sold off the currency. Macmillan told the cabinet that they could be looking at the death of sterling itself. Under normal circumstances, the government would have sought a loan from the United States or the International Monetary Fund, which was largely controlled by the United States. Eisenhower, however, had forbidden both options until a cease-fire could be arranged.[160] The British government consequently faced the very real possibility that while successfully securing the canal they might have lost everything else of worth.

Confronting economic disaster, Eden could do only one thing. At 11:03 a.m., British Standard Time, he sent a telegram to his commander in Egypt, General Sir Charles Keightley, stating: "It may be essential politically to have an immediate cease-fire and to stand fast. Could you maintain the force at present ashore indefinitely from present positions assuming maintenance through Port Said?" When he had heard nothing by 1:00 p.m., he sent another wire: "Is answer 'Yes' or 'No'? Please reply plain soonest." Finally, Keightly replied: "The answer is Yes." Eden informed him that he should be prepared to issue the cease-fire by 5:00 p.m.[161] The prime minister then picked up the telephone to call the American president. Eisenhower was elated with Eden's decision and immediately sent him a telegram: "I was delighted at the opportunity to talk with you on the telephone and to hear that the U.K. will order a cease-fire this evening. ... Let me say again that I will be delighted to have you call me at any time. The telephone connection seemed very satisfactory."[162] Britain's relationship with the United States was secure but it had come at a cost. Having won the battle, the government lost the war and British forces began withdrawing by the end of the month. On December 23, 1956, the last soldier left the territory. For the first time since 1882, there was no British presence in the Suez Canal zone.

In the way it was fought, the Suez campaign was cleaner than most of Britain's other post–Second World War engagements. Yet in the duplicity of its planning, the mistruths the government gave to Commonwealth and other governments, and Eden's refusal to contemplate anything other than a military engagement, Suez was perhaps the dirtiest of all Britain's dirty wars— and it spelled the end of Anthony Eden's short premiership.

V. The endgame for Anthony Eden

On November 23, 1956, Anthony Eden, along with his wife, boarded an aeroplane for Jamaica where he planned to take a "prolonged holiday" on doctor's orders. He was to do so at the home of Ian Fleming. The press did not fail to pick up on the irony of the now discredited prime minister escaping to the home of the legendary author of James Bond, the master of intrigue, after his own clandestine failings. The following day, the United Nations General Assembly passed by sixty-three votes to five a resolution censuring Britain and France for their actions in the Suez Canal zone. For the Conservative Party, the vote was a signal that it was time to change leaders or lose the next general election. Immediately, Harold Macmillan and Rab Butler began jockeying for position. Eden seemed unconcerned. As Lord Bracken (Churchill's First Lord of the Admiralty in 1945) commented to Lord Beaverbrook (of Fleet Street fame) on December 7: "Eden has no intention of giving up No. 10. I should say he was the least rattled of all his ministers. He writes cheerful letters from Jamaica and doesn't seem the least perturbed by all the storms that blow over him."[163]

Eden realized how terribly complacent he had become only when he arrived back in London on December 14. As Viscount Montgomery wrote to Churchill, "In all my military experience I have never known anything to have been so 'bungled' as the Suez affair. You would not have handled it that way. Nor would you have gone off to Jamaica. Under such conditions the captain of the ship does not go sea-bathing—he dies on the bridge."[164] Eden's reception at Downing Street was cold and the reception at the House of Commons on December 17 colder still. His failure on December 18 to answer a simple question for the 1922 Committee (composed solely of Conservative parliamentary backbenchers) further undermined his authority, and on December 20 he was forced to publicly lie to the House of Commons, telling those gathered that he had no foreknowledge of the Israeli invasion of Egypt. Escaping to the prime ministerial estate of Chequers to avoid scrutiny over the Christmas holiday, Eden found no peace as the fever that had dogged him prior to leaving for Jamaica returned. Another holiday was called for but was not possible.[165]

Consequently, on January 9, 1957, Eden informed the cabinet he was tendering his resignation due to ill health. He then went immediately to see the Queen, who accepted it without hesitation.[166] Nine days later, Eden boarded a steamer for New Zealand, where he remained for the next four months. For Eden, it was a sad end to a lifetime's devotion to party and country. As he admitted to Lyttelton on January 28, "This has been a strange experience. Agreeable in that for the first time since 1931 I have nothing to do with politics either Ministerial or opposition front bench, depressing because one cannot help feeling like a carpenter without a bench of tools."[167] This carpenter's time had come and gone, closing in a manner that he would never have predicted. It was now time for new blood in No. 10 Downing Street, a decision that in 1957 was left not to the Conservative Party membership but to Elizabeth II. Following advice from Winston Churchill, the Queen invited the chancellor of the exchequer to the palace and asked him to form a new government. The empire was now in the hands of Harold Macmillan. He would deliver it to its endgame.

Epilogue: The Imperial Endgame after Eden

On February 3, 1960, Harold Macmillan stood before the South African parliament as the first ever serving British prime minister to visit Africa. His six-week tour of the continent had already taken him to Ghana and Nigeria, the first of which achieved independence only weeks after he had moved to No. 10 Downing Street. Now he faced a skeptical audience of parliamentarians who were committed to an apartheid system of white rule. Holding nothing back, Macmillan praised the South Africans for the "immense material progress" they had achieved in sixty years of union but warned them that in the past fifteen years, the processes of nationalism that had given birth to the nation-states of Europe were spreading throughout the rest of the world and had finally come to Africa. Uttering what would become his most famous phrase, he stated: "The wind of change is blowing through this continent, and, whether we like it or not, this growth of national consciousness is a political fact. We must all accept it as a fact, and our national policies must take account of it."[1] Lest there be any misunderstanding, Macmillan clarified his position:

[T]his tide of national consciousness which is now rising in Africa is a fact for which you and we and the other nations of the western world are ultimately responsible. For its causes are to be found in the achievements of western civilisation, in the pushing forward of the frontiers of knowledge, in the applying of science in the service of human needs, in the expanding of food production, in the speeding and

351

multiplying of the means of communication, and perhaps, above all, in the spread of education.[2]

The grant of independence to colonies within the Commonwealth and their concurrent development of a strong national consciousness were not signs that Britain had failed in its imperial mission but rather that it had succeeded. Since the mid-nineteenth century, Macmillan claimed, Britain's liberal imperialism had been predicated on paternalistic notions of social and cultural betterment. Rather than conquest, the end goal had always been to lift the peoples of the world from poverty and ignorance to British levels of civilization, and then to release them into happy independence, a process he believed had now been fulfilled. He warned, however, that there would be grave consequences if by misguided hubris Britain and the other imperial powers attempted to hold onto their colonies once they reached this final stage of political maturity. In the Cold War world, peoples denied freedom might turn to the enemy of their enemy for support, which in this case would be the Soviet Union. Macmillan laid out this risk in stark terms:

As I see it the great issue in this second half of the twentieth century is whether the uncommitted peoples of Asia and Africa will swing to the East or to the West. Will they be drawn into the Communist camp? Or will the great experiments in self-government that are now being made in Asia and Africa, especially within the Commonwealth, prove so successful, and by their example so compelling, that the balance will come down in favor of freedom and order and justice? The struggle is joined, and it is a struggle for the minds of men. What is now on trial is much more than our military strength or our diplomatic and administrative skill. It is our way of life.[3]

For Macmillan, the choice was clear. Only by facilitating the grant of self-government to colonial territories could the British government hope to keep them within the Commonwealth, and only through Commonwealth membership could they remain a guaranteed part of the West. Perhaps ironically, it was the end of the British Empire that would save all that the empire had stood for.

Yet the policy outlined in Macmillan's wind of change speech was not new. On the contrary, it had first been articulated by Labour's Arthur Creech Jones following Britain's failed campaign in Palestine, when the colonial secretary recognized that only an imperial strategy predicated upon devolving power to indigenous peoples could work in the postwar twentieth century. This was a strategy pioneered in the field by Sir Henry Gurney and General Harold Briggs, who understood that before the British could provide stable self-government to their colonies, those elements within colonial society that were opposed to Western, democratic principles had to be separated and ruthlessly purged lest their own anti-Western ideologies spread. This notion was perfected by General Sir Gerald Templer upon his appointment as high commissioner and director of operations in Malaya, when he coined the phrase "the winning of hearts and minds" to describe the emphasis he placed on the provision of social welfare, education, and an increased quality of life in his counterinsurgency doctrine. Templer's ideas were copied and adapted in Kenya and Cyprus by Sir Evelyn Baring, General George Erskine, Field Marshal Sir John Harding, and others who accepted the basic premise that increased participation in government by colonial people was necessary. This policy had the support of Oliver Lyttelton and Alan Lennox-Boyd, and of Anthony Eden and Selwyn Lloyd. When Macmillan spoke before the South African parliament in 1960, he was not articulating fresh doctrine. He was describing Britain's imperial mission as it had been for the previous twelve years.

Since becoming prime minister on January 10, 1957, Macmillan's energies had been consumed by imperial matters. On January 24, 1957, he received a memorandum from the colonial office evaluating what it called "subversive activities" in the colonies. After detailing subversion in twenty separate territories, including Kenya and Cyprus, it asserted that there were three main causes of subversion: anti-colonialism, communism, and Africanism. The latter two were self-explanatory, communism as expected and Africanism a euphemism for the development of pan-Africanism. Anti-colonialism, however, was further divided into three subcategories. The first, Russian anti-colonialism, was based on Lenin's writings on imperialism and capitalism. The report pointed to its hypocrisy, noting that the Soviet Union had "no inhibitions about acquiring colonies under some other name." The second, pioneered by "recently awakened" Asian and African former colonies, "thrives on imagined wrongs, forgets all past benefits, is full of racialism, is riddled with envy and all uncharitableness, is rapacious to a degree, assumes a maturity it has not reached, and has no benevolent intentions towards the weaker of its brethren." The final subcategory, American anti-colonialism, was characterized by "its policy of interference" and its "control without responsibility." Written in the aftermath of the Suez crisis, the report listed this latter subcategory as the most dangerous of all forms of subversion, as it had created "vacuums" in Palestine, the Dutch East Indies, and French Indochina with dire consequences.[4]

With this report on his desk, Macmillan first turned to Malaya, a colony that had improved to such an extent that it did not even warrant a mention in the report. In many ways, Malaya was the great success story of Britain's postwar decolonization and one that Macmillan hoped to draw attention to. In June 1957, the war office's operational research unit, Far East, published a study comparing the emergencies in Malaya and Kenya, providing a sound summary of the government's imperial strategy over the previous decade. It noted that as emergencies were "basically a civil problem," they could only be "permanently resolved by civil measures." More specifically, it stated: "The battle is one for the support of the population and the Civil Administration's first contribution will be to arrange that the population shall be so placed that they can be controlled and given security from the terrorists by the Security Forces." Yet security was not enough, as the report noted: "When a state of reasonable security is attained, the task of the Civil Administration is to win the support of the population by remedying genuine grievances, improving social services and persuading them of the rightness of its aims." Once such social betterment was provided and the indigenous peoples were "on the side" of the government, "action must be taken to identify the population with the fight against the terrorists and to induce them to take increasing responsibility for its conduct."[5] It was a report that could have been written by Gurney, Briggs, Templer, or Erskine.

In nowhere was this model more closely followed, with more success, than in the Federation of Malaya. That is not to say that the campaign had been without cost. Between 1948 and 1957, the communist insurgency killed 1851 members of the security forces and 2461 civilians, while wounding 2526 security force personnel and 1383 civilians. The emergency cost £700 million, £520 million of which had come directly from the British treasury. Yet the toll on the insurgency was even greater, with 6398 killed, 2760 wounded, 1245 captured, and 1938 surrendered.[6] More importantly, the government succeeded in its aims of isolating the insurgents and devolving stable self-government to the multiethnic Malay peoples. In October 1954, Sir Donald MacGillivray—Templer's successor as high commissioner—invited five local political leaders (two Malays, one Chinese, one Indian, and one European) to sit on the director of operations committee. From January 1955 onward, he instructed the chairmen of the SWECs and DWECs to likewise make their committees more representative of the local population. In March 1956, a further step forward was taken, when the British invited Tunka Abdul Rahman, the Malay chief minister and minister for internal defense and security, to become responsible to the executive council for the overall direction of the emergency.[7] As the Malay people of all ethnicities became further entrenched in their own governance, British authorities began to take a step back, allowing the gradual transfer of power. Finally, on August 31, 1957, the British government relinquished all sovereignty over Malaya.[8]

This transfer of power did not mean that the communist threat evaporated overnight and thus British forces could not withdraw as quickly as they had, under very different circumstances, from India and Palestine. A government report written on September 12, 1957, noted that there were still some 1830 active communist insurgents in Malaya and recommended the British army remain for at least another year in a "protector" role, with the director of operations continuing to hold "very wide powers."[9] These last insurgents proved a tougher nut to crack than at first expected. Consequently, British forces remained until July 31, 1960, when the emergency was finally declared over. Its final years stood in marked contrast to its first. In 1951—the first full year the Briggs Plan was initiated and the year that Gurney was killed—there were 2333 major and 3749 minor insurgent incidents. By comparison, in 1959 there were only four major and eight minor incidents, with just one member of the security forces and three civilians killed. In 1960, the insurgents were unable to kill a single individual and the security forces estimated that there were just 100 guerillas left on the peninsula.[10]

Three years after the emergency ended and six years after the grant of independence, Malaya united with Singapore, Sarawak, and Sabah to form the new state of Malaysia, remaining within the Commonwealth. Although Singapore later left the union to become an independent state, the history of Malaysia since its creation has largely been one of success.[11] With the exception of race riots in May 1969, Malaysia has remained a politically stable and democratic state, with an economic system that from 1963 until the late twentieth century saw a steady growth rate in real gross domestic product of close to 7 percent.[12] Upon the formation of the united federation in 1963, Lord Shackleton, the Labour peer and son of the British explorer Sir Ernest Shackleton, proclaimed in the House of Lords: "I was not hopeful, immediately after the war, about the future of Malaysia. ... One saw little chance of the creation of a real political modern State. One was confronted with Communist revolt in the jungles of Malaya, and yet we are now looking at one of the most encouraging developments in the modern world. ... I have said before in this House that it is a great pity that the whole world does not consent to be ruled by the British."[13] It was a sentiment Macmillan, Eden, Churchill, Attlee, Lennox-Boyd, Lyttelton, and Creech Jones would have shared.

In contrast with Malaya's trouble-free final years, the end of the Kenyan emergency experienced more ambiguity. The final outcome was a relatively stable and democratic western nation within the Commonwealth, with the threat of Mau Mau eliminated and Kenya set on the path to modernity, but considerable violence was used to achieve this end, much of it of a highly dubious character. Macmillan's new government got its first taste of this violence on June 25, 1957, when Evelyn Baring (still governor of Kenya) wrote to Alan Lennox-Boyd, whom Macmillan had retained as his colonial secretary. In this letter, Baring introduced a new method being employed in Kenyan detention camps called the "dilution technique of rehabilitation." This involved mixing "intractable" Mau Mau with Mau Mau who had become government cooperators. The hope was that the new intake would succumb to peer pressure and eventually become rehabilitated themselves. The ratio of cooperators to intractables could be as high as 10:1 in especially difficult cases. The problem was how to psychologically "break" those within the new intake who "arrive[d] determined to resist and to cause others to resist." Baring argued that the only way to do this was to offer a "psychological shock" using force immediately upon arrival. The importance of breaking these internees was that once rehabilitated, they could be moved from large central camps to smaller, local camps before eventual release. If they could not be broken, they would be sent with other "irreconcilables" to the Hola camp, the designated resting place for the most difficult detainees. This, however, was far more costly to run and maintain than the local camps. Baring had spoken with Dr Junod of the International Red Cross, who assured him that he had "no doubt in his own mind that if the violent shock was the price to be paid for pushing detainees out to the detention camps near their districts, away from the big camps, and then onward to release, we should pay it." Baring recognized that there were "risks" involved in using such violence, but was sure they were worth taking.[14]

Baring included with his letter a report by Eric Griffiths-Jones, the Kenyan minister for legal affairs, exploring in more detail the use of force in enforcing discipline during the dilution process. It explained that there were two essential factors to be achieved on the arrival of each new intake: first, discipline and authority had to be immediately established over the new detainees; and second, "all physical symbols and souvenirs of their Mau Mau past" had to be removed. To achieve the latter, upon arrival at the camp the hair and beards of all detainees were shorn and their clothing and jewelry removed, after which they were instructed to put on camp clothing. The report noted that the purpose of this was to "condition them psychologically to shed the past and look to the future, with its prospects of release." The achievement of the first goal, discipline and authority, required the use of force upon those who would not cooperate. Griffiths-Jones described how this was implemented when he visited the Mwea camp:

> The detainees were ordered to change into the camp clothes. Any who showed any reluctance or hesitation to do so were hit with fists and/or slapped with the open hand. This was usually enough to dispel any disposition to disobey the order to change. In some cases, however, defiance was more obstinate, and on the first indication of such obstinacy three or four of the European officers immediately converged on the man and "rough-housed" him, stripping his clothes off him, hitting him, on occasion kicking him, and, if necessary, putting him on the ground. Blows struck were solid, hard

ones, mostly with closed fists and about the head, stomach, sides and back. There was no attempt to strike at testicles or any other manifestations of sadistic brutality; the performance was a deliberate, calculated and robust assault, accompanied by constant and imperative demands that the man should do as he was told and change his clothes.

Griffiths-Jones witnessed four intakes, each of twenty men, and noted that in each instance, "the man eventually gave in and put on the camp clothes." He had been warned by the camp guards that this was not always the case. On occasion, a resistor would begin the so-called "Mau Mau moan," which would then be picked up by others in the camp. The camp guards believed it was essential to stop this "moan" to maintain good discipline and order: "[A]ccordingly a resistor who started it was promptly put on the ground, a foot placed on his throat and mud stuffed in his mouth. ... a man whose resistance could not be broken down was in the last resort knocked unconscious."

The violence did not end there, however, as Griffiths-Jones explained: "When changed and shorn, the men were made to squat. ... Each man was asked in turn if he intended to obey. If he said 'Yes', he moved on immediately; if he said 'No' or did not answer, he was immediately struck and, if necessary, compelled to submit by the use of force." Griffiths-Jones related that the whole process was "conducted at speed," with one party finished by the time the next party arrived from the railway station fifteen minutes later. Of the eighty new arrivals he witnessed, twelve needed "minor persuasion," five required "pretty rough treatment," and one had to be "manhandled" to his compound, although the guards had "subdued" him by the time he arrived. All violence was administered by European officers rather than Africans, and the use of violence ceased as soon as the detainees complied: "The whole process was one of rush, hustle and prompt and, if necessary, enforced discipline. The purpose is to compel immediate submission to discipline and compliance with orders, and to do so by a psychological shock treatment which throws off balance and overcomes any disposition towards defiance or resistance."

Once a detainee was in the camp and subdued, the further use of violence was prohibited, as "the dangers of excesses, the impracticability of constant and personal control and restraint by responsible officers in all parts of the camp at all times, and the insidious infection of violence, combine to eliminate any certainty of assurances against abuse." Force was to be an initial shock, but nothing more. The report concluded:

> It cannot be over-emphasised that the use of force on persons in custody is ordinarily abhorrent and illegal, and, even within the strictly limited confines discussed above, potentially dangerous. Its only justification is the necessary enforcement of discipline; it must never be used punitively (save by way of corporal punishment awarded formally and by due process for a proved offence) and, needless to say, it must never be used to extort confessions. When necessarily applied, it must be applied responsibly, deliberately and dispassionately, with adequate safeguards against causing serious injury, under the immediate control of a senior European officer, and in no greater degree and for no longer than its purpose necessitate.[15]

In his report, Griffiths-Jones emphasized that this violence was necessary and, in its own way, restrained. It was only used on the most insolent of detainees and its use was by no means widespread throughout the camp system. Although filled with initial doubt, Lennox-Boyd eventually authorized the continuation of the technique. The consequences of doing so were soon to become clear.

On March 3, 1959—almost two years after the colonial secretary sanctioned the use of greater force in Kenya's detention camps—disaster struck. The rehabilitation process had been proceeding as was hoped for. By 1959, the government had released close to 77,000 of the 80,000 or so Kikuyu detainees it once held in the camps. Most of these men and women were successfully reintegrated into Kenyan society.[16] From the government's perspective, the widespread sweeps and detentions had worked—Mau Mau had quite literally been starved of its population base and the Kikuyu people had been shielded from its influence.[17] Yet there still remained a little over 3000 detainees. In March 1959, the government decided to concentrate 1100 of the most "hardcore" of these in a closed camp at Hola, alongside the camp already existing there. At this new camp, the government applied a philosophy that work would lead to freedom and instructed the warders to engage the detainees in an irrigation-building scheme. Those who refused to cooperate were to be "manhandled" to and from the work zone.[18]

On the morning of March 3, Willoughby Thompson, the British district officer in the Tana River district where the Hola camp was located, was approached by a young prison officer who informed him that a detainee had died and requested that he come to the camp immediately. Thompson, in the middle of adjudicating a land inheritance case, replied that he would come as quickly as possible. After twenty minutes, the prison officer returned to say that another two detainees were dead. Ten minutes after that, a "very much more senior officer" appeared to inform him that "something dreadful had taken place," with perhaps as many as six dead. By the time Thompson arrived at Hola, he found nine corpses with many more wounded, two of whom would later die. The senior prison officer informed him that the men had been working and had collapsed because of the heat, after which several of his younger prison guards panicked and threw buckets of water on them causing them to drown. The camp doctor confirmed that their deaths were most likely caused by drowning.

Thompson immediately rejected this argument, pointing to the "various gashes and bruises" on the bodies, and used his police radio to call Nairobi police headquarters, where he spoke directly with the deputy police commissioner, asking that he, the senior CID officer, the chief native commissioner (who was also the minister for African affairs), and the commissioner of prisons come to Hola at once. The police complied with Thompson's request but the prisons department refused to send anyone other than a junior officer, who immediately accepted the drowning story and released a public statement to that effect. As Thompson later wrote, "[T]he white Prisons Officers closed ranks and the black ones kept their mouths shut." Nevertheless, he and the police constables remained at Hola and the story of what had occurred slowly came out, aided in large part by a British public works engineer who refused to collude with the prisons officers and instead revealed the truth. Eighty-eight detainees had been taken out that morning and asked to dig trenches. When they refused, their African guards set upon them with truncheons and whips, watched over by three European officers, until nine lay dead and twenty-five seriously wounded. When they saw the extent of the damage, the European officers tried to revive the injured, many of whom had water "literally poured down their throats." Evelyn Baring had warned that there were risks involved in allowing greater violence into camp discipline. The events at Hola exceeded even his worst imaginings.

Upon hearing the two conflicting stories (Thompson's and the prison service's), the governor immediately summoned the district officer to Nairobi, where Thompson repeated his account first to Baring and then to the entire war cabinet. The governor took Thompson at his word and, while he was still sitting at the cabinet table, placed a telephone call to Lennox-Boyd revealing the truth. What happened next shocked Thompson: "[T]he Governor [was] told [by Lennox-Boyd] that it would be politically unwise to alter the story [told by the prison service]. I distinctly remember the words (indeed I noted them at the time) 'You would put me in an untenable position in the House.'" Baring, feeling unable to disobey the colonial secretary, issued a statement saying only that the incident was under investigation. He did, however, appoint Thompson to "take over and supervise all that went on at Hola," devolving his district officer duties to a more junior official. Thompson immediately determined that his first priority was to rehabilitate and release as many detainees as quickly as possible. By January 1960, over half had been freed and the remainder followed the next year. One of those interned under Thompson was Fred M. Koinange, who was originally arrested alongside Kenyatta in 1952. Koinange wrote to Thompson on October 23, 1959, following his release. His words provide perhaps the best judgment on Thompson's role there, and on the possibilities of the rehabilitation system if done humanely and without violence:

[A]s you well know I have been in detention camp for seven years and I know enough what sort of life this is. Before I left Hola, I remember I pledge before you that I resumed my normal life. I shall maintain my behavior and see that I am not going to implicate myself with the public activities. This pledge believe me I have always observed and it would be very foolish and unrealistic and would rather call it madness to try to astray myself by implicating myself in this type [of] dirty activity. This would be a self betrayal even before the ink that revoked my detention order got dry. Anyone who may attempt to convince you that I am engaging myself in the Country's wrong affairs is lying you. I shall never forget the little sermon you so generously gave me while in your office. This sermon has always been in my memory and let me assure you this minute that I shall never repeat NEVER let your golden words down.[19]

Thompson's control of Hola was not the end of the affair, however. Pressured by parliamentary questioning led by Labour MP Barbara Castle, Lennox-Boyd established an internal investigation headed by Senior Resident Magistrate W. H. Goudie on March 18, 1959. When the report was published later that spring, it concluded, "In each case death was found to have been caused by shock and hemorrhage *due to multiple bruising caused by violence*. ... There was no serious combined attempt [by the detainees] to attack warders … [and] there was a very considerable amount of beating by warders with batons solely for the purpose of compelling them to work or punishing them for refusing to work."[20] Goudie's report made damning reading for the government. A cabinet office briefing of June 3 informed the prime minister that "the men were illegally beaten to make them work. … [There was] also evidence of scurvy in the camp, without which fewer might have died."[21] Immediately after the report's publication, the Labour opposition demanded a debate in Parliament. This they got on June 16, 1959. Sir Frank Soskice, Labour MP for Newport, began the session by moving, "That this House deplores the circumstances in which eleven men in Hola Detention Camp met their deaths as a result of the use of unlawful violence and regrets the failure of Her Majesty's Government to take immediate steps to set up a public inquiry to ascertain where the responsibility should be placed." Lennox-Boyd offered an alternate motion: "That this House deeply regrets the recent death of eleven men in Hola Detention Camp and fully supports Her Majesty's Government and the Government of Kenya in the steps both remedial and disciplinary that are being taken to prevent a recurrence of such a tragic event."[22]

Ultimately, Soskice's motion was defeated by 314 votes to 255, with Lennox-Boyd's passing by the same division, but the debate was an uncomfortable sitting for the Conservative Party. Behind closed doors, there were some who doubted the wisdom of Lennox-Boyd remaining at the colonial office after such a scandal. His good friend Harold Balfour even wrote directly to him on June 19, asking, "Does the doctrine, in its entire purity, of ministerial responsibility not apply? God knows, I don't want you to go but I have searched and cannot find either from the S[secretary] of S[tate] or the Governor any expression of acceptance of final responsibility."[23] In a subsequent parliamentary debate held on July 27, the right-wing MP Enoch Powell best summed up the concern spreading through the parliamentary benches of the Commons: "We claim that it is our object—and this is something which unites both sides of the House—to leave representative institutions behind us wherever we give up our rule. I cannot imagine that it is a way to plant representative institutions to be seen to shirk the acceptance and the assignment of responsibility, which is the very essence of responsible Government." He continued:

Nor can we ourselves pick and choose where and in what parts of the world we shall use this or that kind of standard. We cannot say, "We will have African standards in Africa, Asian standards in Asia and perhaps British standards here at home." We have not that choice to make. We must be consistent with ourselves everywhere. All Government, all influence of man upon man, rests upon opinion. What we can do in Africa, where we still govern and where we no longer govern, depends upon the opinion which is entertained of the way in which this country acts and the way in which Englishmen act. We cannot, we dare not, in Africa of all places, fall below our own highest standards in the acceptance of responsibility.[24]

The British government could only go so far in its dirty wars in pursuit of a liberal transfer of power. The parliamentary opposition and government backbenchers made that clear in the aftermath of Hola.

Sensing that the tide had turned against them, Lennox-Boyd and Governor Baring tried to make amends for the parliamentary reprimand they had received. Following the debate, Lennox-Boyd wrote to Baring, instructing him to "make a close examination of the lessons which are to be learned from this disaster, so that we may make certain that in future we are in a position not merely to prevent any repetition of such an occurrence, but also to handle, with the greatest efficiency and humanity, the exceedingly difficult problem which is posed by the moral need to do everything that can possibly be done to restore to civilisation and freedom, without danger to the community, the few remaining hundreds of embittered and

365

desperate Mau Mau supporters."[25] Baring replied that his government, and public opinion throughout Kenya, "share that disquiet [present in London] and are most seriously anxious that every possible step should be taken to ensure that never again is there the risk of such a tragedy occurring."[26] True to his word, Baring published a directive laying down certain safeguards to prevent the future use of violence on detainees. Chief among these was the notion that, "When a prisoner refuses to obey a lawful order a Prison Officer shall not use force to hurt the prisoner so as to make him carry out the order or so as to punish him because he has refused to do so. For example, it would be illegal to hit a prisoner until he agreed to obey an order."[27] The abuses of Hola would not be allowed to occur again.

These improvements were too little too late for Baring and Lennox-Boyd, however. Immediately following the October 1959 British general election, in which the Conservative Party increased its contingent in the House of Commons from 345 to 365 members, Macmillan removed Lennox-Boyd from the cabinet, promoting instead Iain Macleod as colonial secretary. Having served as minister of health and minister of labour, Macleod was more interested in domestic politics than the empire, but the Hola affair affected him greatly.[28] He readily accepted Macmillan's offer of the colonial office, although confessed to Peter Goldman of the Conservative Research Department that he hoped to be the last colonial secretary—Macleod's clear intention was that the empire should no longer be an integral part of British foreign policy.[29] In keeping with his disgust at Hola, his first action as colonial secretary was to recall the now discredited Evelyn Baring and instead appoint Sir Patrick Renison to be governor of Kenya, a man who had served with success distinction as governor of British Honduras and British Guiana.[30]

With Lennox-Boyd and Baring gone, the prime minister gave permission to Macleod to hasten the grant of self-government and eventual independence to Kenya. In January 1960, just days before he boarded his plane for the African continent, Macmillan instructed Renison to declare the emergency over.

The British security forces had now defeated the threat from Mau Mau and less than 1000 detainees remained in British custody. With Macmillan proclaiming that the British government would accept the "wind of change" blowing through the empire, Macleod called a conference at Lancaster House composed of all forty members of the Kenyan Legislative Council. At this conference, he was able to persuade the white contingent to accept a compromise whereby Africans would hold thirty-three of the sixty-five elected seats in the Kenyan Legislative Council, with new elections scheduled for February 1961. With an African majority legislature assured from early 1961 onward, Macleod turned his attention to freeing the remaining Kikuyu detainees. All but Jomo Kenyatta were released prior to the February elections, and Kenyatta—the last of the Kikuyu prisoners—arrived home on August 14, 1961.[31]

Following Kenyatta's release, the imperial endgame in Kenya arrived as swiftly as it had in Malaya. In October 1961, Kenyatta was appointed president of the Kenya African National Union (KANU) party. Shortly thereafter, he was elected a member of the legislative council, where he was appointed minister of state for constitutional affairs and economic planning in April 1962. In the May elections that followed, the KANU gained a majority among the African parties, propelling Kenyatta to the prime ministership less than twelve months after being released from British detention. Only days later, on June 1, 1963, the British government granted Kenya responsible government—in essence, full self-government. Kenyatta took advantage of this development and on December 12, 1963, proclaimed full independence. Despite all he had endured in British confinement, he publicly denounced Mau Mau and chose to keep Kenya within the Commonwealth with Elizabeth II as its head of state. Even when the Legislative Assembly voted a year later to declare Kenya a republic and make Kenyatta its president, the nation continued within the Commonwealth, where it remains today. Never again would it succumb to the sort of violence inflicted upon its people by Mau Mau.[32]

If the emergencies in Malaya and Kenya were drawing to their close when Macmillan became prime minister in January 1957, the same could not be said of Cyprus. Less than a month after he arrived in Downing Street, the new prime minister received his first intelligence review from the Cyprus intelligence committee. It informed him that terrorism had "tended to increase during the second half of January." The main violent effort had been devoted to "the throwing of grenades at Security Forces vehicles and the residences of Security Forces families"; "the use of electrically detonated mines also against Security Forces vehicles"; "time bombs" on water supplies, Security Force canteens, and other government buildings; and booby traps, including a new type never seen before, which was "fixed to a door and is designed to explode when the door is opened." The report offered an ominous conclusion: "Outstanding though recent successes have been against the hardcore leaders, two thirds of them are still at large. ... In spite of large-scale counter-terrorist operations, the terrorists' communications and central direction would appear to be effective to judge by the widespread and coordinated intensified activity towards the end of January."[33]

As EOKA violence increased, so too did British casualties, and with them, British frustrations. The Suez crisis and Cyprus's crucial role as a staging point for forces involved there had increased the number of British security forces on the island to more than 30,000, allowing for more "easy" targets for EOKA. By the time Macmillan formed his new government in January 1957, EOKA's "kill rate" had risen from ten per month during the summer of 1956 to twenty-six per month. While many of those deaths were caused by mundane assassination, other attacks were more audacious, such as the one at Lefkonico on October 23, 1956, when EOKA rigged up an explosives device to a water tap often used following rugby practice by the Highland Light Brigade. Triggered by a wire control in a nearby grove, two young women signaled with their handkerchiefs to the bombers as the soldiers gathered for a drink. Two were disemboweled and four seriously injured.[34] The reaction of the British soldier was ugly, if predictable: "Soldiers whose colleagues had been shot or blown up searched Cypriot houses. Many Greek families who had no contact with EOKA found the soldiers rough. When searching for weapons or explosives the soldiers would empty sacks of grain onto the floor or tip a load of fruit and vegetables off a van."[35] EOKA prisoners also alleged torture, and in late 1956 the Nicosia Bar Council set up a Human Rights Commission to investigate and publicize these allegations. Although it had no jurisdiction to act on its findings, the reports of the Human Rights Commission increasingly took up column space in British newspapers, causing further embarrassment to a government that, in the aftermath of the withdrawal for Suez, was coming under increasing scrutiny for its actions in Kenya.[36]

Macmillan carefully read the parliamentary climate and saw that continued aggression in Cyprus would only hurt the Conservative Party. He also realized that following withdrawal from the Suez Canal, British strategic interests no longer needed an island fortress in the eastern Mediterranean. Once he had reached this conclusion, it was no longer imperative for the sovereignty of Cyprus to remain British. The government could therefore move beyond self-government within the empire to instead embrace independence within the Commonwealth in its discussions.[37] Consequently, in March 1957, Macmillan released Archbishop Makarios from his exile in the Seychelles, although the cleric could only return to Athens rather than Cyprus itself.[38] Macmillan was further aided in his pursuit of change when, following a summer and autumn of extreme violence, in October, Harding resigned as governor, allowing the prime minister to replace the soldier with a civilian who might be more attuned to negotiation.[39]

Macmillan chose Sir Hugh Foot, previously colonial secretary to Cyprus from 1943 to 1945, who as the brother of the prominent Labour politician Michael Foot was able to negate some parliamentary opposition to the government's actions in Cyprus.[40] Macmillan had settled on Foot prior to Harding's resignation. Lennox-Boyd first contacted him on October 1, asking if he had any interest in the position, and on October 2 he laid out in a letter a summary of their conversation, which had discussed a five-year appointment as governor during which time a "constitutional experiment" would be made in self-determination. Foot would "regard the five-year period as an opportunity to try to sell to the Cypriots the advantages of con-stitutional development with the hope that at the end of that period, if called on to make their choice they would decide to remain in the British Commonwealth." At the close of his letter, Lennox-Boyd asked Foot if he could give an assurance that he would "work under the instructions of the British Government for a Cyprus settlement that would not be unacceptable to Her Majesty's Government, the Turkish Government and the Greeks, and that he would not resign because the British Government refused to impose something on the Turks."[41]

Foot replied on October 3, stating that he would "do a good job if there were a sporting chance of working representative institutions. I should of course loyally carry out all decisions of H.M.G. I would certainly work wholeheartedly for a settlement that would not be unacceptable to H.M.G., the Turks and the Greeks." However, he added the caveat that, "I believe partition [of the island between Turk and Greek] would be a disaster and am bound to say that if all efforts to reach agreed solution failed I should wish to feel free to ask to be replaced rather than have to put into effect a policy which I felt to be wrong."[42] Lennox-Boyd was unhappy with Foot's reply. He instructed the colonial office to send him a return telegram, asking him to come to London for talks in person on October 9.[43] This Foot agreed to. Lennox-Boyd was clearly more persuasive in the flesh than on paper: Foot accepted the position without any qualification or equivocation.[44]

His appointment did not in any way demean Harding's leaving. Macmillan believed the field marshal had served a nec-essary purpose in Cyprus, telling him on October 17:

I cannot imagine a tougher assignment being given to any man nor can I think of any man who could have discharged it with greater distinction. During the whole of your tenure of office Cyprus has been the centre of bitter political and international controversies. This has made your task doubly hard but you have steered your course with such courage, fairness and skill that I feel no doubt that your Governorship will long be remembered with pride even by those who have not agreed with our policies.[45]

Harding too grasped that it was time to go. In a letter to his son written on October 21, he admitted, "It's never possible to be quite sure that one is right in these matters but I feel as certain as I can be that the time has come when it is best for someone else to take over here with a fresh mind and fresh energy. ... I don't know anything about Sir Hugh Foot, but I am sure there are definite advantages at this stage in having someone in the post who has no connection with the harsh measures I have had to adopt to hold and control the island, and has no military label attached to him."[46] The dirty war in Cyprus had been necessary but now it was time for a less coercive approach.

Nevertheless, the island continued to be plagued with violence. On October 3—the same day Lennox-Boyd requested that Foot come to London—EOKA shot dead two British service-wives. The British reaction was swift, as Mrs J. M. Somerville, the wife of a battery commander from 29 Field Regiment Royal Artillery, recounted in her diary: "All Greek males being rounded up and taken to cages for questioning. Troops not wearing kid gloves and many broken heads. Feel troops are justified in being a bit rough considering what happened. ... Max and Tommy came, Max with several bloody heads to his credit and raring for some more."[47] The following day, Somerville wrote: "Todays funny story. RMP's [Royal Military Police] searching house of Greek Doctor inform him 2 British women shot. Good show, says doctor. Say that again, say RMP's. He does—is taken to own clinic with fractured jaw and no teeth!"[48]

If the security forces on the ground were impressed by such behavior, the incoming governor was less so. On November

27—one week before he was due to be installed—Foot wrote to George Sinclair, the deputy governor in Cyprus, indicating that he planned to make a public statement upon his arrival laying out his hope to offer "a short period [of ceasefire and reflection] (possibly to the end of the year) after which it will be necessary to decide whether it will be possible to pursue, as I earnestly hope, a course of free discussion with a relaxation of security measures or whether on the other hand I shall be left with no choice but to resume full powers and take all necessary measures to deal with the situation." He stressed that it was essential to "let it be known publicly that after a short interval it will be necessary if violence continues to take severe measures. But I think that it is important to give the other side some interval and opportunity to abandon the campaign of violence."[49]

Sinclair attempted to water down Foot's proposal, suggesting that, "Any such period would, we fear, be regarded by EOKA as an 'open season' during which they could commit murder and sabotage with impunity."[50] Foot, however, was not deterred, and upon his arrival on December 3, he delivered a statement telling the Cypriot people:

> I believe that the over-whelming majority of the people of Cyprus will wish to accept the offer of friendship and understanding and co-operation which I make. If there are those who wish to reject it and resort instead to disorder and intimidation they will succeed only in delaying progress towards a just settlement and in making Cyprus suffer; and those who make Cyprus suffer will carry the terrible responsibility and lasting condemnation of their actions. I earnestly ask everyone in the Island to pause today to consider the course we should follow. Cyprus cannot be doomed to a future of hate and fear. The people of this lovely island must one day again work and live together in peace and respect and happiness.[51]

Foot's gamble did not initially pay off, as EOKA murdered three Turks on December 5. On December 7, widespread rioting erupted in Limassol and Nicosia, continuing until December 9 when the security forces imposed a curfew. Had it not been for the curfew, the rioting would have continued.[52] Foot wrote to Lennox-Boyd on December 10, lamenting "what a misery it is to me that we have not got the clear run we had hoped for. Our main effort in the immediate future must and will be directed to checking disorder and preventing a spread of communal strife." He nevertheless remained optimistic: "I still hope that we can contain this outbreak and continue to concentrate on the main aim of urgently finding and declaring a new course for the future."[53] This optimism found expression in what has become known as the Foot Plan, drawn up by the governor in early January 1958. The elements of this plan were fourfold: first, there would be a cessation of violence on all sides and an immediate end to the emergency regulations; second, there would be a period of five to seven years during which constitutional discussions leading to self-government would take place; third, leaders of all communities, including Makarios, would be involved in these discussions; and finally, no final decision would be taken at the end of the five- to seven-year period without the full support and agreement of both the Greek and Turkish governments. The British government agreed with Foot's approach, but first the Turks and then the Greeks denounced it. On February 11, 1958, Foot abandoned it too.[54]

Now that it had settled on this path to self-government and eventual independence, the British government did not give up easily, however. Macmillan himself took the lead from Lennox-Boyd in hammering out a solution and on June 19, 1958, he presented his proposals to Parliament. Described as provisional measures until a permanent constitutional settlement could be reached, they included participation by the British, Greek, and Turkish governments in the fashioning of an eventual constitution; Greek and Turkish representatives appointed to serve alongside the governor in the interim period; and a system of representative government and communal autonomy, whereby there would be separate Houses of Representative for the Greek and Turkish communities and a shared council presided over by the British governor with Greek and Turkish representatives.[55] Westminster approved Macmillan's approach after a full debate on June 26, and in early July the prime minister put his proposals to the Greek and Turkish governments. These governments considered the proposals throughout July and on August 8 Macmillan traveled to Greece to meet with the Greek prime minister face to face. The following day, he traveled to Turkey. Nothing was agreed during these meetings, however, and on August 19 the Greeks rejected the proposals.[56]

Macmillan remained unbowed by Greek intransigence and continued to communicate with both governments throughout the autumn of 1958. His perseverance paid off. In December, the Greek and Turkish governments began to talk for the first time in four years under the cover of a NATO ministerial council and on February 11, 1959, they issued a joint communiqué, stating that they had reached a compromise solution subject to British agreement. There followed a flurry of activity and meetings between the British, Greek, and Turkish governments, and then on February 19—against all odds—an agreement was reached.[57] This stated that the British government would give up sovereignty of Cyprus, which would become an independent republic. The government hoped that upon independence the new republic would join the Commonwealth, but this was not required—to be successful, Commonwealth membership had to be voluntary rather than coerced. Within the new republic, the president would be a Greek-Cypriot, elected by the Greek-Cypriot population, with a Turkish-Cypriot vice president, elected by the Turkish-Cypriot people. The cabinet would consist of seven Greek-Cypriots, chosen by the president, and three Turkish-Cypriots, chosen by the vice president. Throughout the lower levels of government, this 70:30 ratio would be maintained, mirroring the island's demographic mix. Decisions taken by the government required an absolute majority, but to prevent Greek autocracy the vice president was given veto power. Finally, although ceding sovereignty over the island, the British government would retain two military bases totaling ninety-nine square miles, which would remain British soil.[58]

Upon the signing of the February agreement, EOKA declared an immediate cease-fire and Sir Hugh Foot lifted all emergency regulations. The British government then established a joint constitutional committee with a target date of the summer of 1960 for the official transfer of power. This they accomplished, and on August 16, 1960, Foot handed over power to Archbishop Makarios, the newly elected president of the Cyprus Republic. Just as Jomo Kenyatta would do four years later, Makarios chose to keep Cyprus within the Commonwealth as a fully democratic partner of Great Britain and its Western allies. Although the February agreement would eventually break down and in 1963 the United Nations—with British consent—would intervene to introduce a *de facto* partition of Cyprus between its Greek and Turkish constituents, Cyprus remained a member of the Commonwealth, and on May 1, 2004, entered the European Union as a democratic, presidential republic.

The ends of the emergencies in Malaya, Kenya, and Cyprus dominated Macmillan's premiership. As he wrote in his memoirs, "The absorbing claims of foreign, Commonwealth and Colonial affairs, together with the need for frequent journeys abroad, demanded a high proportion of my time and attention."[59] Yet the dirty wars highlighted in this book are only one part of the story of decolonization, albeit a central one. For having forged the processes of devolving self-government to colonial powers in the fires of violent insurgency, the transfer of power in those colonies that did not rebel seemed all the more straightforward in the decade that followed. These included the Gold Coast (renamed Ghana) in 1957, British Somaliland (renamed Somalia) and Nigeria in 1960, Sierra Leone, North Cameroons (annexed into Nigeria), South Cameroons (renamed Cameroun, later the Republic of Cameroon), and Tanganyika (renamed Tanzania) in 1961, Jamaica, Trinidad and Tobago, and Uganda in 1962, Zanzibar (annexed into Tanzania) in 1963, Nyasaland (remained Malawi), Malta, and Northern

Rhodesia (remained Zambia) in 1964, The Gambia in 1965, British Guiana (renamed Guyana), Bechuanaland (remained Botswana), Basutoland (renamed Lesotho), and Barbados in 1966, and Mauritius and Swaziland in 1968.[60] That all of these nations remained within the Commonwealth, none choosing to distance itself from its former colonial master, suggests that the policy adopted by the Labour Party in 1948 and continued by the Conservatives throughout the 1950s and early 1960s had a great deal of wisdom to it.

It is, indeed, an astonishing fact that of the many nations to achieve their independence from the British Empire in the 1950s, 1960s, and 1970s, only one—Aden—chose to abandon the West and instead align itself with the Soviet Union, doing so in 1967 (renamed South Yemen). The story of Aden's emergency (1963–1967) is one which, like the Northern Ireland Troubles, is sadly beyond the scope of this book.[61] Suffice to say that the failed counterinsurgency there was the exception rather than the rule of British decolonization. So successful was government policy in the fifteen years after 1948 that on November 18, 1965, Sir Burke Trend of the colonial office wrote to Sir Roger Hollis, director-general of MI5, informing him that the security service could now close twelve of its security liaison offices in Commonwealth countries. The threat had diminished sufficiently that if needed, MI5 officers could simply be sent on temporary missions from London.[62]

From 1948 to the mid-1960s, the British government did not abandon its imperial mission. Rather it reshaped that mission to better facilitate the conditions of the postwar world. Correctly recognizing that the age of national self-determination and self-government was upon it, and cognizant of the bipolarity of the Cold War environment, the government evolved its strategy to preference the devolution of power to indigenous peoples over the autocratic practice of that power. Not all colonial peoples were willing to accept this Western democratic mantle, however, some being all too keen to rebel against it. Consequently, the government deployed its security forces to ruthlessly quell all contemporaneous opposition in the name of providing greater autonomy to future generations. If there is one clear conclusion to be drawn from the end of Britain's empire, it is that liberal imperialism can only be sustained by illiberal dirty wars. Britain's imperial endgame demonstrates that it is possible to achieve success in each. Whether moral or not is a question best left to philosophers and kings.

Notes

Prologue

1. Ronald Hyam, *Britain's Declining Empire: The Road to Decolonisation, 1918–1968* (Cambridge: Cambridge University Press, 2006), xiii.
2. Ibid., 1.
3. For the most recent incarnation of this interpretation of empire, see Bernard Porter, *The Absent-Minded Imperialists: Empire, Society, and Culture in Britain* (Oxford: Oxford University Press, 2006).
4. John Darwin, *Britain and Decolonization: The Retreat from Empire in the Post-War World* (New York: St. Martin's Press, 1988). For a more recent analysis, see his *The Empire Project: The Rise and Fall of the British World System, 1830–1970* (Cambridge: Cambridge University Press, 2009).
5. Charles Townshend, *Britain's Civil Wars: Counterinsurgency in the Twentieth Century* (London: Faber and Faber, 1986); Thomas Mockaitis, *British Counterinsurgency, 1919–1960* (London: Macmillan Ltd., 1990); and John Newsinger, *British Counter-Insurgency: From Palestine to Northern Ireland* (New York: Palgrave Macmillan, 2002).
6. Caroline Elkins, *Imperial Reckoning: The Untold Story of Britain's Gulag in Kenya* (New York: Henry Holt and Company, 2005); David Anderson, *Histories of the Hanged: The Dirty War in Kenya and the End of Empire* (New York and London: W.W. Norton and Company, 2005); Daniel Branch, *Defeating Mau Mau, Creating Kenya: Counterinsurgency, Civil War, and Decolonization* (Cambridge: Cambridge University Press, 2009); and R. F. Holland, *Britain and the Revolt in Cyprus, 1954–1959* (Oxford: Oxford University Press, 1998). Similar case-studies have also been conducted in the journal literature. For Kenya, see David A. Percox, "Internal Security and Decolonization in Kenya, 1956–1963," *Journal of Imperial and Commonwealth History*, Volume 29, Issue 1 (2001), 92–116; for Malaya, see A. J. Stockwell, "Malaysia: The Making of a Neo-Colony?" *Journal of Imperial and Commonwealth History*, Volume 26, Issue 2 (1998), 138–56; for Cyprus, see Robert Holland, "Never, Never Land: British Colonial Policy and the Roots of Violence in Cyprus, 1950–1954," *Journal of Imperial and Commonwealth History*,

Volume 21, Issue 3 (1993), 148–76; and for Aden, see Spencer Mawby, "Britain's Last Imperial Frontier: The Aden Protectorates, 1952–1959," *Journal of Imperial and Commonwealth History*, Volume 29, Issue 2 (2001), 75–100.

1 The Attlee Years

1. The weather diary from the Kew Observatory records the day's conditions as follows: "Cloudy all day, light and intermittent rain and drizzle in morn, mist in morn."
2. The National Archives [TNA], Colonial Office [CO] 733/457/11, Telegram from George Henry Hall, Secretary of State for the Colonies, to Field Marshal Viscount Gort, British High Commissioner for Palestine, November 3, 1945. For an account of the events of November 1, 1945, see J. Bowyer Bell, *Terror out of Zion: Irgun Zvai Leumi, LEHI, and the Palestine Underground, 1929–1949* (New York: St. Martin's Press, 1977), 145–6.
3. For an analysis of the 1945 General Election, see Kenneth O. Morgan, *Labour in Power, 1945–1951* (Oxford: The Clarendon Press, 1984), 34–44.
4. MacDonald continued as prime minister until 1935 but did so under the guise of a national government rather than a Labour government, with the majority of his ministers and members of parliament coming from the Conservative Party. Throughout his final four years in power, his national government faced the Labour Party in opposition, now under different leadership.
5. This withdrawal occurred on May 21, 1945, on which date Clement Attlee wrote to Churchill explaining his reasons and citing the "party differences" that were held over the "problems of reconstruction of the economic life of the country" as the primary cause. The letter in its entirety is published in Attlee's memoirs, C. R. Attlee, *As It Happened* (New York: The Viking Press, 1954), 190–3.
6. The Conservative Member of Parliament Sir Cuthbert Headlam described the election in his diary as a "truly catastrophic election—never was [there] such a crushing disaster." Sir Cuthbert Headlam, *Parliament and Politics in the Age of Churchill and Attlee: The Headlam Diaries, 1935–1951* [*Diaries*], Thursday, July 26, 1945, edited by Stuart Ball (Cambridge: Cambridge University Press, 1999), 469.
7. Not such a good time to be a member of the Conservative Party. On the day Attlee was invited to form the government, Headlam complained, "The more one thinks over this ghastly election, the more wretched one feels." *Diaries*, 470.

8. Prior to his time in Parliament, Hall had been a coalminer and a trade unionist, and although he had served well in his various wartime roles, he was not known as a specialist in colonial affairs. Indeed, most historians believe that his appointment as colonial secretary had more to do with his personal friendship with Attlee than his political expertise and experience. David Goldsworthy, *Colonial Issues in British Politics, 1945–1961: From 'Colonial Development' to 'Wind of Change'* (Oxford: The Clarendon Press, 1971), 14.

9. The official role of the colonial secretary, according to a 1948 colonial office report, was to be "constitutionally responsible to Parliament for the good government of colonial territories." *The Colonial Empire (1947–1948)* (Colonial Office Annual Report, 1948), 3, quoted in ibid., 42.

10. Quoted in David Fromkin, *A Peace to End All Peace: The Fall of the Ottoman Empire and the Creation of the Modern Middle East* (New York: Owl Books, 1989), 297.

11. For the most comprehensive account of this long and tangled saga, see Isaiah Friedman, *The Question of Palestine, 1914–1918: British-Jewish-Arab Relations* (New York: Schocken Books, 1973).

12. Richard Allen, *Imperialism and Nationalism in the Fertile Crescent: Sources and Prospects of the Arab-Israeli Conflict* (New York: Oxford University Press, 1974), 260–72.

13. Ibid.

14. Roza I. M. El-Eini, *Mandated Landscape: British Imperial Rule in Palestine, 1929–1948* (London and New York: Routledge, 2006), 22.

15. See Y. Porath, *The Emergence of the Palestinian-Arab National Movement, 1918–1929* (London: Frank Cass, 1974), particularly chapters four through seven.

16. For an in-depth analysis of the 1929 riots and their causes, see Bernard Wasserstein, *The British in Palestine: The Mandatory Government and the Arab-Jewish Conflict, 1917–1929* (London: Royal Historical Society, 1978), 215–35.

17. Martin Kolinsky, *Law, Order and Riots in Mandatory Palestine, 1928–35* (London: St. Martin's Press, in association with King's College, London, 1993), 123–58.

18. For a detailed explanation of these statistics, see E. Bromberger, "The Growth of Population in Palestine," *Population Studies*, Volume 2, Number 1 (June 1948), 71–91; and P. J. Loftus, "Features of the Demography of Palestine," *Population Studies*, Volume 2, Number 1 (June 1948), 92–114.

19. Kolinsky, *Law, Order and Riots in Mandatory Palestine*, 172–6.

20. For an account of the development of Palestinian Arab national-
    ism in these years and the outbreak of the revolt, see Y. Porath, *The
    Palestinian Arab National Movement: From Riots to Rebellion, Volume
    Two, 1929–1939* (London: Frank Cass, 1977). For more recent work
    on the Arab revolt, see Jacob Norris, "Repression and Rebellion:
    Britain's Response to the Arab Revolt in Palestine of 1936–1939," *The
    Journal of Imperial and Commonwealth History*, Volume 36, Number
    1 (March 2008), 25–45; and Matthew Hughes, "The Banality of
    Brutality: British Armed Forces and the Repression of the Arab Revolt
    in Palestine, 1936–39," *English Historical Review*, Volume CXXIV,
    Number 507 (April 2009), 313–54.

21. Michael J Cohen, "Appeasement in the Middle East: The British
    White Paper on Palestine, May 1939," *The Historical Journal*, Volume
    16, Number 3 (September 1973), 571.

22. David A. Charters, *The British Army and Jewish Insurgency in Palestine,
    1945–47* (New York: St. Martin's Press, 1989), 15–17.

23. The Irgun commander-in-chief, David Raziel, was even killed on a
    British SOE (Special Operations Executive) operation in Iraq in May
    1941. John Newsinger, *British Counterinsurgency: From Palestine to
    Northern Ireland* (New York: Palgrave Macmillan, 2002), 6.

24. J. Bowyer Bell, *Terror out of Zion: Irgun Zvai Leumi, LEHI, and the
    Palestine Underground, 1929–1949* (New York: St. Martin's Press,
    1977), 62–65. The most detailed account of the Stern Gang can be
    found in Joseph Heller, *The Stern Gang: Ideology, Politics and Terror,
    1940–1949* (London: Frank Cass, 1995).

25. Bell, *Terror out of Zion*, 57–8.

26. For more on *Hashomer Zatzair* and *Betar*, see Elkana Margalit, "Social
    and Intellectual Origins of the Hashomer Hatzair Youth Movement,
    1913–1920," *Journal of Contemporary History*, Volume 4, Number 2
    (April 1969), 25–46; and Lenni Brenner, "Zionist-Revisionism: The
    Years of Fascism and Terror," *Journal of Palestine Studies*, Volume 13,
    Number 1 (Autumn 1983), 66–92.

27. This account of Begin's early life is taken from the following three
    biographies: Eitan Haber, *Menahem Begin: The Legend and the Man*,
    translated by Louis Williams (New York: Delacorte Press, 1978);
    Amos Perlmutter, *The Life and Times of Menachem Begin* (New York:
    Doubleday & Company, Inc., 1987); and Eric Silver, *Begin: The
    Haunted Prophet* (New York: Random House, 1984).

28. Haber, *Menahem Begin*, 99–109.

29. John Keegan, *The Second World War* (New York: Penguin Books,
    1989), 358; Gerhard L. Weinberg, *A World at Arms: A Global History of
    World War II* (Cambridge: Cambridge University Press, 1994), 641–2;

John Keegan, *Collins Atlas of World War II* (New York: HarperCollins, 2006), 119; Gerhard L. Weinberg, *A World at Arms*, 611–16.

30. TNA, CO 733/457/5, Telegram from Sir Harold MacMichael, British High Commissioner in Palestine, to Oliver Stanley, Secretary of State for the Colonies, April 15, 1944.

31. TNA, CO 733/457/5, Telegram from William Ormsby-Gore, 4th Baron Harlech, British High Commissioner to South Africa, to Sir Harold MacMichael, British High Commissioner in Palestine, April 18, 1944.

32. TNA, CO 733/457/5, Telegram from Sir Harold MacMichael, British High Commissioner in Palestine, to William Ormsby-Gore, 4th Baron Harlech, British High Commissioner to South Africa, April 24, 1944.

33. TNA, CO 733/457/5, Telegram from Oliver Stanley, Secretary of State for the Colonies, to Sir Harold MacMichael, British High Commissioner in Palestine, May 15, 1944; Telegram from Sir Harold MacMichael, British High Commissioner in Palestine, to Oliver Stanley, Secretary of State for the Colonies, May 17, 1944; Telegram from Oliver Stanley, Secretary of State for the Colonies, to British consul, Casablanca, June 2, 1944.

34. Bell, *Terror out of Zion*, 114–7.

35. Ibid., 119.

36. Ibid., 120.

37. Ibid., 124.

38. TNA, CO 733/457/12, Letter from Sir John Shaw, Palestine Chief Secretary, to Sir Arthur Dawe, Deputy Under Secretary for the Colonies, December 22, 1944. The emphasis is Shaw's.

39. TNA, CO 733/457/12, Telegram from J. C., British administration in Palestine, to Oliver Stanley, Secretary of State for the Colonies, March 1, 1945.

40. "Obituary: Sir Richard Catling: Police commissioner who dealt with uprisings in Palestine, Malaya, and Kenya: August 22, 1912-March 22, 2005," *The Times*, April 12, 2005.

41. TNA, CO 733/457/5, Report from Richard Catling, Deputy Head of Special Branch, submitted to MI5 in October 1944.

42. Ibid.

43. This sequence of events is summarized in TNA, CO 733/457/5, Letter from A. J. Kellar, MI5, to C. G. Eastwood, Colonial Office, March 14, 1945.

44. Ibid.

45. TNA, CO 733/457/14, Letter from Guy Liddell, Director of B Division (Counter-Espionage), MI5, to C. G. Eastwood, Colonial Office, April 19, 1945.

46. TNA, CO 733/457/12, Report prepared by John Rymer Jones, Inspector General of the Palestine Police, for Sir John Shaw, Palestine Chief Secretary, April 24, 1945.

47. John Keegan, *Collins Atlas of World War II*, 164–7.

48. Bell, *Terror out of Zion*, 136.

49. Ibid., 137.

50. Ibid., 138.

51. TNA, CO 733/457/12, Letter from C. G. Eastwood, Colonial Office, to Lord Killearn, Undersecretary of State for Colonial Affairs, July 29, 1945.

52. Attlee, *As It Happened*, 245.

53. This was true not only for Labour Members of Parliament but also for Conservatives. Sir Cuthbert Headlam, in his diary entry of August 6, wrote: "The news tonight is that some new and fearful form of bomb—something to do with the 'splitting of the atom' (God help us)—has been dropped in Japan—the havoc so fearful that no one can tell how much damage has been done …. It seems that this wretched bomb is so devastating in its effect that it wipes out a whole town at one blow—if this is really the case, it means either the end of war or the end of civilization. Apparently its discovery—the discovery of the bomb—has cost 500 million pounds—it is all beyond comprehension and makes one hate 'Science' more than ever." (Headlam, *Diaries*, 473). Within a month, however, Cuthbert had forgotten these sentiments as the extent of Japanese atrocities became clear and the problem of how to punish the Japanese leaders was raised. On September 7, he wrote: "How to punish these beastly creatures, I cannot imagine—something spectacular, I imagine, should be done, but short of hanging the Emperor and all his war lords I cannot think of anything calculated to impress the Japanese nation. The only sensible thing to do really would be to drop atomic bombs wholesale over the country and thus to destroy the Japanese race as fully as possible—one cannot see what good service they render to humanity." (Ibid., 478).

54. Morgan, *Labour in Power*, 254–62.

55. Cabinet Office [CAB] 81/46, PHP (45)29(0) Final, "The Security of the British Empire": report by the Post-Hostilities Planning Staff for the Chiefs of Staff Committee, June 29, 1945, in S. R. Ashton and S. E. Stockwell, eds, *British Documents on the End of Empire [BDOEE]: Series A: Volume 1: Imperial Policy and Colonial Practice, 1925–1945: Part I: Metropolitan Reorganisation, Defence and International Relations, Political Change and Constitutional Reform* (London: Her Majesty's Stationary Office, 1996), 233–4.

56. This phrase was coined by John Colville, private secretary to both Winston Churchill and Clement Attlee, in his diary entry of August 6,

1945. John Corville, *The Fringes of Power: 10 Downing Street Diaries, 1939–1955* (New York: W.W. Norton & Company, 1985), 612.

57. *Let Us Face the Future: A Declaration of Labour Policy for the Consideration of the Nation* (London: The Labour Party, 1945), 11, quoted in Goldsworthy, *Colonial Issues in British Politics*, 13.

58. Attlee, *As It Happened*, 229.

59. Morgan, *Labour in Power*, 97–8.

60. For details of the welfare state, see ibid., chapter 4 (pages 142–87).

61. Henry Pelling, *The Labour Governments, 1945–51* (New York: St. Martin's Press, 1984), 158.

62. Goldsworthy, *Colonial Issues in British Politics*, 15.

63. Letter from Harry S. Truman, President of the United States, to Winston Churchill, Prime Minister, July 24, 1945, reprinted in Francis Williams, *Twilight of Empire: Memoirs of Prime Minister Clement Attlee* (New York: A.S. Barnes and Co., 1962), 183–4.

64. Letter from Clement Attlee, Prime Minister, to Harry S. Truman, President of the United States, July 31, 1945, reprinted in ibid., 184.

65. Michael J. Cohen, "The Genesis of the Anglo-American Committee on Palestine, November 1945: A Case Study in the Assertion of American Hegemony," *The Historical Journal*, Volume 22, Number 1 (March 1979), 192.

66. Letter from Harry S. Truman, President of the United States, to Clement Attlee, Prime Minister, August 31, 1945, reprinted in Williams, *Twilight of Empire*, 187–9.

67. Ibid.

68. Letter from Clement Attlee, Prime Minister, to Harry S. Truman, President of the United States, September 18, 1945, reprinted in ibid., 189–90.

69. Telegram from Clement Attlee, Prime Minister, to Harry S. Truman, President of the United States, October 25, 1945, summarized in ibid., 191.

70. Ritchie Ovendale, "The Palestine Policy of the British Labour Government, 1945–1946," *International Affairs*, Volume 55, Number 3 (July 1979), 411–12.

71. Ibid., 412.

72. Foreign Office [FO] 371/44557, no 2560, [Anglo-American relations and the position of Britain]: despatch from Lord Halifax (Washington) to Mr Bevin (FO), August 9, 1945, in Ronald Hyam, ed., *BDOEE: Series A: Volume 2: The Labour Government and the End of Empire, 1945–1951: Part II: Economics and International Relations* (London: Her Majesty's Stationary Office, 1992), 304–13. In his report, Lord Halifax offers a brilliant analysis of the differences in

national character between the United States and Great Britain, writing: "In their search for security in a world that modern science has contracted, Americans may be counted upon to display the virtues and defects inherent in a people which, throughout the comparative short span of its history, has seen itself as dedicated to the advancement of human freedoms and blessed beyond the inhabitants of other lands with a moral and democratic way of life. Now that the full strength of their country has become manifest to them, Americans hold that they are bound to take a leading part in the readjustment of international relationships. Faith in the magic of large worlds; an enthusiastic belief that the mere enunciation of an abstract principle is equivalent to its concrete fulfilment; a tendency to overlook the practical difficulties that obstruct the easy solution of current problems; above all, a constant disposition to prefer the emotional to the rational approach—these are amongst the salient traits that are likely in the future, no less than in the past, to provoke Americans to impatience with the more solid, disillusioned and pragmatic British, and to give rise to current misunderstandings between our two Governments. Taken in the aggregate these traits, for all that they at times bear the stamp of arrogant self-righteousness, spring from a core of genuine idealism which requires to be handled with more generosity and imagination and, be it also said, in a less patronising spirit than it has always received. In the meantime, increased contacts with other regions are causing many Americans to shed their ignorance of the outside world." (Ibid., 307).

73. Sir Harold Beeley, working as a civil servant in the Palestine Department of the Foreign Office and later secretary to the Anglo-American committee of inquiry, noted that: "Bevin had two preoccupations in dealing with Palestine. First, he was always afraid that it would poison Anglo-American relations and he wanted very much to secure American support for whatever policy we adopted. That might have led him to take a pro-Zionist position. But his second pre-occupation was the danger of alienating the Arabs—the Arab world as a whole." Bodleian Library of Commonwealth and African Studies at Rhodes House [Rhodes House Library] Library, Oxford, Mss. Brit. Emp. s. 527, "End of Empire" Transcripts, 527/10/1, Transcript of an interview with Sir Harold Beeley, interviewed by Alison Rooper, September 7, 1983.

74. Cohen, "The Genesis of the Anglo-American Committee on Palestine, November 1945," 197.

75. Ibid., 198.

76. Ibid.

77. Ibid., 201.
78. Ibid., 201–4. For a more detailed analysis of the establishment of the Anglo-American committee, see Allen Howard Podet, *The Success and Failure of the Anglo-American Committee of Inquiry, 1945–1946: Last Chance in Palestine* (Lewiston, NY, and Queenston, ON: The Edwin Mellen Press, 1986), 55–81.
79. TNA, CO 733/457/5, Letter from Sir David Petrie, Director-General of MI5, to A. F. Giles, Head of the Criminal Investigation Department, Palestine Police, August 22, 1945.
80. TNA, CO 733/456/12, Letter from A. J. Kellar, MI5, to C. G. Eastwood, Colonial Office, August 24, 1945.
81. TNA, Air Ministry (AIR) 23/6414, Memorandum from H. D. McGregor, Air Commodore, Commanding RAF LEVANT, to Headquarters, Royal Air Force, Middle East, August 28, 1945.
82. TNA, AIR 23/6414, Memorandum from E. R. E. Black, Group Captain, for H. D. McGregor, Air Commodore, Commanding RAF LEVANT, August 31, 1945.
83. TNA, AIR 23/6414, "Administrative Plan for Internal Security Operations in Palestine," September 12, 1945.
84. TNA, CO 733/457/11, Telegram from George Henry Hall, Secretary of State for the Colonies, to Field Marshal Viscount Gort, British High Commissioner for Palestine, November 3, 1945; TNA, CO 733/457/11, Telegram from Ernest Bevin, Secretary of State for Foreign Affairs, to Lord Halifax, British Ambassador to the United States, November 6, 1945; TNA, CO 733/457/11, Telegram from Lord Addison, Secretary of State for Dominion Affairs, to the Prime Ministers of Canada, Australia, New Zealand, and South Africa, November 8, 1945.
85. TNA, CO 733/457/11, Telegram from Ernest Bevin, Secretary of State for Foreign Affairs, to Lord Halifax, British Ambassador to the United States, November 6, 1945.
86. Charters, *The British Army and Jewish Insurgency in Palestine*, 85–92.
87. Bell, *Terror out of Zion*, 146.
88. Charters, *The British Army and Jewish Insurgency in Palestine*, 111.
89. T. A. Heathcote, *The British Field Marshals, 1763–1997: A Biographical Dictionary* (Barnsley, South Yorkshire: Leo Cooper, 1999), 283.
90. John Strawson, "Cunningham, Sir Alan Gordon," in H. C. G. Matthew and Brian Harrison, eds, *Oxford Dictionary of National Biography* (Oxford and New York: Oxford University Press, 2004).
91. *Parliamentary Debates (Hansard)*, House of Commons, Fifth Series, Volume 415, October 29–November 16, 1945 (London: His Majesty's Stationary Office, 1945), November 5, 1945, column 896; ibid., November 2, 1945, column 786.

92. Ibid., November 13, 1945, columns 1927–31.

93. Bell, *Terror out of Zion*, 147.

94. Ibid.

95. Charters, *The British Army and Jewish Insurgency in Palestine*, 112.

96. Bell, *Terror out of Zion*, 150.

97. Ibid., 151.

98. TNA, CO 733/457/11, Report written by Arthur Creech Jones, Undersecretary of State for Colonial Affairs, January 1, 1946.

99. TNA, CO 733/457/11, Telegram from Lieutenant General Sir Alan Cunningham, British High Commissioner in Palestine, to George Henry Hall, Secretary of State for the Colonies, December 29, 1945.

100. TNA, CO 733/457/11, Report written by Arthur Creech Jones, Undersecretary of State for Colonial Affairs, January 1, 1946.

101. TNA, CO 733/457/11, Conclusions of a meeting of the Cabinet, held on January 1, 1946.

102. CAB 131/2, DO(46)40, "[Defence in the Mediterranean, Middle East and Indian Ocean]": Memorandum by Mr Bevin for Cabinet Defence Committee, March 13, 1946, in Ronald Hyam, ed., *BDOEE: Series A: Volume 2: The Labour Government and the End of Empire, 1945–1951: Part III: Strategy, Politics and Constitutional Change* (London: Her Majesty's Stationary Office, 1992), 215–18.

103. CAB 131/2, DO(46)47, "Strategic Position of the British Commonwealth": report by Chiefs of Staff for Cabinet Defence Committee, April 2, 1946, in ibid., 333–40.

104. Bell, *Terror out of Zion*, 153–6.

105. Charters, *The British Army and Jewish Insurgency in Palestine*, 112–17.

106. Imperial War Museum [IWM], Department of Documents (DoD), Roy Hammerton, *Cliff and I: Memories of Army Service from 1944–1948* (Unpublished memoir, July 2004), Papers of R. Hammerton (05/45/1).

107. Charters, *The British Army and Jewish Insurgency in Palestine*, 117.

108. Bell, *Terror out of Zion*, 161.

109. Ibid., 164–6.

110. TNA, War Office [WO] 275/27, "H.Q. British Troops Palestine & Transjordan: Report on Operation AGATHA, 29th June–1st July, 1946," July 9, 1946.

111. Ibid.

112. Charters, *The British Army and Jewish Insurgency in Palestine*, 117–18.

113. TNA, WO 275/27, "Report on Operation AGATHA."

114. Ibid.

115. Charters, *The British Army and Jewish Insurgency in Palestine*, 118.

116. Bodleian Library, Oxford University, Papers of Harold Macmillan [Macmillan Papers], Dep. c. 890, "Palestine: Statement of Information Relating to Acts of Violence," Presented to Parliament by the Secretary of State for the Colonies by Command of His Majesty, July 1946.

117. Bell, *Terror out of Zion*, 169–72.

118. IWM, DoD, Captain Ridley Hugh Clark, MC, *Hugh's Wartime Memoirs* (Unpublished memoir, April 2006), Papers of Captain R. H. Clark, MC (06/38/1).

119. Charters, *The British Army and Jewish Insurgency in Palestine*, 58.

120. *Parliamentary Debates (Hansard)*, House of Commons, Fifth Series, Volume 425, July 8–July 23, 1946 (London: His Majesty's Stationary Office, 1946), July 22, 1946, columns 1689–1844.

121. Morgan, *Labour in Power*, 152–63.

122. *Parliamentary Debates (Hansard)*, House of Commons, Fifth Series, Volume 425, July 23, 1946, columns 1877–8.

123. Ian F. W. Beckett, *Modern Insurgencies and Counter-Insurgencies: Guerillas and Their Opponents Since 1750* (London and New York: Routledge, 2001), 88.

124. Miriam Joyce Haron, "Palestine and the Anglo-American Connection," *Modern Judaism*, Volume 2, Number 2 (May 1982), 201.

125. Ibid., 202. It was not only Bevin who descended into a "black rage." Ritchie Ovendale writes: "The British public was outraged by Truman's statement: seven British soldiers had just been murdered by Zionist terrorists and the British government felt that Truman showed scant appreciation of the needs of British security." Ovendale, "The Palestine Policy of the British Labour Government, 1945–1946," *International Affairs*, 419.

126. Ovendale, "The Palestine Policy of the British Labour Government," 419–21.

127. Ibid., 422.

128. Quoted in ibid., 423.

129. Ibid., 422–4.

130. Quoted in Michael J. Cohen, *Palestine and the Great Powers, 1945–1948* (Princeton: Princeton University Press, 1982), 125.

131. Ibid.

132. Ovendale, "The Palestine Policy of the British Labour Government," 424–5.

133. Cohen, *Palestine and the Great Powers*, 125–6.

134. Ovendale, "The Palestine Policy of the British Labour Government," 425.

135. Cohen, *Palestine and the Great Powers*, 128–30.

136. Quoted in ibid., 130.
137. Quoted in ibid., 132.
138. Quoted in Ovendale, "The Palestine Policy of the British Labour Government," 426.
139. For a more complete overview of the collapse of Anglo-American cooperation, see Martin Jones, *Failure in Palestine: British and United States Policy after the Second World War* (London and New York: Mansell Publishing Limited, 1986), 70–143.
140. Quoted in ibid., 166.
141. Ibid., 167
142. Ibid., 168.
143. Quoted in ibid., 171.
144. Quoted in Wm. Roger Louis, "British Imperialism and the End of the Palestine Mandate," in Wm. Roger Louis and Robert W. Stookey, eds, *The End of the Palestine Mandate* (Austin: University of Texas Press, 1986), 11.
145. A. J. Stockwell, "Gurney, Sir Henry Lovell Goldsworthy," in Matthew and Harrison, eds, *Oxford Dictionary of National Biography*.
146. TNA, CO 967/102, Letter from Henry Gurney, Chief Secretary in Palestine, to John Martin, Assistant Undersecretary at the Colonial Office, October 8, 1946.
147. IWM, DoD, Clark, *Hugh's Wartime Memoirs*, Papers of Captain R. H. Clark, MC (06/38/1).
148. TNA, CO 967/102, Letter from Henry Gurney, Chief Secretary in Palestine, to John Martin, Assistant Undersecretary at the Colonial Office, November 5, 1946.
149. Patricia M. Pugh, "Jones, Arthur Creech," in H. C. G. Matthew and Brian Harrison, eds, *Oxford Dictionary of National Biography* (Oxford: Oxford University Press, 2004).
150. Bell, *Terror out of Zion*, 183.
151. TNA, Prime Minister's Office [PREM] 8/864, Letter from Viscount Montgomery, Chief of the Imperial General Staff, to Clement Attlee, Prime Minister, November 19, 1946.
152. TNA, CAB 21/1686, Minutes of Cabinet Defence Committee Meeting held at No. 10 Downing Street, November 20, 1946.
153. TNA, CO 976/102, Letter from Henry Gurney, Chief Secretary in Palestine, to John Martin, Assistant Undersecretary at the Colonial Office, November 20, 1946.
154. See Priya Satia, *Spies in Arabia: The Great War and the Cultural Foundations of Britain's Covert Empire in the Middle East* (Oxford and New York: Oxford University Press, 2008); and Martin Thomas, *Empires of Intelligence: Security Services and Colonial Disorder after 1914* (Berkeley and Los Angeles: University of California Press, 2008).

155. For more on the reprisals in Ireland, see Benjamin Grob-Fitzgibbon, *Turning Points of the Irish Revolution: The British Government, Intelligence, and the Cost of Indifference, 1912–1921* (New York and Basingstoke, UK: Palgrave Macmillan, 2007), 168–73.

156. TNA, CAB 21/1686, Telegram Exchange between General Sir Miles Dempsey, Commander in Chief Middle East Land Forces, and General Sir Alan Cunningham, High Commissioner in Palestine, forwarded to Arthur Creech Jones, Secretary of State for Colonial Affairs, November 23, 1946.

157. TNA, CO 967/102, Letter from Henry Gurney, Chief Secretary in Palestine, to John Martin, Assistant Undersecretary at the Colonial Office, November 29, 1946.

158. IWM, DoD, Letter from Colonel C. R. W. Norman, Chief of Military Intelligence in Palestine, to his mother, December 15, 1946, Papers of Colonel C. R. W. Norman, OBE (87/57/4).

159. Liddell Hart Centre for Military Archives, King's College, London [LHCMA], General Sir Harold Pyman Papers, 7/1/1, Commander in Chief's Second Agenda, December 17, 1946. Pyman also noted that the Chief of the Imperial General Staff, Viscount Montgomery, was "watching carefully that, should the situation arise, the Army would be allowed full scope."

160. TNA, CAB 21/1686, Note by L. C. Hollis and W. S. Murrie to members of the Cabinet Defence Committee, December 19, 1946.

161. TNA, CAB 21/1686, Memorandum: "Palestine: Use of the Armed Forces," circulated to members of the Cabinet Defence Committee, December 19, 1946.

162. Bevin no doubt also had in mind the reaction of the American government and public. Having just returned from a trip to the United States, he informed Attlee on December 29—just three days before speaking at the cabinet defense committee meeting—that (as Attlee paraphrased to his brother Tom), "Zionism has become a profitable racket over there [in the United States]. A Zionist is defined as a Jew who collects money from another Jew to send another Jew to Palestine. The collector, I gather, takes a good percentage of his collections." Bodleian Library, Oxford University, Ms. Eng. c. 4793, Letter from Clement Attlee to his brother Tom Attlee, December 29, 1946.

163. TNA, CAB 21/1686, Minutes of Cabinet Defence Committee held at No. 10 Downing Street, January 1, 1947.

164. LHCMA, General Sir Harold Pyman Papers, 7/1/1, Cipher Message for General Sir Harold Pyman, Chief of Staff Middle East Land Forces, from Viscount Montgomery, Chief of the Imperial General Staff, January 2, 1947.

165. Rhodes House Library, Oxford University, Mss. Brit. Emp. 332, Papers of Arthur Creech Jones [Creech Jones Papers], Box 60, File 6, Letter from Viscount Montgomery of Alamein, Chief of the Imperial General Staff, to Arthur Creech Jones, Secretary of State for the Colonies, January 2, 1947.

166. Rhodes House Library, Oxford University, Creech Jones Papers, Box 60, File 6, Letter from Viscount Montgomery of Alamein, Chief of the Imperial General Staff, to Arthur Creech Jones, Secretary of State for the Colonies, January 4, 1947.

167. Although the directive itself could not be found, the timing of its transmission is suggested in TNA, CAB 21/1686, "Palestine—Use of the Armed Forces," Memorandum by Arthur Creech Jones, Secretary of State for the Colonies, to the Cabinet Defence Committee, January 15, 1947. Montgomery confirmed this in a cipher message he sent to General Sir Miles Dempsey, the commander in chief MELF, on January 15, in which he noted that he himself had drafted the directive, the purpose of which was to ensure that Cunningham would "use more effective and robust methods in his endeavours to maintain law and order in Palestine." LHCMA, General Sir Harold Pyman Papers, 7/1/2, Cipher Message from Viscount Montgomery of Alamein, Chief of the Imperial General Staff, to General Sir Miles Dempsey, Commander in Chief Middle East Land Forces, January 15, 1947.

168. LHCMA, General Sir Harold Pyman Papers, 7/1/2, Letter from General Sir Harold Pyman, Chief of Staff, Middle East Land Forces, to General Sir Miles Dempsey, Commander in Chief Middle East Land Forces, January 3, 1947.

169. LHCMA, General Sir Harold Pyman Papers, 7/1/2, Diary Entry, January 13, 1947.

170. TNA, CO 967/102, Letter from Henry Gurney, Chief Secretary in Palestine, to John Martin, Assistant Undersecretary at the Colonial Office, January 16, 1947.

171. Bell, *Terror out of Zion*, 186.

172. LHCMA, General Sir Harold Pyman Papers, 7/1/2, Diary Entry, January 21, 1947.

173. Bell, *Terror out of Zion*, 186.

174. IWM, DoD, Letter from Colonel C. R. W. Norman, Chief of Military Intelligence in Palestine, to his mother, February 2, 1947, Papers of Colonel C. R. W. Norman, OBE (87/57/4).

175. IWM, DoD, Letter from Colonel C. R. W. Norman, Chief of Military Intelligence in Palestine, to his mother, February 9, 1947, Papers of Colonel C. R. W. Norman, OBE (87/57/4).

176. TNA, CO 967/102, Letter from Henry Gurney, Chief Secretary in Palestine, to John Martin, Assistant Undersecretary at the Colonial Office, February 8, 1946.

177. Rhodes House Library, Oxford University, Creech Jones Papers, Box 60, File 6, Letter from Viscount Montgomery of Alamein, Chief of the Imperial General Staff, to Arthur Creech Jones, Secretary of State for the Colonies, January 28, 1947.

178. Bell, *Terror out of Zion*, 186–7.

179. Barbara D. Metcalf and Thomas R. Metcalf, *A Concise History of India* (Cambridge: Cambridge University Press, 2002), 203.

180. Ibid., 203–4.

181. Ibid., 206.

182. Ibid., 209.

183. Ibid.

184. Ibid., 211.

185. Ibid., 213.

186. John Darwin, *Britain and Decolonisation: The Retreat from Empire in the Post-War World* (New York: St. Martin's Press, 1988), 94–5.

187. Ibid.

188. Quoted in Stanley Wolpert, *Shameful Flight: The Last Years of the British Empire in India* (Oxford and New York: Oxford University Press, 2006), 131. Not all shared Attlee's sense of optimism. Sir Cuthbert Headlam, a member of the opposition Conservative Party, wrote in his diary on February 20: "It seems to me to be a tremendous gamble and a needless policy of despair—unless there is a settlement by the appointed day what will our position be? Shall we really withdraw our troops and leave India to anarchy and chaos? Such a policy would in my opinion be wholly wrong and a great betrayal of the whole Indian population" (*Diaries*, 489).

189. Morgan, *Labour in Power*, 373.

190. Headlam, *Diaries*, January 8, 1947, 482.

191. Morgan, *Labour in Power*, 337.

192. Ibid., 339–40.

193. *Annual Register* quoted in Pelling, *The Labour Governments*, 165.

194. Ibid., 165–6.

195. Headlam, *Diaries*, February 10, 1947, 486.

196. Ibid., March 2, 1947, 491.

197. Pelling, *The Labour Governments*, 166.

198. Bell, *Terror out of Zion*, 187.

199. Ibid., 190. Bell lists the number of operations launched as sixteen, but Pyman noted in his diary entry of March 2 that there were eighteen, which is the number this author has chosen to cite.

LHCMA, General Sir Harold Pyman Papers, 7/1/3, Diary Entry, March 2, 1947.

200. IWM, DoD, Letter from Colonel C. R. W. Norman, Chief of Military Intelligence in Palestine, to his mother, March 2, 1947, Papers of Colonel C. R. W. Norman, OBE (87/57/4).

201. Bell, *Terror out of Zion*, 190.

202. Ibid.

203. TNA, CO 967/102, Letter from Henry Gurney, Chief Secretary in Palestine, to John Martin, Assistant Undersecretary at the Colonial Office, March 5, 1946.

204. Bell, *Terror out of Zion*, 190–91.

205. LHCMA, General Sir Harold Pyman Papers, 7/1/3, Cipher Message from Viscount Montgomery of Alamein, Chief of the Imperial General Staff, to General Sir Miles Demsey, Commander in Chief Middle East Land Forces, March 4, 1947.

206. LHCMA, General Sir Harold Pyman Papers, 7/1/3, Cipher Message from General Sir Miles Dempsey, Commander in Chief Middle East Land Forces, to Viscount Montgomery of Alamein, Chief of the Imperial General Staff, March 4, 1947.

207. Bell, *Terror out of Zion*, 191.

208. LHCMA, General Sir Harold Pyman Papers, 7/1/3, Cipher Message from Viscount Montgomery of Alamein, Chief of the Imperial General Staff, to General Sir Miles Dempsey, Commander in Chief Middle East Land Forces, March 12, 1947.

209. Bell, *Terror out of Zion*, 191.

210. LHCMA, General Sir Harold Pyman Papers, 7/1/3, Cipher Message from General Sir Miles Dempsey, Commander in Chief Middle East Land Forces, to Viscount Montgomery of Alamein, Chief of the Imperial General Staff, March 20, 1947.

211. TNA, WO 216/666, Memorandum: "Appreciation in Note Form of the Measures Necessary to Maintain Law and Order in Palestine," prepared by Major General Sir Gordon MacMillan, General Officer Commanding Palestine, for Viscount Montgomery, Chief of the Imperial General Staff, March 23, 1947.

212. TNA, CO 967/102, Letter from Henry Gurney, Chief Secretary in Palestine, to John Martin, Assistant Undersecretary at the Colonial Office, May 22, 1947.

213. IWM, DoD, Letter from Colonel C. R. W. Norman, Chief of Military Intelligence in Palestine, to his mother, May 25, 1947, Papers of Colonel C. R. W. Norman, OBE (87/57/4).

214. Bell, *Terror out of Zion*, 191.

215. Ibid., 199–200.

216. Ibid., 200–2.

217. For a full account of these escapes, see ibid., 204–18.

218. Ritchie Ovendale, "The Palestine Policy of the British Labour Government 1947: The Decision to Withdraw," *International Affairs*, Volume 56, Number 1 (January 1980), 88.

219. Bell, *Terror out of Zion*, 219–20.

220. Ovendale, "The Palestine Policy of the British Labour Government 1947," 88.

221. Bell, *Terror out of Zion*, 221–2.

222. Ibid., 224.

223. IWM, DoD, "Review of the Situation in Palestine," A report prepared by Colonel C. R. W. Norman, Chief of Military Intelligence in Palestine, June 22, 1947, Papers of Colonel C. R. W. Norman, OBE (87/57/4).

224. Bell, *Terror out of Zion*, 227–8.

225. IWM, DoD, Letter from Colonel C. R. W. Norman, Chief of Military Intelligence in Palestine, to his mother, July 13, 1947, Papers of Colonel C. R. W. Norman, OBE (87/57/4).

226. Bell, *Terror out of Zion*, 228.

227. For a full account of the *Exodus* saga, see ibid., 229–34. Such duties were also resented by the soldiers. George Lowe, a sergeant with the Intelligence Corps at the time, later recalled: "I think the army as a whole felt that we were trying to be gentlemen in an ungentlemanly situation. Suffering for it, and in fact, immigrants themselves were suffering for it." Rhodes House Library, Oxford University, Mss. Brit. Emp. s. 527, "End of Empire" Transcripts, 527/10/2, Transcript of an interview with George Lowe, interviewed by Alison Rooper, September 7, 1983.

228. IWM, DoD, Kendal George Fleming Chavasse, *Some Memories of my Life* (Unpublished memoir, 1996), Papers of Colonel K. G. F. Chavasse DSO (89/23/1).

229. IWM, DoD, Letter from Colonel C. R. W. Norman, Chief of Military Intelligence in Palestine, to his mother, July 18, 1947, Papers of Colonel C. R. W. Norman, OBE (87/57/4).

230. Bell, *Terror out of Zion*, 235–6.

231. Ibid., 238.

232. IWM, DoD, Letter from Colonel C. R. W. Norman, Chief of Military Intelligence in Palestine, to his mother, August 2, 1947, Papers of Colonel C. R. W. Norman, OBE (87/57/4).

233. WO 216/221, Telegram from General Sir John T. Crocker, Commander in Chief Middle East Land Forces, to Emmanuel Shinwell, Secretary of State for War, August 3, 1947. Crocker sent a similar telegram to the vice chief of the imperial general staff, using the same words quoted to Shinwell but adding that "there

are strong indications that moderate elements representing the majority of the Jewish community are shocked by recent outrage and prepared to provide maximum assistance to Government short of publicly admitting co-operation. Therefore future policy should be to demonstrate by strength to the terrorists the futility of their ways and to the majority of the Jewish population the wisdom of their assisting the Government. Any sign of weakness now either through adoption of less determined policy or because of lack of military strength to back present line of actions would be fatal and would lead to rapid and irrevocable deterioration of situation and final failure of our stewardship. … Pressure is being brought to bear in certain quarters for us to impose martial law. This would be premature and must be avoided if possible." LHCMA, General Sir Harold Pyman Papers, 7/1/8. Cipher Message from Vice Chief of the Imperial General Staff from General Sir John T. Crocker, Commander in Chief Middle East Land Forces, August 3, 1947.

234. WO 216/221, Minute from Vice Chief of the Imperial General Staff to Emmanuel Shinwell, Secretary of State for War, August 4, 1947.

235. PREM 8/623, Note from Hugh Dalton, Chancellor of the Exchequer, to Clement Attlee, Prime Minister, August 11, 1947.

236. TNA, CO 967/102, Letter from Henry Gurney, Chief Secretary in Palestine, to John Martin, Assistant Undersecretary at the Colonial Office, September 1, 1947.

237. This account is taken from Wolpert, *Shameful Flight*, 131–71. Writing in a letter to his brother Tom on August 18, 1947, the prime minister, Clement Attlee, related: "I've just been seeing Mountbatten's private secretary who gave me an account of the extraordinary scenes at the handing over. Mount B was surrounded by about a quarter of a million Indians all violently enthusiastic for him. He has certainly captured the Indian imagination. I doubt if things will go awfully easily now as the Indian leaders know little of administration, but at least we have come out with honour instead, as at one time seemed likely, being pushed out ignominiously with the whole country in a state of confusion." Bodleian Library, Oxford University, Ms. Eng. c. 4793, Letters from Clement Attlee to his brother Tom Attlee, August 18, 1947.

238. Jones, *Failure in Palestine*, 277–80.

239. Quoted in Cohen, *Palestine and the Great Powers*, 276–7.

240. Quoted in ibid., 277. Creech Jones' insistence on an early troop withdrawal made some in the military community decidedly uncomfortable, as evidenced by a note written by General Sir John Crocker, commander in chief MELF, on October 8, while these debates were taking place: "1. Some authority must remain to govern

the country and run the public services. So long as that authority is the British Administration, the Army must remain to support it. 2. If the Civil Authority and Army withdraw without handing over to a new authority, there will be immediate civil chaos which will undoubtedly develop into civil war. 3. Transjordan, Saudi Arabia, Levant States, Iraq, and particularly Egypt would consider this to be a complete breach of trust and our swan song in the Middle East. We would never, thereafter, have any influence in the Middle East. 4. In short, if we wish to remain a great power in the Middle East, we cannot evacuate Palestine before we have handed over the country to some other authorities." LHCMA, General Sir Harold Pyman Papers, 7/1/10, Note written by General Sir John Crocker, Commander in Chief, Middle East Land Forces, October 8, 1947.

241. Cohen, *Palestine and the Great Powers*, 281–300.
242. IWM, DoD, Letter from Colonel C. R. W. Norman, Chief of Military Intelligence in Palestine, to his mother, November 30, 1947, Papers of Colonel C. R. W. Norman, OBE (87/57/4).
243. Bell, *Terror out of Zion*, 255.
244. IWM, DoD, Letter from Colonel C. R. W. Norman, Chief of Military Intelligence in Palestine, to his mother, December 7, 1947, Papers of Colonel C. R. W. Norman, OBE (87/57/4).
245. IWM, DoD, Top Secret Memorandum prepared by Colonel C. R. W. Norman, Chief of Military Intelligence in Palestine, December 11, 1947, Papers of Colonel C. R. W. Norman, OBE (87/57/4).
246. IWM, DoD, Directive No. 279, "Internal Security," Issued by General Headquarters Middle East Land Forces, December 27, 1947, Papers of Major General W. S. Cole, CB, CBE (07/34/06).
247. Bell, *Terror out of Zion*, 266–7.
248. IWM, DoD, Letter from Colonel C. R. W. Norman, Chief of Military Intelligence in Palestine, to his mother, February 22, 1948, Papers of Colonel C. R. W. Norman, OBE (87/57/4).
249. IWM, DoD, Letter from Colonel C. R. W. Norman, Chief of Military Intelligence in Palestine, to his mother, February 29, 1948, Papers of Colonel C. R. W. Norman, OBE (87/57/4).
250. IWM, DoD, Letters from Colonel C. R. W. Norman, Chief of Military Intelligence in Palestine, to his mother, March 14, 20, and 27, 1948, Papers of Colonel C. R. W. Norman, OBE (87/57/4).
251. IWM, DoD, Letter from Second Lieutenant R. Hodges to "Stinger", March 24, 1948, Papers of Second Lieutenant R. Hodges (87/14/1).
252. Templer Study Centre (TSC), National Army Museum (NAM), London, Papers of General Sir Alan Cunningham, NAM 1983-03-104-27, Telegram from General Sir Alan Cunningham, British High Commissioner in Palestine, to Arthur Creech Jones, Secretary of State for the Colonies, March 31, 1948.

253. LHCMA, General Sir Harold Pyman Papers, Cipher Message from General Sir John Crocker, Commander in Chief Middle East Land Forces, to Viscount Montgomery of Alamein, Chief of the Imperial General Staff, April 2, 1948.

254. Rhodes House Library, Oxford University, Creech Jones Papers, Box 60, File 6, Letter from Sir Alan Cunningham, British High Commissioner in Palestine, to Arthur Creech Jones, Secretary of State for the Colonies, April 12, 1948.

255. IWM, DoD, Diary Entry, April 14, 1948, Papers of Major P. F. Towers-Clark (06/43/1).

256. Ibid., Diary Entry, April 16, 1948.

257. Ibid., Diary Entry, April 19, 1948.

258. Ibid., Diary Entry, April 20, 1948.

259. Ibid., Diary Entry, April 21, 1948.

260. Ibid., Diary Entry, April 26, 1948.

261. LHCMA, General Sir Harold Pyman Papers, Cipher Message from Viscount Montgomery of Alamein, Chief of the Imperial General Staff, to General Sir John Crocker, Commander in Chief Middle East Land Forces, April 27, 1948.

262. IWM, DoD, Diary Entry, April 28, 1948, Papers of Major P. F. Towers-Clark (06/43/1).

263. TNA, CO 967/102, Letter from Henry Gurney, Chief Secretary in Palestine, to John Martin, Assistant Undersecretary at the Colonial Office, April 27, 1948.

264. IWM, DoD, Letter from Colonel C. R. W. Norman, Chief of Military Intelligence in Palestine, to his mother, May 2, 1948, Papers of Colonel C. R. W. Norman, OBE (87/57/4).

265. IWM, DoD, (Untitled, unpublished, and undated typescript account), Papers of M. P. Jefferson (99/77/1).

266. Beckett, *Modern Insurgencies and Counter-Insurgencies*, 89.

267. CO 717/167/52849/2/1948, f 302, [Declaration of Emergency]: inward telegram no 641 from Sir Edward Gent, High Commissioner to Malaya, to Arthur Creech Jones, Secretary of State for the Colonies, June 17, 1948, in A. J. Stockwell, ed., *BDOEE: Series B: Volume 3: Malaya: Part II: The Communist Insurrection, 1948–1953* (London: Her Majesty's Stationary Office, 1995), 19–20.

268. This narrative is taken from ibid., 34. The events surrounding Gent's death were highly controversial. As late as January 6, 1949, F. C. R. Douglas, British high commissioner in Malta, wrote to Creech Jones, saying: "When the Parliamentary Delegation was on its way to Ceylon it spent a day here. Among them was Capt. Gammans. He was talking to my wife about Sir Edward Gent's last journey, and said that he travelled by an R.A.F. plane because Malcolm MacDonald would not allow his plane

to be away long enough from Malaya and that the plane was manned by a 'scratch crew.' There seemed to be an insinuation that Malcolm had acted badly and that the R.A.F. were negligent in not providing a crew suitable to the nature of the journey. I think that you should know that this is being said." Rhodes House Library, Oxford University, Creech Jones Papers, Box 26, File 9, Letter from F. C. R. Douglas, British High Commissioner in Malta, to Arthur Creech Jones, Secretary of State for the Colonies, January 6, 1949.

269. CO 537/3686, no 6, [Replacement of Sir Edward Gent]: unnumbered telegram from M. J. MacDonald, Commissioner-General for British territories in Southeast Asia, to Arthur Creech Jones, Secretary of State for the Colonies, Jun 29, 1948, in A. J. Stockwell, ed., *BDOEE: Series B: Volume 3: Malaya: Part II: The Communist Insurrection,* 34–36.

270. CO 537/3686, no 8, [Appointment of new high commissioner]: outward telegram (reply) no 127 from Arthur Creech Jones, Secretary of State for the Colonies, to M. J. MacDonald, Commissioner-General for British territories in Southeast Asia, in ibid., 36.

271. Rhodes House Library, Oxford University, Creech Jones Papers, Box 57, File 2, Letter from Sir Henry Gurney to Arthur Creech Jones, Secretary of State for the Colonies, June 18, 1948.

272. CO 537/3686, no 28, [Appointment of new high commissioner]: outward telegram (reply) no 148 from Arthur Creech Jones, Secretary of State for the Colonies, to M. J. MacDonald, Commissioner-General for British territories in Southeast Asia, July 7, 1948, in A. J. Stockwell, ed., *BDOEE: Series B: Volume 3: Malaya: Part II: The Communist Insurrection,* 46.

273. Rhodes House Library, Oxford University, Creech Jones Papers, Box 57, File 2, Letter from General Sir Alan Cunningham to Arthur Creech Jones, Secretary of State for the Colonies, July 14, 1948.

274. Rhodes House Library, Oxford University, Creech Jones Papers, Box 57, File 2, Letter from Sir Thomas K. Lloyd, Permanent Undersecretary of State at the Colonial Office, to Arthur Creech Jones, Secretary of State for the Colonies, July 22, 1948.

275. CO 537/3687, no 51, [Appointment of Sir Henry Gurney as high commissioner]: inward telegram no 1067 from M. J. MacDonald, Commissioner-General for British territories in Southeast Asia, to Arthur Creech Jones, Secretary of State for the Colonies, August 31, 1948, in ibid., 68–70; and CO 537/3687, no 52, [Appointment of Sir Henry Gurney]: inward telegram no 214 from M. J. MacDonald, Commissioner-General for British territories in Southeast Asia, to Arthur Creech Jones, Secretary of State for the Colonies, September 1, 1948, in A. J. Stockwell, ed., *BDOEE: Series B: Volume 3: Malaya: Part II: The Communist Insurrection,* 70–71.

276. Robert Jackson, *The Malayan Emergency: The Commonwealth's Wars, 1948–1966* (London and New York: Routledge, 1991), 3–4.

277. Ibid., 4–6.

278. Ibid., 6.

279. John A. Nagl, *Learning to Eat Soup with a Knife: Counterinsurgency Lessons from Malaya and Vietnam* (Chicago: The University of Chicago Press, 2002), 60.

280. Anthony Short, *The Communist Insurrection in Malaya, 1948–1960* (New York: Crane, Russak & Company, Inc., 1975), 21.

281. Keegan, *The Second World War*, 256–61.

282. Ibid., 24. For more on this, see Richard Clutterbuck, *Conflict and Violence in Singapore and Malaysia, 1945–1983* (Boulder, CO: Westview Press, 1985), 37–41; and A. J. Stockwell, "Introduction," in A. J. Stockwell, ed., *BDOEE: Series B: Volume 3: Malaya: Part I: The Malayan Union Experiment, 1942–1948* (London: Her Majesty's Stationary Office, 1995), liii–lvi.

283. Stockwell, "Introduction," lv.

284. Clutterbuck, *Conflict and Violence in Singapore and Malaysia,* 37–41.

285. Short, *The Communist Insurrection in Malaya,* 34–41.

286. Not insignificantly, this proposal of federation for Malaya was quite similar to the proposal Foreign Secretary Ernest Bevin made at the same time for a Palestinian Federation with autonomous Jewish and Arab states.

287. Stockwell, "Introduction," lxiii.

288. Quoted in Short, *The Communist Insurrection in Malaya,* 56.

289. Ibid., 59.

290. Quoted in ibid., 60–61.

291. Stockwell, "Introduction," lxiii.

292. CAB 129/28, CP (48) 171, "The Situation in Malaya," Cabinet Memorandum by Arthur Creech Jones, Secretary of State for the Colonies, July 1, 1948, in A. J. Stockwell, ed., *BDOEE: Series B: Volume 3: Malaya: Part II: The Communist Insurrection,* 37–42.

293. PREM 8/1406, CP (48) 190, "The Situation in Malaya": Cabinet memorandum by Arthur Creech Jones, Secretary of State for the Colonies, July 19, 1948, in ibid., 47–48.

294. Short, *The Communist Insurrection in Malaya,* 96–100.

295. Ibid.

296. CAB 128/13, CM 52 (48) 5, [Proscription of the Malayan Communist Party]: Cabinet conclusions, July 19, 1948, in A. J. Stockwell, ed., *BDOEE: Series B: Volume 3: Malaya: Part II: The Communist Insurrection,* 50–51.

297. Short, *The Communist Insurrection in Malaya,* 113–14.

298. Ibid., 114.

299. Ibid., 140.

300. Such was the protest against Dyak trackers and the rumors surrounding their deployment that on November 24, Creech Jones had to assure Sir Gerald Creasy, governor of the Gold Coast, that, "There is no truth whatsoever in the suggestion that they brought or used poison arrows. There is no truth in the suggestion that head hunting is prevalent (as it used to be years ago) among the Dyaks. There is no truth in the statement that the Dyaks were instructed or allowed to cut off bandits' heads or received or were promised any reward for doing so." Rhodes House Library, Oxford University, Creech Jones Papers, Box 26, File 9, Telegram from Arthur Creech Jones, Secretary of State for the Colonies, to Sir Gerald Creasy, Governor of the Gold Coast, November 24, 1948. It should be noted that trackers from Sarawak were reintroduced to Malaya in 1949—once the global furor had died down—and by 1952 there were 264 such trackers serving with the security forces. CO 1022/57, Federal Government Press Statement, March 15, 1952. They remained until the end of the emergency and the withdrawal of British troops in 1960.

301. Richard Stubbs, *Hearts and Minds in Guerilla Warfare: The Malayan Emergency, 1948–1960* (Oxford: Oxford University Press, 1989), 70–71.

302. Short, *The Communist Insurrection in Malaya*, 136–7.

303. IWM, DoD, Major I. S. Gibb, MC, (Unpublished memoir), Papers of Major I. S. Gibb, MC (86/3/1).

304. Quoted in Short, *The Communist Insurrection in Malaya*, 138.

305. CO 537/3758, no 19, Letter from Sir Henry Gurney, British High Commissioner in Malaya, to Sir Thomas Lloyd, Permanent Undersecretary of State at the Colonial Office, October 8, 1948, in A. J. Stockwell, ed., *BDOEE: Series B: Volume 3: Malaya: Part II: The Communist Insurrection,* 73–75.

306. Short, *The Communist Insurrection in Malaya*, 173.

307. Rhodes House Library, Oxford University, Creech Jones Papers, Box 29, File 9, Telegram from Sir Henry Gurney, British High Commissioner in Malaya, to Arthur Creech Jones, Undersecretary of State for the Colonies, October 25, 1948. This telegram is also found in TNA, CO 717/167/52849/2/1948, Telegram from Sir Henry Gurney, British High Commissioner in Malaya, to Arthur Creech Jones, Undersecretary of State for the Colonies, October 25, 1948.

308. Rhodes House Library, Oxford University, Mss. Brit. Emp. s. 527, "End of Empire" Transcripts, 527/9/2, Interview with Hugh Humphrey, Malayan Civil Service, Secretary for Defence and Internal Security, Federation of Malaya, 1953–57, Interviewed by Desmond Smith. No date.

309. Ibid.
310. Stubbs, *Hearts and Minds in Guerilla Warfare*, 74.
311. TNA, CO 537/4762, Letter from J. D. Higham, Assistant Secretary and Head of the Eastern Department, Colonial Office, to Mr Blackburne, November 1948.
312. LHCMA, General Hugh Stockwell Papers, 6/26, "Morale in Palestine," by Major General H. C. Stockwell, Commandant, Royal Military Academy, Sandhurst, c. late 1948.
313. LHCMA, General Hugh Stockwell Papers, 6/26, "Lessons Learned in Palestine," by J. H. M. Hackett, November 17, 1948.
314. LHCMA, General Hugh Stockwell Papers, 6/26, "General Lessons from Palestine, 1945–1948," collated by General Stockwell, 1948.
315. This account is taken from interviews with Mrs Ching Yoong, Mrs Wong Foo Moi, and Mr Chung, survivors of this event, interviewed by Desmond Smith in 1981, transcripts held at the Rhodes House Library, Oxford University, Mss. Brit. Emp. s. 527, "End of Empire" Transcripts, 527/9/4.
316. HM Treasury [T] 220/86, Despatch no 1 from Sir Henry Gurney, British High Commissioner in Malaya, to Arthur Creech Jones, Secretary of State for the Colonies, January 8, 1949, in A. J. Stockwell, ed., *BDOEE: Series B: Volume 3: Malaya: Part II: The Communist Insurrection*, 102–10.
317. CO 927/1/1, no 59, Circular Despatch from George Hall, Colonial Secretary, to Governors, November 12, 1945, in Ronald Hyam, ed., *BDOEE: Series A: Volume 2: The Labour Government and the End of Empire, 1945–1951: Part II: Economics and International Relations*, 14.
318. CO 537/4750, no 35, Letter for Sir Henry Gurney, British High Commissioner in Malaya, to Arthur Creech Jones, Secretary of State for the Colonies, February 28, 1949, in A. J. Stockwell, ed., *BDOEE: Series B: Volume 3: Malaya: Part II: The Communist Insurrection*, 114–16.
319. Bodleian Library, Oxford University, Macmillan Papers, Dep. c. 420, Colonial Office Memorandum No. 27, "Notes on Recent Developments in the Federation of Malaya," February 1949.
320. CO 537/4751, no 80, [Security situation]: Despatch (reply) no 4 from Sir Henry Gurney, British High Commissioner in Malaya, to Arthur Creech Jones, Secretary of State for the Colonies, April 11, 1949, in A. J. Stockwell, ed., *BDOEE: Series B: Volume 3: Malaya: Part II: The Communist Insurrection*, 129–31.
321. Quoted in Noel Barber, *The War of the Running Dogs: The Malayan Emergency: 1948–1960* (New York: Weybright and Talley, 1971), 62.

322. Richard L. Clutterbuck, *The Long, Long War: Counterinsurgency in Malaya and Vietnam* (New York: Frederick A. Praeger, 1966), 43.
323. CO 537/4751, no 80, [Security situation]: Despatch (reply) no 4 from Sir Henry Gurney, British High Commissioner in Malaya, to Arthur Creech Jones, Secretary of State for the Colonies, April 11, 1949, in A. J. Stockwell, ed., *BDOEE: Series B: Volume 3: Malaya: Part II: The Communist Insurrection*, 129–31.
324. CO 537/4773, no 3, [Insurgency and counter-insurgency]: Despatch no 5 from Sir Henry Gurney, British High Commissioner in Malaya, to Arthur Creech Jones, Secretary of State for the Colonies, May 30, 1949, in ibid., 133–43.
325. WO 279/391, "Imperial Policing and Duties in Aid of the Civil Power, 1949," issued by Command of the Army Council, June 13, 1949.
326. Clutterbuck, *The Long, Long War: Counterinsurgency in Malaya and Vietnam*, 52.
327. Ibid., 54.
328. IWM, DoD, Papers of N. A. Martin (02/19/1), Unpublished memoir, written by Martin, titled "The Day the Sun Stopped Shining." Quote taken from pages 66–7.
329. Rhodes House Library, Oxford University, Creech Jones Papers, Box 57, File 2, Despatch from Sir Henry Gurney, British High Commissioner in Malaya, to Arthur Creech Jones, Secretary of State for the Colonies, January 12, 1950.
330. TNA, FO 371/84477, Telegram from Sir Henry Gurney, British High Commissioner in Malaya, to Arthur Creech Jones, Secretary of State for the Colonies, February 23, 1950.
331. Robert Pearce, *Attlee's Labour Governments, 1945–1951* (London and New York: Routledge, 1994), 18.
332. Ibid., 32–3.
333. Ibid., 35.
334. Ibid., 40.
335. Churchill Archives Centre, Churchill College, Cambridge [Churchill Archives Centre], Sir Winston Churchill Papers [CHUR 2], Box 143, Letter from Sir Winston Churchill, Leader of the Conservative Party, to Viscount Montgomery, Chief of the Imperial General Staff, June 4, 1948.
336. Churchill Archives Centre, CHUR 2/143, Letter from Viscount Montgomery, Chief of the Imperial General Staff, to Winston Churchill, Leader of the Conservative Party, June 7, 1948.
337. Churchill Archives Centre, CHUR 2/143, Letter from Viscount Montgomery, Chief of the Imperial General Staff, to Winston Churchill, Leader of the Conservative Party, June 10, 1948.

338. Bodleian Library, Oxford University, Harold Macmillan Papers [Macmillan Papers], Dep. c. 890, Speech given by Harold Macmillan, January 15, 1949, at Bromley, Kent.

339. Churchill Archives Centre, Oliver Lyttelton Papers [CHAN II], Box 4, File 5, Letter from Oliver Lyttelton, Conservative Member of Parliament, to Winston Churchill, Leader of the Conservative Party, March 4, 1949.

340. Ibid.

341. Headlam, *Diaries*, 613.

342. Pelling, *The Labour Governments*, 227.

343. Quoted in ibid., 230.

344. Headlam, *Diaries*, 621.

345. Rhodes House Library, Oxford University, Creech Jones Papers, Box 32, File 3, Letter from Harold J. Locker, London School of Economics, to Arthur Creech Jones, Secretary of State for the Colonies, January 30, 1950.

346. Quoted in Pelling, *The Labour Governments*, 231.

347. Rhodes House Library, Oxford University, Mss. Brit. Emp. s. 525, Transcript of an interview with Oliver Lyttelton, Lord Chandos, interviewed by Max Beloff, Gladstone Professor of Government and Public Administration, February 27, 1970. Lyttelton was not the only man to voice this opinion. The historian David Goldsworthy has written that Griffiths was "characterized by a warm-hearted and rather emotional approach to public affairs." Goldsworthy, *Colonial Issues in British Politics*, 22.

348. Goldsworthy, *Colonial Issues in British Politics*, 22. Griffiths believed Creech Jones to be "one of the outstanding Colonial Secretaries of the twentieth century."

349. PREM 8/1406/2, [Director of Operations]: Minute by Emmanuel Shinwell, Minister of Defense, to Clement Attlee, Prime Minister, March 7, 1950, in A. J. Stockwell, ed., *BDOEE: Series B: Volume 3: Malaya: Part II: The Communist Insurrection*, 194.

350. TNA, FO 371/84477, Telegram from Sir Henry Gurney, British High Commissioner to Malaya, to James Griffiths, Secretary of State for the Colonies, March 9, 1950. The full text of the proposed announcement read as follows: "The Government of the Federation of Malaya has appointed (blank) as Director of Operations to plan, co-ordinate and generally direct anti-bandit operations of Police and fighting forces. The post is a civil one. The Director of Operations will be responsible for the allocation of tasks to various components of the Security Forces available for operations and for deciding, in consultation with heads of the Police Force and fighting services, the priorities between these tasks and general timing and

sequence of their execution. His primary function will be to secure full and effective co-ordination."

351. Edgar O'Ballance, *Malaya: The Communist Insurgent War, 1948–1960* (Hamden, CT: Archon Books, 1966), 106.

352. Short, *The Communist Insurrection in Malaya*, 235.

353. TNA, CAB 21/2510, Memorandum from Sir Norman Brook, Secretary of the Cabinet, to Clement Attlee, Prime Minister, March 29, 1950.

354. TNA, CAB 21/2510, Memorandum from W. Elliot and A. Johnson, Cabinet Office, to the Cabinet, April 5, 1950.

355. Bodleian Library, Oxford University, Macmillan Papers, Dep. c. 420, Colonial Office Memorandum No. 2, "The Political, Economic and Social Development of the British Colonies," by Sir William McLean, March 1950 (revised edition).

356. TNA, CO 875/72/1, Statement by the Federal Government on the Conclusion of Anti-Bandit Month, April 5, 1950.

357. The Ferret Force only lasted from July to November 1948. Composed largely of former Force 136 officers, its purpose was to "go and live in the jungle, to establish good relations with the aborigines and locate and destroy the guerillas either by themselves or in conjunction with regular forces." It was disbanded due to the regular army's dislike of "private armies." Because of its short duration, it did not have a great effect on the course of the emergency. See Short, *The Communist Insurrection in Malaya*, 132–3.

358. See Sir Robert Thompson, *Make for the Hills: Memories of Far Eastern Wars* (London: Leo Cooper, 1989), especially chapter 9.

359. Quoted in Barber, *The War of the Running Dogs*, 96.

360. Ibid., 97.

361. TNA, CAB 21/1681, Directive No. 1, Director of Operations, Malaya, April 16, 1950.

362. Ibid.

363. TNA, CAB 21/1681, Directive No. 2, Director of Operations, Malaya, May 12, 1950.

364. Barber, *The War of the Running Dogs*, 97. Although known as the Briggs Plan, this was in fact written in large part by Thompson.

365. TNA, CAB 21/1861, Federation Plan for the Elimination of the Communist Organisation and Armed Forces in Malaya, May 24, 1950.

366. Ibid.

367. TNA, CO 537/5984, Definition of Terrorism, laid down in the Federation of Malaya Government Gazette, July 13, 1950, No. 32, Vol. III, L.N. 302 in the Emergency (Amendment No. 12) Regs, 1950.

368. Short, *The Communist Insurrection in Malaya*, 384.

369. Quoted in Morgan, *Labour in Power*, 410.
370. Quoted in Pelling, *The Labour Governments*, 235.
371. Churchill Archives Centre, CHAN II 4/15, Letter from Sir Alan Frederick "Tommy" Lascelles to Oliver Lyttelton, Conservative Member of Parliament, April 23, 1950.
372. Churchill Archives Centre, CHAN II 4/15, Letter from Oliver Lyttelton, Conservative Member of Parliament, to Winston Churchill, Leader of the Conservative Party, April 25, 1950.
373. Churchill Archives Centre, CHAN II 4/15, Letter from Winston Churchill, Leader of the Conservative Party, to Oliver Lyttelton, Conservative Member of Parliament, May 3, 1950.
374. Churchill Archives Centre, CHAN II 4/15, Letter from Oliver Lyttelton, Conservative Member of Parliament, to Sir Alan Frederick "Tommy" Lascelles, May 4, 1950.
375. TNA, CAB 21/1681, Minutes of the Chiefs of Staff Meeting to discuss the Use of Special Operations Techniques in Malaya, June 2, 1950.
376. See David Rooney, *Mad Mike: A Life of Michael Calvert* (London: Leo Cooper, 1997), especially chapters 5 and 6.
377. Michael Calvert, *Fighting Mad: One Man's Guerilla War* (Barnsley, South Yorkshire, UK: Pen & Sword, 2004), 94.
378. Michael Asher, *The Regiment: The Real Story of the SAS* (London: Penguin Books, 2008), 277.
379. See Rooney, *Mad Mike*, chapter 7.
380. Asher, *The Regiment*, 287–91.
381. Calvert, *Fighting Mad*, 200–1.
382. Asher, *The Regiment*, 298–9.
383. TNA, WO 32/12362, "The Organization of SAS Troops," August 30, 1949.
384. TNA, WO 32/13867, War Office Report on the Establishment of the Special Air Service Corps, May 22, 1950.
385. Calvert, *Fighting Mad*, 201.
386. Letter from General Harding, Commander in Chief, Far East, to Michael Calvert, quoted in Rooney, *Mad Mike*, 135.
387. Quoted in Asher, *The Regiment*, 302.
388. Ibid., 302–3.
389. Calvert, *Fighting Mad*, 205.
390. Rooney, *Mad Mike*, 137.
391. Ibid., 139.
392. Calvert, *Fighting Mad*, 205–6.
393. Rooney, *Mad Mike*, 143–5.
394. Ibid., 148.
395. Calvert, *Fighting Mad*, 208.

396. "'Mad Mike' of Burma Leads Scout Squadron," *Bulawayo Chronicle*, March 11, 1951, found in TSC, NAM 1997-04-58, Papers relating to 'C' (Rhodesia) Squadron, 22 SAS, Malaya.

397. Quoted in Rooney, *Mad Mike*, 154.

398. Ibid., 149–50.

399. Rhodes House Library, Oxford, Creech Jones Papers, Box 26, File 9, Paper written by the Central Office of Information Reference Division, "A Brief Economic Review of Malaya: 1945/49," June 10, 1950.

400. CAB 129/40, CP (50) 125, Cabinet Memorandum: "Preliminary report on a visit to Malaya and Singapore," by James Griffiths, Secretary of State for the Colonies, June 13, 1950, in A. J. Stockwell, ed., *BDOEE: Series B: Volume 3: Malaya: Part II: The Communist Insurrection*, 231–3.

401. Cab 128/17, CM 37 (5) 1, "Malaya": Cabinet Conclusions on reports by James Griffiths, Secretary of State for the Colonies, and John Strachey, Secretary of State for War, following their visits to Malaya, June 19, 1950, in ibid., 239–42.

402. William Stueck, *The Korean War: An International History* (Princeton: Princeton University Press, 1995), 11.

403. Security Council resolutions quoted in ibid., 12.

404. Max Hastings, *The Korean War* (New York: Simon and Schuster, 1987), 60–61.

405. Ibid., 70.

406. Stueck, *The Korean War*, 72.

407. TNA, CAB 21/1681, Memorandum by James Griffiths, Secretary of State for the Colonies, for the Malaya Committee of the Cabinet, "Malaya—General Background," July 14, 1950.

408. TNA, CAB 21/1681, Memorandum by James Griffiths, Secretary of State for the Colonies, for the Malaya Committee of the Cabinet, "Malaya—Various Matters," July 14, 1950.

409. TNA, CAB 21/1681, Minutes of a Meeting Held by the Malaya Committee of the Cabinet, with Robert Menzies, Prime Minister of Malaya, in attendance, July 17, 1950.

410. Richard Stubbs, "Counter-Insurgency and the Economic Factor: The Impact of the Korean War Prices Boom on the Malayan Emergency" (Occasional Paper No. 19, The Institute of Southeast Asian Studies, 1974), 3.

411. Ibid., 9.

412. Ibid., 13. Please note that all figures given here are in Malaysian dollars. In the exchange rate at the time, one Malaysian dollar equaled 33 U.S. cents, and 2s 4d sterling. See Ibid., 1, footnote 1.

413. Ibid.

414. Cab 21/1681, Memorandum by the British Defence Co-ordination Committee, Far East, August 9, 1950.

415. TNA, AIR 23/8437, "Note on a Meeting Held at Air Headquarters Malaya to Discuss Air/Army Co-operation in the Anti-Bandit Campaign," August 9, 1950.

416. TNA, CAB 21/1681, "The Present Situation in Malaya," A Memorandum by James Griffiths, Secretary of State for the Colonies, to the Malaya Committee of the Cabinet, September 22, 1950.

417. TNA, CO 537/5873, Letter from Sir W. N. P. Jenkin, Technical Adviser to the Malayan Police Intelligence, to the Acting Chief Secretary, Government of the Federation of Malaya, November 10, 1950.

418. TNA, CO 537/5973, Telegram from Sir Henry Gurney, British High Commissioner in Malaya, to Stafford Foster Sutton, Malayan Attorney General, November 15, 1950.

419. TNA, CO 537/5973, Letter from Stafford Foster Sutton, Malayan Attorney General, to Sir Henry Gurney, British High Commissioner in Malaya, November 17, 1950.

420. Short, *The Communist Insurrection in Malaya*, 276.

421. TNA, CAB 21/1682, "An Appreciation of the Military and Political Situation in Malaya," by General Harold Briggs, Director of Operations, Forwarded to the Chief of Staffs Committee of the Cabinet, November 16, 1950.

422. TNA, CAB 21/1682, Minutes of a Meeting Held by the Chiefs of Staff Committee of the Cabinet, November 23, 1950.

423. TNA, CAB 21/1682, Minutes of a Meeting Held Between General Harold Briggs, Director of Operations, and Clement Attlee, Prime Minister, with Sir Henry Gurney and Cabinet Secretaries Present, November 24, 1950.

424. TNA, CAB 21/2884, "Progress Report on Situation in Malaya," by General Harold Briggs, Director of Operations, Malaya, February 15, 1951.

425. TNA, CO 1022/32, Director of Operations Malaya Directive No. 13, "Administration of Chinese Settlements," February 26, 1951.

426. Stubbs, *Hearts and Minds in Guerilla Warfare*, 166.

427. TNA, CO 537/7280, Statement on Collective Fines, February 27, 1951.

428. PREM 8/1406/1, GEN 345/5, "Cabinet Office Summary of a Meeting at 10 Downing Street on 26 Feb Called by Mr Attlee to Consider the [Briggs] Plan's Slow Progress," in A. J. Stockwell, ed., *BDOEE: Series B: Volume 3: Malaya: Part II: The Communist Insurrection*, 277–9.

429. TNA, CAB 21/2884, Minutes of Cabinet Meeting, March 12, 1951.

430. CO 967/145, Letter from Sir Henry Gurney, British High Commissioner in Malaya, to Sir Thomas Lloyd, Permanent

Undersecretary of State at the Colonial Office, March 19, 1951, in A. J. Stockwell, ed., *BDOEE: Series B: Volume 3: Malaya: Part II: The Communist Insurrection*, 286–7.

431. CO 967/145, Letter from Sir Thomas Lloyd, Permanent Undersecretary of State at the Colonial Office, to Sir Henry Gurney, British High Commissioner in Malaya, April 5, 1951, in A. J. Stockwell, ed., *BDOEE: Series B: Volume 3: Malaya: Part II: The Communist Insurrection*, 286–7.

432. TNA, CO 875/71/6, Collection of British Propaganda Leaflets Used in the Anti-Communist Campaign in Malaya, Beginning April 1951.

433. Stubbs, *Hearts and Minds in Guerilla Warfare*, 180.

434. Ibid., 181.

435. Ibid., 182.

436. O'Ballance, *Malaya: The Communist Insurgent War*, 105. See also Clutterbuck, *Conflict and Violence in Singapore and Malaysia*, 193–4.

437. TNA, WO 32/16138, Letter from Emmanuel Shinwell, Minister for Defense, to Clement Attlee, Prime Minister, April 28, 1951.

438. TNA, WO 32/16138, Letter from Emmanuel Shinwell, Minister for Defense, to Field Marshal Sir William Slim, May 3, 1951.

439. TNA, WO 32/16138, Letter from Field Marshal Sir William Slim, Chief of the Imperial General Staff, to Emmanuel Shinwell, Minister of Defense, May 4, 1951.

440. TNA, WO 32/16138, Letter from Emmanuel Shinwell, Minister of Defense, to Clement Attlee, Prime Minister, May 21, 1951.

441. TNA, CAB 21/2884, Combined Appreciation of the Emergency Situation by the High Commissioner and the Director of Operations, June 4, 1951.

442. This account is taken from Barber, *The War of the Running Dogs*, 130–1, and Stubbs, *Hearts and Minds in Guerilla Warfare*, 132.

443. FO 371/93118, no. 2, Telegram from M. V. del Tufo, Malayan Chief Secretary, to James Griffiths, Secretary of State for the Colonies, October 6, 1951, in A. J. Stockwell, ed., *BDOEE: Series B: Volume 3: Malaya: Part II: The Communist Insurrection*, 301–2.

444. See Hastings, *The Korean War*, especially 128–91.

445. Stueck, *The Korean War*, 129.

446. Anthony Farrar-Hockley, "The Post-War Army, 1945–1963," in David G. Chandler and Ian Beckett, eds, *The Oxford History of the British Army* (Oxford: Oxford University Press, 1994), 321.

447. Ibid., 324–8.

448. Quoted in Morgan, *Labour in Power*, 424.

449. Headlam, *Diaries*, 630.

450. Pelling, *The Labour Governments*, 247.

451. Morgan, *Labour in Power*, 439–40.

452. Quoted in Pelling, *The Labour Governments*, 247.
453. Ibid.
454. Ibid., 248.
455. Attlee, *As it Happened*, 276.
456. Pelling, *The Labour Governments*, 249–50.
457. Attlee, *As it Happened*, 285.
458. Pelling, *The Labour Governments*, 249–50.
459. Ibid., 257.
460. Morgan, *Labour in Power*, 484.
461. Ibid., 485–6.
462. Pelling, *The Labour Governments*, 259.

2 The Churchill Years

1. For the most readable biography of Churchill's life, see Roy Jenkins, *Churchill: A Biography* (New York: Farrar, Straus and Giroux, 2001).
2. Winston S. Churchill, Speech to the House of Commons, November 6, 1951, in Robert Rhodes James, ed., *Winston S. Churchill: His Complete Speeches, 1897–1963: Volume VIII, 1950–1963* (New York and London: Chelsea House Publishers, 1974), 8289–8297.
3. Oliver Lyttelton, Viscount Chandos, *The Memoirs of Lord Chandos: An Unexpected View from the Summit* (New York: New American Library, 1963), 328.
4. Ibid., 348.
5. Lockhart proved to be an able and effective replacement for Briggs, a man who inherently understood the intricacies of counterinsurgency warfare. Within days of taking up his position, Lockhart scribbled for himself a note of the "Golden Rules for Anti-Bandit Warfare," which he kept as a constant reminder of the chief operating principles. His rules were as follows: "Always be on the look-out and ready for something new and unexpected. Always be alert, inquisitive and suspicious. Always check anything anyone you don't know left you. Always make certain that movement is covered by fire. Never take anything for granted. Never relax precautions, even if other troops are protecting you. Never do anything in the same way, or at the same time twice running or often. Never imagine that because nothing has happened for some time it won't happen at any moment. Never enter a defile unless its flanks have been searched or it is guarded by other troops. Never move alone or off sight or close range of a comrade. Never do nothing if attacked. Take bold action immediately. Never adopt the obvious course of action simply because it's the easiest. Never leave evidence of a bivouac area.

The bandit intelligence is good. Never underestimate your enemy because he is cunning and often brave." TSC, NAM 1995-01-165-85, "Golden Rules for Anti-Bandit Warfare."

6. Lyttelton, *The Memoirs of Lord Chandos*, 348.

7. PREM 11/122, Minute from Oliver Lyttelton, Secretary of State for the Colonies, to Winston Churchill, Prime Minister, October 30, 1951, in A. J. Stockwell, ed., *BDOEE: Series B: Volume 3: Malaya: Part II: The Communist Insurrection*, 304.

8. Lyttelton, *The Memoirs of Lord Chandos*, 348–349.

9. *Parliamentary Debates (Hansard)*, House of Commons, Fifth Series, Volume 493, October 31–November 16, 1951 (London: His Majesty's Stationary Office, 1951), November 14, 1951, column 984.

10. Lyttelton, *The Memoirs of Lord Chandos*, 337. Lyttelton gives a full, and enlightening, explanation behind his logic for this policy in his memoirs, where he writes: "The reasons for this bald [*sic*] statement are not far to seek. The first reason is that we do not have the force to govern without the consent of the governed. The second is that with modern communications, consent has to be engaged by open and candid discussion of policy. In the days of Queen Victoria we had the force. British power policed the world and kept it at peace. African potentates sought Her Majesty's protection. A stiff letter and a gunboat, or a small show of force, soon calmed disorder and faction. Above all, the white man was supposed to know the answers. No pan-African movement could be conceived, much less brought to birth, because the communications between one part of Africa and another were primitive and too slow to carry the flame of the nationalist aspirations of one territory and set alight the same fire in another. Today the African no longer lives in a world of his own. The newspapers, now the *Guardian* and the *Mirror*, now the *Daily Telegraph* or *The Times*, or *Life*, tell different stories and propose conflicting policies. If the white man knows the answers, they are not all the same answers. ... Even if it were desired to rule without engaging the consent of the governed, and in my opinion it certainly should not be, that consent is a plain necessity in the nineteen-fifties in multi-racial societies. If such a policy is enlightened, well and good, but necessary it surely is" (337–338).

11. TNA, CO 1022/7, Telegram from the Federation of Malaya to Oliver Lyttelton, Secretary of State for the Colonies, November 1, 1951, sent at 10.10 hours.

12. TNA, CO 1022/7, Telegram from the Federation of Malaya to Oliver Lyttelton, Secretary of State for the Colonies, November 1, 1951, sent at 11.10 hours. See also, "Memorandum: Organisation for Dealing with Emergency Matters," November 1951, in General Sir Robert Lockhart Papers, TSC, NAM 1995-01-165-27.

13. FO 371/116969, no 14, Telegram from Malcolm MacDonald, Commissioner-General of British Territories in Southeast Asia, to Sir Thomas Lloyd, Permanent Under Secretary of State at the Colonial Office, November 5, 1951, in A. J. Stockwell, ed., *BDOEE: Series B: Volume 3: Malaya: Part II: The Communist Insurrection*, 306–307.

14. TNA, WO 216/450, "The Military Implications of the Situation in Malaya: Note by the War Office," The War Office, November 19, 1951.

15. TNA, CAB 21/2884, "The Situation in Malaya," Memorandum by Oliver Lyttelton, Secretary of State for the Colonies, November 20, 1951.

16. TNA, CAB 21/2884, "Annex I: Conclusions of the British Defence Co-Ordination Committee (Far East)," November 15, 1951.

17. TNA, CAB 21/2884, "Annex II: The Situation in Malaya," Report from the Colonial Office.

18. TNA, CAB 21/2884, "Annex III: Forces Engaged in Malaya."

19. CAB 128/23, CC 10 (51) 2, "'Malaya': Cabinet conclusions on the current situation and Mr. Lyttelton's forthcoming visit," November 22, 1951, in A. J. Stockwell, ed., *BDOEE: Series B: Volume 3: Malaya: Part II: The Communist Insurrection*, 315–316.

20. Lyttelton, *The Memoirs of Lord Chandos*, 351–352.

21. "The Situation in the Federation of Malaya from the Point of View of the Director of Operations," November 26, 1951, in the General Sir Robert Lockhart Papers, TSC, NAM 1995-01-165-28.

22. Lyttelton, *The Memoirs of Lord Chandos*, 352.

23. Ibid., 359.

24. PREM 11/639, f 51, Telegram from Oliver Lyttelton, Secretary of State for the Colonies, to Winston Churchill, Prime Minister, December 8, 1951, in A. J. Stockwell, ed., *BDOEE: Series B: Volume 3: Malaya: Part II: The Communist Insurrection*, 317–318.

25. CAB 129/ 48, C (51) 59, "Malaya," Cabinet Memorandum by Oliver Lyttelton, Secretary of State for the Colonies, December 21, 1951, in A. J. Stockwell, ed., *BDOEE: Series B: Volume 3: Malaya: Part II: The Communist Insurrection*, 318–331.

26. Quote given in the introduction to ibid., 318.

27. Lyttelton, *The Memoirs of Lord Chandos*, 363.

28. Ibid., 364.

29. PREM 11/121, Letter from Field Marshal Lord Montgomery, Deputy Supreme Allied Commander in Europe, to Oliver Lyttelton, Secretary of State for the Colonies, December 27, 1951, in A. J. Stockwell, ed., *BDOEE: Series B: Volume 3: Malaya: Part II: The Communist Insurrection*, 353–355.

30. Whereas Briggs had been quick to make up his mind and issue orders that were to be obeyed without question, Lockhart followed a more deliberative approach, causing some to question his suitability for overall command of the emergency situation. A perusal of Lockhart's papers makes this difference in approach abundantly clear. On December 12, 1952, for example, Lockhart circulated a memorandum titled, "Points of Policy for Consideration or Review," which asked a series of questions displaying an uncertainty foreign to Briggs: "Is our present system the best we can devise? ... Chinese: Policy towards: is it to be one of encouragement or severity and compulsion or a mixture of both? ... Detention: I understand we haven't sufficient detainees to fill a ship. Is this true?" (TSC, NAM 1995-01-165-36) Such a style of leadership continued until he was relieved. At a meeting on December 17, he raised the possibility of releasing residents from the resettlement villages after four years only to be "shot down" (NAM 1995-01-165-37). On December 22, he released a memorandum listing a number of questions, including such eclectic suggestions as: "Do we 'show the flag' enough? ... Is acting on information the best way of obtaining results or could we do better by trying to dominate areas by more active patrolling, much of which would be devoted to ambushes? ... Is sufficient stress laid on the necessity for cunning, silence and concealment? ... Could we use deception methods at all? ... Would special 'gangster' units be of any value?" In this same memorandum, Lockhart questioned whether the security forces could use elephants as transport and flame throwers as weaponry in the jungle. (NAM 1995-01-165-38) His style was to make a careful study of the situation and then implement a reasoned and researched plan. Lyttelton wished to see a more proactive approach.

31. PREM 11/639, Telegram from Oliver Lyttelton, Secretary of State for the Colonies, to Winston Churchill, Prime Minister, January 4, 1952, in A. J. Stockwell, ed., *BDOEE: Series B: Volume 3: Malaya: Part II: The Communist Insurrection*, 356.

32. Stubbs, *Hearts and Minds in Guerilla Warfare*, 140.

33. Henry Pelling, *Churchill's Peacetime Ministry, 1951–55* (New York and Basingstoke, Hampshire, UK: Macmillan Press, Ltd., 1997), 28.

34. PREM 11/639, Minute from Sir Gerald Templer, soon to be High Commissioner and Director of Operations in Malaya, to Winston Churchill, Prime Minister, January 12, 1952, in A. J. Stockwell, ed., *BDOEE: Series B: Volume 3: Malaya: Part II: The Communist Insurrection*, 361.

35. Stubbs, *Hearts and Minds in Guerilla Warfare*, 140–141; and A. J. Stockwell, ed., *BDOEE: Series B: Volume 3: Malaya: Part II: The Communist Insurrection*, 372.

36. TSC, NAM 1995-01-165-40, General Sir Robert Lockhart Papers, Telegram from General Sir Robert Lockhart, Director of Operations in Malaya, to Field Marshal Sir William Slim, Chief of the Imperial General Staff, January 14, 1952.

37. TSC, NAM 1995-01-165-53, Letter from General Sir Robert Lockhart, Out Going Director of Operations in Malaya, to General Sir Gerald Templer, In Coming Director of Operations in Malaya, January 27, 1952.

38. TNA, CAB 21/2884, Directive to Sir Gerald Templer, High Commissioner and Director of Operations in Malaya, from Oliver Lyttelton, Secretary of State for the Colonies, on behalf of Her Majesty's Government in the United Kingdom, February 7, 1952. A copy is also found in Rhodes House Library, Oxford University, Creech Jones Papers, Box 26, File 9.

39. TSC, NAM 1995-01-165-56, General Sir Robert Lockhart Papers, "A Message to the People of the Federation of Malaya," leaflet issued by General Sir Gerald Templer on his arrival in the Federation of Malaya as High Commissioner and Director of Operations, February 7, 1952.

40. Barber, *The War of the Running Dogs*, 157.

41. Quoted in Stubbs, *Hearts and Minds in Guerilla Warfare*, 145.

42. Rhodes House Library, Oxford University, Mss. Brit. Emp. s. 527, "End of Empire" Transcripts, 527/9/1, Interview with Leslie Davis, Malayan Civil Service, Interviewed by Desmond Smith, August 1981.

43. Stubbs, *Hearts and Minds in Guerilla Warfare*, 146.

44. Quoted in Benjamin Grob-Fitzgibbon, "Securing the Colonies for the Commonwealth: Counterinsurgency, Decolonization, and the Development of British Imperial Strategy in the Postwar Empire," *British Scholar*, Volume II, Issue 1 (September 2009), 31. It should be noted that Templer was the first to coin this oft-repeated phrase.

45. Quoted in Stubbs, *Hearts and Minds in Guerilla Warfare*, 148.

46. TNA, CO 1022/22, Report for Oliver Lyttelton, Secretary of State for the Colonies, by Hugh Fraser, Parliamentary Private Secretary for Mr Lyttelton, January 16, 1952. The Police Jungle Companies had been authorized by Lockhart on November 26, 1951, in his second operation instruction as director of operations. This instruction read, in part: "To maintain permanently a force capable of dealing with well-armed criminals, it was decided to group a specific number of Jungle Squads on a Company basis. This method is designed to improve efficiency and training, and to simplify command and administration. But the essential characteristics of the Jungle Squad, operating under its own Command, have been retained and will be found whether the Company operates as a complete unit, by Platoons or by individual squads. Jungle Companies are not the equivalent of military infantry

companies. ... But it is the intention that they will relieve military units of certain police tasks now being carried out by the military, which can then concentrate on purely military tasks." "Extract from Director of Operations Instruction No. 2," November 26, 1951, General Sir Robert Lockhart Papers, TSC, NAM 1995-01-165-01.

47. Barber, *The War of the Running Dogs*, 147.

48. Stubbs, *Hearts and Minds in Guerilla Warfare*, 143. Young intentionally sought to exude such confidence, as he wrote in an appreciation of the Malaya police force in March 1952: "The immediate tasks of the Commissioner are to inspire leadership, to ensure confidence, to define command, to distinguish responsibility and to secure common and effective standards which will make common purposes possible. In short, to ensure that everyone is given a sufficient definition of his duty, a reasonable instruction and guidance in his task, and afforded the opportunity and time to fulfil it." He was convinced that he would succeed in this task: "The success of the Police in Malaya is not in doubt; it is as certain as the triumph of righteousness itself. The issue is solely how soon can success be achieved. Despite all difficulties, the duty of the Police in Malaya is fortified and indeed inspired by the fact that it is the most difficult, the most dangerous and perhaps even the most important Police responsibility in all the world." TSC, NAM 1995-01-165-14, "An Appreciation of the Basic Situation by the Commissioner," A. E. Young, Commissioner of Police, March 1952.

49. TNA, CO 1022/51, Minutes of Meeting Between Sir Gerald Templer, High Commissioner and Director of Operations in Malaya, and the Cabinet Malaya Committee, January 31, 1952.

50. TNA, CO 1022/51, Telegram from Sir Gerald Templer, High Commissioner and Director of Operations in Malaya, to Oliver Lyttelton, Secretary of State for the Colonies, February 13, 1952.

51. Christopher Andrew, *The Defence of the Realm: The Authorized History of MI5* (London: Allen Lane, 2009), 449–450.

52. TSC, NAM 1995-01-165-58, Papers of General Sir Robert Lockhart, Memorandum from General Sir Gerald Templer, distributed to the Deputy High Commissioner, the Deputy Director of Operations, the GOC Malaya, the Secretary of Defense, and the Commissioner of Police, February 13, 1952.

53. TNA, CO 1022/51, Minutes of Meeting Between Sir Gerald Templer, High Commissioner and Director of Operations in Malaya, and the Cabinet Malaya Committee, January 31, 1952.

54. TNA, WO 216/494, "Malayan Scouts-Special Air Service Regiment," Report by General Headquarters, Far East Land Forces, December 22, 1951.

55. Asher, *The Regiment*, 310. Asher mistakenly suggests that this name change took place in the months prior to Templer being appointed high commissioner. It was, in fact, a decision Templer took himself, on the advice of General Headquarters, Far East Land Forces, shortly after being appointed high commissioner and director of operations, although prior to him arriving in Malaya.

56. Ibid., 323–325.

57. CO 1022/60, no. 3, Telegram from Sir Gerald Templer, High Commissioner and Director of Operations, to Oliver Lyttelton, Secretary of State for the Colonies, February 28, 1952, in A. J. Stockwell, ed., *BDOEE: Series B: Volume 3: Malaya: Part II: The Communist Insurrection*, 373–376.

58. Barber, *The War of the Running Dogs*, 157–159.

59. Stubbs, *Hearts and Minds in Guerilla Warfare*, 165.

60. Ibid., 168–169.

61. TNA, CO 1022/29, Note for UN Brief: "New Villages in the Federation of Malaya," April 1952.

62. Stubbs, *Hearts and Minds in Guerilla Warfare*, 170.

63. TSC, NAM 1995-01-165-69, General Sir Robert Lockhart Papers, General Circular No. 5 of 1952, issuing the High Commissioner's Objective, March 31, 1952.

64. TSC, NAM 1995-01-165-70, General Sir Robert Lockhart Papers, Letter from Major General R. E. Urquhart, Army General Officer Commanding Malaya, to General Sir Gerald Templer, High Commissioner and Director of Operations in Malaya, April 7, 1952.

65. Briggs first introduced food control operations on June 16, 1951, by designating certain "Restricted Articles" that were heavily regulated, and creating "Food Restriction Areas" for communities that consistently violated the Restricted Articles regulations. For specific detail on these regulations, see "Food Movement Control ... Why? A Message from the Director of Operations, Sir Harold Briggs, to the People of Malaya," Issued by the Department of Information, Federation of Malaya, June 16, 1951, in TSC, NAM 1995-01-165-22, General Sir Robert Lockhart Papers.

66. TNA, CO 1022/26, Notes on a meeting held at the Colonial Office, January 14, 1952.

67. TNA, CO 1022/26, Memorandum for Oliver Lyttelton, Secretary of State for the Colonies, to Sir Gerald Templer, High Commissioner and Director of Operations in Malaya, April 7, 1952.

68. TNA, CO 1022/26, Statement on the Use of Chemical Defoliation, April 9, 1952.

69. TNA, CO 1022/26, Press Statement by the Royal Air Force's Far East Air Force, April 14, 1952.

70. TNA, CO 1022/317, Advice Given to Oliver Lyttelton, Secretary of State for the Colonies, by Sir Gerald Templer, High Commissioner and Director Operations in Malaya, April 21, 1952.

71. *Parliamentary Debates (Hansard)*, House of Commons, Fifth Series, Volume 499, April 21–May 2, 1952 (London: His Majesty's Stationary Office, 1952), April 23, 1952, columns 394–395.

72. Ibid.

73. Ibid., April 30, 1952, columns1453–1455.

74. TNA, CO 1022/55, Government Press Statement on Selangor, April 10, 1952.

75. TNA, CO 1022/55, Government Press Statement on Sungei Pelek, April 22, 1952.

76. TNA, CO 1022/55, Telegram from Sir Gerald Templer, High Commissioner and Director of Operations in Malaya, to Oliver Lyttelton, Secretary of State for the Colonies, April 25, 1952.

77. TNA, CO 1022/152, Malayan Federal Government Press Statement, April 30, 1952.

78. TNA, CO 1022/26, "Precautions to be Taken During the Handling of Sodium Trichloroacetate (S.T.C.A.)," Institute for Medical Research, Kuala Lumpur, May 1952.

79. TNA, CO 1022/56, Malayan Federal Government Press Statement, May 11, 1952.

80. TNA, WO 216/541, Letter from Sir Gerald Templer, High Commissioner and Director of Operations in Malaya, to Field Marshal Sir William Slim, Chief of the Imperial General Staff, May 15, 1952.

81. TNA, WO 216/541, Note from Field Marshal Sir William Slim, Chief of the Imperial General Staff, to Lt Col C. H. P. Harrington, Military Assistant to the Chief of the Imperial General Staff, May 15, 1952.

82. TNA, WO 216/541, Letter from Lt Col C. H. P. Harrington, Military Assistant to the Chief of the Imperial General Staff, to Ernest Hall, Deputy Director-General of the Army Medical Service, May 26, 1952.

83. TNA, WO 216/541, Letter from Ernest Hall, Deputy Director-General of the Army Medical Service, to Lt Col C. H. P. Harrington, Military Assistant to the Chief of the Imperial General Staff, May 28, 1952.

84. TNA, WO 216/541, Letter from Field Marshal Sir William Slim, Chief of the Imperial General Staff, to Sir Gerald Templer, High Commissioner and Director of Operations, May 29, 1952.

85. TNA, CO 1022/48, Memorandum from the Executive Council for Sir Gerald Templer, High Commissioner and Director of Operations in Malaya, May 17, 1952.

86. TNA, CO 1022/48, Extract from the Minutes of the Federal Executive Council, May 20, 1952.

87. Churchill Archives Centre, CHAN II 4/17/11, Oliver Lyttelton's Speech at the Corona Club Dinner, June 17, 1952.
88. David Anderson, *Histories of the Hanged: The Dirty War in Kenya and the End of Empire* (New York and London: W.W. Norton & Company, 2005), 47.
89. T. C. McCaskie, "Cultural Encounters: Britain and Africa in the Nineteenth Century," in Philip D. Morgan and Sean Hawkins, eds, *Black Experience and the Empire* (Oxford: Oxford University Press, 2004), 175–177.
90. Elspeth Huxley, *White Man's Country: Lord Delamere and the Making of Kenya: Volume One, 1870–1914* (London: Chatto and Whindus, 1953), 3.
91. See John S. Galbraith, *Mackinnon and East Africa, 1878–1895: A Study in the 'New Imperialism'* (Cambridge: Cambridge University Press, 1972).
92. See G. H. Mungeam, *British Rule in Kenya, 1895–1912: The Establishment of Administration in the East Africa Protectorate* (Oxford: Clarendon Press, 1966), chapter 1.
93. Caroline Elkins, *Imperial Reckoning: The Untold Story of Britain's Gulag in Kenya* (New York: Henry Holt and Company, 2005), 1–12.
94. Carl G. Rosberg, Jr and John Nottingham, *The Myth of "Mau Mau": Nationalism in Kenya* (New York: Frederick A. Praeger, Publishers, 1966), 7–13.
95. East Africa was not the only part of the British Empire to submit to this fate. For a larger history of such tactics, see Ian Hernon's three volumes *Massacre and Retribution*, *The Savage Empire*, and *Blood in the Sand*, now conveniently available in a single compilation, *Britain's Forgotten Wars: Colonial Campaigns of the 19th Century* (Stroud, Gloucestershire, UK: The History Press, 2008).
96. Ibid., 14–16.
97. Elkins, *Imperial Reckoning*, 14.
98. Mungeam, *British Rule in Kenya*, 286–287.
99. See Elspeth Huxley, *White Man's Country: Lord Delamere and the Making of Kenya: Volume Two, 1914–1931* (London: Chatto and Windus, 1953), chapters 16 and 17.
100. Anderson, *Histories of the Hanged*, 21.
101. Elkins, *Imperial Reckoning*, 16.
102. Anderson, *Histories of the Hanged*, 15.
103. Ibid.
104. Ibid., 15–17.
105. Ibid., 18.
106. David Throup, *Economic and Social Origins of Mau Mau, 1945–53* (Athens, OH: Ohio University Press, 1988), 91–100.

107. Denis Judd, *Empire: The British Imperial Experience from 1765 to the Present* (New York: Basic Books, 1996), 350.

108. Anderson, *Histories of the Hanged*, 25.

109. Ibid., 26.

110. See Throup, *Economic and Social Origins of Mau Mau*, chapter 7.

111. Anderson, *Histories of the Hanged*, 29.

112. Elkins, *Imperial Reckoning*, 24–25.

113. Ibid., 27.

114. IWM, DoD, "Mau Mau Oath Ceremonies," 1953, in the Papers of Lt Col J. K. Windeatt (305 90/20/1).

115. Rhodes House Library, Oxford University, Mss. Brit. Emp. s. 525, Interview with Lord Chandos, Oliver Lyttelton, interviewed by Professor Max Beloff, Gladstone Professor of Government and Public Administration, February 27, 1970.

116. Anderson, *Histories of the Hanged*, 44.

117. Ibid., 45–46.

118. Ibid., 46.

119. Ibid.

120. Throup, *Economic and Social Origins of Mau Mau*, 43.

121. Lyttelton, *The Memoirs of Lord Chandos*, 378.

122. Anthony Clayton, "Baring, (Charles) Evelyn, first Baron Howick of Glendale (1903–1973)," in Matthew and Harrison, *Oxford Dictionary of National Biography* (Oxford and New York: Oxford University Press, 2004).

123. Lyttelton, *The Memoirs of Lord Chandos*, 370.

124. Throup, *Economic and Social Origins of Mau Mau*, 225.

125. British Library, Emrys Evans Papers, Add. 58244, Volume X, 2. Ff.110-154, Letter from Sir Evelyn Baring to Paul Emrys Evans, April 14, 1952.

126. Throup, *Economic and Social Origins of Mau Mau*, 280–281.

127. Anderson, *Histories of the Hanged*, 52.

128. Ibid., 52–53.

129. TNA, CO 822/437, Letter from John Whyatt, Attorney General and Member for Law and Order, to P. Rogers, Assistant Undersecretary of State at the Colonial Office, September 2, 1952.

130. Anderson, *Histories of the Hanged*, 52–53.

131. TNA, CO 822/436, Letter from Henry Potter, Acting Governor of Kenya, to P. Rogers, Assistant Undersecretary of State at the Colonial Office, August 17, 1952.

132. Anderson, *Histories of the Hanged*, 53.

133. TNA, CO 822/437, Letter from John Whyatt, Attorney General and Member for Law and Order, to P. Rogers, Assistant Undersecretary

of State at the Colonial Office, September 2, 1952; with attachment, "Law and Order in Kenya: Texts of Eight Bills Published."

134. Anderson, *Histories of the Hanged*, 53.

135. TNA, CO 822/437, Letter from Fenner Brockway, Member of Parliament, to Oliver Lyttelton, Secretary of State for the Colonies, September 19, 1952.

136. Anderson, *Histories of the Hanged*, 53.

137. TNA, CO 822/438, "Memorandum on Mau Mau Intimidation," Criminal Investigation Department, Kenya, September 12, 1952.

138. Anderson, *Histories of the Hanged*, 55–57; and Elkins, *Imperial Reckoning*, 31–32.

139. TNA, CO 822/444, Letter from Sir Evelyn Baring, Governor of Kenya, to Oliver Lyttelton, Secretary of State for the Colonies, October 9, 1952.

140. F. D. Corfield, *Historical Survey of the Origins and Growth of Mau Mau: Presented to Parliament by the Secretary of State for the Colonies by Command of Her Majesty* (London: Her Majesty's Stationary Office, 1960), 159.

141. TNA, CO 822/437, Committee Notes on the Despatch of British Troops to Kenya, September 29, 1952.

142. TNA, CO 822/437, Letter from Earl Alexander, Minister of Defense, to Oliver Lyttelton, Secretary of State for the Colonies, October 1, 1952.

143. TNA, CO 822/437, Letter from Oliver Lyttelton, Secretary of State for the Colonies, to Earl Alexander, Minister of Defense, October 8, 1952.

144. TNA, CO 822/437, Letter from Sir Edward Jacob, Chief Staff Officer and Deputy Military Secretary at the Ministry of Defense, to Earl Alexander, Minister of Defense, October 13, 1952.

145. TNA, CO 822/444, Telegram from Sir Evelyn Baring, Governor of Kenya, to Oliver Lyttelton, Secretary of State for the Colonies, 7:30 a.m., October 17, 1952.

146. Ibid.

147. TNA, CO 822/444, Telegram from Sir Evelyn Baring, Governor of Kenya, to Oliver Lyttelton, Secretary of State for the Colonies, 5:00 p.m., October 17, 1952.

148. TNA, WO 216/561, "An Appreciation of the Situation in Malaya," September 22, 1952.

149. TNA, CO 1022/56, Telegram containing the text of a speech delivered on August 20 to the inhabitants of Permatang Tinggi, from General Sir Gerald Templer, High Commissioner and Director of Operations, to Oliver Lyttelton, Secretary of State for the Colonies, August 20, 1952.

150. TNA, CO 1022/56, "Action Taken Against the Village Under ER. 17D in August 1952," prepared by Director of Operations' Staff, October 9, 1952.

151. TNA, CO 1022/56, "Federal Government Press Statement," August 27, 1952.

152. LHCMA, General Hugh Stockwell Papers, 7/4, "Schedule of DWEC Training Course," and "Director of Operations' Opening Remarks." These four courses were held on Thursday, August 28 to Saturday, August 30; Monday, September 1 to Wednesday, September 3; Friday, September 4 to Sunday, September 7; and Tuesday, September 9 to Thursday, September 11, 1952.

153. TSC, NAM 1995-01-165-75, General Sir Robert Lockhart Papers, "Memorandum to all SWEC Chairmen: SWECs—Organisation and Responsibilities," October 1952.

154. TSC, NAM 1995-01-165-77, General Sir Robert Lockhart Papers, "Brief by the Combined Intelligence Staff: Review of the Security Situation in Malaya," September 30, 1952.

155. TSC, NAM 1995-01-165-76, General Sir Robert Lockhart Papers, Letter from General Sir Gerald Templer, High Commissioner and Director of Operations, to the Director of Information Services, October 5, 1952.

156. TSC, NAM 1995-01-165-76, General Sir Robert Lockhart Papers, Letter from General Sir Robert Lockhart, Deputy Director of Operations, to General Sir Gerald Templer, High Commissioner and Director of Operations, October 6, 1952.

157. TSC, NAM 1995-01-164-14, General Sir Robert Lockhart Papers, "An Appreciation of the Basic Situation by the Commissioner," A. E. Young, Commissioner of Police, March 1952.

158. Short, *The Communist Insurrection in Malaya*, 358.

159. Disappointed with the results of sodium trichloroacetate, A. H. P. Humphrey, a senior civil servant in the Malaya defense department, suggested to J. D. Higham at the colonial office that Imperial Chemical Industries had been "using us as a lucrative field for experiment," and stated that "if you can tweak their tails diplomatically, we should be delighted!" TNA, CO 1022/26, Letter from A. H. P. Humphrey to J. D. Higham, January 19, 1953.

160. TNA, AIR 23/8592, Telegram from the Army Chief of Staff, Malaya, to Advanced Air Headquarters, Malaya, December 8, 1952.

161. TNA, AIR 20/8735, Telegram from the Army Chief of Staff, Malaya, to General Sir Robert Lockhart, Deputy Director of Operations in Malaya, December 11, 1952. CMU was a weed killer first produced by DuPont Company in the United States in 1951. Described by *The Science News Letter* as a "weed killer that attacks both grasses

and broad-leaved weeds, leaving only bare soil in its wake," its chemical composition was 3-(*p*-chlorophenyl)-I,1-dimethyl-urea. See "Weedkiller Attacks Grass and Broad-Leaved Weeds," *The Science News Letter*, Volume 60, Number 20 (November 17, 1951), 311.

162. TNA, CO 1022/26, Letter from E. K. Woodford to R. W. Piper at the Colonial Office, January 14, 1952.

163. TNA, CO 1022/26, Notes on a Meeting Held in Room 228, War Office, January 21, 1953, on the Chemical Control of Vegetation.

164. TNA, CO 1022/26, Letter from H. A. Sargeaunt, Scientific Adviser to the Army Council, to General Sir Gerald Templer, High Commissioner and Director of Operations in Malaya, January 29, 1953.

165. See TNA, CO 1022/26, Letter from E. K. Woodford, Department of Agriculture, Oxford University to R. W. Piper of the Colonial Office; TNA, CO 1022/26, Letter from R. W. Piper at the Colonial Office to G. E. Blackman, Department of Agriculture, University of Oxford, February 1953; TNA, CO 1022/27, Letter from A. H. P. Humphrey, Defence Department, Government of Malaya, to T. C. Jerrom of the Colonial Office, March 11, 1953; TNA, AIR 23/8592, "Chemical Destruction of CT Food Crops," May 25, 1953; TNA, AIR 20/8735, "Destruction of Crops by Chemical Means," May 28, 1953; TNA, AIR 20/8735, "Destruction of C. T. Foodcrops—Progress Report for May 1953," June 4, 1953; TNA, CO 1022/27, "Destruction of Terrorists' Crops in Malaya," June 9, 1953; TNA, AIR 23/8592, Director of Operations Instruction No. 27, "The Destruction of CT Cultivation Areas," August 12, 1953; and TNA, AIR 20/8735, Operation Research Section (Malaya), Technical Note No. 2/53, "Crop Destruction by Chemicals—Experimental Programme," August 20, 1953.

166. TSC, NAM 1995-01-165-78, "Monthly Average Comparisons for the years 1951 and 1952," Operations Information Branch, Federal Police H.Q., January 2, 1953.

167. Transcript of interview with Sir Michael Blundell, interviewed November 1984 by Allan Segal, Rhodes House Library, Oxford University, Mss. Brit. Emp. s. 527, "End of Empire" Transcripts, 527/8/1.

168. Elkins, *Imperial Reckoning*, 36–37; and Anderson, *Histories of the Hanged*, 63.

169. Anderson, *Histories of the Hanged*, 63.

170. Quoted in Anderson, *Histories of the Hanged*, 68.

171. Ibid., 88–89.

172. Lyttelton, *The Memoirs of Lord Chandos*, 382.

173. Ibid.
174. Quoted in Elkins, *Imperial Reckoning*, 50.
175. Lyttelton, *The Memoirs of Lord Chandos*, 383.
176. Ibid., 380.
177. TNA, CO 822/428, Telegram from Oliver Lyttelton, Secretary of State for Colonial Affairs, to Sir Evelyn Baring, Governor of Kenya, November 8, 1952.
178. *Parliamentary Debates (Hansard)*, House of Commons, Fifth Series, Volume 507, November 4–November 21, 1952 (London: His Majesty's Stationary Office, 1952), November 7, 1952, column 459.
179. TNA, CO 822/438, Telegram from Sir Evelyn Baring, Governor of Kenya, to Oliver Lyttelton, Secretary of State for the Colonies, November 13, 1952.
180. TNA, CO 822/438, Telegram from Sir Evelyn Baring, Governor of Kenya, to Oliver Lyttelton, Secretary of State for the Colonies, November 15, 1952.
181. TNA, CO 822/439, Telegram from Sir Evelyn Baring, Governor of Kenya, to Oliver Lyttelton, Secretary of State for the Colonies, November 18, 1952.
182. Anderson, *Histories of the Hanged*, 89–90; and Elkins, *Imperial Reckoning*, 38.
183. TNA, CO 822/439, Telegram from Sir Evelyn Baring, Governor of Kenya, to Oliver Lyttelton, Secretary of State for the Colonies, November 23, 1952.
184. TNA, CO 822/450, Telegram from Sir Evelyn Baring, Governor of Kenya, to Oliver Lyttelton, Secretary of State for Colonial Affairs, November 24, 1952.
185. Anderson, *Histories of the Hanged*, 90.
186. Elkins, *Imperial Reckoning*, 38.
187. Anderson, *Histories of the Hanged*, 70.
188. *Parliamentary Debates (Hansard)*, House of Commons, Fifth Series, Volume 508, November 24–December 5, 1952 (London: His Majesty's Stationary Office, 1952), November 25, 1952, column 381.
189. TNA, CO 822/462, Telegram from Oliver Lyttelton, Secretary of State for the Colonies, to Sir Evelyn Baring, Governor of Kenya, November 25, 1952.
190. TNA, CO 822/462, Internal Colonial Office Memorandum Prepared by Oliver Lyttelton, Secretary of State for the Colonies, December 1, 1952.
191. TNA, CO 822/462, Telegram from Sir Evelyn Baring, Governor of Kenya, to Oliver Lyttelton, Secretary of State for the Colonies, December 1, 1952.
192. Andrew, *The Defence of the Realm*, 456.

193. This list of proposals is given in TNA, CO 822/450, Telegram from Sir Evelyn Baring, Governor of Kenya, to Oliver Lyttelton, Secretary of State for the Colonies, November 28, 1952.

194. Andrew, *The Defence of the Realm*, 456.

195. TNA, CO 822/450, Telegram from Sir Evelyn Baring, Governor of Kenya, to Oliver Lyttelton, Secretary of State for the Colonies, November 28, 1952.

196. Elkins, *Imperial Reckoning*, 98.

197. *Parliamentary Debates (Hansard)*, House of Commons, Fifth Series, Volume 508, November 24–December 5, 1952 (London: His Majesty's Stationary Office, 1952), November 25, 1952, column 345.

198. TNA, CO 822/439, Telegram from Sir Evelyn Baring, Governor in Kenya, to Oliver Lyttelton, Secretary of State for the Colonies, December 3, 1952.

199. Anderson, *Histories of the Hanged*, 64.

200. Ibid., 65.

201. Ibid., 66–67; and Elkins, *Imperial Reckoning*, 41–46.

202. TNA, CO 822/439, Note of a Meeting held in the Secretary of State's Room on Monday, December 15, 1952.

203. Anderson, *Histories of the Hanged*, 72–73.

204. Ibid., 91.

205. TNA, CO 822/439, Telegram from Sir Evelyn Baring, Governor of Kenya, to Oliver Lyttelton, Secretary of State for the Colonies, January 15, 1953.

206. TNA, CO 822/439, Telegram from Oliver Lyttelton, Secretary of State for the Colonies, to Sir Evelyn Baring, Governor of Kenya, January 15, 1953.

207. Anderson, *Histories of the Hanged*, 354.

208. Short, *The Communist Insurrection in Malaya*, 383–384.

209. See Bell, *Terror out of Zion*, descriptions throughout.

210. TNA, CO 822/439, Telegram from Sir Evelyn Baring, Governor of Kenya, to Oliver Lyttelton, Secretary of State for the Colonies, January 17, 1953.

211. Anderson, *Histories of the Hanged*, 93–95; Elkins, *Imperial Reckoning*, 42.

212. Quoted in Elkins, *Imperial Reckoning*, 42.

213. Ibid., 43.

214. Anderson, *Histories of the Hanged*, 92.

215. TNA, WO 276 / 411, "Appreciation of the Situation," by Major-General W.R.N. Hinde, March 5, 1953.

216. Anderson, *Histories of the Hanged*, 125–126.

217. Rhodes House Library, Oxford University, Mss. Brit. Emp. s. 527, "End of Empire" Transcripts, 527/8/3, Interview with Sir Anthony

Swann, District Commissioner in Kiamba, Kenya, Interviewed by Allan Segal, February 1985.

218. Peter Hewitt, *Kenya Cowboy: A Police Officer's Account of the Mau Mau Emergency,* 3rd edn (Johannesburg, South Africa: 30 Degrees South Publishers, 2008), 134–6.

219. Anderson, *Histories of the Hanged,* 133.

220. Ibid., 137.

221. For a detailed account of these trials, see ibid., 151–177.

222. TNA, CO 822/440, Telegram from Sir Evelyn Baring, Governor of Kenya, to Oliver Lyttelton, Secretary of State for the Colonies, April 24, 1953.

223. TNA, WO 32/21722, Emergency Directive No. 1, Issued by Major General W. R. N. Hinde, Director of Operations, Kenya, April 12, 1953.

224. TNA, CO 822/440, Telegram from Sir Evelyn Baring, Governor of Kenya, to Oliver Lyttelton, Secretary of State for the Colonies, April 20, 1953.

225. Ibid.

226. Quoted in Anderson, *Histories of the Hanged,* 180.

227. Ibid.

228. Hinde, to his credit, volunteered to remain in Kenya as deputy director of operations, with much reduced authority and responsibility. Baring accepted this offer and Hinde served under Erskine for the remainder of the Mau Mau uprising.

229. Huw Bennett, "Erskine, Sir George Watkin Eben James," in Matthew and Harrison, *Oxford Dictionary of National Biography.*

230. TNA, CO 822/440, Telegram from Sir Evelyn Baring, Governor of Kenya, to Oliver Lyttelton, Secretary of State for the Colonies, May 18, 1953.

231. Anderson, *Histories of the Hanged,* 151–154.

232. Brian Lapping, *End of Empire* (New York: St. Martin's Press, 1985), 427.

233. Quoted in Elkins, *Imperial Reckoning,* 52.

234. Ibid.

235. Anderson, *Histories of the Hanged,* 259. See also TNA, WO 32/21722, "Memorandum on Captain Griffiths," December 9, 1953; and WO 32/21722, Telegram from GHQ East Africa to War Office, December 9, 1953.

236. Quoted in ibid., 52–53.

237. Quoted in ibid., 52.

238. Churchill Archives Centre, CHAN II 4/9, Private Comments from Edwina Mountbatten for herself, June 1, 1953.

239. Churchill Archives Centre, CHAN II 4/9, Letter from Oliver Lyttelton to Sir Winston Churchill, June 4, 1953.

240. Churchill Archives Centre, CHAN II 4/9, Letter from Oliver Lyttelton to Edwina Mountbatten, June 4, 1953.

241. Churchill Archives Centre, CHAN II 4/9, Letter from Edwina Mountbatten to Oliver Lyttelton, July 7, 1953.

242. Churchill Archives Centre, CHAN II 4/9, Letter from Oliver Lyttelton to Edwina Mountbatten, July 14, 1953.

243. This viewpoint was expressed fully in a speech to the American seminar in London on July 8, 1953. In this lecture, Lyttelton stated: "Our policy is to give an increasing measure of responsibility for their own affairs to the colonial peoples in conditions that assure to the people a fair standard of living and freedom from aggression from any quarter. ... We know that Africa is stirring: it is true that there is no pan-African nationalism, but in each and all of these territories aspirations towards some form of self-government have become vocal. The reasons are not far to seek. ... Indeed, this vast continent, which has so far made little or no contribution to the progress, enlightenment, art, or literature of the world, has come suddenly to see, as it were, a blinding flash of light, to be conscious of age-long civilisations, and to the African the march of time and the march of man has become a living reality. We want to help him. This is a simple objective." Churchill Archives Center, CHAN II 4/17/12.

244. TNA, WO 291/1731, Operational Research Section (Malaya), Memorandum No. 6/53, "Statistical Survey of Activities by Security Forces in Malaya, From May 1952 to April 1953," July 10, 195, Prepared by Lt Col R. S. Hawkins.

245. TNA, CO 1022/50, Internal Memorandum, "Special Operational Volunteer Force," June 17, 1953; TNA, CO 1022/50, Press Release: Special Operational Volunteer Force, no date.

246. IWM, DoD, Typescript Manuscript, no date, Papers of Captain Peter Head (97/36/1).

247. TNA, CO 1022/58, Telegram from General Sir Gerald Templer, High Commissioner and Director of Operations in Malaya, to Oliver Lyttelton, Secretary of State for the Colonies, August 28, 1953.

248. TNA, CO 1022/58, Telegram from Oliver Lyttelton, Secretary of State for the Colonies, August 29, 1953.

249. Anderson, *Histories of the Hanged*, 261.

250. TNA, WO 276/409, "Appreciation of Operation 'Buttercup'," by Executive Officer, District Emergency Committee, Fort Hall District, August 1953.

251. Anderson, *Histories of the Hanged*, 262.
252. TNA, WO 216/856, Letter from General George Erskine, Commander-in-Chief East Africa, to General Sir Harold Redman, Vice Chief of the Imperial General Staff, July 28, 1953.
253. TNA, WO 216/856, Letter from Antony Head, Secretary of State for War, to Oliver Lyttelton, Secretary of State for Colonial Affairs, August 17, 1953.
254. Anderson, *Histories of the Hanged*, 262.
255. TNA, CO 822/496, "Emergency Directive No. 9: Surrender Policy," July 28, 1953.
256. Erskine followed up Directive No. 9 with "Emergency Directive No. 10: Directive on the Treatment of Surrendered Terrorists" (July 28, 1953), which expressly forbid the ill-treatment of surrendered insurgents. TNA, CO 822/496.
257. TNA, CO 822/496, Memorandum from Henry S. Potter, Chief Secretary in Kenya, "Prosecution of Surrendered Terrorists," July 28, 1953.
258. TNA, CO 822/496, Memorandum: "Surrender Policy," August 20, 1953.
259. TNA, CO 822/496, Telegram from Oliver Lyttelton, Secretary of State for the Colonies, to the Deputy Governor, Kenya, August 21, 1953.
260. TNA, CO 822/496, Surrender Leaflet, Issued by Evelyn Baring, Governor of Kenya, and George Erskine, Commander-in-Chief East Africa, August 24, 1953.
261. Anthony Clayton, *Counter-Insurgency in Kenya: A Study of Military Operations Against Mau Mau* (Nairobi, Kenya: Transafrica Publishers, 1976), 25.
262. Quoted in Elkins, *Imperial Reckoning*, 94. The full transcript of this trial is available in the following archival records: TNA, CO 822/472.
263. TNA, CO 822/499, Letter from E. J. Twining, Governor of Tanganyika, to W. L. Gorell-Barnes at the Colonial Office, November 25, 1953.
264. TNA, CO 822/499, "Report on the case of the Queen versus Brian Hayward," December 5, 1953.
265. TNA, CO 822/499, Letter from E. J. Twining, Governor of Tanganyika, to W. L. Gorell-Barnes at the Colonial Office, November 25, 1953.
266. TNA, CO 822/499, Telegram from Sir Evelyn Baring, Governor of Kenya, to Oliver Lyttelton, Secretary of State for the Colonies, November 28, 1953.
267. IWM, DoD, "Message to be Distributed to all Officers of the Army, Police and the Security Forces," November 30, 1953, Papers of Lt Col J. K. Windeatt.

268. TNA, CO 822/499, Telegram from John Whyatt, Attorney General of Kenya, to Oliver Lyttelton, Secretary of State for the Colonies, December 15, 1953.

269. TNA, CO 822/499, Telegram from Sir Evelyn Baring, Governor of Kenya, to Oliver Lyttelton, Secretary of State for the Colonies, December 17, 1953.

270. TNA, CO 822/499, Telegram from Sir Evelyn Baring, Governor of Kenya, to Oliver Lyttelton, Secretary of State for the Colonies, December 22, 1953.

271. Henry Swanzy, "Quarterly Notes," *African Affairs*, Volume 53, Number 212 (July 1954), 200.

272. *Parliamentary Debates (Hansard)*, House of Commons, Fifth Series, Volume 521, November 23–December 11, 1953 (London: His Majesty's Stationary Office, 1953), December 10, 1953, columns 2182–2183.

273. TNA, WO 32/21722, Memorandum on the McLean Court of Inquiry, by General George Erskine, Commander in Chief East Africa, January 1, 1954.

274. TNA, WO 32/21722, Memorandum: "Court of Inquiry—Action to be Taken as a Result Of," From George Erskine, Commander-in-Chief East Africa, to the Commanders of 39 Brigade, 49 Brigade, 70 Brigade, 6th Battalion King's African Rifles, 4th Battalion King's African Rifles, Kenya Regiment, 156 Mobile Column, and the Armed Car Squadron, January 1, 1954.

275. Churchill Archives Centre, CHAN II 4/5, Letter from Oliver Lyttelton, Secretary of State for the Colonies, to Sir Winston Churchill, Prime Minister, July 27, 1954.

276. Churchill Archives Centre, CHAN II 4/10, Letter from Oliver Lyttelton, Secretary of State for the Colonies, to Sir Thomas Lloyd, Permanent Undersecretary of State at the Colonial Office, July 29, 1954. Lyttelton offered just one criticism of Lloyd: "No praise without qualification is ever worth giving, and the only small admonition that I will leave behind me is that prolixity is an insidious vice, and that the English language should be used to disclose rather than to conceal the meaning."

277. Churchill Archives Centre, CHAN II 4/10, Letter from Oliver Lyttelton, Secretary of State for the Colonies, to J. S. Crossley, August 10, 1954.

278. Churchill Archives Centre, CHAN II 4/5, Letter from Sir Winston Churchill, Prime Minister, to Oliver Lyttelton, Secretary of State for the Colonies, July 29, 1954.

279. Churchill Archives Centre, CHAN II 4/5, Letter from Oliver Lyttelton, Secretary of State for the Colonies, to Sir Winston Churchill, Prime Minister, December 3, 1953.

280. Quoted in John Cloake, *Templer: Tiger of Malaya: The Life of Field Marshal Sir Gerald Templer* (London: Harrap, 1985), 317.

281. Ibid., 319.

282. Quoted in ibid., 260.

283. Ibid.

284. Stubbs, *Hearts and Minds in Guerilla Warfare*, 180.

285. Rhodes House Library, Mss. Brit. Emp. 332, Creech Jones Papers, Box 21, File 3, "Report to the Secretary of State for the Colonies by the Parliamentary Delegation to Kenya, January 1954," Presented to the Secretary of State for the Colonies to Parliament by Command of Her Majesty, February 1954.

286. Daniel Branch, *Defeating Mau Mau, Creating Kenya: Counterinsurgency, Civil War, and Decolonization* (Cambridge: Cambridge University Press, 2009), 91.

287. TNA, WO 276/453, Operation Report: "Enemy Situation Rift Valley Province," April 21, 1954.

288. Anderson, *Histories of the Hanged*, 232–235.

289. "Devonshire Regiment's Conduct in Kenya 'More than Vindicated': Their Job if Difficult and Dangerous," by Brigadier Ralph Rayner, *The Western Morning News*, February 12, 1954, found in IWM, DoD, Papers of Lieutenant Colonel J. K. Windeatt.

290. LHCMA, Rex Charles Mace Papers, Rex Charles Mace, "East Africa Artillery: 156 (East Africa) Independent Heavy Anti-Aircraft Battery: Brief History of the East African Artillery: Operations in Kenya, 1952–1955," no date.

291. For a full account of Operation Wedgwood, see Anderson, *Histories of the Hanged*, 273–279. The official records can be found in TNA, WO 276 / 454.

292. For the most comprehensive account of Operation Anvil, see Anderson, *Histories of the Hanged*, 200–205.

293. Quoted in Branch, *Defeating Mau Mau*, Creating Kenya, 106. Erskine made this comment in a report published on April 25, 1955.

294. Anderson, *Histories of the Hanged*, 205 and 212.

295. Philippa Levine, *The British Empire: Sunrise to Sunset* (Harlow, UK: Pearson Education Limited, 2007), 90.

296. R.F. Holland, *Britain and the Revolt in Cyprus, 1954–1959* (Oxford: Oxford University Press, 1998), 5.

297. Ibid., 7–8.

298. Ibid., 1–5.

299. Ibid., 9–13.

300. Ibid., 13.

301. Ibid., 15–16.

302. TNA, CO 537 / 2486, "The Future of Cyprus in Relation to the Withdrawal from Palestine," November 14, 1947.
303. Holland, *Britain and the Revolt in Cyprus*, 18.
304. Quoted in ibid., 20.
305. Quoted in ibid., 22.
306. Quoted in ibid., 27.
307. Ibid., 30–33.
308. Colin Barker, "Armitage, Sir Robert Perceval (1906–1900)," in Matthew and Harrison, *Oxford Dictionary of National Biography*.
309. Quoted in Holland, *Britain and the Revolt in Cyprus*, 35.
310. Ibid.
311. Ibid., 37.
312. *Parliamentary Debates (Hansard)*, House of Commons, Fifth Series, Volume 531, July 26–October 29, 1954 (London: His Majesty's Stationary Office, 1954), July 28, 1954, columns 505–506.
313. Ibid., column 508.
314. Lyttelton, *The Memoirs of Lord Chandos*, 420.
315. *Parliamentary Debates (Hansard)*, July 28, 1954, columns 549 and 552.
316. Holland, *Britain and the Revolt in Cyprus*, 37.
317. Philip Murphy, "Boyd, Alan Tindal Lennox-, first Viscount Boyd of Merton (1904–1993)," in Matthew and Harrison, *Oxford Dictionary of National Biography*.
318. TNA, WO 216 / 874, Letter and Appreciation of the Situation in Malaya from Lieutenant General G.K. Bourne, Director of Operations in Malaya, to Field Marshal Sir John Harding, Chief of the Imperial General Staff, July 17, 1954.
319. TNA, WO 216 / 874, "Director Operations, Federation of Malaya: Planning Directive for 1955," August 11, 1954.
320. IWM, DoD, "Patrol Action in the Mt. Kenya Forest," by Lt Col M. C. Hastings, DSO, no date, in the Papers of Lt Col J. K. Windeatt.
321. IWM, DoD, "The Tana River Incident," by Major P. Burdick, no date, in the Papers of Lt Col J. K. Windeatt.
322. TNA, WO 276/233, "The Use and Value of Heavy Bombing," September 1954.
323. TNA, AIR 23/8617, "Forecast of R.A.F. bombing effort in Kenya subsequent to 1st February, 1955," by Air Vice Marshal S. O. Rufton, December 20, 1954.
324. TNA, WO 276/ 545, "A Handbook on Anti-Mau Mau Operations," General Headquarters, East Africa, Nairobi, November 27, 1954.
325. TNA, WO 276/461, "Forecast of Security Force Operations in 1955," December 6, 1955.

326. TNA, CO 822/778, Telegram from Sir Evelyn Baring, Governor of Kenya, to Alan Lennox-Boyd, Secretary of State for the Colonies, December 13, 1954.

327. Clayton, *Counter-Insurgency in Kenya*, 27.

328. TNA, CO 822/778, "Operation 'First Flute,'" Report by General Erskine, April 12, 1955.

329. Anderson, *Histories of the Hanged*, 269–270.

330. British Library, Add. 58244, Emrys Evans Papers, Vol. X, ff. 154, Letter from Sir Evelyn Baring, Governor of Kenya, to Paul Emrys Evans, January 10, 1955.

331. TNA, CO 822/778, Telegram from Sir Evelyn Baring, Governor of Kenya, to Alan Lennox-Boyd, Secretary of State for the Colonies, January 5, 1955.

332. Churchill Archives Centre, Churchill College, Cambridge, CHAN II/4/17/14, Speech by Oliver Lyttelton at the Royal Institute of International Affairs' City Meeting, January 17, 1955.

333. Colville, *The Fringes of Power: 10 Downing Street Diaries, 1939–1955*, 654.

334. For a firsthand account of this event, see ibid., 668–670.

335. Ibid., 679.

336. Jenkins, *Churchill*, 847.

337. Ibid., 850–861.

338. Colville, *The Fringes of Power*, 706.

339. Ibid., 708.

340. Ibid., 709.

341. Pelling, *Churchill's Peacetime Ministry*, 176.

3 The Eden Years

1. Holland, *Britain and the Revolt in Cyprus*, 52.

2. Ibid., 52 and 55.

3. For a more detailed account of this progression, see ibid., chapter 2.

4. See David Carlton, *Anthony Eden: A Biography* (London: Allen Lane, 1981), chapters 1–9.

5. Ibid., 369–370.

6. Victor Rothwell, *Anthony Eden: A Political Biography, 1931–57* (Manchester: Manchester University Press, 1992), 166.

7. Bodleian Library, Oxford, Harold Macmillan Papers, Dep. c. 295, Note from Harold Macmillan, Minister of Defence, to Antony Head, Secretary of State for War, November 11, 1954.

8. Ibid., Letter from Harold Macmillan, Minister of Defence, to Winston Churchill, Prime Minister, December 1954.

9. Ibid., Letter from Harold Macmillan, Minister of Defence, to Antony Head, Secretary of State for War, January 18, 1955.

10. Ibid., Letter from Harold Macmillan, Minister of Defence, to Viscount Swinton, February 5, 1955.
11. Quoted in Holland, *Britain and the Revolt in Cyprus*, 56.
12. Ibid., 56.
13. Quoted in ibid., 57.
14. Bodleian Library, Oxford, Harold Macmillan Papers, Dep. c. 904, Letter from Harold Macmillan, Foreign Secretary, to The Earl of Halifax, April 26, 1955.
15. TNA, CO 926/517, Letter from the Colonial Secretary, Cyprus, to Sir John Martin, Colonial Office, April 27, 1955.
16. TNA, CO 1035/98, Note on action taken to strengthen the Intelligence Organization in Cyprus, July 1955.
17. TNA, FO 371/117640, Telegram from Alan Lennox-Boyd, Secretary of State for the Colonies, June 20, 1955.
18. Holland, *Britain and the Revolt in Cyprus*, 59–60.
19. TNA, FO 317/117642, Paper on the Future of Cyprus, Colonial and Foreign Offices, June 25, 1955.
20. TNA, FO 371/117640, Telegram from Sir Robert Armitage, Governor of Cyprus, to Alan Lennox-Boyd, Secretary of State for the Colonies, June 28, 1955.
21. Holland, *Britain and the Revolt in Cyprus*, 61.
22. TNA, FO 371/117640, Note on the Colonial Office viewpoint by J. G. Ward of the Foreign Office, June 29, 1955.
23. Holland, *Britain and the Revolt in Cyprus*, 61.
24. TNA, FO 371/117640, Telegram from Sir Robert Armitage, Governor of Cyprus, to Alan Lennox-Boyd, Secretary of State for the Colonies, June 30, 1955.
25. Special Collections Department, University of Birmingham, Lord Avon (Anthony Eden) Papers, AP 20/20/28, Memorandum from Anthony Eden, Prime Minister, to Alan Lennox-Boyd, Secretary of State for Colonial Affairs, July 1, 1955.
26. TNA, FO 371/117642, Brief for Secretaries of State, "Conference on East Mediterranean and Cyprus," July 2, 1955.
27. TNA, FO 371/117642, Letter from Alan Lennox-Boyd, Secretary of State for the Colonies, to Anthony Eden, Prime Minister, July 6, 1955.
28. TNA, FO 371/117642, Notes on Cabinet Meeting, July 7, 1955.
29. Holland, *Britain and the Revolt in Cyprus*, 62.
30. Special Collections Department, University of Birmingham, Lord Avon Papers, AP 20/22/60, Telegram from Alan Lennox-Boyd, Secretary of State for the Colonies, to Anthony Eden, Prime Minister, July 10, 1955.
31. Ibid.
32. Holland, *Britain and the Revolt in Cyprus*, 64.

33. Ibid., 66.
34. Ibid., 70.
35. Bodleian Library, Oxford, Harold Macmillan Papers, Dep. c. 300, Letter from Harold Macmillan, Secretary of State for Foreign Affairs, to Selwyn Lloyd, Minister of Defence, August 11, 1955.
36. Bodleian Library, Oxford, Harold Macmillan Papers, Dep. c. 904, Memorandum from Harold Macmillan, Secretary of State for Foreign Affairs, to Anthony Eden, Prime Minister, August 16, 1955.
37. Holland, *Britain and the Revolt in Cyprus*, 71.
38. Bodleian Library, Oxford, Harold Macmillan Papers, Dep. c. 904, Memorandum from Harold Macmillan, Secretary of State for Foreign Affairs, to Anthony Eden, Prime Minister, August 19, 1955.
39. Special Collections Department, University of Birmingham, Lord Avon Papers, AP 20/20/57, Memorandum from Anthony Eden, Prime Minister, to Harold Macmillan, August 19, 1955.
40. Holland. *Britain and the Revolt in Cyprus*, 72.
41. Bodleian Library, Oxford, Harold Macmillan Papers, Dep. c. 301, Memorandum from Harold Macmillan, Secretary of State for Foreign Affairs, to Anthony Eden, Prime Minister, August 29, 1955.
42. Stella Soulioti, *Fettered Independence: Cyprus, 1878–1964: Volume One: The Narrative* (Minneapolis, MN: Minnesota Mediterranean and East European Monographs, Modern Greek Studies, University of Minnesota, 2006), 29–32.
43. Special Collections Department, University of Birmingham, Lord Avon Papers, AP 20/20/64, Memorandum from Anthony Eden, Prime Minister, to Harold Macmillan, Secretary of State for Foreign Affairs, August 30, 1955.
44. Holland, *Britain and the Revolt in Cyprus*, 78.
45. IWM, DoD, Papers of Field Marshal Lord Harding of Petherton (96/40/1), Letter from Anthony Eden, Prime Minister, to Field Marshal Sir John Harding, Chief of the Imperial General Staff, September 24, 1955.
46. Holland, *Britain and the Revolt in Cyprus*, 79–82.
47. TNA, WO 216/875, Letter from Lieutenant-General Sir Geoffrey Bourne, Director of Operations in Malaya, to General Sir Gerald Templer, Chief of the Imperial General Staff, October 3, 1955.
48. TNA, CAB 21/2906, Memorandum from GHQ East Africa to the War Office, May 26, 1955.
49. TNA, CAB 21/2906, Telegram from Sir Evelyn Baring, Governor of Kenya, to Alan Lennox-Boyd, Secretary of State for the Colonies, June 3, 1955.

50. TNA, WO 276/430, War Council Directive No. 4: Withdrawal of Surrender Offer, June 8, 1955.
51. TNA, AIR 23/8617, Appreciation by the Commander in Chief of the Operational Situation in Kenya in June, 1955.
52. TNA, WO 276/460, Report of a Special Force in Kenya by R. C. Catling, Commissioner of Police, Kenya, July 4, 1955.
53. Harvey Sicherman, *Aden and British Strategy, 1839–1968* (Philadelphia, PA: Foreign Policy Research Institute, 1972), 1–17.
54. Ibid., 28.
55. Ronald Hyam, *Britain's Declining Empire: The Road to Decolonisation, 1918–1968* (Cambridge: Cambridge University Press, 2006), 288–289.
56. TNA, CO 1015/844, Telegram from Sir Tom Hickinbotham, Governor of Aden Colony, to Alan Lennox-Boyd, Secretary of State for the Colonies, May 22, 1955.
57. TNA, CO 1015/844, Telegram from Sir Tom Hickinbotham, Governor of Aden Colony, to Alan Lennox-Boyd, Secretary of State for the Colonies, June 13, 1955.
58. TNA, CO 1015/844, Letter from Frank Cooper at the Air Ministry to Sir Bernard Reilly at the Colonial Office, June 18, 1955, with attached report, "Brief Note on R.A.F. Offensive Operations in Aden, 1946–1951."
59. *Parliamentary Debates (Hansard)*, House of Commons, Fifth Series, Volume 543, June 27–July 15, 1955 (London: Her Majesty's Stationary Office, 1955), July 13, 1955, columns 1930–1931.
60. TNA, CO 1015/843, Memorandum from J.C. Morgan of the Colonial Office to General Cecil Llewelyn Firbank, Director of Infantry, War Office, July 1, 1955.
61. TNA, CO 1015/844, Telegram from Sir Tom Hickinbotham, Governor of Aden, to Alan Lennox-Boyd, Secretary of State for the Colonies, July 15, 1955.
62. TNA, CO 1015/844, Memorandum on Punitive Air Action, July 18, 1955.
63. *Parliamentary Debates (Hansard)*, House of Commons, Fifth Series, Volume 544, July 18–July 28, 1955 (London: Her Majesty's Stationary Office, 1955), July 20, 1955, columns 374.
64. Bodleian Library, Oxford, Harold Macmillan Papers, Dep. c. 300, Letter from Harold Macmillan, Secretary of State for Foreign Affairs, to Selwyn Lloyd, Minister of Defense, July 29, 1955.
65. David Hunt, "Harding, John, first Baron Harding of Petherton (1896–1989)," in Matthew and Harrison, *Oxford Dictionary of National Biography* (Oxford and New York: Oxford University Press, 2004).

66. Holland, *Britain and the Revolt in Cyprus*, 85.

67. Ibid., 86.

68. Special Collections Department, University of Birmingham, Lord Avon Papers, AP 20/22/192, Telegram from Field Marshal Sir John Harding, Governor of Cyprus, to Anthony Eden, Prime Minister, October 8, 1955.

69. Holland, *Britain and the Revolt in Cyprus*, 86–87.

70. Special Collections Department, University of Birmingham, Lord Avon Papers, AP 20/22/198, Telegram from Field Marshal Sir John Harding, Governor of Cyprus, to Anthony Eden, Prime Minister, October 11, 1955.

71. Ibid., AP 20/22/199, Statement by Field Marshal Sir John Harding, Governor of Cyprus, October 11, 1955.

72. Ibid., AP 20/22/200, Telegram from Field Marshal Sir John Harding, Governor of Cyprus, to Anthony Eden, Prime Minister, October 11, 1955.

73. Bodleian Library, Oxford, Harold Macmillan Papers, Dep. c. 301, Memorandum from Harold Macmillan, Foreign Secretary, to Anthony Eden, Prime Minister, October 12, 1955.

74. Holland, *Britain and the Revolt in Cyprus*, 87.

75. Special Collections Department, University of Birmingham, Lord Avon Papers, AP 20/20/94, Memorandum from Anthony Eden, Prime Minister, to Sir Thomas Lloyd, Permanent Undersecretary of State for Colonial Affairs, October 13, 1955.

76. Ibid., AP 20/22/195, Telegram from Field Marshal Sir John Harding, Governor of Cyprus, to Anthony Eden, Prime Minister, October 10, 1955.

77. Ibid., AP 20/22/207, Telegram from Field Marshal Sir John Harding, Governor of Cyprus, to Anthony Eden, Prime Minister, October 14, 1955.

78. TNA, CO 926/455, Memorandum by the Cyprus Intelligence Committee, "The Nature of EOKA, Its Political Background, and Sources of Direction," October 18, 1955.

79. TNA, CO 926/518, Telegram from Field Marshal Sir John Harding, Governor of Cyprus, to Alan Lennox-Boyd, Secretary of State for the Colonies, October 24, 1955.

80. Holland, *Britain and the Revolt in Cyprus*, 90–91.

81. Ibid., 89.

82. TNA, CO 926/351, "A Law to authorize the Use of Her Majesty's Forces in the Performance of Police Duties," enacted October 28, 1955.

83. IWM, DoD, MISC 93 (1391), Red Card: "Instructions to Individuals for Opening Fire in Cyprus," 1955.

84. Holland, *Britain and the Revolt in Cyprus*, 93.

85. TNA, CO 926/519, Telegram from Field Marshal Sir John Harding, Governor of Cyprus, to Alan Lennox-Boyd, Secretary of State for the Colonies, November 18, 1955.

86. TNA, WO 276/431, GHQ East Africa, Instruction No. 35, December 21, 1955. For operational details on the establishment of these teams, see: TNA, WO 276/431, Memorandum by R. C. Catling, Commissioner of Kenya Police, "Future Employment of Special Force Teams," December 21, 1955; and TNA, WO 276/431, Letter from R. C. Catling, Commissioner of Kenya Police, to The Senior Assistant Commissioner of Police, Nyeri Area, December 21, 1955.

87. TNA, WO 276/431, Special Force Operations since Inception, January 1956. The named leaders killed were Major Kalasinga, General M'Wariama, Brigadier Nguku, Major General Ochieng, Brigadier Wanjoki, General Dishon, General Murange, Field Marshal Maoharia Kimemia, General Oakuri Karuri, Colonel Wanjiru, General Kuratwende, and Field Marshal Chumali.

88. For more on these early operations, see TNA, WO 276/431, Letter from Headquarters, the Kenya Police, to Brigadier R. M. P. Carver, Chief of Staff, General Headquarters, East Africa, October 24, 1955; TNA, WO 276/431, Memorandum: Elimination of Terrorist Leaders by Special Forces, November 19, 1955; TNA, WO 276/431, Memorandum: Future Use of Special Forces, November 24, 1955; TNA, WO 276/431, Memorandum: Recent Successful Operation in Bamboo Forest, November 29, 1955.

89. TNA, WO 276/430, Memorandum from R. M. P. Carver, Chief of Staff, General Headquarters, East Africa, to all Security Force units, October 26, 1955.

90. TNA, WO 276/430, Memorandum by the Minister of Legal Affairs, "Captured and Surrendered Terrorists," November 5, 1955.

91. TNA, WO 276/430, Letter from R. C. Catling, Commissioner of Kenya Police, to Brigadier R. M. P. Carver, Chief of Staff, General Headquarters, East Africa, November 16, 1955.

92. TNA, WO 276/430, "War Council Instruction No. 18: The Treatment of Surrendered Terrorists and Captured Terrorists," November 23, 1955.

93. IWM, DoD, General T. H. Birbeck Papers, "Security Forces Hit the Terrorists Hard on Mount Kenya," by a Military Observer, February 19, 1956; and "Special Patrol: South West Mount Kenya," by General T. H. Birkbeck, March 1956.

94. TNA, AIR 23/8741, "Operational Research Branch Memorandum No. 13: An Analysis of the Types of Target Attacked During Offensive Air Operations in Malaya in 1955," May 1956.

95. TNA, CO 1035/83, "Intelligence Centre, Aden," Report Forwarded by Sir Tom Hickinbotham, Governor of Aden, to Alan Lennox-Boyd, Secretary of State for the Colonies, February 19, 1956; and CO 1035/83, "Directive for the Officer in Charge of the Protectorate Section of the Intelligence Centre, Aden," February 18, 1956.

96. TNA, CO 926/543, Telegram from Field Marshal Sir John Harding, Governor of Cyprus, to Alan Lennox-Boyd, Secretary of State for the Colonies, December 4, 1955.

97. TNA, CO 926/543, Telegram from Field Marshal Sir John Harding, Governor of Cyprus, to Alan Lennox-Boyd, Secretary of State for the Colonies, December 9, 1955.

98. Ibid.

99. Holland, *Britain and the Revolt in Cyprus*, 104–105.

100. TNA, WO 32/16260, Telegram from Field Marshal Sir John Harding, Governor of Cyprus, to Alan Lennox-Boyd, Secretary of State for the Colonies, December 11, 1955.

101. TNA, CO 1035/98, Letter and Accompanying Report from A. M. MacDonald, Security Intelligence Advisor at the Colonial Office, to Field Marshal Sir John Harding, Governor of Cyprus, December 22, 1955.

102. For more on policing reforms in Cyprus, see David M. Anderson, "Policing and Communal Conflict: the Cyprus Emergency, 1954–60," in David M. Anderson and David Killingray, eds, *Policing and Decolonisation: Politics, Nationalism and the Police, 1917–65* (Manchester: Manchester University Press, 1992), 187–217.

103. TNA, WO 32/16260, Telegram from Field Marshal Sir John Harding, Governor of Cyprus, to Alan Lennox-Boyd, Secretary of State for the Colonies, January 7, 1956.

104. Holland, *Britain and the Revolt in Cyprus*, 108–109.

105. Ibid., 110–113.

106. Ibid., 113–114.

107. Ibid., 116.

108. IWM, DoD, Papers of Field Marshal Lord Harding of Petherton, GCB CBE DSO MC (96/40/1), Letter from Field Marshal Sir John Harding, Governor of Cyprus, to his son John Charles Harding, March 4, 1956.

109. D. Smith, quoted in Holland, *Britain and the Revolt in Cyprus*, 116.

110. Ibid., 117–119.

111. Ibid., 120–130.

112. Ibid., 134.

113. TNA, CO 926/543, Telegram from Field Marshal Sir John Harding, Governor of Cyprus, to Alan Lennox-Boyd, Secretary of State for the Colonies, May 25, 1956.

114. TNA, CO 926/543, Memorandum by Field Marshal Sir John Harding, "Collective Fines in Cyprus," June 1956.

115. TNA, CO 926/543, Telegram from Field Marshal Sir John Harding, Governor of Cyprus, to Alan Lennox-Boyd, Secretary of State for the Colonies, June 9, 1956.

116. TNA, AIR 8/1921, Telegram from the Commander-in-Chief, Middle East Land Forces, to the Air Ministry, London, June 18, 1956.

117. TNA, CO 1035/118, Report by the Cabinet Committee on Counter-Subversion in the Colonial Territories, "Short Review of Subversion in the Colonial Empire," June 20, 1956.

118. TNA, CO 926/581, Chiefs of Staff Committee Report, "Relief of Parachute Battalions in Cyprus," July 6, 1956.

119. TNA, WO 32/16260, Memorandum from Field Marshal Sir General Templer, Chief of the Imperial General Staff, to Alan Lennox-Boyd, Secretary of State for the Colonies, July 26, 1956.

120. "Extracts from a Speech by Colonel Nasser of 26 July 1956 announcing the Nationalization of the Suez Canal Company," in D. C. Watt, ed., *Documents on the Suez Crisis, 26 July to 6 November 1956* (London: Royal Institute of International Affairs, 1957), 44–49.

121. Telegram from Anthony Eden, Prime Minister, to Dwight D. Eisenhower, President of the United States, July 27, 1956, in Peter G. Boyle, ed., *The Eden-Eisenhower Correspondence, 1955–1957* (Chapel Hill: The University of North Carolina Press, 2005), 153–154.

122. Robert Kubicek, "British Expansion, Empire, and Technological Change," in Andrew Porter, ed., *The Oxford History of the British Empire: Volume III: The Nineteenth Century* (Oxford: Oxford University Press, 1999), 252.

123. P. J. Cain and A. G Hopkins, *British Imperialism, 1688–2000*, 2nd edn (London: Pearson Education Limited, 2002), 312–313.

124. Richard Aldous, *The Lion and the Unicorn: Gladstone vs. Disraeli* (New York: W. W. Norton & Company, 2006), 262–263.

125. Cain and Hopkins, *British Imperialism*, 314.

126. Kubicek, "British Empire, Expansion, and Technological Change," 252.

127. Cain and Hopkins, *British Imperialism*, 316.

128. Keith Kyle, *Suez: Britain's End of Empire in the Middle East* (London: I.B. Tauris Publishers, 2003), 14–18.

129. Ibid., 18–21.

130. See Joel Gordon, *Nasser's Blessed Movement: Egypt's Free Officers and the July Revolution* (Oxford: Oxford University Press, 1992).

131. Wm. Roger Louis, "The Dissolution of the British Empire," in Judith M. Brown and Wm. Roger Louis, eds, *The Oxford History of the British Empire: Volume IV: The Twentieth Century* (Oxford: Oxford University Press, 1999), 340–341.

132. Ibid., 341–342.

133. Telegram from Anthony Eden, Prime Minister, to Dwight D. Eisenhower, President of the United States, January 16, 1956, in Boyle, ed., *The Eden-Eisenhower Correspondence*, 110.

134. Special Collections Department, University of Birmingham, Lord Avon Papers, AP 20/21/16, Top Secret Memorandum from Anthony Eden, Prime Minister, to Sir Walter Monckton, Minister of Defense, January 19, 1956.

135. This information is revealed in Telegram from Anthony Eden, Prime Minister, to Dwight D. Eisenhower, President of the United States, March 5, 1956, in Boyle, ed., *The Eden-Eisenhower Correspondence*, 119.

136. Special Collections Department, University of Birmingham, Lord Avon Papers, AP 20/24/161, Telegram from Selwyn Lloyd, Secretary of State for Foreign Affairs, to Anthony Eden, Prime Minister, March 7, 1956.

137. Ibid., AP 20/24/313, Telegram from Anthony Eden, Prime Minister, to Prime Ministers of Canada, Australia, New Zealand, and South Africa, July 28, 1956.

138. Letter from Dwight D. Eisenhower, President of the United States, to Anthony Eden, Prime Minister, July 31, 1956, in Boyle, ed., *The Eden-Eisenhower Correspondence*, 156–157.

139. Letter from Anthony Eden, Prime Minister, to Dwight D. Eisenhower, President of the United States, August 5, 1956, in ibid., 158–159.

140. TNA, CO 1035/24, Report by the Joint Intelligence Committee, "Egyptian Nationalisation of the Suez Canal Company," August 3, 1956.

141. Special Collections Department, University of Birmingham, Lord Avon Papers, AP 20/25/7, Telegram from Anthony Eden, Prime Minister, to Sidney Holland, Prime Minister of New Zealand, August 4, 1956.

142. TNA, CO 1035/24, Report by the Joint Intelligence Committee, "Considerations Affecting Action by Egypt in the Event of Armed Intervention," August 7, 1956.

143. TNA, CO 1035/24, Report by the Joint Intelligence Committee, "Political and Military Effects in the Middle East of Certain Developments in the Suez Canal Situation," August 17, 1956.

144. Letter from Anthony Eden, Prime Minister, to Dwight D. Eisenhower, President of the United States, August 27, 1956, in Boyle, ed., *The Eden-Eisenhower Correspondence*, 161.

145. TNA, CO 1035/24, Memorandum from Alan Lennox-Boyd, Secretary of State for the Colonies, to the Lord Privy Seal, "Effects in Colonial Territories of Developments in the Suez Canal Situation," September 7, 1956.

146. Special Collections Department, University of Birmingham, Lord Avon Papers, AP 20/21/195, Memorandum from Anthony Eden, Prime Minister, to Selwyn Lloyd, Foreign Secretary, September 24, 1956.

147. Ibid., AP 20/25/74, Telegram from Selwyn Lloyd, Foreign Secretary, to Anthony Eden, Prime Minister, October 8, 1956.

148. Letter from Dwight D. Eisenhower, President of the United States, to Anthony Eden, Prime Minister, October 11, 1956, in Boyle, ed., *The Eden-Eisenhower Correspondence*, 174.

149. For a fuller account of these talks and the resulting protocol, see Kyle, *Suez*, 314–331.

150. For an insider's accounts from the American perspective on these events, see Chester L. Cooper, *The Lion's Last Roar: Suez, 1956* (New York: Harper & Row, Publishers, 1978), chapter 8.

151. "Anglo-French Ultimatum to the Governments of Egypt and Israel," October 30, 1956, in Watt, ed., *Documents on the Suez Crisis*, 85–86.

152. Letter from Dwight D. Eisenhower, President of the United States, to Anthony Eden, Prime Minister, October 30, 1956, in Boyle, ed., *The Eden-Eisenhower Correspondence*, 181.

153. Kyle, *Suez*, 382.

154. Special Collections Department, University of Birmingham, Lord Avon Papers, AP 20/25/111, Telegram from Sidney Holland, Prime Minister of New Zealand, to Anthony Eden, Prime Minister, November 1, 1956.

155. TNA, CO 1035/20, Telegram from Alan Lennox-Boyd, Secretary of State for the Colonies, to Commonwealth and other British Imperial Governments, November 2, 1956.

156. Kyle, *Suez*, 392–396.

157. Ibid., 461–464; and Farrar-Hockley, "The Post War Army," in Chandler and Beckett, eds, *The Oxford History of the British Army*, 334–337.

158. Quoted in Kyle, *Suez*, 406.

159. Ibid., 428.

160. Ibid., 464–465.

161. Ibid., 469.

162. Telegram from Dwight D. Eisenhower, President of the United States, to Anthony Eden, Prime Minister, November 6, 1956, in Boyle, ed., *The Eden-Eisenhower Correspondence*, 184–5.

163. Quoted in Carlton, *Anthony Eden*, 463.

164. Churchill Archives Centre, Churchill College, Cambridge, CHUR 2/143, Letter from Viscount Montgomery of Alamein to Sir Winston Churchill, December 6, 1956.
165. Rothwell, *Anthony Eden*, 244–245.
166. Carlton, *Anthony Eden*, 464.
167. Churchill Archives Centre, Churchill College, Cambridge, CHAN II 4/6, Letter from Anthony Eden to Oliver Lyttelton, January 28, 1957.

Epilogue

1. Harold Macmillan, "The Wind of Change," Speech given to the South African Parliament, February 3, 1960, reprinted in *Great Speeches of the 20th Century: No. 4: The Wind of Change*, with a forward by Douglas Hurd (London: Guardian News & World, 2007), 9.
2. Ibid., 9–10.
3. Ibid., 10.
4. TNA, CO 1035/139, Colonial Office Memorandum, "Survey of Subversive Activities in the Colonies, 1957," January 24, 1957. The report also highlighted what it considered the hypocrisy of American anti-colonialism, writing: "For so anti-Colonial a power it is strange to find that the US has Colonies, 'possessions' is the word legally used. They are Puerto Rico, conquered from Spain; New Mexico (and with it Utah, Arizona, Nevada, Wyoming, and part of California) acquired by war from Mexico, with subsequent compensation of $15 million; the Virgin Islands, bought from Denmark; Alaska, bought from Czarist Russia; Louisiana, bought from France; Hawaii, secured by cession from us; American Samoa, secured by agreement with us and with Imperial Germany; the Carolines, Marshalls, and Marianas obtained by United Nations trusteeship; and the Panama Canal Zone, acquired by threat of war."
5. TNA, WO 291/1670, Operational Research Unit Far East: Report No. 1/57, "A Comparative Study of the Emergencies in Malaya and Kenya," June 1957.
6. TNA, WO 106/5990, "Review of the Emergency in Malaya from June 1948 to August 1957, by the Director of Operations, Malaya," September 12, 1957, 6.
7. Ibid., 14.
8. For more on these constitutional developments, see Short, *The Communist Insurrection in Malaya, 1948–1960*; and Stubbs, *Hearts and Minds in Guerilla Warfare*.
9. TNA, WO 106/5990, "Review of the Emergency in Malaya from June 1948 to August 1957, by the Director of Operations, Malaya," September 12, 1957, 26.

10. Stubbs, *Hearts and Minds in Guerilla Warfare*, 241.
11. Richard Clutterbuck offers some caveats to this interpretation in his book *Conflict and Violence in Singapore and Malaysia, 1945–1983*.
12. Stubbs, *Hearts and Minds in Guerilla Warfare*, 261.
13. *Parliamentary Debates (Hansard)*, House of Lords, Fifth Series, Volume 252 (London: Her Majesty's Stationary Office, 1963), July 26, 1963, columns 972–3.
14. TNA, CO 822/1251, Letter from Evelyn Baring, Governor of Kenya, to Alan Lennox-Boyd, Secretary of State for the Colonies, June 25, 1957.
15. TNA, CO 822 / 1251, "'Dilution' Detention Camps: Use of Force in Enforcing Discipline," Report by Eric Griffiths-Jones, Kenyan Minister for Legal Affairs, June 25, 1957.
16. For an account of the lives of detainees within these camps, see Derek R. Peterson, "The Intellectual Lives of Mau Mau Detainees," *Journal of African History*, Number 49 (2008), 73–91.
17. Lapping, *End of Empire*, 434. This argument, and the figures that support it, contradict those put forward by Caroline Elkins in her controversial book *Imperial Reckoning: The Untold Story of Britain's Gulag in Kenya* (which was originally and more provocatively titled *Britain's Gulag: The Brutal End of Empire in Kenya* in its British publication). There is much of use for the imperial historian within Elkins' work, but ultimately she pushes her argument too far. Relying primarily on oral testimonies from former Kikuyu detainees collected some forty years after the event in question, Elkins alleges that rather than 80,000 detainees, the British government in fact detained "some 1.5 million people, or nearly the entire Kikuyu population." (p. xiv) She then details conditions of extraordinary brutality, torture, and violence, before claiming, "at the very least it is safe to assume that the official figure of some 11,000 Mau Mau killed is implausible given all that has been uncovered." (p. 366) Her sensational conclusion is that there were between "130,000 and 300,000 Kikuyu" who were "unaccounted for" in the emergency. The clear implication is that these hundreds of thousands died at the hands of the British in the camps. Putting aside the problems with her methodology and its reliance on oral testimony (a criticism raised by Lawrence James in the *Sunday Times*, Nicholas Best in the *Daily Telegraph*, and Richard Dowden in the *Guardian*, among others), she provides no indication whatsoever as to why the official government figures ought to be discounted, particularly when British civil servants were so meticulous about documenting other areas of colonial life, the good as well as the bad. There are other reasons to be cautious about Elkins' analysis. Taking a more empirical approach than Elkins, John Blacker in his article "The Demography of Mau Mau: Fertility

and Mortality in Kenya in the 1950s: A Demographer's Viewpoint," *African Affairs*, Volume 106, Issue 423 (April 2007), has shown that the emergency engendered perhaps 50,000 excess deaths, of whom some 26,000 were children under the age of 10 due to malnutrition and 24,000 (17,000 males and 7000 females) were due to violence (pp. 225–6). As the British government itself acknowledged the deaths of 11,503 Mau Mau, together with 1086 executions, this leaves just over 11,000 unaccounted for adults, several thousand of whom died at the hands of Mau Mau. While still a number far higher than in Palestine, Malaya, or Cyprus—and a number that deserves careful investigation—it is hardly the hundreds of thousands put forward by Elkins. Finally, as Pascal James Imperato has documented in his review article "Differing Perspectives on Mau Mau," *African Studies Review*, Volume 48, Number 3 (December 2005), there is an underlying political agenda to Elkins' scholarship: "Elkins is a prominent political activist who for some time has been campaigning for monetary compensation for the alleged victims of British efforts at defeating Mau Mau. ... [T]hrough inappropriate analogies and inflammatory rhetoric, Elkins attempts not so much to present truth supported by incontrovertible evidence, but rather to solicit broad public support for her crusade on behalf of Mau Mau adherents and sympathizers who were detained. In effect, her book is less a serious scholarly narrative and more a political brief crafted in popular language in the interests of a group of people whom she considers victims of a past wrong and worthy of reparations." (pp. 148–9) Without uncovering any evidence to contradict the official figures, and bearing in mind the very serious questions raised about Elkins' work by other scholars, in this book I have treated her interpretation with caution, while using some of the information she provides when it can be verified by other sources. It should be noted, however, that Elkins has attempted to respond to these criticisms, most recently in a seminar paper given at the Washington History Seminar, an initiative of the National History Center, on September 27, 2010. The video recording of this seminar session, complete with the presentation and question-and-answer session that followed, can be found on the following website: www.wilsoncenter.org.

18. Lapping, *End of Empire*, 434. Lennox-Boyd later described to parliament the theory behind this: "Experience has shown, time after time, that unless hard core detainees can be got to start working, their rehabilitation is impossible. Once they have started working, there is a psychological break-though and astonishing results are then achieved." After he had made this statement, the colonial secretary was asked by Labour MP Sydney Silverman, "Who told the

right hon. Gentleman that? Stalin?" *Parliamentary Debates (Hansard)*, House of Commons, Fifth Series, Volume 607, June 15–June 26, 1959 (London: Her Majesty's Stationary Office, 1959), June 16, 1959, column 270.

19. This letter, and all other documents aiding this account of the Hola affair, is found in the Papers of W. H. Thompson, DoD, IWM.

20. Quoted in Elkins, *Imperial Reckoning*, 347. Italics in original document.

21. TNA, CAB 21/2906, Cabinet Office Briefing for Harold Macmillan, Prime Minister, "Hola Detention Camp," June 3, 1959.

22. This entire debate can be found in *Parliamentary Debates (Hansard)*, House of Commons, Fifth Series, Volume 607, June 15–June 26, 1959 (London: Her Majesty's Stationary Office, 1959), June 16, 1959, columns 248–383.

23. Bodleian Library, Oxford, Mss. Eng. C. 3395, Alan Lennox-Boyd Papers, Letter from Harold Balfour to Alan Lennox-Boyd, Secretary of State for the Colonies, June 19, 1959.

24. *Parliamentary Debates (Hansard)*, House of Commons, Fifth Series, Volume 610, July 27–September 18, 1959 (London: Her Majesty's Stationary Office, 1959), July 27, 1959, column 237.

25. TNA, CAB 21/2906, Despatch from Alan Lennox-Boyd, Secretary of State for the Colonies, to Evelyn Baring, Governor of Kenya, July 1959.

26. TNA, CAB 21/2906, Despatch from Evelyn Baring, Governor of Kenya, to Alan Lennox-Boyd, Secretary of State for the Colonies, July 1959.

27. TNA, CAB 21/2906, Telegram from Evelyn Baring, Governor of Kenya, to Alan Lennox-Boyd, Secretary of State for the Colonies, July 7, 1959.

28. Lapping, *End of Empire*, 435–6.

29. David Goldsworthy, "Macleod, Iain (1913–1970)," in Matthew and Harrison, *Oxford Dictionary of National Biography* (Oxford and New York: Oxford University Press, 2004).

30. D. W. Throup, "Renison, Sir Patrick Muir (1911–1965)," in ibid.

31. Anderson, *Histories of the Hanged*, 334.

32. Hyam, *Britain's Declining Empire*, 278–82; Lapping, *The End of Empire*, 436–45; and Anderson, *Histories of the Hanged*, 330–6.

33. TNA, CO 926/670, Cyprus Intelligence Committee, "Intelligence Review for the Second Half of January 1957," February 7, 1957.

34. Holland, *Britain and the Revolt in Cyprus*, 154.

35. Lapping, *End of Empire*, 331.

36. Holland, *Britain and the Revolt in Cyprus*, 171–2.

37. Ibid., 171–81.

38. Alan Lennox-Boyd announced Makarios' release on March 28. The archbishop left the Seychelles on April 6 and arrived in Athens on April 17. Soulioti, *Fettered Independence*, 44.

39. Holland, *Britain and the Revolt in Cyprus*, 206.

40. Lapping, *End of Empire*, 337–8.

41. Rhodes House Library, Oxford, Mss. Medit. s. 35, Papers of Sir Hugh Foot, Box 2, File 4, Telegram from Alan Lennox-Boyd, Secretary of State for the Colonies, to Sir Hugh Foot, October 2, 1957.

42. Ibid., Telegram from Sir Hugh Foot to Alan Lennox-Boyd, Secretary of State for the Colonies, October 3, 1957.

43. Ibid., Telegram from the Colonial Office to Sir Hugh Foot, October 3, 1957.

44. Holland, *Britain and the Revolt in Cyprus*, 207.

45. IWM, DoD, Papers of Field Marshal Lord Harding of Petherton, Letter from Harold Macmillan, Prime Minister, to Field Marshal Sir John Harding, Governor of Cyprus, October 17, 1957.

46. Ibid., Letter from Field Marshal Sir John Harding, Governor of Cyprus, to his son, John Charles Harding, October 21, 1957.

47. IWM, DoD, Papers of Mrs J. M. Somerville, Diary Entry, October 3, 1957.

48. Ibid., Diary Entry, October 4, 1957.

49. Ibid., Telegram from Sir Hugh Foot, Incoming Governor of Cyprus, to George Sinclair, Deputy Governor of Cyprus, November 27, 1957.

50. Ibid., Telegram from George Sinclair, Deputy Governor of Cyprus, to Sir Hugh Foot, Incoming Governor of Cyprus, November 27, 1957.

51. Rhodes House Library, Oxford, Mss. Medit. s. 35, Papers of Sir Hugh Foot, Box 13, File 3, Statement to the People of Cyprus made by Sir Hugh Foot, after taking the oath as Governor and Commander in Chief of Cyprus, December 3, 1957.

52. Holland, *Britain and the Revolt in Cyprus*, 219–20.

53. Rhodes House Library, Oxford, Mss. Medit. s. 35, Papers of Sir Hugh Foot, Box 1, File 1, Telegram from Sir Hugh Foot, Governor of Cyprus, to Alan Lennox-Boyd, Secretary of State for the Colonies, December 10, 1957.

54. Soulioti, *Fettered Independence*, 45.

55. Harold Macmillan, *Riding the Storm, 1956–1959* (New York: Harper & Row, Publishers, 1971), 669–70.

56. Ibid., 671–87.

57. For a detailed discussion of this process, see ibid., 689–96.

58. For more detail of this agreement, see Soulioti, *Fettered Independence*, 71–105.

59. Macmillan, *Riding the Storm*, 702.

60. Hyam, *Britain's Declining Empire*, 411–12.
61. For information on the Aden emergency, see Spencer Mawby, *British Policy in Aden and the Protectorates, 1955–67: Last Outpost of a Middle East Empire* (London and New York: Routledge, 2005); Karl Pieragostini, *Britain, Aden, and South Arabia: Abandoning Empire* (New York: St. Martin's Press, 1991); Peter Hinchcliffe, John T. Ducker, and Maria Holt, *Without Glory in Arabia: The British Retreat from Aden* (London: I.B. Tauris, 2006); and Jonathan Walker, *Aden Insurgency: The Savage War in South Arabia, 1962–1967* (Staplehurst, Kent, UK: Spellmount Limited, 2005). Since the publication of these works, new archival documents have been released, particularly on the military dimensions of the conflict, which will allow a full account to be told by future historians. Most significantly, these include the Dean-Drummond Papers at the Liddell Hart Centre for Military Archives, King's College, London.
62. TNA, CO 1035/171, Letter from Sir Burke Trend, Colonial Office, to Sir Roger Hollis, Director General of MI5, November 18, 1965.

Bibliography

Unpublished Primary Sources

Bodleian Library, Oxford University, Oxford

Letters from Clement Attlee to his brother Tom Attlee
Letters from Harold Macmillan to Lady Waverley
Papers of:
Lennox-Boyd, Alan
Macmillan, Harold

British Library, London

Papers of:
Emrys Evans

Churchill Archives Centre, Churchill College, Cambridge

Papers of:
Chandos, 1st Viscount (Oliver Lyttelton)
Churchill, Sir Winston

Imperial War Museum, Department of Documents, London

Papers of:
Baines, Brigadier D. F. A. T., MBE
Bird, F. W., MBE GM
Birkbeck, Major General T. H., CB CBE DSO
Chavasse, Colonel K. G. F., DSO
Clark, Captain R. H., MC
Cole, Major General W. S., CB CBE
Darling, General Sir Kenneth, GBE KCB DSO
Gibb, Major I. S., MC
Green, J. C. A.
Hammerton, R.
Harding of Petherton, Field Marshal Lord, GCB CBE DSO MC

Harrison, Major W. C., MBE GM
Head, Captain P.
Hodges, Second Lieutenant R.
Jefferson, M. P.
Martin, N. A.
MISC 93
Norman, Colonel C. R. W., OBE
Shepheard, Major General J. K., CB DSO OBE
Somerville, Mrs J. M.
Thompson, Major W. H.
Towers-Clark, Major P. F.
Windeatt, Lieutenant Colonel J. K., OBE

Liddell Hart Centre for Military Archives, King's College, London

Papers of:
Deane-Drummond, Major General Anthony John
Mace, Colonel Rex Charles
Pyman, Sir Harold English
Stockwell, General Sir Hugh Charles
Talbot, Major General Dennis Edmund Blaquière

National Archives, Kew, Richmond-Upon-Thames

Admiralty
ADM 1: Correspondence and Papers

Air Ministry
AIR 8: Department of the Chief of the Air Staff: Registered Files
AIR 20: Papers accumulated by the Air Historical Branch
AIR 23: Royal Air Force Overseas Commands: Reports and Correspondence

Cabinet Office
CAB 21: Registered Files (1916–65)
CAB 182: Joint Intelligence Committee: Sub-Committees, Working Parties etc: Minutes, Memoranda and Papers

Colonial Office
CO 537: Confidential General and Confidential Original Correspondence
CO 717: Federated Malay States: Original Correspondence
CO 733: Palestine Original Correspondence
CO 822: East Africa: Original Correspondence
CO 850: Personnel: Original Correspondence
CO 875: Public Relations Department, later Information Department: Registered Files

Bibliography

CO 926: Mediterranean Department, Predecessor and Successors: Registered Files, Mediterranean Colonies (MED Series)
CO 967: Private Office Papers
CO 968: Defence Department and Successor: Original Correspondence
CO 1015: Central Africa and Aden: Original Correspondence
CO 1022: South East Asia Department: Original Correspondence
CO 1027: Information Department: Registered Files (INF Series)
CO 1035: Intelligence and Security Departments: Registered Files (ISD Series)

Foreign Office
FO 371: Political Departments: General Correspondence from 1906–66

Ministry of Defence
DEFE 24: Defence Secretariat Branches and their Predecessors: Registered Files
DEFE 25: Chief of Defence Staff: Registered Files (CDS, SCDS and ACDS (OPS) Series)

Prime Minister's Office
PREM 8: Correspondence and Papers, 1945–51
PREM 11: Correspondence and Papers, 1951–64

War Office
WO 32: Registered Files (General Series)
WO 106: Directorate of Military Operations and Military Intelligence, and Predecessors: Correspondence and Papers
WO 216: Office of the Chief of the Imperial General Staff: Papers
WO 231: Directorate of Military Training, later Directorate of Army Training: Papers
WO 275: Sixth Airborne Division, Palestine: Papers and Reports
WO 276: East Africa Command: Papers
WO 279: Confidential Print
WO 291: Military Operational Research Unit, Successor and Related Bodies: Reports and Papers
WO 337: Headquarters British Forces Gulf Area: Files

Rhodes House Library (Bodleian Library of Commonwealth and Africa Studies at Rhodes House), Oxford University, Oxford
Mss. Brit. Emp. 332, Papers of Arthur Creech Jones
Mss. Brit. Emp. s. 395, Transcript of interview with Sir Hugh Foot, Lord Caradon, interviewed by W. P. Kirkman, African and Commonwealth Correspondent for *The Times* and Secretary of the University of Cambridge Appointments Board, April 23, 1971.

Mss. Brit. Emp. s. 525, Transcript of interview with Oliver Lyttelton, Lord Chandos, interviewed by Professor Max Beloff, Gladstone Professor of Government and Public Administration, February 27, 1970
Mss. Brit. Emp. s. 527, "End of Empire" Transcripts
Mss. Medit. s. 35, Papers of Sir Hugh Foot, Lord Caradon

Special Collections Department, University of Birmingham, Birmingham
Papers of:
Lord Avon (Anthony Eden)

Templer Study Centre, National Army Museum, London
NAM 1983-03-104, Papers of General Sir Alan Cunningham
NAM 1989-08-144, Papers of Field Marshal Lord Harding of Petherton
NAM 1995-01-165, Papers of General Sir Robert Lockhart
NAM 2001-06-1, "A Study of United Kingdom Emergency Operations from 1950 to 1966," by the Unison Planning Staff (Ministry of Defence), 1967
NAM 2001-08-889, A Collection of 19 Documents on the Presence of the British Army in East Africa

Published Primary Sources, Memoirs, and Autobiographies

Let Us Face the Future: A Declaration of Labour Policy for the Consideration of the Nation (London: The Labour Party, 1945).
Parliamentary Debates (Hansard), House of Commons, Fifth Series, Volumes 415–610 (London: His Majesty's Stationary Office).
——, House of Lords, Fifth Series, Volume 252.
"Weedkiller Attacks Grass and Broad-Leaved Weeds," *The Science News Letter*, Volume 60, Number 20 (November 17, 1951).
Ashton, S. R. and Stockwell, S. E., eds, *British Documents on the End of Empire: Series A: Volume 1: Imperial Policy and Colonial Practice, 1925–1945: Part I: Metropolitan Reorganisation, Defence and International Relations, Political Change and Constitutional Reform* (London: Her Majesty's Stationary Office, 1996).
Attlee, C. R., *As It Happened* (New York: The Viking Press, 1954).
Boyle, Peter G., ed., *The Eden-Eisenhower Correspondence, 1955–1957* (Chapel Hill: The University of North Carolina Press, 2005).
Calvert, Michael, *Fighting Mad: One Man's Guerilla War* (Barnsley, South Yorkshire, UK: Pen & Sword, 2004).
Colville, John, *The Fringes of Power: 10 Downing Street Diaries, 1939–1955* (New York: W.W. Norton & Company, 1985).

Cooper, Chester L., *The Lion's Last Roar: Suez, 1956* (New York: Harper & Row, Publishers, 1978).

Corfield, F. D., *Historical Survey of the Origins and Growth of Mau Mau: Presented to Parliament by the Secretary of State for the Colonies by Command of Her Majesty* (London: Her Majesty's Stationary Office, 1960).

Headlam, Sir Cuthbert, *Parliament and Politics in the Age of Churchill and Attlee: The Headlam Diaries, 1935–1951*, edited by Stuart Ball (Cambridge: Cambridge University Press, 1999).

Hewitt, Peter, *Kenya Cowboy: A Police Officer's Account of the Mau Mau Emergency*, 3rd edn (Johannesburg, South Africa: 30 Degrees South Publishers, 2008).

Hyam, Ronald, ed., *British Documents on the End of Empire: Series A: Volume 2: The Labour Government and the End of Empire, 1945–1951: Part II: Economics and International Relations* (London: Her Majesty's Stationary Office, 1992).

——, ed., *British Documents on the End of Empire: Series A: Volume 2: The Labour Government and the End of Empire, 1945–1951: Part III: Strategy, Politics and Constitutional Change* (London: Her Majesty's Stationary Office, 1992).

James, Robert Rhodes, ed., *Winston S. Churchill: His Complete Speeches, 1897–1963: Volume VIII, 1950–1963* (New York and London: Chelsea House Publishers, 1974).

Lyttelton, Oliver, *Lord Chandos, The Memoirs of Lord Chandos: An Unexpected View from the Summit* (New York: New American Library, 1963).

Macmillan, Harold, *Riding the Storm, 1956–1959* (New York: Harper & Row, Publishers, 1971).

——, "The Wind of Change," Speech given to the South African Parliament, February 3, 1960, reprinted in *Great speeches of the 20th Century: No. 4: The Wind of Change*, with a forward by Douglas Hurd (London: Guardian News & World, 2007), 9.

Stockwell, A. J., ed., *British Documents on the End of Empire: Series B: Volume 3: Malaya: Part I: The Malayan Union Experiment, 1942–1948* (London: Her Majesty's Stationary Office, 1995).

——, ed., *British Documents on the End of Empire: Series B: Volume 3: Malaya: Part II: The Communist Insurrection, 1948–1953* (London: Her Majesty's Stationary Office, 1995).

——, ed., *British Documents on the End of Empire: Series B: Volume 3: Malaya: Part III: The Alliance Rout to Independence, 1953–1957* (London: Her Majesty's Stationary Office, 1995).

Swanzy, Henry, "Quarterly Notes," *African Affairs*, Volume 53, Number 212 (July 1954).

Thompson, Sir Robert, *Make for the Hills: Memories of Far Eastern Wars* (London: Leo Cooper, 1989).

Watt, D. C., ed., *Documents on the Suez Crisis, 26 July to 6 November 1956* (London: Royal Institute of International Affairs, 1957).

Secondary Sources

Books

Allen, Richard, *Imperialism and Nationalism in the Fertile Crescent: Sources and Prospects of the Arab-Israeli Conflict* (New York: Oxford University Press, 1974).

Anderson, David, *Histories of the Hanged: The Dirty War in Kenya and the End of Empire* (New York and London: W.W. Norton & Company, 2005).

——, and Killingray, David, eds., *Policing and Decolonisation: Politics, Nationalism and the Police, 1917–65* (Manchester: Manchester University Press, 1992).

Andrew, Christopher, *The Defence of the Realm: The Authorized History of MI5* (London: Allen Lane, 2009).

Asher, Michael, *The Regiment: The Real Story of the SAS* (London: Penguin Books, 2008).

Barber, Noel, *The War of the Running Dogs: The Malayan Emergency: 1948–1960* (New York: Weybright and Talley, 1971).

Beckett, Ian F. W., *Modern Insurgencies and Counter-Insurgencies: Guerillas and Their Opponents Since 1750* (London and New York: Routledge, 2001).

Bell, J. Bowyer, *Terror out of Zion: Irgun Zvai Leumi, LEHI, and the Palestine Underground, 1929–1949* (New York: St. Martin's Press, 1977).

Branch, Daniel, *Defeating Mau Mau, Creating Kenya: Counterinsurgency, Civil War, and Decolonization* (Cambridge: Cambridge University Press, 2009).

Brown, Judith M. and Louis, Wm. Roger, eds, *The Oxford History of the British Empire: Volume IV: The Twentieth Century* (Oxford: Oxford University Press, 1999).

Cain, P. J. and Hopkins, A. G., *British Imperialism, 1688–2000,* 2nd edn (London: Pearson Education Limited, 2002).

Carlton, David, *Anthony Eden: A Biography* (London: Allen Lane, 1981).

Chandler, David and Beckett, Ian, eds, *The Oxford History of the British Army* (Oxford: Oxford University Press, 1994).

Charters, David A., *The British Army and Jewish Insurgency in Palestine, 1945–47* (New York: St. Martin's Press, 1989).

Clayton, Anthony, *Counter-Insurgency in Kenya: A Study of Military Operations Against Mau Mau* (Nairobi, Kenya: Transafrica Publishers, 1976).

Clutterbuck, Richard L., *Conflict and Violence in Singapore and Malaysia, 1945–1983* (Boulder, CO: Westview Press, 1985).

Clutterbuck, Richard L., *The Long, Long War: Counterinsurgency in Malaya and Vietnam* (New York: Frederick A. Praeger, 1966).

Cohen, Michael J., *Palestine and the Great Powers, 1945–1948* (Princeton: Princeton University Press, 1982).

Darwin, John, *Britain and Decolonisation: The Retreat from Empire in the Post-War World* (New York: St. Martin's Press, 1988).

——, *The Empire Project: The Rise and Fall of the British World System, 1830–1970* (Cambridge: Cambridge University Press, 2009).

El-Eini, Roza, *Mandated Landscape: British Imperial Rule in Palestine, 1929–1948* (London and New York: Routledge, 2006).

Elkins, Caroline, *Imperial Reckoning: The Untold Story of Britain's Gulag in Kenya* (New York: Henry Holt and Company, 2005).

Friedman, Isaiah, *The Question of Palestine, 1914–1918: British-Jewish-Arab Relations* (New York: Schocken Books, 1973).

Galbraith, John S., *Mackinnon and East Africa, 1878–1895: A Study in the 'New Imperialism'* (Cambridge: Cambridge University Press, 1972).

Goldsworthy, David, *Colonial Issues in British Politics, 1945–1961: From 'Colonial Development' to 'Wind of Change'* (Oxford: The Clarendon Press, 1971).

Gordon, Joel, *Nasser's Blessed Movement: Egypt's Free Officers and the July Revolution* (Oxford: Oxford University Press, 1992).

Grob-Fitzgibbon, Benjamin, *Turning Points of the Irish Revolution: The British Government, Intelligence, and the Cost of Indifference, 1912–1921* (New York and Basingstoke, UK: Palgrave Macmillan, 2007).

Haber, Eitan, *Menahem Begin: The Legend and the Man*, translated by Louis Williams (New York: Delacorte Press, 1978).

Hastings, Max, *The Korean War* (New York: Simon and Schuster, 1987).

Heathcote, T. A., *The British Field Marshals, 1763–1997: A Biographical Dictionary* (Barnsley, South Yorkshire: Leo Cooper, 1999).

Heller, Joseph, *The Stern Gang: Ideology, Politics and Terror, 1940–1949* (London: Frank Cass, 1995).

Hernon, Ian, *Britain's Forgotten Wars: Colonial Campaigns of the 19th Century* (Stroud, Gloucestershire, UK: The History Press, 2008).

Hinchcliffe, Peter, Ducker, John T. and Holt, Maria, *Without Glory in Arabia: The British Retreat from Aden* (London: I.B. Tauris, 2006).

Holland, R. F., *Britain and the Revolt in Cyprus, 1954–1959* (Oxford: Oxford University Press, 1998).

Huxley, Elspeth, *White Man's Country: Lord Delamere and the Making of Kenya, Volumes One and Two, 1870–1914 and 1914–1931* (London: Chatto and Windus, 1953).

Hyam, Ronald, *Britain's Declining Empire: The Road to Decolonisation, 1918–1968* (Cambridge: Cambridge University Press, 2006).

Jackson, Robert, *The Malayan Emergency: The Commonwealth's Wars, 1948–1966* (London and New York: Routledge, 1991).

Jenkins, Roy, *Churchill: A Biography* (New York: Farrar, Straus and Giroux, 2001).

John Cloake, *Templer: Tiger of Malaya: The Life of Field Marshal Sir Gerald Templer* (London: Harrap, 1985), 317.

Jones, Martin, *Failure in Palestine: British and United States Policy After the Second World War* (London and New York: Mansell Publishing Limited, 1986).

Judd, Denis, *Empire: The British Imperial Experience from 1765 to the Present* (New York: Basic Books, 1996).

Keegan, John, *Collins Atlas of World War II* (New York: HarperCollins, 2006).

——, *The Second World War* (New York: Penguin Books, 1989).

Kolinsky, Martin, *Law, Order and Riots in Mandatory Palestine* (New York: St. Martin's Press, in association with King's College, London, 1993).

Kyle, Keith, *Suez: Britain's End of Empire in the Middle East* (London: I.B. Tauris Publishers, 2003).

Lapping, Brian, *End of Empire* (New York: St. Martin's Press, 1985).

Levine, Philippa, *The British Empire: Sunrise to Sunset* (Harlow, UK: Pearson Education Limited, 2007).

Louis, Wm. Roger and Stookey, Robert W., *The End of the Palestine Mandate* (Austin: University of Texas Press, 1986).

Matthew, H. C. G. and Harrison, Brian, *Oxford Dictionary of National Biography* (Oxford and New York: Oxford University Press, 2004).

Mawby, Spencer, *British Policy in Aden and the Protectorates, 1955–67: Last Outpost of a Middle East Empire* (London and New York: Routledge, 2005).

Metcalf, Barbara D. and Metcalf, Thomas R., *A Concise History of India* (Cambridge: Cambridge University Press, 2002).

Mockaitis, Thomas R., *British Counterinsurgency, 1919–1960* (London: Macmillan Ltd., 1990).

Morgan, Kenneth O., *Labour in Power, 1945–1951* (Oxford: The Clarendon Press, 1984).

Morgan, Philip D. and Hawkins, Sean, eds, *Black Experience and the Empire* (Oxford: Oxford University Press, 2004).

Mungeam, G. H., *British Rule in Kenya, 1895–1912: The Establishment of Administration in the East Africa Protectorate* (Oxford: Clarendon Press, 1966).

Nagl, John, *Learning to Eat Soup with a Knife: Counterinsurgency Lessons from Malaya and Vietnam* (Chicago: The University of Chicago Press, 2002).

Newsinger, John, *British Counterinsurgency: From Palestine to Northern Ireland* (New York: Palgrave Macmillan, 2002).

O'Ballance, Edgar, *Malaya: The Communist Insurgent War, 1948–1960* (Hamden, CT: Archon Books, 1966).

Pearce, Robert, *Attlee's Labour Governments, 1945–1951* (London and New York: Routledge, 1994).

Pelling, Henry, *Churchill's Peacetime Ministry, 1951–55* (New York and Basingstoke, Hampshire, UK: Macmillan Press, Ltd., 1997).

——, *The Labour Governments, 1945–51* (New York: St. Martin's Press, 1984).

Perlmutter, Amos, *The Life and Times of Menachem Begin* (New York: Doubleday & Company, Inc., 1987).

Pieragostini, Karl, *Britain, Aden, and South Arabia: Abandoning Empire* (New York: St. Martin's Press, 1991).

Podet, Allen Howard, *The Success and Failure of the Anglo-American Committee of Inquiry, 1945–1946: Last Chance in Palestine* (Lewiston, NY, and Queenston, ON: The Edwin Mellen Press, 1986).

Porath, Y., *The Emergence of the Palestinian-Arab National Movement, 1918–1929* (London: Frank Cass, 1974).

——, *The Palestinian Arab National Movement: From Riots to Rebellion, 1929–1939*, vol. 2 (London: Frank Cass, 1977).

Porter, Andrew, ed., *The Oxford History of the British Empire: Volume III: The Nineteenth Century* (Oxford: Oxford University Press, 1999).

Porter, Bernard, *The Absent-Minded Imperialists: Empire, Society, and Culture in Britain* (Oxford: Oxford University Press, 2006).

Rooney, David, *Mad Mike: A Life of Michael Calvert* (London: Leo Cooper, 1997).

Rosberg, Carl G., Jr and Nottingham, John, *The Myth of "Mau Mau": Nationalism in Kenya* (New York: Frederick A. Praeger, Publishers, 1966).

Rothwell, Victor, *Anthony Eden: A Political Biography, 1931–57* (Manchester: Manchester University Press, 1992).

Satia, Priya, *Spies in Arabia: The Great War and the Cultural Foundations of Britain's Covert Empire in the Middle East* (Oxford and New York: Oxford University Press, 2008).

Short, Anthony, *The Communist Insurrection in Malaya, 1948–1960* (New York: Crane, Russak & Company, Inc., 1975).

Silver, Eric, *Begin: The Haunted Prophet* (New York: Random House, 1984).

Soulioti, Stella, *Fettered Independence: Cyprus, 1878–1964: Volume One: The Narrative* (Minneapolis, MN: Minnesota Mediterranean and East European Monographs, Modern Greek Studies, University of Minnesota, 2006).

Stubbs, Richard, *Hearts and Minds in Guerilla Warfare: The Malayan Emergency, 1948–1960* (Oxford: Oxford University Press, 1989).

Stueck, William, *The Korean War: An International History* (Princeton: Princeton University Press, 1995).

Thomas, Martin, *Empires of Intelligence: Security Services and Colonial Disorder After 1914* (Berkeley and Los Angeles: University of California Press, 2008).

Throup, David, *Economic and Social Origins of Mau Mau, 1945–53* (Athens, OH: Ohio University Press, 1988).

Townshend, Charles, *Britain's Civil Wars: Counterinsurgency in the Twentieth Century* (London: Faber and Faber, 1986).

Walker, Jonathan, *Aden Insurgency: The Savage War in South Arabia, 1962–1967* (Staplehurst, Kent, UK: Spellmount Limited, 2005).

Wasserstein, Bernard, *The British in Palestine: The Mandatory Government and the Arab-Jewish Conflict, 1917–1929* (London: Royal Historical Society, 1978).

Weinberg, Gerhard L., *A World at Arms: A Global History of World War II* (Cambridge: Cambridge University Press, 1994).

Williams, Francis, *Twilight of Empire: Memoirs of Prime Minister Clement Attlee* (New York: A.S. Barnes and Co., 1962).

Wolpert, Stanley, *Shameful Flight: The Last Years of the British Empire in India* (Oxford and New York: Oxford University Press, 2006).

Articles, Essays, and Chapters

Anderson, David M., "Policing and Communal Conflict: the Cyprus Emergency, 1954–60," in Anderson, David M. and Killingray, David, eds, *Policing and Decolonisation: Politics, Nationalism and the Police, 1917–65* (Manchester: Manchester University Press, 1992).

Baker, Colin, "Armitage, Sir Robert Perceval (1906–1990)," in H. C. G. Matthew and Brian Harrison, *Oxford Dictionary of National Biography* (Oxford and New York: Oxford University Press, 2004).

Bennett, Huw, "Erskine, Sir George Watkin Eben James (1899–1965)," in H. C. G. Matthew and Brian Harrison, *Oxford Dictionary of National Biography* (Oxford and New York: Oxford University Press, 2004).

Blacker, John, "The Demography of Mau Mau: Fertility and Mortality in Kenya in the 1950s: A Demographer's Viewpoint," *African Affairs*, Volume 106, Issue 423 (April 2007).

Brenner, Lenni, "Zionist-Revisionism: The Years of Fascism and Terror," *Journal of Palestine Studies*, Volume 13, Number 1 (Autumn 1983).

Bromberger, E., "The Growth of Population in Palestine," *Population Studies*, Volume 2, Number 1 (June 1948)

Clayton, Anthony, "Baring, (Charles) Evelyn, first Baron Howick of Glendale (1903–1973)," in H. C. G. Matthew and Brian Harrison, *Oxford Dictionary of National Biography* (Oxford and New York: Oxford University Press, 2004).

Cohen, Michael J., "Appeasement in the Middle East: The British White Paper on Palestine, May 1939," *The Historical Journal*, Volume 16, Number 3 (September 1973).

Cohen, Michael J., "The Genesis of the Anglo-American Committee on Palestine, November 1945: A Case Study in the Assertion of American Hegemony," *The Historical Journal*, Volume 22, Number 1 (March 1979).

Goldsworthy, David, "Macleon, Iain," in H.C.G. Matthew and Brian Harrison, *Oxford Dictionary of National Biography* (Oxford and New York: Oxford University Press, 2004).

Grob-Fitzgibbon, Benjamin, "Securing the Colonies for the Commonwealth: Counterinsurgency, Decolonization, and the Development of British Imperial Strategy in the Postwar Empire," *British Scholar*, Volume 2, Issue 1 (September 2009).

Farrar-Hockley, Anthony, "The Post-War Army, 1945–1963," in Chandler, David, and Beckett, Ian, eds, *The Oxford History of the British Army* (Oxford: Oxford University Press, 1994).

Haron, Miriam Joyce, "Palestine and the Anglo-American Connection," *Modern Judaism*, Volume 2, Number 2 (May 1982).

Harvey Sicherman, *Aden and British Strategy, 1839–1968* (Philadelphia, PA: Foreign Policy Research Institute, 1972), 1–17.

Holland, Robert, "Never, Never Land: British Colonial Policy and the Roots of Violence in Cyprus, 1950–1954," *Journal of Imperial and Commonwealth History*, Volume 21, Issue 3 (1993).

Matthew Hughes, "The Banality of Brutality: British Armed Forces and the Repression of the Arab Revolt in Palestine, 1936–39," *English Historical Review*, Volume CXXIV, Number 507 (April 2009).

Hunt, David, "Harding, John, first Baron Harding of Petherton (1896–1989)," in H. C. G. Matthew and Brian Harrison, *Oxford Dictionary of National Biography* (Oxford and New York: Oxford University Press, 2004).

Imperato, Pascal James, "Differing Perspectives on Mau Mau," *African Studies Review*, Volume 48, Number 3 (December 2005).

Loftus, P. J., "Features of the Demography of Palestine," *Population Studies*, Volume 2, Number 1 (June 1948).

Louis, Wm. Roger, "British Imperialism and the End of the Palestine Mandate," in Lewis, Wm. Roger and Stookey, Robert W., eds, *The End of the Palestine Mandate* (Austin: University of Texas Press, 1986).

——, Roger, "The Dissolution of the British Empire," in Judith M. Brown and Wm. Roger Louis, eds, *The Oxford History of the British Empire: Volume IV: The Twentieth Century* (Oxford: Oxford University Press, 1999).

Margalit, Elkana, "Social and Intellectual Origins of the Hashomer Hatzair Youth Movement, 1913–1920," *Journal of Contemporary History*, Volume 4, Number 2 (April 1969).

Mawby, Spencer, "Britain's Last Imperial Frontier: The Aden Protectorates, 1952–1959," *Journal of Imperial and Commonwealth History*, Volume 29, Issue 2 (2001).

McCaskie, T. C., "Cultural Encounters: Britain and Africa in the Nineteenth Century," in Philip D. Morgan and Sean Hawkins, eds, *Black Experience and the Empire* (Oxford: Oxford University Press, 2004).

Norris, Jacob, "Repression and Rebellion: Britain's Response to the Arab Revolt in Palestine of 1936–39," *Journal of Imperial and Commonwealth History*, Volume 36, Number 1 (March 2008).

Ovendale, Ritchie, "The Palestine Policy of the British Labour Government, 1945–1946," *International Affairs*, Volume 55, Number 3 (July 1979).

——, "The Palestine Policy of the British Labour Government 1947: The Decision to Withdraw," *International Affairs*, Volume 56, Number 1 (January 1980).

Percox, David A., "Internal Security and Decolonization in Kenya, 1956–1963," *Journal of Imperial and Commonwealth History*, Volume 29, Issue 1 (2001).

Peterson, Derek R., "The Intellectual Lives of Mau Mau Detainees," *Journal of African History*, Number 49 (2008).

Pugh, Patricia M., "Jones, Arthur Creech," H. C. G. Matthew and Brian Harrison, eds, *Oxford Dictionary of National Biography* (Oxford and New York: Oxford University Press, 2004).

Stockwell, A. J., "Gurney, Sir Henry Lovell Goldsworthy," in H. C. G. Matthew and Brian Harrison, *Oxford Dictionary of National Biography* (Oxford and New York: Oxford University Press, 2004).

——, "Introduction," in A. J. Stockwell, ed., *British Documents on the End of Empire: Series B: Volume 3: Malaya: Part I: The Malayan Union Experiment, 1942–1948* (London: Her Majesty's Stationary Office, 1995).

——, "Malaysia: The Making of a Neo-Colony?" *Journal of Imperial and Commonwealth History*, Volume 26, Issue 2 (1998).

Strawson, John, "Cunningham, Sir Alan Gordon," in H. C. G. Matthew and Brian Harrison, eds, *Oxford Dictionary of National Biography* (Oxford and New York: Oxford University Press, 2004).

Stubbs, Richard, "Counter-Insurgency and the Economic Factor: The Impact of the Korean War Prices Boom on the Malayan Emergency" (Occasional Paper No. 19, The Institute of Southeast Asian Studies, 1974).

Throup, D. W., "Renison, Sir Patrick Muir," in H.C.G. Matthew and Brian Harrison, *Oxford Dictionary of National Biography* (Oxford and New York: Oxford University Press, 2004).

Index

Abrahams, Abraham, 32
Acheson, Dean, 55, 148
Aden, 317, 327–328, 337, 338,
    376
  collective punishment in,
    314–315, 316
  history of, 313
Aden Protectorate Levies (APL),
    315–316
Ainsworth, J. D., 211
air force, *see* Royal Air Force
    (RAF)
Alexander, Albert Victor, 24, 69
Alexander, Lord, 186, 225
Ali, Husain ibn, 7
Anglo-American Committee of
    Inquiry (Palestine), 29–31,
    35–36, 39, 51–58, 385n73
Arab-Israeli War (1948), 100
Arab Revolt, 10, 17
Armitage, Sir Robert, 286, 301,
    304–305, 306–308, 329
  makes case for the declaration
    of an emergency in Cyprus,
    304–305
  replaced as governor of
    Cyprus, 309–310
army, *see* British Army
Army Air Corps, 142
Army Medical Service, 206
Ataturk, Kemal, 283
Attlee, Clement, 6, 23, 35, 65,
    77, 89–90, 127–128, 130,
        131, 139, 140–141, 164–165,
        168, 169–170, 173, 175, 284,
        340, 357, 379n5
    and the Briggs Plan in Malaya,
        156–157, 159–160
    correspondence with Truman,
        26–27, 55, 56, 58
    on the Palestine problem, 24,
        52, 61–62, 70
    on the King David Hotel
        bombing, 51
    on nationalization, social
        justice, and the welfare
        state, 25
    resignation of, 172
Asquith, Herbert Henry, 174, 283
Auchinleck, Sir Claude, 35
Australia, 33, 85, 91, 141, 151,
        342, 346
Awbery, Stanley, 201

Baldwin, Stanley, 174, 299
Balfour, A. J.,
    and the Balfour Declaration,
        7, 8, 93
Balfour, Harold, 364
Barbados, 376
Baring, Sir Evelyn, 225–226, 235,
        239, 241, 248, 249, 254, 258,
        264, 268, 269, 280, 311, 324,
        353
    and abuse in Kenya, 272–274,
        365–366

appointed governor of Kenya, 218

arrival in Kenya, 222

asks Lyttelton for permission to declare a state of emergency in Kenya, 223–224, 225

biography of, 217–218

briefs the cabinet on Mau Mau (1952), 243–244

and capital punishment, 241, 245–246, 254

and collective punishment, 235–236, 237–238, 241, 244

correspondence with Erskine, 256

declares emergency in Kenya, 233–234

entertains demands from the white settler community, 246–247

forms war council in Kenya, 279

and the Haywood case, 272–273

recalled from Kenya, 365–366

on "rehabilitation" in Kenya, 357–358, 362

recommends the removal of sanctions in some areas of Kenya, 293–294

removes Hinde as director of operations, 255

requests delegation from MI5, 240

requests a Director of Operations for Kenya, 238

and "screening" in Kenya, 236–237, 254

and the trial of Jomo Kenyatta, 242–243

Barker, Lieutenant General Sir Evelyn Hugh, 46, 70, 72, 80

Basutoland, 376

Batang Kali massacre, 119–120

Bavin, E. W., 19

Bayly–Pike, D. F., 232

Beaverbrook, Lord, 349

Bechuanaland, 376

Beeley, Sir Harold, 385n73

Begin, Menachem, 11–13, 18

Ben–Eliezer, Arieh, 11, 13, 18

Ben Gurion, David, 39, 40

Benn, William Wedgwood, *see* Stansgate, 1st Viscount

Betar, 12

Bergson, Peter,
and the Bergson Group, 18–20

Berlin, Isaiah, 19

Bevan, Aneurin, 168, 170, 171

Bevin, Ernest, 5–6, 24, 27–28, 33, 41–42, 74, 92, 130, 131, 148, 156, 169, 385n73
and the Anglo-American Committee of Inquiry, 29–31, 35–36, 52–58
death of, 170
on the Palestine problem, 68–69

Bingley, Dick, 245

Birkbeck, Lieutenant Colonel, 118–119

Black, Group Captain E. R. E., 32–33

Black Watch, 266

Blackman, C. E., 232

Blood, Sir Bindon, 173

Blundell, Michael, 219, 222, 233, 234

Boothby, Robert, 169

Botswana, 376

Boucher, Major General Sir Charles, 112, 113, 117, 119, 122, 124

Bourne, Lieutenant General Geoffrey C., 185, 277,
on Malaya, 289–291, 310–311

Bowyer, Eric, 234, 240
Bracken, Lord, 349
Briggs, General Sir Harold, 134,
    146, 147–148, 153, 171, 176,
    178, 182, 185, 189, 196, 226,
    250, 254, 285, 289, 353, 355
  appointed Director of
    Operations in Malaya,
    132–133
  concerns about the Briggs Plan,
    155–157
  establishes the Briggs Plan,
    135–138
  on food denial and collective
    punishment, 159
  and intelligence in Malaya,
    154–155
  and resettlement of squatters in
    Malaya, 157–159
  retirement of, 176
  on the success of the Briggs
    Plan, 165–166
Briggs Plan, the, 135–138,
    146–148, 149–150, 151,
    152–166, 227, 356
British Army, 142, 148–149, 214
  and abuse in Kenya, 274–275
  and the Briggs Plan (Malaya),
    136–137, 157
  in Cyprus, 302, 307–308, 309,
    321–322, 323, 329, 330, 333,
    334, 368–369, 371
  in Kenya, 233, 234, 236, 238,
    248, 249, 257, 264–265,
    266–267, 279, 281, 291–292,
    293, 324, 325
  lessons from Palestine for
    Malaya, 117–119
  in Malaya, 110–111,
    112–114, 121–125, 126,
    143–144, 147, 152–153, 180,
    191, 195, 226, 228–229,
    262–263, 290–291

  on Mau Mau oathing practices,
    215–216
  in Palestine, 34, 36–38, 44–48,
    61, 73, 86–87, 89, 94, 95,
    394n227
  and "screening" of Kikuyu
    population in Kenya, 237
  see also individual regiments
    and units by name
British Guiana, 366, 376
British Honduras, 366
British Parliament, see House of
    Commons
British Petroleum (BP), 313
British Security Coordination
    (New York), 19
British Sixth Airborne Division
    (see also Parachute Regiment),
    37–38, 44–45, 117–119
British Somaliland, 337, 375
Brittain, R. W., 232
Brockway, Fenner, 221, 240–241
Brook, Sir Norman, 54
Brooke, Sir Alan, 41
Brownjohn, General N. C. D., 154
Budd, Lieutenant D. J., 280
Bufton, Air Vice Marshal S. O.,
    292–293
Burdick, Major P., 291–292
Burma, 185
Burton, Special Agent (FBI), 19
Butler, Rab, 300, 349
Byrnes, James F., 33
  and the Anglo-American
    Committee of Inquiry, 29–31,
    52, 54–55

Cadogan, Sir Alexander, 85
Calvert, Michael "Mad Mike",
    141–146, 193
Cameroon, 375
Campbell-Bannerman, Sir
    Henry, 174

Canada, 33, 85, 91, 342, 346

capital punishment, 84, 86–87, 89, 138, 241, 245–246, 253–254, 321, 332, 334

Cassino, battles of, 13

Castle, Barbara, 363

Catling, Richard,
  biography of, 17
  and Kenya, 312, 326–327
  trip to the United States from Palestine, 17–20

Cecil, Lord Hugh, 174

Chamberlain, Neville, 299

Chavasse, Colonel K. G. F., 88

Chilevicius, Jankelis, 13–14, 18–20, 31

China, 104, 107, 151, 167, 336

China Communist Party, 104

China, General, *see* Itote, Waruhiu

Church of Scotland, 244

Churchill, Lord Randolph, 173

Churchill, Sir Winston, 6, 23, 26, 127, 130, 139–140, 141–142, 171, 176, 182, 198, 259, 260, 299, 300–301, 341, 349–350, 357
  appoints Alan Lennox-Boyd colonial secretary, 288
  appoints Templer Malayan high commissioner and director of operations, 186
  biography of, 173–175
  correspondence with Viscount Montgomery, 128–129
  failing health of, 294
  meeting with Lyttelton to discuss Malaya, 184–185
  and the resignation of Oliver Lyttelton, 275–277
  resignation of, 295–296, 301
  return to the premiership (1951), 172

Clark, Captain Ridley Hugh, 50, 59

Codnor, Michael, 189

collective punishment, 159, 195–196, 198, 201–203, 216–217, 227–228, 235–236, 237–238, 239, 241, 242, 244, 314–315, 316, 322, 328–329, 334–336,

colonial office, 24, 26, 33, 43, 70–71, 105–106, 107, 116–117, 121, 127, 133, 176, 177, 186, 207–208, 212, 217, 219, 224–225, 239, 243–244, 284–285, 288, 294, 301, 305, 313, 314, 329, 364, 370, 376
  and Aden, 315–316
  and the Anglo-American Committee of Inquiry, 29
  and crop destruction in Malaya, 198–199
  disagreement with the war office over Palestine, 65–68
  joint paper on Cyprus, 302–304
  memorandum on imperial security (1957), 353–354
  and relations with MI5, 20–21, 239–240
  requests legislation to quell Mau Mau in Kenya, 220–221
  view of the Malayan Emergency, 191

Colonial Development Corporation, 146

Colonial Development and Welfare Fund, 146

colonial secretary, position of, 380n9

Colqhoun, Brigadier, 119

Colville, John, 294, 295

Conservative Party, 51, 128–130, 140, 169, 295, 298, 299, 349–350, 364, 369, 376
  colonial policy of, 177, 425n243

Conservative Party – *continued*
  and general election of 1945,
    379n6, 379n7
  and general election of 1950,
    127, 130–131
  and general election of 1951,
    171–172, 175
  and general election of 1955, 300
  and general election of
    1959, 366
Crawford, Sir Frederick,
    270–271
Creasy, Sir Gerald, 400n300
Creech Jones, Arthur, 40–41, 63,
    70, 74, 83, 98, 100, 112, 117,
    137, 170, 171, 177, 178, 185,
    284, 353, 357
  biography of, 60
  correspondence with Sir Henry
    Gurney, 114–115, 120–123,
    125–127
  correspondence with Malcolm
    MacDonald on Malaya,
    101–103
  and the end of the British
    mandate in Palestine, 96–97
  loses his parliamentary seat
    (1950), 127, 131
  meeting with Cunningham and
    Montgomery, 71–72
  on the declaration of a Malayan
    emergency, 108–111
  on the Palestine problem,
    61–62, 68, 92–93
Crete, 284
Cripps, Stafford, 128, 169, 170
Crocker, General Sir John T., 89,
    96, 99
Cromer, Lord, 217
Crookshank, Lieutenant Colonel
    A. K., 152
Cunningham, Lieutenant General
    Sir Alan, 36–37, 39–40, 41,

    45–46, 49, 60–61, 66, 73, 87,
    102, 118
  biography of, 34–35
  and the end of the British
    mandate in Palestine, 96–100
  meeting with Creech Jones and
    Montgomery, 71–72
  ordered to change course in
    Palestine, 70, 72
  proclaims martial law in
    Palestine, 79–80
  supports the policy of Gurney
    and Creech Jones in
    Palestine, 63–65
  suspends martial law in
    Palestine, 82
Cypriot Police, 297–298, 301,
    304–305, 307, 309, 321–322,
    334
  Special Branch, 302, 307,
    329–330
  terrorist attacks against, 302,
    308, 321, 329, 331, 368
Cyprus, 300–302, 313, 316, 337,
    338, 342, 346, 353, 354,
    368–372
  alleged human rights abuses
    in, 369
  capital punishment in, 321,
    332, 334
  collective punishment in, 322,
    328–329, 334–336
  curfews in, 307–308, 328–329,
    373
  emergency regulations in, 306,
    321–322, 334
  end of the emergency in,
    373–375
  EOKA violence in, 297–298,
    302, 306–307, 308–309, 322,
    323, 329, 331, 332, 334,
    368–369, 371, 372–373
  history of, 282–287

and intelligence, 329–330
offered self-government and a
    path to self-determination, 323
parliamentary statement on,
    287–288
strategic value of, 285, 302–304
tripartite conference
    concerning, 304–306, 307,
    308–309
Cyprus Regiment, 284
Czechoslovakia, 85, 91, 341

Dalton, Hugh, 24, 77–78, 89–90,
    130, 131–132, 170
D'Arcy, Lieutenant General J. C.,
    34, 36–37, 39, 46
Davidesca, Joseph, 32
Davies, Eric, 221
Dawe, Sir Arthur, 15–16
death penalty, see capital
    punishment
Defence Security Office (DSO), 32
Del Tufo, M. V., 137–138
Demetriou, Andreou, 332, 334
Dempsey, General Sir Miles,
    63–65, 72, 73, 81, 82, 89
Devonshire Regiment, 280,
    291–292
Directorate of Technical
    Investigation (war office), 142
Disraeli, Benjamin, 282, 339
District War Executive Committee
    (DWEC), see Malaya
dominions office, 33
Douglas, F. C. R., 397–398n268
Dow, Sir Hugh, 97
Driberg, Thomas, 201
Dulles, John Foster, 341, 344
Dunn, Group Captain P. H.,
    152–153
Dutch East Indies, 354
Dyak trackers (in Malaya), 112,
    400n300

East Africa Artillery, 280
East African Association (EAA), 212
East African Protectorate, 210–211
East India Company, see English
    East India Company
Easter Rising (Ireland), see Irish
    Easter Rising
Eastwood, Christopher, 20, 21,
    23, 32, 64
Eden, Anthony, 51, 175, 286, 301,
    305–308, 317, 318, 320,
    323–324, 340, 353, 357
    becomes prime minister,
        295–296, 298
    biography of, 298–300
    on Cypriot self-determination,
        320–321
    correspondence with
        Eisenhower, 338, 341, 342,
        344, 345, 348
    replaces Armitage with Harding
        as governor of Cyprus,
        309–310
    resignation of, 349–350
    and the Suez Crisis, 339,
        341–349
Egypt, 42, 100, 171, 224–225, 256,
    283, 338–341, 343–346, 350
Eisenhower, President Dwight D.,
    and the Suez Crisis, 338, 341,
    342, 344, 347–348
Elizabeth II, Queen, 187–188,
    295–296, 350, 367
Elliot, Air Marshal Sir
    William, 156
Emrys Evans, Paul, 218, 293
English East India Company,
    103, 313
Enosis, 282–288, 297–298, 304,
    306, 309, 318, 320, 321, 323,
    329, 331, 332–333, 334
EOKA, see Ethniki Organosis
    Kyprion Agoniston

Erskine, Lieutenant General Sir
George "Bobbie," 269, 279,
280, 281, 293, 353, 355
and abuse in Kenya, 270–275
appointed commander in chief
in Kenya, 255
biography of, 255–256
concerns about Kenya,
257–258, 266
introduces surrender policy,
267–268
strategy in Kenya, 264–268
Ethniki Organosis Kyprion Agoniston
(EOKA), 304–305, 306, 309,
321–322, 331, 334–335
campaign of violence of,
297–298, 302, 306–307,
308–309, 322, 323, 329, 331,
332, 334, 368–369, 371,
372–373
declares ceasefire, 375
European Union, 375
Exodus, the, 87–88, 394n227

Farouk I, King, 341
Federal Bureau of Investigation
(FBI), 19–21, 31
Federal War Council, *see* Malaya
Fergusson, Charles, 245
Ferret Force (Malaya), 135
Field, William, 200, 202
Fiji, 217
Firbank, General Cecil Llewelyn,
315
Fleming, Ian, 349
Foot, Sir Hugh, 369–371,
371–373, 375
Foot, Michael, 369
"Force 136", 105
foreign office, 33
joint paper on Cyprus,
302–304
Foster Sutton, Stafford, 155

France, 42, 87–88, 151, 315, 343,
345–346, 349
Frankfurter, Justice Felix, 55
Franks, Lieutenant Colonel Brian,
142–143
Fraser, Hugh, 177, 191
Freeman, John, 170
Freeman, Peter, 314
French Indochina, 151, 185, 354

Gaitskell, Hugh, 170
Gambia, 376
Gandhi, Mohandas, 91
General China, *see* Itote, Waruhiu
general election, 139–140
of 1945, 6, 23, 379n6, 379n7
of 1950, 127, 130–131
of 1951, 170–172
of 1955, 300
of 1959, 366
Gent, Sir Edward, 100–101, 106,
107, 108, 109, 397–398n268
George VI, King, 6, 130, 139, 140,
172, 175, 187, 295
Germany, 25, 88, 256, 284, 315
Ghana, 351, 375
Gibb, Lieutenant I. S., 113–114
Gibbs, Michael, 79
Gibson, Anthony, 248
Giles, A. F., 31–32
Girouard, Sir Percy, 211
Gloucestershire Regiment,
167–168
Gold Coast, 375, *see also* Ghana
Goldman, Peter, 366
Gort, Field Marshal 6th Viscount,
John Standish Vereker, 34
Goschen, George, 339
Goudie, W. H., 363–364
Grady, Ambassador Henry F., 52,
54–55
Grantham, Sir Alexander, 102
Granville, Second Earl, 299

Gray, W. N., 110, 112, 121,
    154–155, 179
Great Calcutta Killing, 76
Greece, 42, 282–288, 298,
    301–302, 303–304, 305–306,
    308–309, 336, 369, 370,
    373–375
Green Howards, 124–125
Griffiths, Captain G. S. L., 257
Griffiths, James, 132, 146–147,
    156, 161, 167, 176, 178, 185,
    285, 287–288
  on the Briggs Plan, 153
  on the strategic importance of
    Malaya, 149–150
Griffiths-Jones, Eric, 358–360
Grivas, Lieutenant Colonel
    George, 331
  and beginning of EOKA
    campaign of violence,
    297–298
Guatemala, 85, 91
Guinness, Walter Edward, *see*
    Moyne, 1st Baron
Gurkha Rifles, 152, 180, 289
Gurney, Sir Henry, 60–61, 62, 72,
    82, 100, 112, 117, 118, 119,
    133–134, 137–138, 152, 170,
    171, 176, 178, 179, 185, 189,
    196, 250, 286, 289, 353, 355,
    356
  appointed high commissioner
    in Malaya, 102–103
  arrival in Palestine, 58
  biography of, 58–59
  and the Briggs plan, 146–148,
    156–157, 165–166
  correspondence with Arthur
    Creech Jones, 114–115,
    120–123, 125–127
  correspondence with John
    Martin, 59, 62–63, 65, 72–73,
    74, 80, 83, 90, 99
  death of, 166–167
  introduces Sir Harold Briggs to
    Sir Robert Thompson, 135
  offers his resignation, 160–161
  on emergency strategy in
    Malaya, 114–115, 153–154
  on the end of the Palestine
    mandate, 99
  on the police in Malaya,
    120–121, 122–123, 154–155
  on the use of the army in
    Malaya, 121–123
  suggests the appointment of
    a Director of Operations for
    Malaya, 126–127, 132
Guyana, 376

Hackett, Lieutenant Colonel John,
    117–118
Hadden, R. E., 232
Hadingham, Superintendent K. P.,
    50
Haganah, the, 47, 48, 51, 64
  terrorist campaign of, 37–38, 94
Hale, Leslie, 240–241
Halifax, 1st Earl of, E. F. L. Wood,
    28–29, 33, 301–302,
    384–386n72
  and the Anglo-American
    Committee of Inquiry, 29–31
Hall, Ernest, 206
Hall, George Henry, 5–7, 23–24,
    26, 29, 31, 33, 35, 39–41,
    47–48, 53–54, 59–60, 62, 64,
    380n8
Harding, Field Marshal Sir John,
    143, 144, 160, 277, 289, 307,
    353
  appointed governor of Cyprus,
    310
  biography of, 317–318
  and collective punishment in
    Cyprus, 328–329

Harding, Field Marshal Sir
John – *continued*
declares state of emergency in
Cyprus, 323–324
and deportation of Makarios,
332–333
meetings with Makarios,
318–320, 322–323, 331–332
resignation as governor of
Cyprus, 369–371
strategy in Cyprus, 321–322,
330–331
visit to London, 331
Harding, John Charles, 333
Harlech, 4th Baron, William
Ormsby-Gore, 13–14
Harrington, Lieutenant Colonel
C. H. P., 206
Harrison, Earl G., 27
Hashomer Hatzair, 11
Hastings, Major M. C., 291
Haywood, Brian, 270–273
Head, Antony, 266, 274, 301, 311
Head, Captain Peter, 262–263
Headlam, Sir Cuthbert, 78–79,
130, 130–131, 168–169,
379n6, 379n7, 383n53,
392n188
Helpern, Jeremiah, 32
Henderson, Ian, 279, 280
Hesselberger, Kitty, 245
Hickinbotham, Sir Tom, 314, 316,
327–328
Higham, J. D., 116, 420n159
Highland Light Brigade, 368–369
Hinde, Major General W. R. N.
"Looney," 258, 268, 424n228
appointed director of military
operations in Kenya, 248
develops military plan for the
Kenyan emergency, 249–251
promoted director of
operations, 254

removed as director of
operations, 255
Hiroshima, 25, 142
Hobley, C. W., 211
Hodges, Second Lieutenant
R., 95–96
Hola Affair, 360–365
Holland, Sidney, 343, 346
Hollis, L. C., 65
Hollis, Sir Roger, 376
Hong Kong, 143, 144, 185, 256
Hopkinson, Henry, 287–288
House of Commons, 51, 52, 56,
78, 98, 107, 169, 173, 175,
176, 200–202, 221, 233, 241,
244, 264, 274, 284, 294, 296,
298, 299, 314, 316, 347, 350,
366, 373–374
cross-party delegation to Kenya
(1954), 278–279
debate on the Hola Affair
(Kenya), 364–365
debate on India, 90–91
debate on Palestine, 35–36
photographs of Mau Mau
atrocities placed in, 235
statement on Cyprus, 287–288
House of Lords, 356–357
Humphrey, A. H. P., 420n159
Humphrey, Hugh, 115–116
Hvass, Kenya Reserve Police
officer, 273

Imjin River, battle of, 167–168
Imperial Chemical Industries
(ICI), 198, 420n159
Imperial East Africa Company,
209
India, 74–77, 85, 90–91, 97, 104,
128, 208, 256, 284, 301, 313,
317, 346, 356, 395n237
Indian Civil Service, 75, 217
Indian Mutiny, 75

Indian National Congress, 74–76
Indian Police Service, 154
Indochina, *see* French Indochina
Information Services Department
  (Malaya), 163
Intelligence Corps, 394n227
International Monetary
  Fund, 348
International Red Cross, 358
Iran, 85, 91, 171, 313
Iraq, 63, 100
Ireland, 64
Irgun Zvai Leumi (the IZL), 10–11,
  38, 48, 51, 66, 87, 93, 123,
  334
  beginning of revolt of (1944),
    12–13
  ceasefire of (1945), 22–23
  hanging of two police
    sergeants, 89
  terrorist campaign of, 14–15,
    22, 32, 33, 38, 43–44, 45,
    48–51, 54, 61, 62–63, 73, 79,
    80–81, 84–86, 88–89, 95
Irish Easter Rising, 18–19
Irish War of Independence, 256
Israel, 100, 313, 343, 345, 350,
  see also Palestine
Italy, 42, 284
Itote, Waruhiu (General China),
  279–280

Jabotinsky, Eric, 18
Jabotinsky, Vladimi Ze'ev, 12
Jacob, Sir Edward, 225
Jamaica, 349, 350, 375
Japan, 24–25, 104–106
Jefferson, Second Lieutenant
  Michael, 100
Jenkin, Sir William, 154–155, 176
Jewish Agency, 5–6, 11, 22–23,
  39, 40, 51, 55, 59, 61, 63, 69,
  73, 281

declaration of the state of
  Israel, 100
founding of, 8
collaboration with British
  government, 15–17,
  60–61, 64
and Operation Agatha, 46–48
Jinnah, Muhammad Ali, 76, 91
Jones, Arthur Creech, *see* Creech
  Jones, Arthur
Jordan, 100
Junod, Dr., 358

Kagorani, Douglas, 244
Kaplan, Ruth, 19
Karolis, Michael, 321, 322, 334
Kearns, G. H., 232
Keates, Richard Geoffrey, 270
Keightley, General Sir Charles, 348
Keith-Roach, Edward, 9
Kellar, A. J., 20, 32, 64, 240
Kenya, 216, 217, 218, 221, 224,
  225, 226, 246, 258, 278, 286,
  288, 300, 308, 316, 317, 318,
  328, 329–330, 334, 336, 337,
  338, 346, 353, 354, 369
  assassination of Chief Waruhiu
    wa Kungu, 222–223
  beginning of Mau Mau violence
    in, 208, 216–217
  capital punishment in, 241,
    245–246, 253–254
  casualty statistics in, 249, 261,
    441–442n17
  Christianity in, 211
  collective punishment in,
    216–217, 235–236, 237, 239,
    241, 242, 244
  development of Mau Mau in,
    213–217
  emergency legislation in,
    220–221, 234
  end of emergency in, 366–367

Kenya – *continued*
  founding of, 211
  history of, 208–214
  Hola Affair, 360–365, 366
  Indian immigration into, 209
  intelligence in, 239–240, 250
  Lari massacre, 251–252, 255,
    257, 260, 268
  lessons from Malaya for,
    267–268
  the "McLean Court", 274–275
  MI5 in, 239–240
  oathing in, 213–216
  propaganda in, 267–268,
    269–270
  "rehabilitation" in, 327,
    357–365
  "screening" in 236–237, 239,
    254, 270–273, 281
  surrender policy, 267–270,
    279–280, 325–327
Kenya African National Union
  (KANU), 367
Kenya African Union (KAU), 213,
  215, 219–220, 233, 240, 243
Kenya Police, 233–234, 236, 238,
  239, 242, 245, 247, 248,
  249–250, 252–253, 256, 257,
  264, 266, 267, 279, 281, 293,
  325, 327, 330, 361–362
  abuse by, 270–275, 278–279
  Criminal Investigation
    Department (CID), 221–222,
    268–269, 326, 361–362
  and "screening" of Kikuyu
    population, 237
  Special Branch, 233, 240, 250,
    264, 268–269, 280, 312,
    325, 326
  tribal police, 249, 252, 327
Kenya Police Reserve (KPR), 249,
  270, 273–274, 281
Kenya Regiment, 249, 264, 270

Kenyatta, Johnstone (Jomo), 212,
  219–220, 224, 225, 240, 375
  arrest of, 233
  assumes the presidency of the
    KAU, 213
  release of, 367
  trial of, 242–243
Keynes, John Maynard, 128
Keyser, Major, 234
Killearn, 1st Baron, Sir Miles
  Lampson, 23
Kikuyu, 217, 219–220, 238–239,
  241, 245, 247, 249, 250, 251,
  253, 255, 256, 261, 270
  abuse of, 270–275
  early relations with British
    settlers, 210–211
  establishment of political
    organizations, 211–212,
    see also Kikuyu Association
    (KA), East African Association
    (EAA), Local Native Councils
    (LNC), Kikuyu Central
    Association (KCA), and Kenya
    Africa Union (KAU)
  and Mau Mau, 216–217
  migration of, 212–213, 217
  and oathing, 213–216
  "screening" of, 236–237, 239,
    244, 254, 270–273, 281
  special tax imposed on,
    243–244
Kikuyu Association (KA), 211
Kikuyu Central Association (KCA),
  212, 213
Kikuyu Home Guard, 236–237,
  250, 251–253, 256, 257, 265,
  267, 275, 281, 292, 327
Kimathi, Dedan, 324
King David Hotel bombing
  (Palestine), 48–51, 54
King's African Rifles, 225, 252,
  253, 257, 264, 266, 280, 327

King's Royal Rifle Corps, 256
Kohn, Leo, 55
Koinange family, 233, 240, 363
Kook, Hillel, *see* Peter Bergson
Korea, *see* North Korea and South
    Korea
Korean War, 148–149, 150–152,
    167–168, 217, 295

Labour Party, 23, 127–131, 167,
    169–172, 173, 175, 176, 177,
    216, 221, 299, 314, 347, 364,
    376
  1945 manifesto of, 25–26
  and general election of 1945, 6
  and general election of 1950,
    127, 130–131
  and general election of 1951,
    170–172
Lai Tek, 104–105, 106–107
Lampson, Sir Miles, *see* Killearn,
    1st Baron
Lancashire Fusiliers, 233, 234,
    238, 253, 266
Lancaster House conference, 367
Lari massacre, 251–252, 255, 257,
    260, 268
Lascelles, Sir Alan Frederick
    "Tommy", 139–140
Lathbury, General G. W., 293,
    311–312, 324, 327
Lau Tong Tui (Special Service
    Corps of the MPABA), 111
Lawson, Jack, 24
League of Nations, 7–8
Lebanon, 100
Lennox-Boyd, Alan, 200–201,
    291, 293, 300, 301, 311, 321,
    322, 328, 329, 332–333, 334,
    335, 342, 344, 346, 353, 357
  and Aden, 314–315, 316
  appointed colonial secretary,
    288

biography of, 288
and Cyprus, 302, 304–307, 309,
    318–319, 369–370, 373
fall of, 365–366
meetings with Makarios,
    306, 332
and "rehabilitation" in Kenya,
    357, 360, 362, 364–365
visit to Cyprus, 306–307
Liddell, Guy, 20, 21
Livingstone, David, 209
Lloyd, Sir Thomas, 102, 114,
    160–161, 178–179, 240,
    320–321
Lloyd, Selwyn, 286, 300, 302, 307,
    317, 341, 344, 345, 353
Lloyd George, David, 174
Local Native Councils (LNC), 212
Locker, Harold, 131
Lockhart, General Sir Robert, 176,
    181, 182, 185, 230–231, 232,
    409–410n5, 412n30
  assessment of the Malayan
    Emergency by, 187
Lohamel Herut Israel (LEHI),
    10–11, 38, 48, 51
  terrorist campaign of, 15, 32,
    38, 45, 81, 84–85, 86
Luca, Chief, 252
Lyttelton, Oliver, 129–130, 132,
    139–140, 175–176, 191, 192,
    194, 199, 216, 221, 223, 225,
    239, 240, 241, 245–246, 248,
    255, 258, 262, 263–264, 269,
    273, 278, 282, 314, 350, 353,
    357, 410n10, 442–443n18
  appoints Baring as governor of
    Kenya, 217–218
  appoints Templer high
    commissioner and director of
    operations in Malaya, 185–187
  appoints Armitage governor of
    Cyprus

Index

Lyttelton, Oliver – *continued*
  articulates Conservative Party
    colonial policy, 177, 425n243
  comments on Kenya (1955), 294
  correspondence with Edwina
    Mountbatten, 258–261
  criticism of Labour Party
    colonial policy, 177
  and crop destruction in Malaya,
    200–201
  and Cyprus, 282, 286, 287, 288
  delegates all executive authority
    in Malaya to the Director of
    Operations, 178
  discomfort with Mau Mau, 235
  first thoughts on the Malayan
    Emergency, 176–180, 182–184
  grants Baring permission to
    declare an emergency in
    Kenya, 224
  meeting with Churchill and
    Montgomery to discuss
    Malaya, 184–185
  questioned in parliament about
    collective punishments in
    Malaya, 201–203
  on the role of the colonial
    office, 207–208
  rejects Baring's request for a
    Director of Operations in
    Kenya, 237–238, 243
  resignation of, 275–277, 288
  suggests merging the
    positions of Malayan high
    commissioner and director
    of operations into a single
    supremo, 180
  visit to Kenya, 234–235, 256–257
  visit to Malaya, 177, 180–182

MacArthur, General Douglas, 148
MacDonald, A. M., 240, 243, 328,
    329–330

MacDonald, James G., 56
MacDonald, Malcolm, 101–103,
    153, 178–179, 397–398n268
MacDonald, Ramsey, 6,
    379n4,
Mace, Rex Charles, 280
MacGillivray, Sir Donald, 182,
    277, 355
Mackinnon, William, 209
MacKintosh, Angus, 177
Macleod, Ian, 366–367
MacMichael, Sir Harold, 13–14, 15
MacMillan, Major General Sir
    Gordon, 80, 83, 89
Macmillan, Harold, 129, 300, 317,
    347–348, 349, 357
  becomes prime minister,
    350, 353
  on the Cyprus question,
    300–302, 307–309, 320,
    369–371, 373–375
  and Kenya, 357, 364, 366–367
  and Malaya, 354
  and "Wind of Change" speech,
    351–353
Makarios, Archbishop, 298, 306,
    309, 318–320, 321, 322–323,
    331–334, 369, 373, 375
Malawi, 375
Malay Regiment, 180
Malaya, 128, 130, 144, 176, 185,
    208, 216, 217, 235–236, 243,
    247, 249–250, 254, 261, 279,
    285, 288, 292, 300, 308, 310,
    316, 317, 318, 327, 328,
    329–330, 336, 337, 338, 346,
    353, 367
  anti-bandit month (1950),
    133–134
  capital punishment in, 138
  casualty statistics in, 121, 125,
    165, 232–233, 261, 355
  Chinese squatters in, 114–116

collective punishment in, 159,
195–196, 198, 201–203,
227–228
declaration of emergency in,
101, 108
District War Executive Committee
(DWEC), 135–136, 182, 194,
228–229, 290, 334, 355
Dyak trackers in, 112, 400n300
end of emergency in, 354–357
as example for Kenya, 267–268
Federal Executive Council,
182–183, 194
Federal Joint Intelligence
Advisory Committee, 136
Federal War Council, 135–136,
156–157, 182–183, 194
Ferret Force, 135, 404n357
food control in, 159, 198–201,
204–205, 231–232, 263,
415n65
history of, 103–108
emergency regulations, 101
and the Korean War, 150–152
lessons from Palestine for,
117–119
New Villages in, 196–198, 227,
228, 263
propaganda in, 134, 137,
161–164, 181, 183, 206–207
repatriation of Chinese
squatters, 115–116, 125
resettlement of squatters within
Malaya, 134, 137, 150, 154,
156, 157–159, 165, 196–197,
227
rewards for insurgent captures,
203–204
Special Operational Volunteer
Force, 262
State War Executive Committee
(SWEC), 135–136, 182, 194,
228–229, 290, 355

use of Dyak trackers in, 112
war office appreciation of the
situation (1952), 226–227
"white areas" in, 263–264,
277–278, 289, 294
Malayan Civil Service, 115, 134,
147, 158–159, 181, 185, 190
Malayan Communist Party
(MCP), 104–105, 106–108,
112, 134, 149, 163–164,
203–204, 290
Malayan Federation, 107, *see also*
Malaya
Malayan People's Anti-British
Army (MPABA), 108,
111–112, 124, *see also*
Malayan Races Liberation
Army (MRLA)
Malayan People's Anti-Japanese
Army (MPAJA), 105–106, 108
Malayan Police, 109, 110,
112–113, 120–121, 122–124,
126, 143, 147, 152–153, 180,
182, 190–191, 196, 203, 226,
227, 230–231, 290
auxiliary police, 134, 180
and the Briggs Plan, 136–137,
154, 157, 158–159
Criminal Investigation
Department (CID), 120, 155,
164, 165
jungle squads, 147, 191, 263,
413–414n46
Special Branch, 120, 121, 136,
155, 165, 192
Malayan Races Liberation Army
(MRLA), 124–125, 206, 249,
see also Malayan People's
Anti-British Army (MPABA)
Malayan Scouts (SAS), 144–146,
180, 191, 193, *see also* Special
Air Service (SAS)
Malayan Security Service, 101

Malayan Union, 106–107
Malaysia, 356–357, *see also* Malaya
Malta, 375
Marriot, Cyril, 97
Mathenge, Stanley, 324
Martin, John, 59, 62–63, 65, 72–73, 74, 80, 83, 90, 99
Martin, Norman, 125
Mau Mau, 219–220, 223, 224, 226, 233, 235, 236, 242, 243, 246, 249, 250, 254, 256, 261, 264–266, 269, 270–271, 278–280, 281–282, 291–293, 311–312, 326–327, 334, 366, 367
  beginning of violent campaign, 208, 216–217
  campaign of violence, 221–222, 234, 237–239, 244–245, 247–248, 251–253
  declared an illegal organization, 216
  and Lari massacre, 251–252
  and oathing, 214–216, 221–222
  "rehabilitation" of, 357–361
  "Special Force" teams, 324–325
Mauritius, 225, 376
Mbotela, Tom, 238, 239
McEwen, Ian, 19
McGregor, Air Commodore H. D., 32–33
McLean, Lieutenant General Sir Kenneth, 274–275
McLeod, Major General, 224–225
McMahon, Sir Henry, 7
Mead, James, 55–56
Meiklejohn, Ian, 237, 238, 239, 240
Menzies, Robert, 141, 150
Menzies, Sir Stewart, 141
Meridor, Yaacov, 11, 16, 18, 21
Merlin, Samuel, 19

MI5 (the Security Service), 329, 376
  operations in Aden, 328
  operations in Cyprus, 302, 321
  operations in Kenya, 239–240, 243
  operations in Malaya, 191–192
  operations in Palestine, 17–22, 31–32, 34
MI6 (the Secret Intelligence Service), 31, 141
Michael, Charilaos, 332
Middle East,
  strategic importance to Britain of, 42–43, 69, 303
Milverton, Lord, Sir Arthur Richards, 101–102
ministry of defence, 224
Minnery, Colonel, 271
Mitchell, Sir Phillip, 217, 218, 220
Monckton, Sir Walter, 337, 341
Montgomery, 1st Viscount of Alamein, Bernard Law Montgomery, 63, 64, 80, 83, 96, 99, 105, 132, 137, 164, 248, 277, 349–350
  correspondence with Churchill, 128–129
  and martial law in Palestine, 81, 82
  meeting with Churchill and Lyttelton to discuss Malaya, 184–185
  meeting with Creech Jones and Cunningham, 70–72
  on the Palestine problem, 61–62, 69–70, 74
  visits to Palestine, 65
Morgan, J. C., 315–316
Morrison, Herbert, 56, 130, 171
Morton, Jack, 192
Mountbatten, Countess Edwina, 258–261, 262

Mountbatten, Lord Louis, 91, 105, 395n237

Mouskos, Mihail Christdoulou, *see* Makarios

Movement for Colonial Freedom, 221

Moyne, 1st Baron, Walter Edward Guinness, 23

Mugo, Ndegwa, 244

Muhogo, Richard, 244

Murrie, M.S., 65

Muslim League, 75–76

Nagahu, Muthura, 248

Nagasaki, 25, 142

Nasser, Colonel Gamal Abel, 338, 341–345

Nathan, Robert, 55

Nderi, Senior Chief, 234, 235, 240

Nehru, Jawaharlal, 91, 258–261

Nelson, Lieutenant Colonel, 118

Netherlands, the, 85, 91

New Zealand, 33, 151, 342, 343, 346, 350

Ngahu, Stephen, 244

Nigeria, 351, 375

Niles, David, 55

Njeru, Elijah Gideon, 270

Norman, Colonel C. R. W., 65, 74, 79, 83–84, 86, 87, 88, 89, 93, 94–95, 99–100

North Korea, 140, 148

Northern Ireland, 376

Northern Rhodesia, *see* Rhodesia

Northumberland Fusiliers, 266

Nutting, Anthony, 301

Nyasaland, 375

Nye, Sir Archibald, 102

Omdurman, battle of, 174

Operation Agatha (Palestine), 45–48, 52–53, 61, 62, 281

Operation Anvil (Kenya), 281–282

Operation Bellicose (Palestine), 36–37

Operation Buttercup (Kenya), 264–265

Operation Carnation (Kenya), 266

Operation Elephant (Palestine), 80, 81–82

Operation First Flute (Kenya), 293

Operation Hammer (Kenya), 293

Operation Hannibal (Kenya), 327

Operation Helsby (Malaya), 193–194

Operation Hippo (Palestine), 80, 81–82

Operation Jock Scott (Kenya), 224, 233–234, 240, 242

Operation Musketeer (Egypt), 345–349

Operation Overlord (Normandy), 13

Operation Polly (Palestine), 73

Operation Primrose (Kenya), 266

Operation Question (Malaya), 205

Operation Schemozzle I and II (Kenya), 327

Operation Tiger (Palestine), 87

Operation Wedgewood (Kenya), 280

Ormsby-Gore, William, *see* Harlech, 4th Baron

O'Rorke, Michael, 218–219, 222

Paget, General Sir Bernard, 44–45, 63

Pakenham, Lord, 69

Pakistan, 76, 91, 346

Palestine, 42, 108, 110, 115, 117, 123, 128, 133, 137, 161, 216, 281, 284, 285, 313, 334, 346, 353, 354, 356

and the Anglo-American Committee of Inquiry, 29–31

Palestine – *continued*
  capital punishment in, 84,
    86–87, 89
  casualty statistics, 100
  created a Mandate, 7–8
  curfews in, 37, 44, 47, 51, 72,
    87, 117–118
  discussion of reprisals in, 63–65,
    117–118
  history of, 7–10
  introduction of capital
    punishment for terrorist
    offences, 84
  IZL hanging of two police
    sergeants, 89
  Jewish immigration into, 9, 10,
    22, 26–27, 41, 52, 54, 58
  lessons from for Malaya,
    117–119
  London conference (1946), 57
  London conference (1947), 74
  martial law proclaimed in,
    79–80
  partitioned by the United
    Nations, 93
  riots of 1929, 9
  riots of 1933, 10
  riots of 1945, 36–37, 38
  White Paper of 1930, 9
  White Papers of 1939, 10, 11,
    26, 41
Palestine Police, 16, 32, 34,
    48–50, 67
  anti-terrorist operations of,
    37–38, 44–48
  Criminal Investigation
    Department (CID), 14–15, 17,
    31–32, 38, 80, 84
  Special Branch, 17
  terrorist attacks against, 14–15,
    33, 37–38, 43, 45, 48–50, 61,
    84, 87, 88–89
  transferred to Malaya, 110

Pan Malayan Malay Congress, 107
Parachute Regiment, the, 36–37,
    44–45, 117–118, 337, 347
Parliament, British, *see* House
    of Commons and House of
    Lords
Paskin, John, 177
Patterson, Robert, 55
Percival, General Arthur, 105
Peru, 85, 91
Pethick-Lawrence, 1st Baron,
    Frederick William
    Pethick-Lawrence, 77
Petrie, Sir David, 31–32
Pharazyn, Kenya Police Reserve
    officer, 273–274
Phillip, Prince, 295
Pike, Brigadier, 141
Poole, Brigadier Robert G. C., 81
Portal, Lord, 185
Potter, Henry, 218–220, 221, 223,
    268–269
Potsdam Conference, 25, 127
Poullis, Constable, 321
Powell, Enoch, 364–365
Protocol of Sèvres, 345
Pyman, General Sir Harold, 65,
    70, 72

Quit India Movement, 75

RAF, see Royal Air Force
RAF Regiment, 112
Rahman, Tunka Abdul, 355
Raziel, David, 381n23
Redman, Lieutenant General Sir
    Harold, 266
Rees-Williams, David, 131
Renison, Sir Patrick, 366
Revisionist Party, 15
Rhodesia, 145, 218, 225, 376
Richards, Sir Arthur, *see*
    Milverton, Lord

Roach, Special Agent (FBI), 19
Roberts, Brigadier General
    Douglas
Robertson, General Sir Brian,
    185, 255
Rogers, Philip, 219–220, 225
Rosenman, Sam, 55
Rothschild, Lionel de, 339
Royal Air Force (RAF), 134,
    148–149
  in Aden and the Western Aden
    Protectorate, 314–316
  in Cyprus, 283, 330, 333,
    334, 336
  in Egypt, 345–346
  in Kenya, 265, 269, 292–293
  in Malaya, 110–111, 112,
    121–122, 145, 147, 152–153,
    161, 164, 180, 198–200,
    231–232, 327
  in Palestine, 32–33, 37, 43–44,
    61, 89
Royal Armoured Corps, 180
Royal Army Pay Corps, 81
Royal Artillery, 262–263, 371
Royal Australian Air Force
    (RAAF), 180
Royal Electrical and Mechanical
    Engineers (REME), 38
Royal Engineers, 118, 137
Royal Geographical Society, 209
Royal Inniskilling Fusiliers, 266
Royal Irish Fusiliers, 88
Royal Leicestershire Regiment,
    100, 334
Royal Marines, 99, 203, 347
Royal Military Academy,
    Sandhurst, 117, 118, 255
Royal Military Academy,
    Woolwich, 341
Royal Military Police, 47, 49, 371
Royal Navy, 180, 283, 330
Royal Scots Fusiliers, 174

Royal Signals, 47
Royal Tank Regiment, 347
Ruben, Jack Lionel, 270
Ruck family, 247–248
Rymer Jones, Captain J. M., 21, 34

Sabah, 356
Sandhurst, see Royal Military
    Academy, Sandhurst
Sarawak, 112, 356
Sargeaunt, H. A., 232
Saudi Arabia, 337, 347
Sawyer, Kenya Reserve Police
    officer, 273–274
Scobie, Lieutenant General Sir
    Robert, 185
Scots Guards, 119–120
Seaforth Highlanders, 112
Secret Intelligence Service, see MI6
Security Intelligence Far East
    (SIME), 240
Security Intelligence Middle East
    (SIME), 21, 240
Security Service, see MI5
Selwyn Lloyd, see Lloyd, Selwyn
Seychelles Islands, 333, 369
Shackleton, Ernest, 356
Shackleton, Lord, 356–357
Shaw, Sir John, 49, 58
  collaboration with Jewish
    Agency, 15–16
Shertok, Moshe, 5–6, 15, 33,
    39, 40
Shinwell, Emanuel, 78, 89, 130,
    132, 153–154, 156, 164–165,
    171, 201–202
Siam, 103
Sierra Leone, 375
Sillitoe, Sir Percy, 192, 239–240,
    243
Silver, Rabbi Abba Hillel, 55, 56, 85
Silverman, Sydney, 202,
    442–443n18

Simpson, Raynes, 245
Sinclair, George, 372
Singapore, 101, 143, 180, 185, 356
Sixth Airborne Division, *see*
    British Sixth Airborne
    Division
Slade, Humphrey, 234
Slim, Field Marshal Sir William,
    132–133, 143, 150, 156, 160,
    164, 180, 205–206, 289
Snyder, John W., 55
Somaliland, 337, 375
Somerville, J. M., 371
Soskice, Sir Frank, 364
South Africa, 33, 218, 342, 351
South Korea, 140, 148, 346
South Rhodesia, *see* Rhodesia
South Yemen, 376
Soviet Union, 25, 41–43, 107,
    151, 341, 343, 354, 376
Special Air Service (SAS), 141–143,
    145, 193–194, 289–290, 310,
    see also Malayan Scouts (SAS)
Special Investigations Branch
    (RMP), 49
Spencer-Chapman, Lieutenant
    Colonel Freddie, 104–106
Sri Lanka, 101
Stanley, Henry, 209
Stanley, Oliver, 13–14, 16
Stansgate, 1st Viscount, William
    Wedgwood Benn, 24
State War Executive Committee
    (SWEC), *see* Malaya
Stephens, Donald, 302, 313, 321
Sterling, David, 141
Stern, Avraham, 11
Stokes, Richard, 315
Storrs, Sir Ronald, 283
Stockwell, General Hugh,
    117–119, 277
Stratchey, John, 130, 146–147,
    149, 150, 156, 171

Sudan, 341
Suez Canal, 42, 282, 287, 338,
    342, 369
    history of, 338–341
    war over, 345–349, 368
Swann, Anthony, 252
Swaziland, 376
Sweden, 85, 91
Switzerland, 91
Sykes-Picot Agreement, 7
Synes, C. B., 198
Syria, 100
Sytner, Joseph, 23, 32

Tanganyika, 217, 225, 270–272,
    375
Tanzania, *see* Tanganyika
Taylor, Inspector J. C., 48–49
Taylor, Major, 118
Tedder, Lord, 54
Templer, Field Marshal Sir Gerald,
    206–207, 208, 227, 232, 235,
    238, 247, 249, 250, 261–262,
    289, 307, 311–312, 317,
    337–338, 353, 355
    appointed chief of the imperial
      general staff, 310
    appointed high commissioner
      and director of operations in
      Malaya, 185–187
    arrival in Malaya, 187–189
    and collective punishment,
      195–196, 201–203, 227–228
    on the Cyprus question,
      300–301
    establishes the Special
      Operational Volunteer Force,
      262
    establishes "white areas" in
      Malaya, 263–264, 277–278,
      294
    establishment of New Villages
      in Malaya, 196–198

and food control operations,
198–201, 231–232
increases rewards for insurgent
captures, 203–204
and intelligence in Malaya,
191–193, 205, 230
and the police in Malaya,
190–191, 230–231
and propaganda, 206–207
reorganization of administrative
structure in Malaya, 194–195,
228–229
resignation as high
commissioner and director of
operations in Malaya,
277–278
and special forces in Malaya,
193–194
strategy in Malaya,
189–191
Thacker, Ransley, 242–243
Thompson, Sir Robert, 134–135
Thompson, Willoughby, 361–364
Thomson, Joseph, 209
Thuku, Harry, 212
Towers-Clark, Major P.F., 97–99
Trend, Sir Burke, 376
Trinidad and Tobago, 375
Truman, Harry S., 148, 167, 186
and the Anglo-American
Committee of Inquiry, 52,
55–58
correspondence with Attlee,
26–27, 55, 56, 58
Turkey, 42, 282–284, 303–304,
306, 308–309, 336, 370,
373–375

Uffelmann, F. B., 232
Uganda, 217, 375
Ulster Rifles, 167
Union of South Africa, see South
Africa

Union of Soviet Socialist
Republics (USSR), see Soviet
Union
United Malays National
Organization (UMNO), 107
United Nations, 79, 85, 88, 90,
92–93, 96, 97–98, 148,
151–152, 196–197, 221, 286,
287, 346, 349, 375
United Nations Special
Committee on Palestine
(UNSCOP), 85, 86, 91–92
United States, 33, 34, 51, 151,
295, 344, 354, 384–385n72,
440n4
and Anglo-American
Committee of Inquiry,
29–31
and Korea, 148–149
and Palestine, 26–27
and the Suez Crisis, 347–348
Urabi, 340
Urquhart, Major General
R. E., 198
Uruguay, 85, 91

Vereker, John Standish, see Gort,
Field Marshal 6th Viscount
Vietnam, see French Indochina

Wagner, Robert, 56
Wainaini, Headman, 251
Wallace, Henry, 56
war office, 142–143, 144, 179,
193, 248, 249, 274, 286–287,
289, 311
appreciation of the situation in
Malaya (1952), 226–227
disagreement with the colonial
office over Palestine, 65–68
Malaya as priority of, 150
report comparing Kenya and
Malaya, 354–355

Waruhiu wa Kungu, Chief, 222–223
Wavell, Sir Arthur, 35
Weizmann, Chaim, 5–6, 33
Western Aden Protectorate, 313–317, *see* also Aden
Westminster Parliament, *see* House of Commons
White, Dick, 192
Whitehall, 98, 105, 133, 164
Whyatt, John, 219, 220–221, 222, 224, 242, 247, 273, 325–326, 327
Wickham, Sir Charles, 67
Wilson, Evan, 19
Wilson, Harold, 170
Wingate, Orde, 141
Wood, E.F.L., *see* Halifax, 1st Earl of

Woodford, E. K., 232
Woodhouse, Captain John, 145
Wooley, Sir Charles, 284
World Zionist Organization, 5–6
Wright, Sir Andrew, 285

Yamashita, General Tomoyuki, 105
Yeldham, Colonel, 198
Yemen, 313, 314, 315, 317, 337
Young, Arthur, 191, 231, 414n48
Young, Lieutenant R. H., 280
Yugoslavia, 42, 85, 91

Zakos, Andreas, 332
Zambia, 376
Zanzibar, 375